The CAR Book

2018

by

Jack Gillis

and

Amy Curran
Richard Eckman

Foreword by

Jason Levine
Center for Auto Safety

A Center for Auto Safety Publication

ACKNOWLEDGMENTS

Co-author, Richard "Ricky" Eckman again did an extraordinary job of managing and organizing this 38th edition of *The Car Book*. It is a monumental effort as, literally, thousands of data points go into compiling the book and all of its ratings. As a 27 year veteran of *The Car Book*, Amy Curran prepared all of the graphics necessary to clearly present the data and managed the logistics necessary to get a printed book in the hands of the public. Thanks to Amy, Ricky, and the team, consumers have the information they need to make a smart, sensible new car choice.

For 37 years, this effort would not have been possible without the essential contributions from the staff of the Center for Auto Safety, including Michael Brooks, Jon Robinson, and the Center's new Executive Director, Jason Levine.

As always, the most important factor in being able to bring this information to the American car buyer for 38 years is the encouragement, support, and love from my brilliant and beautiful wife, Marilyn Mohrman-Gillis. For her and our four terrific children–Katie, John, Brian and Brennan–I am eternally grateful.

—J.G.

This edition of The Car Book is dedicated to the memory of
Clarence M. Ditlow, III
One of the Most Effective Safety Advocates in America's History
A True Friend and Great Mentor Who Saved Inumerable Lives

JASON LEVINE, CENTER FOR AUTO SAFETY

There has never been a more important moment in car safety. More than 37,000 people died in motor vehicle crashes in 2016 according to the National Highway Traffic Safety Administration. That is a 5.6 percent increase from 2015. The year before, in 2015, traffic deaths rose 7 percent from 2014. More Americans died per vehicle mile traveled in 2016 than in 2015. Recalls are on the rise as well. There were 51 million vehicles recalled in 2016, an increase of almost 400 percent from 2011. What happened?

Until recently, there was widespread agreement among Presidents, Congress, and the Department of Transportation, that preventing motor vehicle crashes was an important governmental function. To achieve this public policy goal meant passing laws and writing regulations to create a level playing field for safety so that all car manufacturers would be required to comply, and safety would not be reserved for the rich or granted only at the whims of industry. The law, and law enforcement authorities, used to protect consumers from false advertising when car shopping or when they were sold a lemon. Even when there was Congressional gridlock, or bureaucratic malaise, responsible public figures and organizations took to the streets, the airwaves, and the courts to pressure auto manufacturers to do the right thing by their consumers – and everyone else on the road whose lives and limbs could be impacted by their vehicles.

Times sure have changed.

The President's proposed budget underfunds NHTSA, the nation's only cop on the car safety beat, making costly investigations more difficult to undertake and showing how little he thinks of the need for auto safety. One year into the new administration, no one has even been nominated to run NHTSA. Despite the lack of leadership and funding, NHTSA still has the authority to set safety standards and require safety defect recalls, yet the agency has too often become a rubber stamp for manufacturer solutions to safety problems which are almost always the least expensive course of action.

The Federal Trade Commission (FTC), the agency charged with preventing false advertising, decided it is fine for used cars to be sold as "safe" even with dangerous unrepaired recalls (like Takata airbags or GM ignition switches). The FTC apparently concluded that if the recall is buried somewhere in the mountains of required paperwork consumers sign when buying a used car from a dealership that would be enough to ensure safety for the 34 million used cars that are sold in the United States every year.

What will the future hold? As the technology for autonomous vehicles, creeps ever closer to reality Congress is working on bills that bend over backwards to give industry whatever it wants. The proposed laws could preempt state laws designed to protect residents, both drivers and pedestrians, while failing to require a national standard for the robot cars. Congress is even contemplating allowing these robot-cars on the road without a cyber-security standard, or a standard for the electronics of the vehicles (such as sensors or radar), and does not require the government to verify the safety of the vehicle before it hits the highway or showroom closest to your house. The auto manufacturers and technology companies who stand to gain the most from producing these vehicles are being given a legislative EZ-Pass from pesky requirements such as proving why their robot-cars do not need to meet safety standards. Except those standards were written to protect all of us from the inevitable crashes that happen when two-ton vehicles travel at 65 miles-per-hour. The advanced safety technology promised by robot-cars could change the world and make our roads safer if implemented in a thoughtful, deliberate fashion with plans for how the new technology will interact with the existing 281 million cars on our roads. Yet, a rush to market that results in an inevitable, preventable, tragedy will only set back the cause of safety.

Meanwhile, as the press gets swept up in futuristic stories about how robot-cars will be here any day now, dangerous defects continue to plague the cars that we drive every day.

What can you do to help stop the bad old days from returning? Be your own best advocate – check for recalls at www.safercar.gov, ask about any Technical Service Bulletins for your car the next time you bring it in for service. (The Center for Auto Safety has led the fight to make this information available to everyone and not just car dealers.) Contact your members of Congress and tell them how important car safety is to you, both today and tomorrow. When you shop for a new car, be sure to use *The Car Book* to understand how your options rate against each other. Finally, your continued support of the Center makes possible our work on your behalf fighting for safer, higher quality, and more fuel-efficient vehicles. Please visit www.autosafety.org to learn more.

JACK GILLIS

The 2018 models are electric! Never before have consumers had such a variety of electric car choices so we've updated our special section at the back of the book with 31 new EVs ranging from subcompact to minivans. Based on family size and driving needs of the typical family, EVs would work for nearly half of Americans! They work like your cell phone—imagine plugging them in each night and then gliding silently and smoothly throughout your driving day in a high-tech, low maintenance vehicle.

If you're not into electric, the safety features in the 2018s have never been better. While the autonomous vehicle is still years down the road, many of the new models have great crash avoidance systems from keeping you in your lane to automatically stopping you before a crash to making sure you know what's behind you before incurring a tragic back up situation. In fact, by mid-2018 all vehicles will have life-saving back up cameras—even the low-priced subcompacts!

In order to make you both a smarter and safer car buyer, The Car Book documents these improvements and puts them at your fingertips. We've rated the 2018s for the number of safety features they have so you can easily find the top performers. The good news is that many of the new, life-saving features are becoming available on the less expensive vehicles.

On the "gee wiz" front, automakers are adding cameras to see the kids in the backseat of your minivan (Honda), push button and Bluetooth enabled starting systems, back seat TV screens, digital dashboards that you can personalize and improved fuel efficiency, thanks to government standards.

Amazingly, this is the 38th year we've been bringing consumers the information they need to make a smart and safe vehicle choice. Not only are vehicles getting better, so is the buying experience. More dealers are abandoning the difficult negotiation process in favor of a straightforward posted price. So with lots of new electronics, improved safety features, and some improvements in the showroom, The Car Book is ready to guide you to a great new 2018 vehicle!

Working closely with the Center for Auto Safety, our goal is to sift through the myriad of government and industry data on cars and present the information so you can actually use it. Thirty-eight years ago, The Car Book was the first publication to give you the ability to make an informed choice on one of the most important and complex items that you will ever purchase. In setting out to change the way people buy their cars, The Car Book was able to change the way car companies made them.

In keeping with The Car Book's philosophy of making it as easy as possible to identify the truly good performers in the government crash tests, we provide a unique Car Book Combined Crash Test Rating which combines all of the complex government testing into a simple, straightforward number. In addition, we take the step of comparing the vehicles on a relative basis to each other so you can easily tell which ones are truly the best performers.

Before The Car Book, consumers had no idea which warranties were better, what you could expect to pay for typical repairs, which cars cost the most and least to insure, or how they stacked up in government complaints. Now you have this information all in one place.

Our exclusive car-by-car ratings at the end of the book provide an overview of all the criteria you need to make a good choice. Here, you'll be able to quickly assess key features and see how the car you're interested in stacks up against its competition so you can make sure your selection is the best car for you.

While the choices get better each year, it's still a challenge to separate the lemons from the peaches. There are differences in how cars protect you in a crash, how much they cost to maintain, and the benefits of their warranties. Nevertheless, by using The Car Book, there's no reason why your next car shouldn't last at least 150,000 miles. Finally, our "Showroom Strategies" section will give you the keys to getting the best deal.

The information in The Car Book is based on data collected and developed by our staff, the U.S. Department of Transportation, and the Center for Auto Safety. With all of this information in hand, you'll find some great choices for 2018.

Drive on!

—Jack

USING THE BUYING GUIDE

T he "Buying Guide" provides a quick comparison of the 2018 cars in terms of their safety, warranty, fuel economy, complaint rating, and price range—arranged by size class. To fully understand the information in the charts, it is important to read the related section in the book.

Overall Rating: This shows how well this car stacks up on a scale of 1 to 10 when compared to all others on the market. Because safety is the most important component of our ratings, cars with no crash test results at the time of printing are not given an overall rating.

Combined Crash Test Rating: This indicates how well the car performed in the government's frontal and side crash test programs compared to this year's vehicles tested to date. See pages 19-27 for details. Note: In order to qualify for a *Best Bet*, the vehicle may not have any Poor or Very Poor crash test or safety feature ratings.

Safety Feature Rating: This is an evaluation of how many extra safety features are available in comparison to all the vehicles. See pages 74-78.

Warranty Rating: This is an overall comparative assessment of the car's warranty. See pages 35-37.

Fuel Economy: This is the EPA city/highway mpg for, what is expected to be, the most popular version of each model.

Complaint Rating: This is based on complaints received by the U.S. Department of Transportation. If not rated, the vehicle is too new to have a complaint rating. See page 53.

Price Range: This will give you a general idea of the "sticker," or manufacturer's suggested retail price (MSRP).

 Indicates a *Car Book* Best Bet. See pages 13-18.

 ABOUT THE CAR BOOK BEST BETS

It is important to consult the specific chapters to learn more about how *The Car Book* ratings are developed and to look on the car pages, beginning on page 79, for more details on these vehicles. In order to be considered as a "Best Bet" the vehicle must have a crash test rating as safety is a critical factor in gaining that recognition. *Vehicles with "Poor" (3 or 4) or "Very Poor" (1 or 2) in Combined Crash Tests, or Front or Side Crash Test Ratings, or an additional injury warning will not qualify as a "Best Bet." In addition, vehicles with a poor or very poor safety feature rating will not qualify as a "Best Bet."* Because most people are considering vehicles in the same size category, the "Best Bets" beginning on page 13 are by size—indicating how these vehicles compared against others in the same size class.

You will note that some of our "Best Bets" have some "not so good" ratings on the next pages. Nevertheless, these vehicles still rise to the top in their size class. This points to the trade offs we often make when buying a new vehicle.

Vehicle	Pg #	Overall Rating	Combined Crash Test Rating	Safety Features Rating	Warranty Rating	Fuel Economy Rating	Complaint Rating	Price Range
Subcompact								
BMW i3	95			Average	Very Good	137/111	Poor	$42-$47,000
Chevrolet Sonic	119	9	Good	Good	Average	25/34	Average	$15-$21,000
Chevrolet Spark	120	5	Very Poor	Good	Average	29/38	Poor	$13-$17,000
Fiat 500	132	2	Very Poor	Very Poor	Average	27/34	Very Poor	$14-$31,000
Ford Fiesta	141	2	Poor	Very Poor	Poor	27/37	Very Poor	$14-$19,000
Honda Fit	155	9	Very Good	Poor	Very Poor	33/41	Good	$16-$21,000
Hyundai Accent	159			Very Poor	Very Good	28/38		$14-$17,000
Hyundai Veloster	166	6	Poor	Poor	Very Good	28/36	Poor	$18-$23,000
Kia Rio	179			Poor	Very Good	28/37		$14-$20,000
Mazda MX-5	204			Very Poor	Very Poor	27/36	Average	$24-$34,000
Mini Hardtop	215	6	Poor	Poor	Very Good	27/35	Good	$20-$30,000
Mitsubishi Mirage	216	3	Very Poor	Very Poor	Very Good	37/43	Poor	$13-$16,000
Nissan Versa	230	1	Very Poor	Very Poor	Very Poor	31/40	Average	$11-$15,000
Toyota Prius C	249	5	Very Poor	Poor	Very Poor	53/46	Very Good	$20-$24,000
Toyota Yaris	257	5	Very Poor	Very Poor	Very Poor	30/36	Very Good	$15-$19,000
Compact								
Acura ILX	79			Good	Average	25/35		$27-$34,000
Audi A3	83	6	Average	Very Good	Good	24/33	Poor	$31-$49,000
Audi A4	84	2	Very Poor	Average	Good	25/33	Poor	$36-$50,000
BMW 2 Series	90			Average	Very Good	23/35	Very Good	$34-$47,000
BMW 3 Series	91	7	Average	Good	Very Good	23/36	Good	$34-$48,000
BMW 4 Series	92			Good	Very Good	23/35	Good	$42-$59,000
Buick Cascada	100			Very Poor	Good	20/27	Average	$33-$37,000
Cadillac ATS	106	4	Very Poor	Good	Very Good	21/33	Average	$34-$49,000
Chevrolet Bolt	110			Very Good	Average	128/110	Very Poor	$36-$40,000
Chevrolet Cruze	114	8	Average	Good	Average	29/40	Very Good	$16-$23,000
Chevrolet Volt	125	7	Poor	Good	Average	43/42	Very Poor	$33-$37,000
Ford C-MAX	134	5	Poor	Poor	Poor	42/37	Very Poor	$24-$30,000
Ford Focus	143	5	Good	Poor	Poor	26/38	Very Poor	$16-$29,000
Honda Civic	153	10	Average	Average	Very Poor	31/41	Good	$19-$26,000
Hyundai Elantra	160			Good	Very Good	28/37	Average	$16-$22,000
Kia Forte	177			Very Poor	Very Good	29/37	Average	$16-$22,000
Kia Soul	182	7	Good	Average	Very Good	25/30	Average	$16-$35,000
Lexus IS	190	8	Average	Very Good	Good	21/30	Very Good	$37-$43,000

Vehicle	Pg #	Overall Rating	Combined Crash Test Rating	Safety Features Rating	Warranty Rating	Fuel Economy Rating	Complaint Rating	Price Range
Compact (cont.)								
Lexus RC	192			Good	Good	22/32	Very Good	$40-$45,000
Mazda 3	202	6	Poor	Average	Very Poor	28/37	Very Good	$18-$24,000
Mercedes-Benz B	205			Poor	Poor	85/82	Very Poor	$39-$39,000
Mercedes-Benz C	206	1	Poor	Very Good	Poor	22/30	Average	$39-$67,000
Mercedes-Benz CLA	207			Good	Poor	24/37	Very Poor	$3-$49,000
Mini Countryman	214			Poor	Very Good	24/32		$26-$31,000
Nissan Leaf	223			Poor	Very Poor	126/101		$30-$36,000
Nissan Sentra	228	5	Very Poor	Very Poor	Very Poor	30/39	Very Good	$16-$21,000
Subaru Impreza	235	5	Average	Good	Poor	20/27	Average	$18-$24,000
Toyota 86	242			Very Poor	Very Poor	25/34	Very Good	$26-$29,000
Toyota Corolla	245	8	Poor	Very Good	Very Poor	27/36	Very Good	$18-$22,000
Toyota Corolla iM	246			Average	Very Poor	28/36	Very Good	$18-$19,000
Toyota Prius	248	7	Average	Very Good	Very Poor	54/50	Poor	$23-$30,000
Toyota Prius Prime	250			Very Good	Very Poor	55/53	Average	$27-$33,000
Toyota Yaris iA	258	6	Average	Very Poor	Very Poor	32/40	Poor	$15-$17,000
Volkswagen Beetle	260	3	Poor	Very Poor	Very Good	25/33	Good	$19-$32,000
Volkswagen Golf	261	5	Average	Average	Very Good	25/36	Poor	$19-$29,000
Volkswagen Jetta	262	7	Good	Poor	Very Good	28/39	Average	$17-$28,000
Intermediate								
Acura TLX	82	9	Very Good	Very Good	Average	23/33	Poor	$33-$45,000
Audi A5	85			Very Good	Good	24/34		$42-$52,000
Audi A6	86	7	Good	Good	Good	20/29	Very Good	$47-$61,000
BMW 5 Series	93	6	Poor	Good	Very Good	23/34	Good	$52-$73,000
Buick Regal	105			Very Good	Good	22/32		$27-$36,000
Chevrolet Camaro	111	4	Good	Poor	Average	19/28	Good	$26-$42,000
Chevrolet Corvette	113			Very Poor	Average	15/25	Average	$55-$83,000
Chevrolet Malibu	117	9	Average	Very Good	Average	27/36	Very Good	$21-$27,000
Ford Fusion	144	4	Poor	Good	Poor	21/32	Poor	$22-$36,000
Ford Fusion Energi	145	8	Good	Good	Poor	40/36	Very Poor	$33-$41,000
Ford Mustang	146	6	Good	Poor	Poor	19/28	Average	$24-$54,000
Honda Accord	152			Very Good	Very Poor	23/34		$22-$34,000
Hyundai Sonata	164	9	Very Good	Average	Very Good	25/35	Average	$22-$32,000
Infiniti Q50	167	3	Poor	Average	Very Good	20/29	Average	$34-$52,000
Kia Optima	178	9	Good	Good	Very Good	24/34	Average	$22-$30,000
Lexus ES	187	5	Good	Very Good	Good	21/31	Poor	$38-$41,000
Lexus GS	188			Very Good	Good	19/29	Poor	$46-$56,000
Lincoln MKZ	197	4	Poor	Average	Very Good	18/27	Average	$35-$47,000
Mazda 6	203	6	Good	Average	Very Poor	26/38	Good	$21-$30,000

Vehicle	Pg #	Overall Rating	Combined Crash Test Rating	Safety Features Rating	Warranty Rating	Fuel Economy Rating	Complaint Rating	Price Range
Intermediate (cont.)								
Nissan Altima	219	4	Average	Poor	Very Poor	27/38	Good	$22-$32,000
Nissan Maxima	224	4	Good	Poor	Very Poor	22/30	Good	$32-$40,000
Subaru Legacy	236	7	Very Good	Good	Poor	26/36	Average	$22-$31,000
Tesla Model 3	238			Good	Very Good	131/120		$35-$450,000
Toyota Avalon	243	8	Good	Very Good	Very Poor	21/31	Good	$33-$42,000
Toyota Camry	244	8	Very Good	Very Good	Very Poor	28/39		$24-$34,000
Toyota Prius V	251	9	Average	Good	Very Poor	44/40	Very Good	$26-$30,000
Volkswagen Passat	263	4	Average	Poor	Very Good	25/36	Poor	$22-$33,000
Volvo S60	265	9	Good	Good	Good	25/36	Very Good	$33-$47,000
Volvo V60	266			Good	Good	25/36	Very Poor	$38-$49,000
Large								
BMW 7 Series	94			Very Good	Very Good	21/29	Average	$83-$96,000
Buick LaCrosse	104	5	Average	Very Good	Good	21/31	Good	$30-$43,000
Cadillac CT6	107			Very Good	Very Good	18/27	Good	$54-$88,000
Cadillac XTS	109	8	Very Good	Good	Very Good	18/28	Good	$45-$72,000
Chevrolet Impala	116	4	Average	Good	Average	18/28	Good	$27-$36,000
Chrysler 300	126	1	Very Poor	Average	Poor	19/30	Poor	$28-$40,000
Dodge Challenger	128	4	Good	Very Poor	Poor	19/30	Very Good	$26-$63,000
Dodge Charger	129	2	Poor	Average	Poor	19/31	Poor	$28-$66,000
Ford Taurus	147	3	Average	Poor	Poor	19/29	Good	$27-$42,000
Genesis G80	148			Very Good	Very Good	19/27	Very Good	$41-$59,000
Lincoln Continental	194	6	Very Good	Good	Very Good	17/26	Very Poor	$44-$64,000
Mercedes-Benz E	208	3	Average	Very Good	Poor	22/30	Average	$52-$69,000
Mercedes-Benz S	213			Very Good	Poor	19/28	Good	$89-$147,000
Tesla Model S	239	10	Very Good	Very Good	Very Good	88/90	Very Poor	$69-$135,000
Minivan								
Chrysler Pacifica	127	8	Good	Good	Poor	18/28	Very Poor	$26-$43,000
Honda Odyssey	157	9	Good	Very Good	Very Poor	19/28		$29-$44,000
Kia Sedona	180			Poor	Very Good	18/25	Good	$26-$41,000
Toyota Sienna	254	2	Average	Very Good	Very Poor	18/25	Poor	$29-$47,000
Small SUV								
Acura RDX	81	9	Very Good	Good	Average	19/27	Good	$35-$40,000
Audi Q3	87			Very Poor	Good	20/28	Very Good	$32-$37,000
BMW X1	96			Average	Very Good	22/32	Poor	$33-$35,000
Buick Encore	102	10	Good	Good	Good	23/30	Very Good	$24-$32,000
Chevrolet Equinox	115	4	Average	Average	Average	26/32		$23-$37,000
Chevrolet Trax	124	10	Good	Good	Average	24/30	Very Good	$21-$28,000
Fiat 500X	133			Poor	Average	22/31	Poor	$19-$27,000

Vehicle	Pg #	Overall Rating	Combined Crash Test Rating	Safety Features Rating	Warranty Rating	Fuel Economy Rating	Complaint Rating	Price Range
Small SUV (cont.)								
Ford EcoSport	135			Poor	Poor	27/29		$19-$26,000
Ford Escape	137	6	Good	Average	Poor	22/31	Average	$23-$33,000
GMC Terrain	150	5	Average	Poor	Average	26/30	Good	$24-$39,000
Honda CR-V	154	10	Very Good	Good	Very Poor	26/32	Good	$24-$33,000
Honda HR-V	156	5	Poor	Very Poor	Very Poor	28/34	Average	$19-$26,000
Hyundai Kona	161			Good	Very Good			
Hyundai Tucson	165	8	Poor	Good	Very Good	24/28	Very Poor	$22-$31,000
Infiniti QX30	168			Good	Very Good	24/33	Very Poor	$29-$38,000
Infiniti QX50	169			Poor	Very Good	17/24	Very Good	$34-$36,000
Jeep Compass	173	4	Very Poor	Very Poor	Poor	22/30	Poor	$20-$29,000
Jeep Renegade	175	1	Very Poor	Poor	Poor	22/31	Very Poor	$17-$27,000
Jeep Wrangler	176			Very Poor	Poor	17/21		$23-$37,000
Kia Sportage	183	9	Good	Average	Very Good	22/29	Good	$23-$34,000
Land Rvr Rng Rvr Evoque	185			Average	Good	21/30	Average	$41-$54,000
Lexus NX	191	5	Good	Good	Good	22/28	Good	$35-$39,000
Lincoln MKC	195	6	Poor	Average	Very Good	19/26	Good	$33-$48,000
Mazda CX-3	199	10	Very Good	Average	Very Poor	29/34	Very Good	$19-$26,000
Mazda CX-5	200	4	Average	Poor	Very Poor	26/32	Average	$24-$30,000
Mercedes-Benz GLA	209			Good	Poor	23/31	Average	$32-$49,000
Mercedes-Benz GLC	210			Very Good	Poor	21/28	Very Poor	$39-$54,000
Mitsu. Outlander Sport	218	4	Poor	Average	Very Good	23/29	Good	$19-$27,000
Nissan Juke*	222	2	Very Poor	Poor	Very Poor	26/31	Good	$20-$30,000
Subaru Crosstrek	233	5	Average	Good	Poor	27/33		$21-$26,000
Subaru Forester	234	4	Average	Good	Poor	24/32	Good	$22-$36,000
Toyota RAV4	252	9	Good	Very Good	Very Poor	22/29	Very Good	$24-$32,000
Volkswagen Tiguan	264			Poor	Very Good	22/27		$25-$37,000
Mid-Size SUV								
Acura MDX	80	7	Good	Very Good	Average	18/27	Poor	$44-$58,000
Audi Q5	88			Poor	Good	23/27		$41-$50,000
Audi Q7	89	3	Average	Good	Good	19/25	Poor	$49-$65,000
BMW X3	97			Good	Very Good	22/29		$39-$47,000
BMW X5	98	5	Good	Good	Very Good	18/27	Very Good	$55-$72,000
BMW X6	99			Average	Very Good	18/24	Poor	$60-$104,000
Buick Envision	103			Very Good	Good	21/27	Poor	$36-$45,000
Cadillac XT5	108	3	Poor	Good	Very Good	19/25	Very Poor	$40-$63,000
Dodge Durango	130	2	Poor	Good	Poor	18/25	Very Poor	$29-$62,000
Dodge Journey	131	1	Very Poor	Poor	Poor	19/25	Very Poor	$22-$34,000
Ford Edge	136	9	Very Good	Good	Poor	20/30	Poor	$29-$40,000

*Based on 2017 ratings.

Vehicle	Pg #	Overall Rating	Combined Crash Test Rating	Safety Features Rating	Warranty Rating	Fuel Economy Rating	Complaint Rating	Price Range
Mid-Size SUV (cont.)								
Ford Explorer	139	3	Average	Average	Poor	17/23	Very Poor	$31-$53,000
GMC Acadia	149	2	Poor	Good	Average	18/25	Very Poor	$32-$47,000
Honda Pilot	158	8	Good	Average	Very Poor	19/27	Poor	$30-$43,000
Hyundai Santa Fe	162			Good	Very Good	18/25	Very Poor	$30-$41,000
Hyundai Santa Fe Sport	163	5	Average	Average	Very Good	21/27	Very Poor	$24-$37,000
Infiniti QX60	170	5	Average	Average	Very Good	19/26	Average	$43-$44,000
Jeep Cherokee	172	5	Average	Good	Poor	21/28	Very Poor	$24-$37,000
Jeep Grand Cherokee	174	4	Average	Very Poor	Poor	14/22	Very Poor	$30-$47,000
Kia Sorento	181	6	Good	Poor	Very Good	21/28	Poor	$25-$45,000
Land Rvr Rng Rvr Sport	186			Average	Good	14/19	Very Good	$65-$94,000
Lexus RX	193	4	Poor	Good	Good	20/28	Very Good	$43-$53,000
Lincoln MKX	196	5	Very Poor	Average	Very Good	17/25	Poor	$39-$56,000
Mazda CX-9	201			Average	Very Poor	20/26	Very Good	$31-$44,000
Mercedes-Benz GLE	211			Very Good	Poor	18/23	Average	$53-$101,000
Mitsubishi Outlander	217	4	Average	Average	Very Good	24/29	Poor	$23-$31,000
Nissan Murano	225			Poor	Very Poor	21/28	Good	$29-$40,000
Nissan Pathfinder	226			Poor	Very Poor	19/26	Poor	$29-$43,000
Nissan Rogue	227	3	Very Poor	Average	Very Poor	25/32	Very Good	$23-$31,000
Porsche Macan	231			Average	Good	17/23	Very Good	$47-$77,000
Subaru Outback	237	8	Very Good	Good	Poor	25/33	Poor	$25-$35,000
Tesla Model X	240	10	Very Good	Very Good	Very Good	89/90	Very Poor	$79-$140,000
Toyota 4Runner	241	2	Very Poor	Poor	Very Poor	17/21	Very Good	$34-$44,000
Toyota Highlander	247	9	Good	Very Good	Very Poor	18/24	Very Good	$30-$47,000
Volkswagen Atlas	259	6	Very Good	Good	Very Good	18/25		$30-$48,000
Volvo XC60	267			Very Good	Good	22/28		$40-$51,000
Large SUV								
Buick Enclave	101	4	Average	Average	Good	18/26		$39-$55,000
Cadillac Escalade	122	3	Good	Average	Very Good	14/21	Good	$76-$97,000
Cadillac Escalade ESV	121	4	Average	Average	Very Good	14/20	Good	$80-$99,000
Chevrolet Suburban	121	2	Average	Poor	Average	15/22	Poor	$50-$67,000
Chevrolet Tahoe	122	4	Good	Poor	Average	16/22	Average	$47-$65,000
Chevrolet Traverse	123	4	Average	Average	Average	18/27		$32-$52,000
Ford Expedition	138			Good	Poor	17/22	Good	$48-$75,000
Ford Flex	142			Very Poor	Poor	16/23	Poor	$30-$40,000
GMC Yukon	122	5	Good	Poor	Average	16/22	Poor	$49-$69,000
GMC Yukon XL	121	4	Average	Poor	Average	15/22	Average	$52-$72,000
Infiniti QX80	171			Good	Very Good	14/20	Good	$63-$89,000
Land Rover Range Rover	184			Average	Good	14/19	Good	$85-$140,000

Vehicle	Pg #	Overall Rating	Combined Crash Test Rating	Safety Features Rating	Warranty Rating	Fuel Economy Rating	Complaint Rating	Price Range
Large SUV (cont.)								
Lexus GX	189			Very Good	Good	15/20	Very Good	$51-$63,000
Lincoln Navigator	198			Average	Very Good	16/21		$72-$93,000
Mercedes-Benz GLS	212			Very Good	Poor	17/22	Good	$67-$124,000
Nissan Armada	220			Good	Very Poor	14/19	Good	$44-$60,000
Toyota Sequoia	253			Good	Very Poor	13/17	Very Good	$48-$67,000
Volvo XC90	268	8	Very Good	Very Good	Good	22/28	Very Poor	$45-$104,000
Compact Pickup								
Chevrolet Colorado	112	2	Poor	Very Poor	Average	20/27	Average	$20-$33,000
GMC Canyon	112	1	Poor	Very Poor	Average	20/26	Poor	$20-$33,000
Nissan Frontier	221	1	Poor	Very Poor	Very Poor	15/21	Average	$18-$35,000
Toyota Tacoma	255	2	Very Poor	Good	Very Poor	19/23	Poor	$24-$39,000
Standard Pickup								
Chevrolet Silverado	118	7	Very Good	Poor	Average	16/22	Very Good	$28-$55,000
Ford F-150	140	9	Very Good	Poor	Poor	17/23	Very Good	$27-$57,000
GMC Sierra	151	5	Very Good	Poor	Average	16/22	Average	$29-$56,000
Nissan Titan	229	1	Good	Very Poor	Very Poor	15/21	Very Poor	$35-$55,000
Ram 1500	232	2	Very Poor	Very Poor	Very Poor	13/19	Average	$27-$53,000
Toyota Tundra	256			Very Good	Very Poor	13/18	Very Good	$32-$50,000

BEST BETS

F ollowing is our list of the highest rated 2018 vehicles in each size category. The ratings are based on expected performance in nine important categories–Combined Crash Rating, Safety Features, Rollover, Preventive Maintenance, Repair Costs, Warranty, Fuel Economy, Complaints, and Insurance Costs–with the heaviest emphasis placed on safety. (See box on page 6.)

BMW 3 SERIES — COMPACT

Combo Crash Tests	6	Warranty	9
Safety Features	7	Fuel Economy	7
Rollover	9	Complaints	8
PM	4	Insurance	3
Repair Costs	2	**OVERALL RATING...**	**7**

Page 91

KIA SOUL — COMPACT

Combo Crash Tests	8	Warranty	9
Safety Features	5	Fuel Economy	6
Rollover	4	Complaints	6
PM	4	Insurance	1
Repair Costs	8	**OVERALL RATING...**	**7**

Page 182

TOYOTA PRIUS — COMPACT

Combo Crash Tests	5	Warranty	2
Safety Features	9	Fuel Economy	10
Rollover	7	Complaints	4
PM	9	Insurance	5
Repair Costs	5	**OVERALL RATING...**	**7**

Page 248

ACURA TLX — INTERMEDIATE

Combo Crash Tests	10	Warranty	6
Safety Features	8	Fuel Economy	6
Rollover	8	Complaints	3
PM	5	Insurance	10
Repair Costs	3	**OVERALL RATING...**	**9**

Page 82

HYUNDAI SONATA

Page 164

INTERMEDIATE

Combo Crash Tests 9	Warranty. 10
Safety Features 6	Fuel Economy. 7
Rollover 7	Complaints 5
PM 5	Insurance 5
Repair Costs. 8	**OVERALL RATING. . . 9**

TOYOTA AVALON

Page 243

INTERMEDIATE

Combo Crash Tests 8	Warranty. 2
Safety Features 10	Fuel Economy. 5
Rollover 7	Complaints 8
PM 6	Insurance 5
Repair Costs. 4	**OVERALL RATING. . . 8**

TOYOTA CAMRY

Page 244

INTERMEDIATE

Combo Crash Tests 9	Warranty. 2
Safety Features 10	Fuel Economy. 8
Rollover 8	Complaints . . . .–
PM 6	Insurance 5
Repair Costs. 3	**OVERALL RATING. . . 8**

AUDI A6

Page 86

INTERMEDIATE

Combo Crash Tests 8	Warranty. 7
Safety Features 7	Fuel Economy. 4
Rollover 9	Complaints 9
PM 4	Insurance 3
Repair Costs. 1	**OVERALL RATING. . . 7**

SUBARU LEGACY

INTERMEDIATE

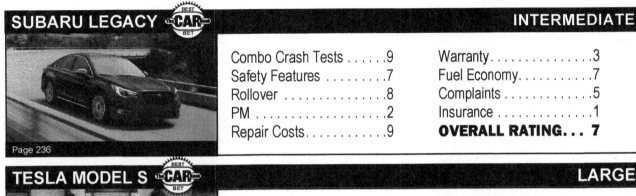

Page 236

Combo Crash Tests	9	Warranty	3
Safety Features	7	Fuel Economy	7
Rollover	8	Complaints	5
PM	2	Insurance	1
Repair Costs	9	**OVERALL RATING... 7**	

TESLA MODEL S

LARGE

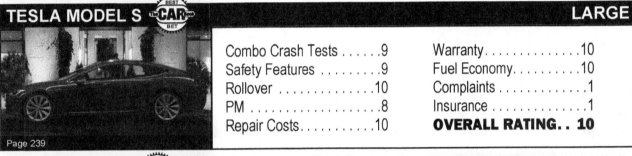

Page 239

Combo Crash Tests	9	Warranty	10
Safety Features	9	Fuel Economy	10
Rollover	10	Complaints	1
PM	8	Insurance	1
Repair Costs	10	**OVERALL RATING.. 10**	

CADILLAC XTS

LARGE

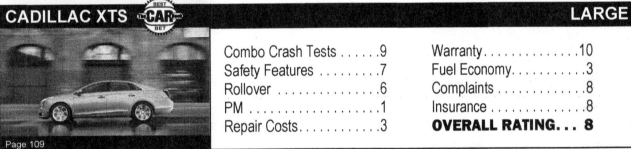

Page 109

Combo Crash Tests	9	Warranty	10
Safety Features	7	Fuel Economy	3
Rollover	6	Complaints	8
PM	1	Insurance	8
Repair Costs	3	**OVERALL RATING... 8**	

HONDA ODYSSEY

MINIVAN

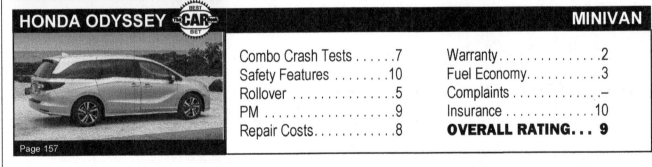

Page 157

Combo Crash Tests	7	Warranty	2
Safety Features	10	Fuel Economy	3
Rollover	5	Complaints	–
PM	9	Insurance	10
Repair Costs	8	**OVERALL RATING... 9**	

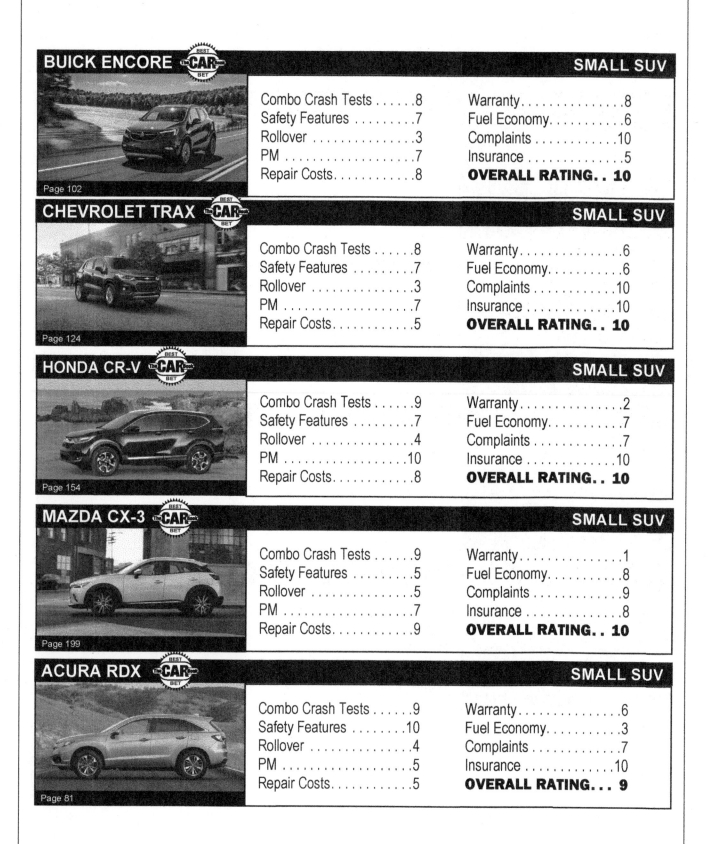

BUICK ENCORE

SMALL SUV

Combo Crash Tests 8
Safety Features 7
Rollover 3
PM 7
Repair Costs 8

Warranty 8
Fuel Economy 6
Complaints 10
Insurance 5
OVERALL RATING . . 10

Page 102

CHEVROLET TRAX

SMALL SUV

Combo Crash Tests 8
Safety Features 7
Rollover 3
PM 7
Repair Costs 5

Warranty 6
Fuel Economy 6
Complaints 10
Insurance 10
OVERALL RATING . . 10

Page 124

HONDA CR-V

SMALL SUV

Combo Crash Tests 9
Safety Features 7
Rollover 4
PM 10
Repair Costs 8

Warranty 2
Fuel Economy 7
Complaints 7
Insurance 10
OVERALL RATING . . 10

Page 154

MAZDA CX-3

SMALL SUV

Combo Crash Tests 9
Safety Features 5
Rollover 5
PM 7
Repair Costs 9

Warranty 1
Fuel Economy 8
Complaints 9
Insurance 8
OVERALL RATING . . 10

Page 199

ACURA RDX

SMALL SUV

Combo Crash Tests 9
Safety Features 10
Rollover 4
PM 5
Repair Costs 5

Warranty 6
Fuel Economy 3
Complaints 7
Insurance 10
OVERALL RATING . . . 9

Page 81

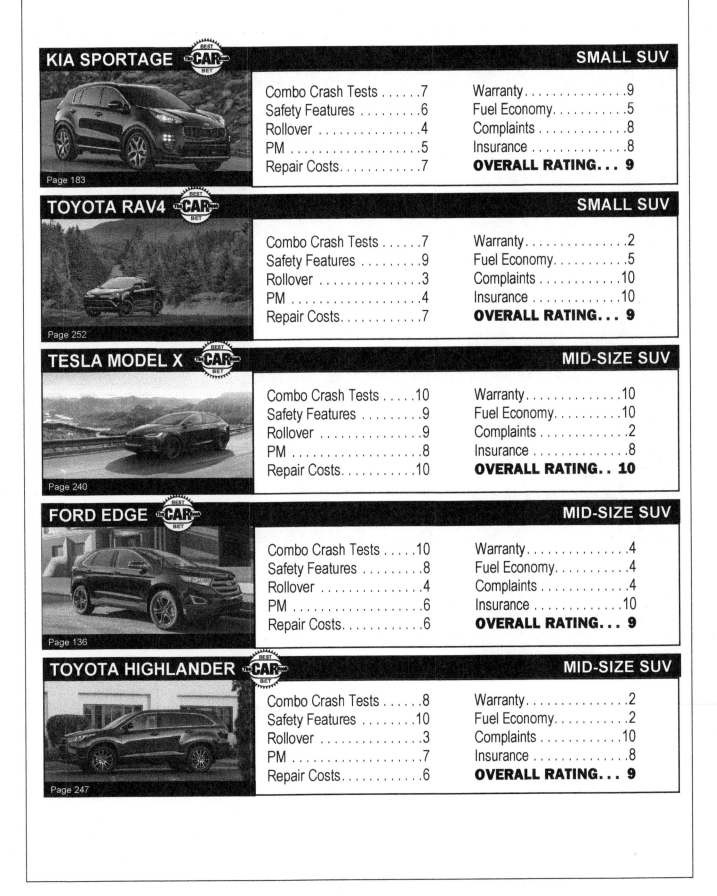

KIA SPORTAGE — SMALL SUV

Page 183

Combo Crash Tests	7	Warranty	9
Safety Features	6	Fuel Economy	5
Rollover	4	Complaints	8
PM	5	Insurance	8
Repair Costs	7	**OVERALL RATING...**	**9**

TOYOTA RAV4 — SMALL SUV

Page 252

Combo Crash Tests	7	Warranty	2
Safety Features	9	Fuel Economy	5
Rollover	3	Complaints	10
PM	4	Insurance	10
Repair Costs	7	**OVERALL RATING...**	**9**

TESLA MODEL X — MID-SIZE SUV

Page 240

Combo Crash Tests	10	Warranty	10
Safety Features	9	Fuel Economy	10
Rollover	9	Complaints	2
PM	8	Insurance	8
Repair Costs	10	**OVERALL RATING..**	**10**

FORD EDGE — MID-SIZE SUV

Page 136

Combo Crash Tests	10	Warranty	4
Safety Features	8	Fuel Economy	4
Rollover	4	Complaints	4
PM	6	Insurance	10
Repair Costs	6	**OVERALL RATING...**	**9**

TOYOTA HIGHLANDER — MID-SIZE SUV

Page 247

Combo Crash Tests	8	Warranty	2
Safety Features	10	Fuel Economy	2
Rollover	3	Complaints	10
PM	7	Insurance	8
Repair Costs	6	**OVERALL RATING...**	**9**

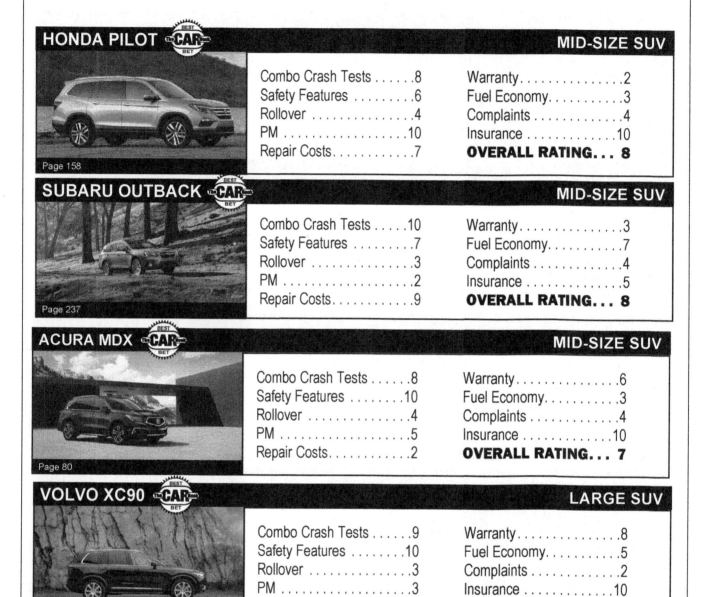

HONDA PILOT
MID-SIZE SUV

Page 158

Combo Crash Tests	8	Warranty	2
Safety Features	6	Fuel Economy	3
Rollover	4	Complaints	4
PM	10	Insurance	10
Repair Costs	7	**OVERALL RATING...**	**8**

SUBARU OUTBACK
MID-SIZE SUV

Page 237

Combo Crash Tests	10	Warranty	3
Safety Features	7	Fuel Economy	7
Rollover	3	Complaints	4
PM	2	Insurance	5
Repair Costs	9	**OVERALL RATING...**	**8**

ACURA MDX
MID-SIZE SUV

Page 80

Combo Crash Tests	8	Warranty	6
Safety Features	10	Fuel Economy	3
Rollover	4	Complaints	4
PM	5	Insurance	10
Repair Costs	2	**OVERALL RATING...**	**7**

VOLVO XC90
LARGE SUV

Page 268

Combo Crash Tests	9	Warranty	8
Safety Features	10	Fuel Economy	5
Rollover	3	Complaints	2
PM	3	Insurance	10
Repair Costs	2	**OVERALL RATING...**	**8**

CRASH TESTS

Safety is likely the most important factor that most of us consider when choosing a new car. In the past, evaluating safety was difficult. Now, thanks to the information in *The Car Book*, it's much easier to pick a safe vehicle. The bottom line: For the greatest protection, you'll want the maximum number of safety features (See Safety Checklist, pages 76-78) and good crash test results (the following tables).

A key factor in occupant protection is how well the car protects you in a crash. This depends on its ability to absorb the force of the impact rather than transfer it to the occupant.

In the frontal test, the vehicle impacts a solid barrier at 35 mph. In the side test, a moving barrier is crashed into the side of the vehicle at 38.5 mph. A second side test simulates hitting a tree or roadside pole by smashing a vehicle onto a vertical pole at the driver's door at 20 mph. The only occupant in this side pole test is a small female dummy in the driver seat.

The dummies measure the impact on the head, chest, neck and thighs.

Not all 2018 vehicles have undergone a crash test. The good news is that by carrying forward previous tests from cars that haven't changed, we have results for 130 2018 models. The bad news is that there are 67 models for which we don't have crash test results.

How the Cars are Rated: The combined crash test ratings are based on the *relative* performance of the 2018 vehicles tested to date. *This is a big difference from the government's "star" program.* Rather than large groups of undifferentiated vehicles in the government's star ratings, *The Car Book* rates them from best to worst. This means that those manufacturers really working on safety each year will rise to the top.

The first column provides *The Car Book's* Combined Crash Test Rating. The cars are rated from 10 Best to 1 Worst. The front is weighted 60%, the side 36%, and the pole test 4% with results compared among all new 2018 crash tests to date.

Next are the individual front and side tests. Again, relative to all other 2018 vehicles with crash test results, we indicate if the vehicle was Very Good, Good, Average, Poor or Very Poor. For side tests, the cars are rated separately from the trucks. Because of their construction, the dynamics of a side test are different in cars and light trucks.

The next five columns indicate the likelihood of the occupant sustaining a life-threatening injury. The percent likelihood is listed for the driver and front passenger in the front test, the driver and rear passenger in the side test, and the driver in the side pole test. Lower percentages mean a lower likelihood of being seriously injured if there is a crash test of this type. This information is taken directly from the government's analysis of the crash test results.

USING CRASH TEST DATA

TIP One of the most important results of our being the first to publish crash test data, and later develop our relative comparative ratings, is that it has put enormous pressure on the manufacturers to improve. Whereas years ago, when competition was based on style and horsepower, thanks to *The Car Book*, today's manufacturers are feverously competing on safety features. While the most important factors in evaluating the safety of today's vehicles are crash test performance and advanced safety features, size and weight do play a role. It is important to compare vehicles in the size classes that follow. For example, in a frontal collision between a subcompact and SUV rated 'Very Good," you'll be better off in the SUV. Nevertheless, selecting the best performers in whatever size class you are buying, is fundamental to protecting yourself. And remember, these tests are conducted with fully belted dummies, if you are not wearing your safety belt, then test results do not really apply.

CRASH TESTS

Crash Test Performance (10=Best, 1=Worst)	Combined Car Book Crash Test Rating	Test Type	Car Book Crash Test Rating-Index (Lower numbers are better)	Likelihood of Life Threatening Injury				
				Front Fixed Barrier		Side Moving Barrier		Side Pole
				Front Driver	Front Pass.	Side Driver	Side Pass.	Pole Driver
Subcompact								
Chevrolet Sonic	7	Front	Very Good-157	8.3%	8.1%			
		Side	Very Poor-153			9.5%	7.6%	3.8%
Chevrolet Spark	2	Front	Very Poor-228	13.6%	10.7%			
		Side	Poor-147			9.2%	6.8%	5.6%
Fiat 500	1	Front	Very Poor-256	11.4%	16.0%			
		Side	Poor-148			5.3%	8.%	15.8%
Ford Fiesta	3	Front	Average-199	8.2%	12.8%			
		Side	Very Poor-154			8.9%	8.2%	3.6%
Honda Fit	9	Front	Good-175	9.2%	9.1%			
		Side	Good-85			6.8%	2.5%	3.5%
Hyundai Veloster	4	Front	Poor-205	12.4%	9.2%			
		Side	Poor-131			6.9%	7.8%	1.5%
Mini Hardtop	4	Front	Average-194	10.7%	9.7%			
		Side	Very Poor-250			7.5%	18.7%	8.6%
Mitsubishi Mirage	2	Front	Poor-218	12.6%	10.5%			
		Side	Very Poor-210			7.5%	11.8%	22.1%
Nissan Versa	1	Front	Very Poor-244	10.2%	15.8%			
		Side	Very Poor-206			11.2%	12.1%	3.5%
Toyota Prius C	2	Front	Poor-206	11.7%	10.1%			
		Side	Very Poor-196			17.7%	5.2%	5.1%
Toyota Yaris	2	Front	Poor-217	9.9%	13.1%			
		Side	Average-111			7.7%	4.6%	2.9%
Compact								
Audi A3	6	Front	Average-197	11.2%	9.6%			
		Side	Average-113			7.0%	5.1%	4.2%
Audi A4	2	Front	Very Poor-276	12.9%	16.9%			
		Side	Average-119			4.3%	8.2%	2.6%
BMW 3 Series	6	Front	Average-194	11.6%	8.9%			
		Side	Average-108			7.9%	4.3%	2.3%
Cadillac ATS	2	Front	Very Poor-237	10.3%	14.9%			
		Side	Poor-138			7.5%	7.4%	4.8%
Chevrolet Cruze	5	Front	Good-176	9.0%	9.5%			
		Side	Very Poor-192			8.7%	12.7%	2.6%
Chevrolet Volt	4	Front	Poor-216	8.4%	14.5%			
		Side	Good-95			6.0%	4.7%	1.4%

CRASH TESTS

Crash Test Performance (10=Best, 1=Worst)	Combined Car Book Crash Test Rating	Test Type	Car Book Crash Test Rating-Index (Lower numbers are better)	Likelihood of Life Threatening Injury				
				Front Fixed Barrier		Side Moving Barrier		Side Pole
				Front Driver	Front Pass.	Side Driver	Side Pass.	Pole Driver
Compact (cont.)								
Ford C-MAX	3	Front	Poor-212	10.3%	12.2%			
		Side	Poor-129			9.2%	4.1%	9.1%
Ford Focus	8	Front	Good-178	8.4%	10.3%			
		Side	Good-95			6.7%	3.9%	2.6%
Honda Civic	5	Front	Average-197	9.3%	11.5%			
		Side	Poor-153			4.9%	10.0%	9.6%
Kia Soul	8	Front	Good-180	7.6%	11.2%			
		Side	Good-81			4.7%	4.0%	2.6%
Lexus IS	5	Front	Poor-219	12.4%	10.9%			
		Side	Good-85			5.6%	2.8%	7.1%
Mazda 3	4	Front	Poor-209	10.3%	11.7%			
		Side	Poor-119			11.5%	2.4%	2.8%
Mercedes-Benz C	3	Front	Average-203	7.8%	13.6%			
		Side	Very Poor-170			5.7%	12.2%	4.8%
Nissan Sentra	2	Front	Very Poor-242	11.8%	14.%			
		Side	Average-118			6.6%	6.5%	1.7%
Subaru Impreza	6	Front	Good-181	10.0%	9.1%			
		Side	Poor-127			8.5%	5.2%	5.6%
Toyota Corolla	4	Front	Poor-217	9.6%	13.4%			
		Side	Average-105			3.6%	6.7%	5.6%
Toyota Prius	5	Front	Average-203	10.3%	11.1%			
		Side	Average-116			6.5%	2.%	23.2%
Toyota Yaris iA	5	Front	Poor-205	9.9%	11.7%			
		Side	Average-111			7.7%	4.6%	2.9%
Volkswagen Beetle	3	Front	Poor-216	9.6%	13.2%			
		Side	Poor-125			7.3%	6.0%	5.3%
Volkswagen Golf	5	Front	Average-198	9.8%	11.1%			
		Side	Average-116			9.1%	3.9%	3.6%
Volkswagen Jetta	7	Front	Average-200	10.0%	11.1%			
		Side	Very Good-78			4.2%	3.9%	3.8%
Intermediate								
Acura TLX	10	Front	Very Good-156	7.3%	8.9%			
		Side	Very Good-58			4.4%	1.7%	3.4%
Audi A6	8	Front	Very Good-163	9.3%	7.7%			
		Side	Average-115			8.1%	3.9%	7.0%

CRASH TESTS

Crash Test Performance (10=Best, 1=Worst)	Combined Car Book Crash Test Rating	Test Type	Car Book Crash Test Rating-Index (Lower numbers are better)	Likelihood of Life Threatening Injury				
				Front Fixed Barrier		Side Moving Barrier		Side Pole
				Front Driver	Front Pass.	Side Driver	Side Pass.	Pole Driver
Intermediate (cont.)								
BMW 5 Series	4	Front	Very Poor-233	13.1%	11.7%			
		Side	Good-85			8.4%	0.8%	5.5%
Chevrolet Camaro	7	Front	Average-201	10.7%	10.5%			
		Side	Very Good-78			5.9%	2.3%	4.7%
Chevrolet Malibu	5	Front	Poor-223	10.4%	13.3%			
		Side	Very Good-73			6.0%	1.2%	6.4%
Ford Fusion	3	Front	Very Poor-226	8.7%	15.2%			
		Side	Average-117			6.3%	6.2%	4.1%
Ford Fusion Energi	7	Front	Very Good-154	7.3%	8.7%			
		Side	Very Poor-158			14.6%	3.6%	4.7%
Ford Mustang	8	Front	Very Good-162	7.0%	9.9%			
		Side	Poor-140			3.3%	10.4%	7.0%
Hyundai Sonata	9	Front	Very Good-147	7.5%	7.8%			
		Side	Average-114			5.8%	6.2%	4.6%
Infiniti Q50	4	Front	Very Poor-246	10.7%	15.6%			
		Side	Very Good-68			6.5%	1.2%	2.6%
Kia Optima	7	Front	Good-175	7.3%	11.0%			
		Side	Poor-128			4.2%	9.3%	2.2%
Lexus ES	7	Front	Good-190	9.5%	10.5%			
		Side	Good-96			5.5%	3.3%	10.5%
Lincoln MKZ	3	Front	Very Poor-226	8.7%	15.2%			
		Side	Average-117			6.3%	6.2%	4.1%
Mazda 6	7	Front	Good-185	7.6%	11.7%			
		Side	Good-96			8.2%	2.5%	3.5%
Nissan Altima	6	Front	Very Good-165	7.2%	10.0%			
		Side	Very Poor-189			17.7%	4.4%	4.9%
Nissan Maxima	7	Front	Good-185	8.7%	10.8%			
		Side	Average-111			6.0%	4.3%	11.4%
Subaru Legacy	9	Front	Very Good-168	9.1%	8.5%			
		Side	Good-80			3.3%	4.7%	4.0%
Toyota Avalon	8	Front	Average-194	10.1%	10.4%			
		Side	Very Good-63			4.1%	1.2%	9.1%
Toyota Camry	9	Front	Very Good-170	8.4%	9.3%			
		Side	Good-80			3.5%	4.8%	2.5%
Toyota Prius V	6	Front	Poor-211	10.3%	12.0%			
		Side	Very Good-70			4.3%	1.5%	10.5%
Volkswagen Passat	5	Front	Very Poor-238	12.6%	12.8%			
		Side	Very Good-76			4.4%	3.1%	5.3%

CRASH TESTS

| Crash Test Performance (10=Best, 1=Worst) | Combined Car Book Crash Test Rating | Test Type | Car Book Crash Test Rating-Index (Lower numbers are better) | Likelihood of Life Threatening Injury | | | | |
| | | | | Front Fixed Barrier | | Side Moving Barrier | | Side Pole |
				Front Driver	Front Pass.	Side Driver	Side Pass.	Pole Driver
Intermediate (cont.)								
Volvo S60	7	Front	Very Good-157	8.3%	8.1%			
		Side	Very Poor-153			9.5%	7.6%	3.8%
Large								
Buick LaCrosse	5	Front	Good-188	8.1%	11.6%			
		Side	Very Poor-168			11.6%	7.7%	2.9%
Cadillac XTS	9	Front	Very Good-160	7.6%	9.1%			
		Side	Good-88			4.2%	4.3%	6.7%
Chevrolet Impala	6	Front	Good-173	7.5%	10.6%			
		Side	Poor-142			10.1%	6.1%	2.9%
Chrysler 300	2	Front	Very Poor-236	12.7%	12.5%			
		Side	Poor-120			12.9%	0.8%	5.1%
Dodge Challenger	7	Front	Average-204	11.7%	9.8%			
		Side	Very Good-56			4.7%	1.4%	2.6%
Dodge Charger	3	Front	Very Poor-232	14.3%	10.4%			
		Side	Average-110			12.2%	0.6%	3.8%
Ford Taurus	6	Front	Very Good-164	8.4%	8.7%			
		Side	Very Poor-154			8.3%	8.3%	5.8%
Lincoln Continental	10	Front	Very Good-158	7.6%	8.9%			
		Side	Very Good-67			3.9%	3.0%	3.4%
Mercedes-Benz E	5	Front	Poor-206	9.6%	12.1%			
		Side	Good-87			6.4%	2.4%	6.8%
Tesla Model S	9	Front	Good-180	9.4%	9.5%			
		Side	Very Good-58			3.5%	1.5%	7.9%
Minivan								
Chrysler Pacifica	8	Front	Very Good-159	8.7%	7.9%			
		Side	Poor-93			5.8%	4.3%	3.2%
Honda Odyssey	7	Front	Good-180	9.5%	9.4%			
		Side	Good-58			2.3%	3.4%	3.1%
Toyota Sienna	6	Front	Average-197	8.6%	12.1%			
		Side	Average-71			2.9%	4.0%	4.5%
Small SUV								
Acura RDX	9	Front	Very Good-149	7.0%	8.5%			
		Side	Good-62			2.2%	2.9%	7.9%
Buick Encore	8	Front	Very Good-165	8.3%	9.0%			
		Side	Average-66			3.3%	3.0%	5.4%
Chevrolet Equinox	6	Front	Very Good-166	7.6%	9.8%			
		Side	Very Poor-230			6.2%	18.0%	5.6%

CRASH TESTS

Crash Test Performance (10=Best, 1=Worst)	Combined Car Book Crash Test Rating	Test Type	Car Book Crash Test Rating-Index (Lower numbers are better)	Likelihood of Life Threatening Injury				
				Front Fixed Barrier		Side Moving Barrier		Side Pole
				Front Driver	Front Pass.	Side Driver	Side Pass.	Pole Driver
Small SUV (cont.)								
Chevrolet Trax	8	Front	Very Good-165	8.3%	9.0%			
		Side	Average-66			3.3%	3.0%	5.4%
Ford Escape	8	Front	Good-179	8.3%	10.5%			
		Side	Good-60			2.0%	3.5%	5.0%
GMC Terrain	6	Front	Very Good-166	7.6%	9.8%			
		Side	Very Poor-230			6.2%	18.%	5.6%
Honda CR-V	9	Front	Very Good-155	7.5%	8.6%			
		Side	Good-58			2.9%	2.3%	6.1%
Honda HR-V	3	Front	Poor-214	11.9%	10.8%			
		Side	Average-70			4.4%	2.6%	5.1%
Hyundai Tucson	4	Front	Poor-210	11.2%	11.1%			
		Side	Average-72			3.7%	1.7%	12.8%
Jeep Compass	2	Front	Poor-211	11.3%	11.1%			
		Side	Very Poor-120			4.1%	8.1%	4.4%
Jeep Renegade	2	Front	Poor-207	10.4%	11.6%			
		Side	Very Poor-187			3.8%	15.8%	2.4%
Kia Sportage	7	Front	Average-195	10.9%	9.6%			
		Side	Good-59			3.5%	1.6%	7.4%
Lexus NX	7	Front	Very Good-153	7.7%	8.3%			
		Side	Very Poor-108			10.9%	0.9%	6.5%
Lincoln MKC	3	Front	Poor-213	8.9%	13.7%			
		Side	Poor-84			2.5%	5.8%	3.4%
Mazda CX-3	9	Front	Very Good-169	8.5%	9.2%			
		Side	Good-62			4.8%	1.8%	3.2%
Mazda CX-5	6	Front	Good-173	8.6%	9.5%			
		Side	Very Poor-128			2.7%	10.1%	4.5%
Mitsubishi Outlander Sport	4	Front	Average-203	10.0%	11.3%			
		Side	Poor-97			2.8%	6.3%	6.8%
Subaru Crosstrek	5	Front	Average-201	10.0%	11.2%			
		Side	Average-65			4.3%	2.%	5.6%
Subaru Forester	6	Front	Poor-205	9.0%	12.7%			
		Side	Good-56			3.1%	2.6%	2.9%
Toyota RAV4	7	Front	Average-204	10.6%	10.9%			
		Side	Very Good-49			3.2%	1.1%	6.5%

CRASH TESTS

Crash Test Performance (10=Best, 1=Worst)	Combined Car Book Crash Test Rating	Test Type	Car Book Crash Test Rating-Index (Lower numbers are better)	Likelihood of Life Threatening Injury				
				Front Fixed Barrier		Side Moving Barrier		Side Pole
				Front Driver	Front Pass.	Side Driver	Side Pass.	Pole Driver
Mid-Size SUV								
Acura MDX	7	Front	Very Good-168	8.3%	9.2%			
		Side	Average-68			2.5%	4.2%	3.6%
Audi Q7	6	Front	Average-195	10.0%	10.6%			
		Side	Average-67			3.7%	3.5%	2.0%
BMW X5	8	Front	Good-177	8.9%	9.7%			
		Side	Average-62			2.4%	3.1%	6.7%
Cadillac XT5	3	Front	Average-199	8.2%	12.7%			
		Side	Very Poor-104			4.7%	5.6%	7.2%
Dodge Durango	3	Front	Very Poor-226	14.1%	9.9%			
		Side	Average-63			6.4%	0.6%	2.9%
Dodge Journey	2	Front	Poor-222	9.6%	14.0%			
		Side	Very Poor-154			5.7%	9.7%	9.1%
Ford Edge	10	Front	Very Good-161	8.3%	8.5%			
		Side	Good-53			2.6%	2.7%	2.9%
Ford Explorer	5	Front	Good-183	10.4%	8.8%			
		Side	Poor-94			5.1%	3.5%	9.9%
GMC Acadia	3	Front	Poor-204	9.1%	12.4%			
		Side	Very Poor-121			5.0%	7.7%	4.0%
Honda Pilot	8	Front	Good-189	9.9%	10.0%			
		Side	Very Good-46			2.5%	1.0%	8.1%
Hyundai Santa Fe Sport	6	Front	Good-184	9.2%	10.1%			
		Side	Average-71			3.6%	3.2%	6.3%
Infiniti QX60	6	Front	Average-196	11.2%	9.5%			
		Side	Average-64			4.9%	1.8%	4.2%
Jeep Cherokee	5	Front	Very Poor-228	11.2%	13.1%			
		Side	Very Good-45			3.2%	1.7%	1.6%
Jeep Grand Cherokee	6	Front	Good-178	9.4%	9.3%			
		Side	Poor-93			8.3%	2.3%	2.4%
Kia Sorento	7	Front	Good-177	8.8%	9.7%			
		Side	Poor-84			3.2%	5.3%	3.7%
Lexus RX	3	Front	Very Poor-251	13.7%	13.2%			
		Side	Good-54			3.1%	2.2%	3.7%
Lincoln MKX	2	Front	Very Poor-313	16.1%	18.1%			
		Side	Poor-81			5.3%	2.3%	8.3%

CRASH TESTS

Crash Test Performance (10=Best, 1=Worst)	Combined Car Book Crash Test Rating	Test Type	Car Book Crash Test Rating-Index (Lower numbers are better)	Likelihood of Life Threatening Injury				
				Front Fixed Barrier		Side Moving Barrier		Side Pole
				Front Driver	Front Pass.	Side Driver	Side Pass.	Pole Driver
Mid-Size SUV (cont.)								
Mitsubishi Outlander	5	Front	Average-195	12.4%	8.0%			
		Side	Poor-91			3.8%	4.7%	7.8%
Nissan Rogue	1	Front	Very Poor-240	10.5%	15.%			
		Side	Very Poor-116			6.5%	4.6%	10.4%
Subaru Outback	10	Front	Very Good-168	9.1%	8.5%			
		Side	Very Good-50			2.9%	1.9%	4.0%
Tesla Model X	10	Front	Very Good-152	8.3%	7.5%			
		Side	Very Good-43			3.3%	1.1%	3.1%
Toyota 4Runner	1	Front	Very Poor-255	11.9%	15.5%			
		Side	Poor-88			7.1%	0.9%	11.7%
Toyota Highlander	8	Front	Average-192	11.2%	9.0%			
		Side	Very Good-45			2.4%	1.1%	7.3%
Volkswagen Atlas	9	Front	Good-182	10.1%	9.0%			
		Side	Very Good-43			2.0%	1.7%	5.6%
Large SUV								
Buick Enclave	5	Front	Average-191	7.1%	12.9%			
		Side	Poor-74			4.4%	3.5%	2.3%
Cadillac Escalade	6	Front	Poor-209	10.1%	12.%			
		Side	Very Good-45			3.%	0.4%	8.6%
Cadillac Escalade ESV	5	Front	Average-199	9.5%	11.5%			
		Side	Average-69			4.5%	1.0%	12.2%
Chevrolet Suburban	6	Front	Average-195	10.4%	10.2%			
		Side	Average-69			4.5%	1.0%	12.2%
Chevrolet Tahoe	8	Front	Good-185	9.7%	9.7%			
		Side	Very Good-45			3.%	0.4%	8.6%
Chevrolet Traverse	5	Front	Average-191	7.1%	12.9%			
		Side	Poor-74			4.4%	3.5%	2.3%
GMC Yukon	8	Front	Good-185	9.7%	9.7%			
		Side	Very Good-45			3.0%	0.4%	8.6%
GMC Yukon XL	6	Front	Average-195	10.4%	10.2%			
		Side	Average-69			4.5%	1.0%	12.2%
Volvo XC90	9	Front	Very Good-170	9.3%	8.5%			
		Side	Good-54			3.7%	2.3%	1.1%
Compact Pickup								
Chevrolet Colorado	3	Front	Poor-223	10.4%	13.3%			
		Side	Poor-73			6.0%	1.2%	6.4%
GMC Canyon	3	Front	Poor-223	10.4%	13.3%			
		Side	Average-73			6.%	1.2%	6.4%
Nissan Frontier	4	Front	Very Poor-357	18.5%	21.1%			
		Side	Very Good-37			3.0%	0.5%	4.1%

CRASH TESTS

Crash Test Performance (10=Best, 1=Worst)	Combined Car Book Crash Test Rating	Test Type	Car Book Crash Test Rating-Index (Lower numbers are better)	Likelihood of Life Threatening Injury				
				Front Fixed Barrier		Side Moving Barrier		Side Pole
				Front Driver	Front Pass.	Side Driver	Side Pass.	Pole Driver
Compact Pickup (cont.)								
Toyota Tacoma	1	Front	Very Poor-258	14.2%	13.5%			
		Side	Very Poor-115			10.1%	1.0%	12.7%
Standard Pickup								
Chevrolet Silverado	9	Front	Good-172	9.4%	8.7%			
		Side	Good-54			2.4%	1.6%	9.8%
Ford F-150	10	Front	Very Good-167	8.1%	9.4%			
		Side	Very Good-43			3.6%	0.70%	3.9%
GMC Sierra	9	Front	Good-172	9.4%	8.7%			
		Side	Good-54			2.4%	1.6%	9.8%
Nissan Titan	7	Front	Average-200	11.5%	9.7%			
		Side	Very Good-46			4.1%	0.9%	2.0%
Ram 1500	2	Front	Very Poor-228	12.6%	11.7%			
		Side	Poor-85			7.2%	0.6%	10.7%
Toyota Tundra		Front	Very Poor-236	12.0%	13.2%			
		Side	No Index-			2.7%		7.5%

CHILD SAFETY

Incorrect Child Safety Seat Installation: Surveys show up to 85 percent of parents do not install their child seats properly. Incorrect installation of a child safety seat can deny the child lifesaving protection and may even contribute to further injuring the child. Read the installation instructions carefully. If you have any questions about the correct installation in your particular car, go to www.safercar.gov/parents. There you will find a list of inspection stations near you where you can go for a free check up and advice by trained experts.

Child Safety Seat Recalls: Manufacturers are required to put address cards in child seat packages. Mail the registration card as soon as you open the box! You can also register your own seat at www.safercars.gov/parents for notification about recalls on your particular seat(s). These are the only ways you will receive notification of a seat recall. Keep a copy of the manufacturer's address and contact the manufacturer if you move. To find out if the seat you are using has ever been recalled go to www.nhtsa.gov/recalls#car-seats. You can also contact the Auto Safety Hotline at 800-424-9393.

Seat Belts for Kids: How long should young children use car seats? For children, a car seat is twice as effective in preventing injury as an adult lap and shoulder harness, so use it for as long as possible. Most children can start using seat belts at 4'9" or when they are tall enough for the shoulder belt to cross the chest, not the neck. The lap section of the belt should be snug and as low on the hips as possible. If the shoulder belt crosses the face or neck, use a booster seat.

AUTOMATIC SAFETY PROTECTION

The concept of automatic safety protection is not new. Automatic fire sprinklers in public buildings, oxygen masks in airplanes, purification of drinking water, and pasteurization of milk are all commonly accepted forms of automatic safety protection. Airbags and other new safety features provide automatic crash protection in cars.

Automatic crash protection comes in two basic forms. First, the airbags, and seat belt pretensioners protect occupants from collision forces. The second form of ACP includes technology intended to prevent crashes entirely, such as Automatic Emergency Braking.

The first form of automatic crash protection protects people from what is called the "second collision," when the occupant collides with the interior of the vehicle. Because the "second collision" occurs in less than a tenth of a second, providing automatic, rather than manual, protection dramatically improves the chances of escaping injury.

Since airbags were introduced over 30 years ago, they have been so successful in saving lives that car makers now include a variety of types which deploy from as many as 10 different areas of the interior.

The automatic control of safety features was first introduced with anti-lock brakes. Today, Electronic Stability Control (ESC) and other automatic functions such as Collision Avoidance Braking and Lane Departure Warnings are improving the safety of new cars.

Electronic Stability Control (ESC) takes advantage of anti-lock brake technology and helps minimize the loss of control. Each car maker will have its own name for this feature, but they all work in a similar fashion.

ESC, which is now required in all light vehicles, uses speed sensors on each wheel to determine if one or more of the wheels is locking up or skidding. ESC then uses these speed sensors, and a unit that determines the steering angle, to monitor what's happening with the vehicle. A special control device measures the steering and rotation of the tires in order to detect when a vehicle is about to go in a direction different from the one indicated by the steering wheel–or out of control! This will typically occur during a hard turn or on slippery surfaces. The control unit will sense whether the car is over-steering (turning sharper than you intended resulting in the back wheels slipping sideways) or under-steering (continuing to move forward despite your intended turn). When either of these events occur, the control unit will automatically apply the brakes to the appropriate wheels to correct the situation and, in some cases, automatically slow down the engine.

ESC will not keep the vehicle under control in severely out of control situations nor does it work as well on curvey roads as on straight roads. Nevertheless, according to the Insurance Institute for Highway Safety, ESC can reduce the chance of a single vehicle crash by over 50% and is particularly effective in reducing rollovers. Its benefit is that it will prevent more typical losses of control from escalating into a crash. For more details on key automatic safety features, see pages 76-78.

! TELEMATICS !

Telematic systems are subscription-based services ($100-$300 per year) that use a combination of cellular technology and global positioning systems to provide a variety of safety and convenience features. The main safety feature is automatic crash notification (ACN) which connects the vehicle's occupants to a call center that directs emergency medical teams to the car. ACN is activated by pressing a button on the dash or rear view mirror or automatically activates if the airbag deploys. The call center receives the exact location of your vehicle and notifies a local emergency response team. This can reduce the time it takes for an emergency team to reach your vehicle. Other safety features can include roadside assistance, remote door unlocking, stolen vehicle tracking, and driving directions.

Caution! Some manufacturers are adding cell phone capability to the ACN system. Talking on the ACN, or any cell phone, while driving increases the risk of a crash by 4 times—about the same effect as drinking and driving.

WHAT'S COMING IN THE FUTURE

CRASHWORTHINESS AND OCCUPANT PROTECTION

Among the great successes in auto safety are the improved occupant protection from air bags and better designed safety belts. Recently, new regulations and technologies have resulted in a dramatic reduction in rollover casualties. Rollovers, especially SUVs and pickups, had been responsible for one third of all road fatalities.

Today, all new light vehicles under 10,000 pounds have electronic stability control systems to keep them under better control, much stronger roofs, and side curtain air bags with improved designs to control ejection even when one is not wearing a safety belt. As a consequence, rollover fatalities in recent models have dropped by about 70%.

REAR END COLLISIONS

Although the crashworthiness of new vehicles is dramatically better than in cars of the past, there is still a problem in rear impacts. The front seat and backs of some vehicles are still so weak that they will collapse and cause even belted occupants to slide into the rear seat or even out the back window when a vehicle is hit from behind. Children in the rear seat – which is where they should be – are, tragically, right in the path of a collapsing front seat. While it is important to carry children in the rear seat for their safety, if possible the child should be placed behind an unoccupied seat or behind the seat occupied by the smallest adult.

Research and testing has shown how to design seating systems that can protect both the people in these seats, and the kids sitting behind them. Unfortunately, we have little data on which vehicles have strong seatbacks. We do know that Mercedes-Benz and BMW vehicles do have strong seatbacks. The Insurance Institute for Highway Safety (iihs.org) has ratings of head restraints in some vehicles for rear impact safety of a seat occupant that can differentiate relatively safe from unsafe vehicles in rear impacts.

WHAT'S NEXT?

Three major changes are occurring in motor vehicle design. First, the fuel economy standards are becoming more rigorous. Cars in 2025 will have to go twice as far on a gallon of gas as they did only a few years ago. Second, advances in electronics, sensors and computing power are being used to both improve safety and take over more of the driving. Third, electric vehicles are breaking into showrooms.

While current safety improvements have been to protect people when crashes occur, most future technology will be devoted to reducing the potential that a crash will even occur. Advanced sensors, electronics and computers will either warn a driver of a potential collision or actually take over control of the vehicle to avoid a crash.

Unquestionably, the self-driving car is coming, but today's vehicles are already "computers on wheels". Computers control emissions, transmissions, crash sensing, braking and many other critical actions. Manufacturers now offer systems that not only *warn* about vehicles in your blind spot, inadvertent lane changing or upcoming crashes, but actually *take action* to avoid collisions.

Lane Keeping Assist monitors the location of the vehicle within a lane and makes an automatic correction if the vehicle drifts out of the center. It also warns if a driver attempts to change lanes when it is not safe to do so.

Smart cruise control, which can vary travel speeds automatically according to traffic conditions, is becoming common.

Automatic braking, that will slow or stop a car when a potential rear end collision or pedestrian is sensed, is available in many cars.

Because of the popularity of these life-saving devices, manufacturers are putting systems, with varying degrees of effectiveness and reliability, on the market. Both NHTSA and IIHS are developing tests and ratings for the performance of such systems. For some of these features, lane changing and forward crash warnings, NHTSA has voluntary standards which define good performance. We've indicated which of these features do and do not meet the government performance standards on the car rating pages.

The good news is that more and more of this technology is becoming available in the cars most of us buy. Unfortunately, too many times these important safety features come with options you may not want, but have to pay for, to get the safety feature. Nevertheless, whether buying for yourself or your new teenage driver, we believe taking advantage of the safety features in today's new vehicles is critically important.

Rollover

Until a few years ago, more than 10,000 people died in rollovers every year. Half of these casualties were thrown out of the vehicle during the rollover and many others suffered head and neck injuries from collapsing roofs. The auto industry denied that anything could be done to reduce this toll even though the 2003 Volvo XC90 had several features that offered rollover occupant protection.

The risk that a vehicle will rollover is a significant safety challenge, especially with sport utility vehicles, pickups and vans. Because of their relatively high center of gravity, they are less stable than most passenger cars. As a result, they are more likely to roll over on a sharp turn or if they go out of control.

There are a few reasons why rollovers occur: drifting off the side of the road where the vehicle "trips" on an obstacle and rolls; responding with a major steering correction in this situation; or, over-steering–making too sharp a turn and having your rear wheels skid out, turning the vehicle sideways.

As a result of a major campaign by the Center for Auto Safety and others, the government is finally requiring new vehicles to have certain rollover protections including:

Electronic Stability Control: ESC automatically applies braking to wheels selectively when a vehicle is on the verge of going out of control. (See page 28.) This can keep the vehicle from sliding and rotating sideways, making it vulnerable to rolling over. ESC has substantially reduced the likelihood of a rollover.

Ejection Control: This feature is designed to keep passengers in the car, even if they are not wearing their safety belts. Ejection control includes improved designs that keep the glass in place even when the window breaks and window curtain air bags that cover the side windows in a rollover. These air curtains cushion the occupant and reduce the chances that they will be ejected.

Roof Strength: Until recently, roof strength requirements were weak and few manufacturers designed roofs that could hold up when a vehicle rolled over. Prodded by the rollover roof crush tests sponsored by the Center for Auto Safety, the government doubled the force that a roof must sustain when the front corner is pushed down at an angle, and required that the test be conducted sequentially on both sides. The result: Most new vehicle roofs can withstand a force of more than four times the weight of the vehicle.

Padding in the Roof: This standard requires energy absorbing padding and helps reduce the likelihood of a concussion or other head injury if your head strikes the roof.

Rollover Estimates

Electronic stability control has dramatically reduced the incidents of rollover by preventing a vehicle from getting into a position where it could rollover. Nevertheless, there are still situations in which a vehicle could find itself in a position where a rollover could occur. A rollover position generally occurs when the vehicle turns sideways and continues to move in a sideways direction. When the ESC fails to prevent a vehicle from getting in this position, the likelihood of an actual rollover is directly related to the vehicle's center of gravity. The higher the center of gravity, the more likely the vehicle is to rollover when in a rollover position.

To approximate a vehicle's center of gravity, the government uses a formula, called the Static Stability Index. It is based on the ratio of the height of the car's center of gravity to half of its track width (the lateral distance between two wheels). Using the SSI the government further develops a "risk of rollover" percentage. The higher the percentage, the more likely the vehicle is to rollover, if in a rollover position.

You can't use this information to exactly predict rollovers. However, all things being equal, if two vehicles are in the same rollover situation, the one with the lower percentage is less likely to roll over. Because this formula doesn't consider such things as driver behavior, vehicle weight, and the effectiveness of the vehicle's ESC, experts do not believe it tells the whole story. We agree, and have urged the government to provide an even better rollover rating system.

The good news: In buying a new vehicle, you can be reasonably confident, thanks to the new standards, that it will have a reasonable level of rollover resistance and, should it roll over, good protection in most situations.

STATIC STABILITY INDEX

Vehicle	SSI (High=Better)/ Chance of Rollover		Vehicle	SSI (High=Better)/ Chance of Rollover		Vehicle	SSI (High=Better)/ Chance of Rollover	
Acura ILX	11.1%	Moderate	Ford Fiesta	14.3%	High	Mercedes-Benz B	15.5%	High
Acura MDX	15.5%	High	Ford Flex	16.9%	High	Mercedes-Benz C	11.1%	Low
Acura RDX	15.5%	High	Ford Focus	11.6%	Moderate	Mercedes-Benz CLA	11.1%	Moderate
Acura TLX	9.9%	Low	Ford Fusion	10.9%	Low	Mercedes-Benz E	9.7%	Low
Audi A3	10.9%	Low	Ford Fusion Energi	10.9%	Low	Mercedes-Benz GLA	13.3%	Moderate
Audi A4	9.9%	Low	Ford Mustang	8.0%	Very Low	Mercedes-Benz GLE	18.5%	Very High
Audi A5	9.5%	Very Low	Ford Taurus	11.3%	Moderate	Mercedes-Benz GLS	19.8%	Very High
Audi A6	8.6%	Very Low	Genesis G80	10.5%	Low	Mercedes-Benz S	10.7%	Low
Audi Q3	14.3%	High	GMC Acadia	16.4%	High	Mini Hardtop	11.1%	Low
Audi Q5	15.5%	High	GMC Sierra	17.4%	High	Mitsubishi Mirage	16.4%	High
Audi Q7	15.5%	High	GMC Terrain	16.4%	High	Mitsubishi Outlander	16.4%	High
BMW 2 Series	10.9%	Low	Honda Accord	10.3%	Low	Mitsubishi Outlander Sport	19.1%	Very High
BMW 3 Series	9.5%	Very Low	Honda Civic	9.3%	Very Low	Nissan Altima	10.3%	Low
BMW 4 Series	9.5%	Very Low	Honda CR-V	16.4%	High	Nissan Armada	21.2%	Very High
BMW 5 Series	9.3%	Very Low	Honda Fit	14.7%	High	Nissan Frontier	19.8%	Very High
BMW 7 Series	10.5%	Low	Honda HR-V	15.5%	High	Nissan Maxima	9.5%	Very Low
BMW i3	14.0%	High	Honda Odyssey	13.6%	Moderate	Nissan Murano	15.5%	High
BMW X1	14.7%	High	Honda Pilot	16.4%	High	Nissan Pathfinder	16.9%	High
BMW X5	17.9%	Very High	Hyundai Elantra	10.7%	Low	Nissan Rogue	16.4%	High
Buick Cascada	10.5%	Low	Hyundai Santa Fe	15.5%	High	Nissan Sentra	11.8%	Moderate
Buick Enclave	15.9%	High	Hyundai Santa Fe Sport	15.1%	High	Nissan Titan	19.8%	Very High
Buick Encore	17.9%	Very High	Hyundai Sonata	10.5%	Low	Nissan Versa	14.3%	High
Buick Envision	17.9%	Very High	Hyundai Tucson	15.5%	High	Ram 1500	21.9%	Very High
Buick LaCrosse	9.9%	Low	Hyundai Veloster	10.5%	Low	Subaru Crosstrek	15.9%	High
Buick Regal	10.5%	Low	Infiniti Q50	9.7%	Low	Subaru Forester	16.9%	High
Cadillac ATS	10.1%	Low	Infiniti QX30	12.1%	Moderate	Subaru Impreza	9.5%	Very Low
Cadillac CT6	10.5%	Low	Infiniti QX50	15.5%	High	Subaru Legacy	10.1%	Low
Cadillac Escalade	21.9%	Very High	Infiniti QX60	17.9%	High	Subaru Outback	17.4%	High
Cadillac Escalade ESV	21.2%	Very High	Infiniti QX80	21.2%	Very High	Tesla Model 3	10.7%	Low
Cadillac XT5	16.9%	High	Jeep Cherokee	16.9%	High	Tesla Model S	5.7%	Very Low
Cadillac XTS	11.8%	Moderate	Jeep Compass	18.5%	Very High	Tesla Model X	9.0%	Very Low
Chevrolet Bolt	17.4%	High	Jeep Grand Cherokee	16.9%	High	Toyota 4Runner	24.6%	Very High
Chevrolet Camaro	8.0%	Very Low	Jeep Renegade	17.9%	High	Toyota 86	8.2%	Very Low
Chevrolet Colorado	21.9%	Very High	Jeep Wrangler	25%	Very High	Toyota Avalon	10.7%	Low
Chevrolet Corvette	6.6%	Very Low	Kia Forte	10.7%	Low	Toyota Camry	9.9%	Low
Chevrolet Cruze	10.7%	Low	Kia Optima	9.9%	Low	Toyota Corolla	11.8%	Moderate
Chevrolet Equinox	18.5%	Very High	Kia Rio	11.8%	Moderate	Toyota Corolla iM	11.1%	Moderate
Chevrolet Impala	12.1%	Moderate	Kia Sedona	14.0%	Moderate	Toyota Highlander	16.9%	High
Chevrolet Malibu	10.3%	Low	Kia Sorento	15.1%	High	Toyota Prius	10.7%	Low
Chevrolet Silverado	17.4%	High	Kia Soul	14.7%	High	Toyota Prius C	11.8%	Moderate
Chevrolet Sonic	10.1%	Low	Kia Sportage	14.7%	High	Toyota Prius Prime	12.4%	Moderate
Chevrolet Spark	17.9%	High	Land Rover Range Ro-ver	19.1%	Very High	Toyota Prius V	13.6%	Moderate
Chevrolet Suburban	20.4%	Very High	Land Rvr Range Rvr Evoque	14.3%	High	Toyota RAV4	16.9%	High
Chevrolet Tahoe	21.9%	Very High	Land Rvr Range Rvr Sport	16.9%	High	Toyota Sequoia	19.1%	Very High
Chevrolet Traverse	16.9%	High	Lexus ES	11.1%	Low	Toyota Sienna	14.0%	Moderate
Chevrolet Trax	17.9%	High	Lexus GS	10.9%	Low	Toyota Tacoma	19.1%	Very High
Chevrolet Volt	9.3%	Very Low	Lexus GX	26%	Very High	Toyota Tundra	21.9%	Very High
Chrysler 300	11.3%	Moderate	Lexus IS	9.5%	Very Low	Toyota Yaris	13.6%	Moderate
Chrysler Pacifica	11.6%	Moderate	Lexus NX	15.9%	High	Toyota Yaris iA	13.3%	Moderate
Dodge Challenger	11.1%	Low	Lexus RC	9.7%	Low	Volkswagen Atlas	15.9%	High
Dodge Charger	10.1%	Low	Lexus RX	16.4%	High	Volkswagen Beetle	10.5%	Low
Dodge Durango	21.2%	Very High	Lincoln Continental	10.7%	Low	Volkswagen Golf	13.3%	Moderate
Dodge Journey	18.5%	Very High	Lincoln MKC	16.9%	High	Volkswagen Jetta	11.1%	Low
Fiat 500	14.3%	High	Lincoln MKX	14.0%	Moderate	Volkswagen Passat	10.7%	Low
Fiat 500X	15.9%	High	Lincoln MKZ	10.9%	Low	Volkswagen Tiguan	17.9%	High
Ford C-MAX	14.7%	High	Lincoln Navigator	21.9%	Very High	Volvo S60	10.1%	Low
Ford EcoSport	19.1%	Very High	Mazda CX-3	13.6%	Moderate	Volvo V60	11.6%	Moderate
Ford Edge	15.5%	High	Mazda CX-5	16.9%	High	Volvo XC60	14.0%	High
Ford Escape	19.1%	Very High	Mazda CX-9	16.9%	High	Volvo XC90	17.9%	High
Ford Expedition	21.9%	Very High	Mazda Mazda3	10.5%	Low			
Ford Explorer	17.4%	High	Mazda Mazda6	10.3%	Low			
Ford F-150	19.1%	Very High	Mazda MX-5	8.0%	Very Low	*Calculated		

As gas prices bounce up and down, regular driving still takes a big bite out of our pocketbooks. Even at today's lower gas prices, the average household spends $1,500 a year on gas. The good news is that higher fuel efficiency standards are forcing car companies to provide more fuel efficient vehicles. Buying right and practicing more fuel efficient driving will make a huge difference in your vehicle's operating costs. With the current low gas prices, many consumers are buying fuel inefficient vehicles. Beware, when gas prices go back up, and they will, you'll be stuck with a budget-busting gas guzzler.

Using the EPA ratings is the best way to incorporate fuel efficiency in selecting a new car. By comparing these ratings, even among cars of the same size, you'll find that fuel efficiency varies greatly. One compact car might get 36 miles per gallon (mpg) while another compact gets only 22 mpg. If you drive 15,000 miles a year and you pay $2.15 per gallon for fuel, the 36 mpg car will save you $570 a year over the "gas guzzler." Imagine what's going to happen when gas prices go back up!

Today, thanks to changes in the way the EPA estimates miles per gallon, the numbers more closely match what you can expect from the vehicle.

Octane Ratings: Once you've purchased your car, you'll be faced with choosing the right gasoline. Oil companies spend millions of dollars trying to get you to buy so-called higher performance or high octane fuels. Using high octane fuel can add considerably to your gas bill, and the vast majority of vehicles do not need it. Check your owner's manual and only use the recommended octane rating, which is usually 87. Very few vehicles require "premium" gasoline.

The octane rating of a gasoline is not a measure of power or quality. It is simply a measure of the gas' resistance to engine knock, which is the pinging sound you hear when the air and fuel mixture in your engine ignites prematurely during acceleration.

Your engine may knock when accelerating a heavily loaded car uphill or when the humidity is low. This is normal and does not mean you need a higher-octane gasoline. When buying, consider the impact of a high octane gas car. It will increase your fuel costs by around 25%.

FIVE FACTORS AFFECTING FUEL ECONOMY

1. Engine Power: The smaller the engine the better your fuel efficiency. A 10% increase in the size of your engine can increase your fuel consumption rate by 6%. Smaller engines can be cheaper to maintain as well. With new engine designs and turbocharging, manufacturers can get more power out of smaller engines.

2. Transmission: Most automatic transmissions today can achieve as high a fuel economy as a manual transmission. Well-designed transmissions with more gears and continuously variable transmissions will generally achieve better fuel economy.

3. Cruise Control: Using cruise control can save fuel because driving at a constant speed uses less fuel than changing speeds frequently.

4. Hybrids: Most manufacturers offer hybrid vehicles that have both gasoline and electric engines. Hybrids can offer 30% better fuel economy and lower emissions.

5. Electrics: All-electric vehicles can keep you out of the gas station altogether. See our new section on page 269.

TWELVE WAYS TO SAVE MONEY AT THE PUMP

Here are a few simple things you can do that will save you a lot of money. Specific savings are based on gas at $2.45.

1. Pump 'Em Up: 27% of vehicles have tires that are under-inflated. Properly inflated tires can improve mileage by 3%, which is like getting 7 cents off a gallon of gas. Check the label on your door or glove box to find out what the pressure range should be for your tires. Don't use the "max pressure" written on your tire. Electronic gauges are fast, easy to use and accurate. Don't rely on the numbers on the air pump. The good news–all new cars must have a low tire pressure warning on the dash.

2. Check Your Air Filter: A dirty air filter by itself can rob a car by as much as 10% percent of its mileage. If an engine doesn't get enough air, it will burn too much gasoline. Replacing a dirty filter can in effect knock up to 25 cents off a gallon of gas.

3. Straighten Out: Not only does poor wheel alignment cause your tires to wear out faster and cause poor handling, but it can cause your engine to work harder and reduce your fuel efficiency by 10%.

4. Be A Regular: Check your owner's manual. Very, very few cars actually need high-octane gas. Using 87-octane (regular) gas can save you over 28 cents per gallon over mid-grade and 52 cents over premium.

5. Tune Up: A properly tuned engine is a fuel saver. Have a trusted mechanic tune your engine to factory specifications and you could save up to 8 cents a gallon.

6. Check Your Cap: It is estimated that nearly 15% of the cars on the road have broken or missing gasoline caps. This hurts your mileage and can harm the environment by allowing your gasoline to evaporate. Many Ford products have a capless gas filler, which is a great convenience.

7. Don't Speed: A car moving at 55 mph gets better fuel economy than the same car at 65 mph. For every 5 mph you reduce your highway speed, you can reduce fuel consumption by 7%, which is like getting 17 cents off a gallon of gas.

8. Don't Idle: An idling car gets 0 mpg. Cars with larger engines typically waste more gas at idle than cars with smaller engines. If you're stopped for more than a minute, consider turning your engine off. Some new cars do that automatically.

9. Drive Smoother: The smoother your accelerations and decelerations, the better your mileage. A smooth foot can save 38 cents a gallon.

10. Combo Trips: Short trips can be expensive because they usually involve a "cold" vehicle. For the first mile or two before the engine gets warmed up, a cold vehicle only gets 30 to 40% of the mileage it gets at full efficiency. Combine your trips.

11. Lose Weight: For every 100 pounds you carry around, you lose 1 to 2% in fuel efficiency. Remove extra items from your trunk or the rear of your SUV. Empty your roof rack—50% of engine power, traveling at highway speed, is used in overcoming aerodynamic drag or wind resistance.

12. Choose Your Gas Miser: If you own more than one vehicle, choosing to drive the one with better gas mileage will save you money. If you drive 15,000 miles per year, half in a vehicle with 20 mpg and half with a 30 mpg vehicle and switch to driving 75% of your trips in the 30 mpg vehicle, you will save $153 annually with gas at $2.45.

FUEL ECONOMY

Get up-to-date information about fuel economy at www.fueleconomy.gov, a website created by the Department of Energy and the EPA. There you'll find the EPA's Fuel Economy Guide, allowing you to compare fuel economy estimates for today's models and back to 1985. You'll also find out about the latest technological advances pertaining to fuel efficiency. The site is extremely useful and easy to navigate. Also, see the Fuel Factor section on our car rating pages.

FUEL ECONOMY MISERS AND GUZZLERS

Because the success of the EPA program depends on consumers' ability to compare the fuel economy ratings easily, we have included key mileage figures on our ratings pages. Listed below are the best and worst of this year's ratings according to annual fuel cost. The complete EPA fuel economy guide is available at www.fueleconomy.gov.

FUEL ECONOMY MISERS AND GUZZLERS

Vehicle	Specifications	MPG (city/hwy)	Annual Fuel Cost
THE BEST			
Electric Vehicles (EV)*			
BMW I3 BEV	Automatic, RWD	137/111	$550
Chevrolet Bolt EV	Automatic, FWD	128/110	$550
Hyundai Ioniq Electric	Automatic, FWD	150/122	$500
Nissan LEAF	Automatic, FWD	124/101	$600
Kia Soul Electric	Automatic, FWD	124/93	$600
Plug In Hybrid Electric Vehicles (PHEVs)*			
Chevrolet Volt	1.5L, 4 cyl., Continuously Variable, FWD	43/42	$650
Ford Fusion Energi Plug-in Hybrid	2.0L, 4 cyl., Continuously Variable, FWD	43/41	$750
Chrysler Pacifica Hybrid	3.6L, 6 cyl., Continuously Variable, FWD	32/33	$900
Audi A3 e-tron ultra	1.4L, 4 cyl., 6-sp. Automated Manual-Selectable, FWD	34/39	$1,000
Gas			
Hyundai Ioniq	1.6L, 4 cyl., 6-sp. Automated Manual, FWD	55/54	$674
Toyota Camry Hybrid LE	2.5L, 4 cyl., 6-sp. Selectable Cont. Variable, FWD	51/53	$708
Kia Niro	1.6L, 4 cyl., 6-sp. Automated Manual, FWD	51/46	$754
Chevrolet Malibu	1.8L, 4 cyl., Continuously Variable, FWD	49/43	$794
Toyota Prius c	1.5L, 4 cyl., Continuously Variable, FWD	48/43	$803
Toyota Camry Hybrid XLE/SE	2.5L, 4 cyl., 6-sp. Selectable Cont. Variable, FWD	44/47	$810
Kia Optima Hybrid	2.0L, 4 cyl., 6-sp. Automated Manual, FWD	39/46	$872
Ford Fusion Hybrid	2.0L, 4 cyl., Continuously Variable, FWD	43/41	$873
Ford C-MAX Hybrid	2.0L, 4 cyl., Continuously Variable, FWD	42/38	$914
Mitsubishi Mirage	1.2L, 43cyl., Continuously Variable, FWD	37/43	$926
Lincoln MKZ Hybrid	2.0L, 4 cyl., Continuously Variable, FWD	41/38	$927
Toyota Avalon	2.5L, 4 cyl., 6-sp. Selectable Cont. Variable, FWD	40/39	$929
Lexus ES 300h	2.5L, 4 cyl., 6-sp. Selectable Cont. Variable, FWD	40/39	$929
Mitsubishi Mirage	1.2L, 3 cyl., 5-sp. Manual, FWD	33/41	$1,004
Honda Civic 4Dr	1.5L, 4 cyl., Continuously Variable, FWD	32/42	$1,007
Honda Fit	1.5L, 4 cyl., Continuously Variable, FWD	33/40	$1,017
Hyundai Elantra	1.4L, 4 cyl., 7-sp. Automated Manual, FWD	32/40	$1,032
Toyota Yaris iA	1.5L, 4 cyl., 6-sp. Semi-Automatic, FWD	32/40	$1,032
Honda Civic 2Dr	1.5L, 4 cyl., Continuously Variable, FWD	31/40	$1,049
Ford Focus	1.0L, 3 cyl., 6-sp. Manual, FWD	30/40	$1,065
THE WORST**			
Mercedes-Benz AMG G 63	5.5L, 8 cyl., 7-sp. Automatic, 4WD	15/15	$3,337
Jeep Grand Cherokee TrackHawk	6.2L, 8 cyl., 8-sp. Automatic, AWD	11/17	$3,252
Lexus LX 570	5.7L, 8 cyl., 7-sp. Semi-Automatic, 4WD	13/18	$2,921
Dodge Durango SRT	6.4L, 8 cyl., 8-sp. Automatic, AWD	13/19	$2,838
Jeep Grand Cherokee SRT	6.4L, 8 cyl., 8-sp. Automatic, AWD	13/19	$2,838
Mercedes-Benz AMG GLE 63	5.5L, 8 cyl., 7-sp. Automatic, 4WD	14/18	$2,820
Chevrolet Camaro	6.2L, 8 cyl., 10-sp. Semi-Automatic, RWD	12/21	$2,684
BMW M6 Convertible	4.4L, 8 cyl., 7-sp. Automated Manual, RWD	14/20	$2,668
Chevrolet Camaro	6.2L, 8 cyl., 10-sp. Manual, RWD	14/20	$2,668
Mercedes-Benz AMG SL 65	6.0L, 12 cyl., 7-sp. Automatic, RWD	13/22	$2,613
Chevrolet Corvette	6.2L, 8 cyl., 8-sp. Semi-Automatic, RWD	13/13	$2,546
Toyota Tundra	5.7L, 8 cyl., 6-sp. Semi-Automatic, 4WD	13/17	$2,483
Toyota Sequoia	5.7L, 8 cyl., 6-sp. Semi-Automatic, 4WD	13/17	$2,483
Toyota Sequoia	5.7L, 8 cyl., 6-sp. Semi-Automatic, RWD	13/17	$2,483
Chevrolet Colorado	3.6L, 6 cyl., 8-sp. Automatic, RWD	15/15	$2,450
GMC Canyon	3.6L, 6 cyl., 8-sp. Automatic, RWD	15/15	$2,450
RAM 1500	5.7L, 8 cyl., 6-sp. Automatic, 4WD	13/18	$2,410
Toyota Tundra	5.7L, 8 cyl., 6-sp. Automatic, RWD	13/18	$2,410
Nissan Armada	5.6L, 8 cyl., 7-sp. Semi-Automatic, 4WD	13/18	$2,410
Toyota Land Cruiser	5.7L, 8 cyl., 8-sp. Semi-Automatic, 4WD	13/18	$2,410

Note: 2018 annual fuel cost based on driving 15,000 miles and a projected regular gas price of $2.45; #=Premium Required; *=Annual cost based on epa estimate for electric use; **=Fuel Economy rating based on hybrid function only; annual cost based on epa estimate for gas and electric use; ***=Low volume exotic vehicles (over $120,000) and cargo vans were excluded.

COMPARING WARRANTIES

After buying your car, maintenance will be a significant portion of your operating costs. The strength of your warranty and the cost of repairs after the warranty expires will determine these costs. Comparing warranties and repair costs, before you buy, can save you thousands of dollars down the road.

Along with your new car comes a warranty which is a promise from the manufacturer that the car will perform as it should. Most of us never read the warranty until it is too late. In fact, because warranties are often difficult to read and understand, most of us don't really know what our warranty covers.

To keep your warranty in effect, you must operate and maintain your car according to the instructions in your owner's manual. It is important to keep a record of all maintenance performed on your car.

Do not confuse a warranty with a service contract. A service contract must be purchased separately while a warranty is yours at no extra cost when you buy the car.

Warranties are difficult to compare because they contain fine print and confusing language. The following table will help you compare this year's warranties. Because the table does not contain all the details about each warranty, review the actual warranty to understand its fine points. You have the right to inspect a warranty before you buy—it's the law.

The table provides information on five critical items in a warranty:

The **Basic Warranty** covers most parts against manufacturer's defects. Tires, batteries, and items added to the car at the time of sale are covered under separate warranties. The table describes coverage in terms of months and miles. For example, 48/50 means the warranty is good for 48 months or 50,000 miles, whichever comes first. This is the most important part of your warranty because it covers the items most likely to fail. We give the basic warranty the most weight.

The **Power Train Warranty** often lasts longer than the basic warranty. Because each manufacturer's definition of the power train is different, it is important to find out exactly what your warranty will cover. Power train coverage should include the engine, transmission, and drive train. Some luxury cars will cover additional systems such as steering, suspension, and electrical systems. We give the powertrain warranty less weight than the basic because it doesn't cover as much as the basic warranty. Even with less weight in our rating, it can have a lot of influence in the overall index if it is very long.

The **Corrosion Warranty** usually applies only to actual holes due to rust. Read this section carefully because many corrosion warranties do not apply to what the manufacturer may describe as cosmetic rust or bad paint.

The **Roadside Assistance** column indicates whether or not the manufacturer offers a program for helping with breakdowns, lockouts, jump starts, flat tires, running out of gas, and towing. Some have special limitations or added features. Because each one is different, check yours carefully.

The **Scheduled Maint. (Free)** column indicates whether or not free scheduled maintenance is included and for how long. These programs cover parts scheduled to be replaced such as filters. If there is an asterisk next to the coverage, that means the manufacturer also covers the cost of <u>any</u> parts that need to be replaced because of wear. Covering the cost of "wear" parts is a terrific feature and offered by very few manufacturers.

The last column, the **Warranty Rating Index**, provides an overall assessment of this year's warranties. **The higher the Index number, the better the warranty.** We give the most weight to the basic and power train components of the warranties. Roadside assistance was weighted somewhat less, and the corrosion warranty received the least weight.

Finally, we also considered special features such as extra coverage on batteries or wheel alignment. These benefits added to the overall ratings, whereas certain limitations (shortened transferability) took away from the rating.

The best ratings are in **_BOLD_**.

WARRANTY COMPARISON

Manufacturer	Basic Warranty	Power Train Warranty	Corrosion Warranty	Roadside Assistance	Scheduled Maint. (Free)	Index	Warranty Rating
Acura[1]	48/50	72/70	60/75	48/50		1106	Average
Audi	48/50	48/50	144/180	48/Unlimited	12/5	1203	Good
BMW[2]	48/50	48/50	144/180	48/Unlimited	48/50	1288	Very Good
Buick	48/50	72/70	72/90	72/90	24/24	1259	Good
Cadillac[3]	48/50	72/70	72/90[4]	72/70	48/50	1320	Very Good
Chevrolet	36/36	60/60[5]	72/90	60/60	24/24	1062	Average
Chrysler[6]	36/36	60/60[7]	60/75	60/60		1010	Poor
Dodge[8]	36/36	60/60[9]	60/75	60/60		1010	Poor
Fiat[10]	48/50	48/50	60/75[11]	48/50		1014	Average
Ford[12]	36/36	60/60	60/Unlimited	60/60		989	Poor
Genesis[13]	60/60	120/100	72/Unlimited	60/60	36/36	1578	Very Good
GMC	36/36	60/60	72/90	60/60	24/24	1026	Average
Honda[14]	36/36	60/60	60/Unlimited	36/36		912	Very Poor
Hyundai[15]	60/60	120/100[16]	84/Unlimited	60/Unlimited		1469	Very Good
Infiniti[17]	48/60	72/70	84/Unlimited	60/Unlimited		1299	Very Good
Jeep[18]	36/36	60/60[19]	36/Unlimited	60/60		964	Poor
Kia[20]	60/60	120/100[21]	60/10	60/60		1276	Very Good
Land Rover	60/60	60/60	72/Unlimited	36/50	12/15	1169	Good
Lexus[22]	48/50	72/70	72/Unlimited	48/Unlimited	12/10	1200	Good
Lincoln[23]	48/50	72/70	60/Unlimited	72/70[24]	24/24	1271	Very Good
Mazda	36/36	60/60	36/Unlimited	36/36		846	Very Poor
Mercedes-Benz[25]	48/50	48/50	48/50	48/50		937	Poor
Mini	48/50	48/50	144/Unlimited	48/Unlimited	36/36	1280	Very Good
Mitsubishi	60/60	120/100	84/100[26]	60/Unlimited		1429	Very Good
Nissan	36/36	60/60	60/Unlimited			798	Very Poor
Porsche	48/50	48/50	144/180	48/50		1157	Good
Ram	60/60	60/60	36/Unlimited			930	Very Poor
Subaru[27]	36/36	60/60	60/Unlimited	48/50		972	Poor
Tesla	48/50	96/Unlimited	48/50	48/50		1357	Very Good
Toyota	36/36	60/60	60/Unlimited	24/Unlimited	25/25	926	Very Poor
Volkswagen	72/72	72/72	120/120	36/36	12/12	1374	Very Good
Volvo	48/50	48/50	120/Unlimited	48/Unlimited	36/36	1220	Good

[1] Wheel Alignment and Balancing 12/12
[2] Free Scheduled Maintenance includes wear parts but is not transferable
[3] Wheel Alignment and Balancing 12/7.5
[4] All Corrosion 48/50
[5] All Corrosion 36/36
[6] Wheel Alignment and Balancing 12/12
[7] All Corrosion 36/Unlimited
[8] Wheel Alignment and Balancing 12/12
[9] All Corrosion 36/Unlimited
[10] Wheel Alignment and Balancing 12/12
[11] All Corrosion 36/Unlimited

[12] Wheel Alignment and Balancing 12/12; Brake Pads 12/18
[13] Free Scheduled Maintenance includes wear parts but is not transferable
[14] Wheel Alignment and Balancing 12/12
[15] Wheel Alignment and Balancing 12/12; Wear Items 12/12
[16] Only transferable up to 60/60
[17] Wheel Alignment and Balancing 12/12
[18] Wheel Alignment and Balancing 12/12
[19] All Corrosion 36/Unlimited
[20] Wheel Alignment and Balancing 12/12

[21] Transferable only to 60/60
[22] Wheel Alignment and Balancing 12/12
[23] Wheel Alignment and Balancing 12/12; Brake Pads 12/18
[24] Lifetime for original owner
[25] Wheel Alignment and Balancing 12/12
[26] Transferable only up to 60/60
[27] Wear Items 36/36

SECRET WARRANTIES AND TECHNICAL SERVICE BULLETINS

If dealers report a lot of complaints about a certain part or system and the manufacturer determines that the problem is due to faulty design or assembly, the manufacturer may permit dealers to repair the problem at no charge to the customer, even though the warranty is expired. In the past, this practice was often reserved for customers who made a big fuss. The availability of the free repair was never publicized, which is why we call these "secret warranties."

Manufacturers deny the existence of secret warranties. They call these free repairs "policy adjustments" or "goodwill service." Whatever they are called, most consumers never hear about them. Many secret warranties are disclosed in technical service bulletins that the manufacturers send to dealers. These bulletins outline free repair or reimbursement programs, as well as other problems and their possible causes and solutions.

Technical service bulletins from manufacturers must, by law, be sent to, and be on file at, the National Highway Traffic Safety Administration (NHTSA). In 2012, Congress required NHTSA to make all of these bulletins, and an accompanying index, publicly available through NHTSA's website. However, the agency did not take sufficient steps to fulfill this obligation, so in February of 2016, the Center for Auto Safety sued the Secretary of Transportation, and forced the DOT to comply with the congressional mandate to begin publishing all service bulletins and related manufacturer communications. While progress has been made, as of the date of publication, the NHTSA service bulletin database remains incomplete. The Center for Auto Safety will continue to actively monitor the agency's progress to ensure a complete and up-to-date service bulletin system is available for consumers soon.

To view service bulletins on your vehicle, visit www.nhtsa.gov/recall to look up your vehicle by VIN, or make and model, and then click on "Manufacturer Communications" to view a list of all available communications between the automaker and dealers, the great majority of which are service bulletins.

If you find that a secret warranty is in effect and repairs are being made at no charge after the warranty has expired, contact the Center for Auto Safety, at contact@autosafety.org, or by mail at 1825 Connecticut Ave. NW, #330, Washington, DC 20009. The Center will publish the information on our website so that other owners can benefit.

Secret Warranty Disclosure Laws: Spurred by the proliferation of secret warranties and the failure of the FTC to take action, California, Connecticut, Virginia, Wisconsin, and Maryland have passed legislation that requires consumers to be notified of secret warranties on their cars. Several other states have introduced similar warranty bills. You can find out more online through your state attorney general or consumer protection division website.

Typically, disclosure laws require the following: direct notice to consumers within a specified time after the adoption of a warranty adjustment policy; notice of the disclosure law to new car buyers; reimbursement within a number of years after payment to owners who paid for covered repairs before they learned of the extended warranty service; and dealers must inform consumers who complain about a covered defect that it is eligible for repair under warranty.

If you live in a state with a secret warranty law already in effect, write your state attorney general's office (in care of your state capitol) for information. To encourage passage of such a bill, contact your state representatives (in care of your state capitol).

LITTLE SECRETS OF THE AUTO INDUSTRY

TIP Some state lemon laws require dealers and manufacturers to give you copies of technical service bulletins on problems affecting your vehicle. These bulletins may alert you to a secret warranty on your vehicle or help you make the case for a free repair if there isn't a secret warranty. See page 58 for an overview of your state's lemon law. If you would like to see the complete law, go to www.autosafety.org/lemon-laws-state to view your state's lemon laws. To see technical service bulletins on your vehicle you can also use the Center for Auto Safety's "Learn Everything About Your Car" features at www.autosafety.org.

KEEPING IT GOING

Comparing maintenance costs before you buy can help decide which car to purchase. These costs include preventive maintenance servicing—such as changing the oil and filters—as well as the cost of repairs after your warranty expires. The following tables enable you to compare the costs of preventive maintenance and nine likely repairs.

Preventive Maintenance: The first column in the table is the periodic servicing, specified by the manufacturer, that keeps your car running properly. For example, regularly changing the oil and oil filter. Every owner's manual specifies a schedule of recommended servicing for at least the first 60,000 miles and many now go to 100,000 miles. The tables on the following pages estimate the labor cost of following this preventive maintenance schedule for 60,000 miles, the length of a typical warranty. Service parts are not included in this total.

Repair Costs: The tables also list the costs for nine repairs that typically occur during the first 100,000 miles. There is no precise way to predict exactly when a repair will be needed. But if you keep a car for 75,000 to 100,000 miles, it is likely that you will experience many of these repairs at least once. The last column provides a relative indication of how expensive these nine repairs are for many cars. Repair cost is rated as Very Good if the total for nine repairs is in the lowest fifth of all the cars rated, and Very Poor if the total is in the highest fifth.

Most repair shops use "flat-rate manuals" to estimate repair costs. These manuals list the approximate time required for repairing many items. Each automobile manufacturer publishes its own manual and there are several independent manuals as well. For many repairs, the time varies from one manual to another. Some repair shops even use different manuals for different repairs. To determine a repair bill, a shop multiplies the time listed in its manual by its hourly labor rate and then adds the cost of parts.

Some dealers and repair shops create their own maintenance schedules which call for more frequent (and thus more expensive) servicing than the manufacturer's recommendations. If the service recommended by your dealer or repair shop doesn't match what the manufacturer recommends, make sure you understand and agree to the extra items. Our cost estimates are based on published repair times multiplied by a nationwide average labor rate of $90 per hour and include the cost of replaced parts and related adjustments.

Prices in the following tables may not predict the exact costs of these repairs. For example, labor rates for your area may be more or less than the national average. However, the prices will provide you with a relative comparison of costs for various automobiles.

Finally, for many of the electric vehicles you'll see a $0. That's because the EV doesn't have that part. This is one reason why EVs can be less expensive to maintain.

! SAVE YOUR RECEIPTS !

Keeping it going means taking advantage of your warranty and, if you've purchased a service agreement, getting what's coming to you. Because warranties and service agreements don't cover consumer abuse, sometimes the repair shop may try to blame the mechanical problem on your failure to properly maintain the vehicle. Unscrupulous service providers do this in order to keep from having to reimburse you for the repair. According to the Center for Auto Safety, a common claim is to blame the problem on your failure to regularly change the oil. To insure that you get the warranty coverage you have a right to, or the service contract coverage you paid for, religiously keep your receipts. That's the best way to prove that you're not the one at fault.

	PM Costs to 60,000 Miles	REPAIR COSTS									
		Front Brake Pads	Starter	Fuel Injector	Fuel Pump	Struts/ Shocks	Timing Belt/Chain	Water Pump	Muffler	Headlamps	Relative Repair Cost*
Subcompact											
BMW i3	999	154	0	0	0	232	0	855	0	1478	Vry. Gd.
Chevrolet Sonic	540	220	323	122	400	159	408	390	685	789	Vry. Gd.
Chevrolet Spark	540	204	267	163	421	181	855	427	454	871	Good
Fiat 500	630	170	308	403	569	98	365	453	324	703	Vry. Gd.
Ford Escape	756	185	408	192	375	219	1065	305	1591	926	Poor
Ford Fiesta	828	164	274	127	284	154	419	273	458	679	Vry. Gd.
Honda Fit	477	151	387	271	439	398	511	285	255	674	Vry. Gd.
Hyundai Accent	864	149	357	343	419	121	453	235	368	338	Vry. Gd.
Hyundai Veloster	882	158	351	170	431	289	367	296	411	765	Vry. Gd.
Kia Rio	774	165	371	229	334	197	454	274	429	633	Vry. Gd.
Mazda MX-5	864	191	354	239	473	349	479	265	624	1482	Average
Mini Cooper	918	205	542	209	576	358	807	468	503	1350	Poor
Mitsubishi Mirage	612	182	502	280	132	226	459	459	422	1329	Good
Nissan Versa	594	191	401	284	502	196	437	213	373	697	Vry. Gd.
Toyota Prius C	558	161	0	495	510	149	1188	714	275	1141	Average
Toyota Yaris	486	176	407	261	456	149	621	246	275	340	Vry. Gd.
Compact											
Acura ILX	576	170	594	489	533	349	444	357	357	928	Good
Audi A3	1377	191	554	367	364	468	508	555	602	1063	Average
Audi A4	972	222	810	360	587	821	722	708	668	601	Vry. Pr.
BMW 2 Series	999	247	614	489	285	311	1195	751	809	746	Poor
BMW 3 Series	945	247	614	489	280	588	1200	751	891	920	Vry. Pr.
Buick Cascada	1251	273	346	328	351	312	508	588	1074	1078	Average
Cadillac ATS	1179	268	686	643	573	341	649	725	1189	1071	Vry. Pr.
Chevrolet Bolt	828	184	0	0	0	130	0	375	0	1023	Vry. Gd.
Chevrolet Cruze	963	176	451	291	389	184	478	661	614	620	Good
Chevrolet Volt	1080	198	0	139	465	155	886	427	661	1007	Good
Ford C-MAX	594	172	0	153	436	255	633	561	359	1363	Good
Ford Focus	882	163	251	234	302	122	713	243	314	678	Vry. Gd.
Honda Civic	423	151	609	192	522	200	569	302	321	692	Good
Hyundai Elantra	981	131	340	227	303	190	493	246	371	821	Vry. Gd.
Kia Forte	585	165	213	203	314	174	499	309	322	589	Vry. Gd.
Kia Soul	954	165	389	266	295	170	589	329	435	999	Good
Lexus IS	756	156	959	643	452	351	1322	547	448	1496	Vry. Pr.
Lexus RC	801	156	788	571	506	297	1349	637	439	1690	Vry. Pr.
Mazda 3	792	177	338	282	575	208	461	292	430	722	Vry. Gd.
Mercedes-Benz B	864	180	0	0	0	450	0	0	0	1013	Vry. Gd.
Mercedes-Benz C	1287	192	532	346	838	423	404	666	931	1063	Poor
Mercedes-Benz CLA	1269	152	959	622	678	250	432	470	617	1010	Poor
Mini Countryman	918	220	478	216	406	362	852	437	622	859	Average
Nissan Leaf	666	164	0	0	0	232	0	658	0	1385	Vry. Gd.
Nissan Sentra	702	175	343	356	504	168	592	318	422	649	Vry. Gd.
Subaru Impreza	1008	175	540	230	430	382	567	368	392	464	Good
Toyota 86	972	190	642	584	696	355	689	389	619	983	Poor
Toyota Corolla	549	153	421	324	458	188	1107	284	412	651	Good
Toyota Corolla iM	513	156	476	309	427	333	640	259	387	533	Vry. Gd.
Toyota Prius	558	183	0	648	492	164	1199	358	470	1263	Average
Toyota Prius Prime	558	161	0	292	442	351	1297	693	285	699	Good
Toyota Yaris iA	536	139	402	218	160	286	504	240	249	686	Vry. Gd.
AVERAGE OF ALL VEHICLES	$890	$206	$446	$346	$478	$309	$796	$471	$630	$953	

	PM Costs to 60,000 Miles	Front Brake Pads	Starter	Fuel Injector	Fuel Pump	Struts/ Shocks	Timing Belt/Chain	Water Pump	Muffler	Headlamps	Relative Repair Cost*
Compact (cont.)											
Volkswagen Beetle	918	185	539	337	434	336	881	487	900	1112	Poor
Volkswagen Golf	1089	182	687	214	369	421	553	466	467	606	Good
Volkswagen Jetta	918	170	670	431	543	410	600	679	721	742	Poor
Intermediate											
Acura TLX	936	152	800	637	488	335	418	312	709	1457	Poor
Audi A5	972	222	676	351	514	471	718	714	791	662	Poor
Audi A6	972	248	880	1620	572	426	650	661	680	614	Vry. Pr.
BMW 5 Series	567	249	604	424	543	492	1330	706	1061	1048	Vry. Pr.
Buick Regal	1251	306	617	332	401	279	514	788	1110	1058	Poor
Chevrolet Camaro	1251	300	335	380	618	282	702	435	873	705	Average
Chevrolet Corvette	1278	334	364	517	642	232	1300	303	1368	1385	Vry. Pr.
Chevrolet Malibu	711	250	369	337	416	247	532	492	656	495	Good
Ford Fusion	684	259	260	312	261	113	638	185	568	931	Vry. Gd.
Ford Fusion Energi	846	163	0	125	305	132	578	213	401	1026	Vry. Gd.
Ford Mustang	603	209	191	207	231	166	824	260	917	1446	Average
Honda Accord	504	159	519	475	569	263	423	322	455	1088	Average
Hyundai Sonata	891	158	294	241	336	154	711	313	645	821	Good
Infiniti Q50	882	168	487	405	494	547	743	263	613	1442	Poor
Kia Optima	864	165	231	266	323	165	598	255	322	625	Vry. Gd.
Lexus ES	864	189	529	427	467	458	1502	403	514	1421	Vry. Pr.
Lexus GS	657	155	827	721	465	243	1801	593	551	1677	Vry. Pr.
Lincoln MKZ	684	195	277	377	473	300	1179	346	1054	1423	Vry. Pr.
Mazda 6	799	184	240	548	528	239	549	226	360	699	Good
Nissan Altima	954	187	330	335	403	237	648	268	410	700	Vry. Gd.
Nissan Maxima	828	173	400	417	457	234	885	411	660	911	Average
Subaru Legacy	1188	170	440	220	426	330	621	368	268	498	Vry. Gd.
Tesla Model 3	702	188	0	0	0	278	0	880	0	1314	Vry. Gd.
Toyota Avalon	864	199	529	427	467	359	1529	403	389	611	Poor
Toyota Camry	864	189	547	454	476	323	1493	457	392	1109	Poor
Toyota Prius V	558	206	0	459	510	146	1262	714	289	470	Good
Volkswagen Passat	918	171	720	253	480	384	944	462	715	671	Average
Volvo S60	909	229	507	398	834	226	497	487	669	566	Average
Volvo V60	1116	221	453	398	834	234	594	487	550	602	Average
Large											
BMW 7 Series	1251	303	720	597	579	2104	1371	829	1052	1979	Vry. Pr.
Buick LaCrosse	1251	273	433	201	481	774	1159	435	607	1106	Vry. Pr.
Cadillac CT6	1179	306	643	566	563	367	658	653	791	1044	Vry. Pr.
Cadillac Escalade	1278	204	316	362	611	809	1201	371	1248	1561	Vry. Pr.
Cadillac XTS	1242	250	413	385	577	279	958	503	706	1374	Poor
Chevrolet Impala	1251	246	376	435	499	205	761	494	622	703	Average
Chrysler 300	630	208	236	225	427	879	746	361	1729	1236	Vry. Pr.
Dodge Challenger	630	415	288	206	731	263	670	270	959	1445	Poor
Dodge Charger	630	267	237	206	586	155	634	298	1084	660	Good
Ford Flex	801	154	207	207	257	187	1024	521	962	811	Average
Ford Taurus	909	163	207	180	342	179	1013	572	764	760	Good
Genesis G80	1044	233	451	215	422	341	1231	372	585	1091	Poor
Lincoln Continental	900	209	259	305	417	490	1134	490	1083	1444	Vry. Pr.
Mercedes-Benz E	1017	187	826	510	488	311	1139	758	1121	1223	Vry. Pr.
Mercedes-Benz S	1017	217	677	442	518	763	399	945	1466	1633	Vry. Pr.
Tesla Model S	702	212	0	0	0	306	0	1017	0	1422	Vry. Gd.
AVERAGE OF ALL VEHICLES	**$890**	**$206**	**$446**	**$346**	**$478**	**$309**	**$796**	**$471**	**$630**	**$953**	

40

	PM Costs to 60,000 Miles	Front Brake Pads	Starter	Fuel Injector	Fuel Pump	Struts/ Shocks	Timing Belt/ Chain	Water Pump	Muffler	Headlamps	Relative Repair Cost*
REPAIR COSTS											
Minivan											
Chrysler Pacifica	504	272	448	192	485	309	886	339	950	613	Average
Honda Odyssey	540	167	544	200	487	146	352	468	648	717	Good
Kia Sedona	990	165	248	321	394	218	742	316	548	401	Vry. Gd.
Toyota Sienna	1116	153	530	418	666	176	1367	538	551	697	Poor
Small SUV											
Acura RDX	909	387	534	262	531	268	332	414	521	1382	Average
Audi Q3	972	191	705	396	321	660	758	641	384	1266	Poor
BMW X1	783	244	698	539	619	425	1290	770	1043	1350	Vry. Pr.
Buick Encore	720	320	268	111	432	198	723	360	607	664	Good
Chevrolet Equinox	1278	306	445	459	726	161	811	469	1017	810	Poor
Chevrolet Trax	774	180	309	115	552	222	1030	496	797	1005	Average
Fiat 500X	630	170	308	403	569	98	365	453	324	703	Vry. Gd.
Ford EcoSport	756	183	332	213	443	278	975	202	488	1050	Good
Honda CR-V	504	151	600	345	485	234	416	257	407	769	Good
Honda HR-V	747	159	631	149	461	211	443	317	395	787	Good
Hyundai Kona	801	135	382	148	312	220	464	427	627	705	Vry. Gd.
Hyundai Tucson	972	161	349	305	327	189	306	331	580	643	Vry. Gd.
Infiniti QX30	720	172	431	372	463	298	799	736	687	1605	Vry. Pr.
Infiniti QX50	594	175	550	311	498	298	799	746	687	1502	Vry. Pr.
Jeep Compass	450	180	367	127	440	356	501	337	465	386	Vry. Gd.
Jeep Renegade	945	304	727	136	386	484	546	377	541	459	Good
Jeep Wrangler	405	224	237	291	562	139	742	381	386	267	Vry. Gd.
Kia Sportage	927	165	231	237	322	241	526	349	624	1472	Good
Land Rover Range Rover Evoque	855	280	575	511	688	604	614	298	715	532	Average
Lexus NX	1431	144	565	576	494	241	1305	524	826	664	Poor
Lincoln MKC	855	204	242	186	385	181	980	545	799	1417	Poor
Mazda CX-3	774	183	364	358	321	226	417	247	402	733	Vry. Gd.
Mazda CX-5	711	165	383	350	330	224	396	240	473	626	Vry. Gd.
Mercedes-Benz GLA	486	323	724	551	546	435	396	882	830	1372	Vry. Pr.
Mercedes-Benz GLC	1062	332	668	541	520	484	383	837	830	1395	Vry. Pr.
Mitsubishi Outlander Sport	792	174	504	351	683	274	519	523	459	1165	Average
Nissan Juke	945	187	504	311	660	212	843	251	401	441	Good
Subaru Crosstrek	1008	170	540	230	430	373	567	368	394	468	Good
Subaru Forester	1026	175	585	528	450	339	621	455	404	504	Good
Toyota RAV4	963	194	511	288	575	125	1072	321	300	603	Good
Volkswagen Tiguan	1053	170	670	410	543	420	609	678	739	734	Poor
Volvo XC40	738	215	415	246	654	226	648	406	620	633	Good
Mid-Size SUV											
Subaru Ascent	1062	186	559	227	454	547	290	459	330	471	Vry. Gd.
Acura MDX	936	308	562	1327	681	284	378	508	728	1226	Vry. Pr.
Audi Q5	972	258	726	459	592	431	780	695	894	661	Vry. Pr.
Audi Q7	1080	268	1006	753	466	728	1410	382	984	752	Vry. Pr.
BMW X3	1242	247	720	534	586	515	1069	856	1164	1697	Vry. Pr.
BMW X5	1053	308	684	530	624	568	1807	750	2060	2262	Vry. Pr.
BMW X6	1107	335	639	440	781	491	817	1157	1628	2460	Vry. Pr.
Buick Envision	1170	278	437	206	486	766	794	440	611	1111	Poor
Cadillac XT5	1251	206	404	425	366	168	1044	516	935	974	Poor
Dodge Durango	918	224	475	233	519	426	931	306	539	867	Average
Dodge Journey	585	224	404	237	728	330	922	415	1411	331	Poor
Ford Edge	855	220	178	233	389	254	999	298	823	1067	Average
AVERAGE OF ALL VEHICLES	**$890**	**$206**	**$446**	**$346**	**$478**	**$309**	**$796**	**$471**	**$630**	**$953**	

	PM Costs to 60,000 Miles	REPAIR COSTS									
		Front Brake Pads	Starter	Fuel Injector	Fuel Pump	Struts/ Shocks	Timing Belt/ Chain	Water Pump	Muffler	Headlamps	Relative Repair Cost*
Mid-Size SUV (cont.)											
Ford Explorer	909	163	225	207	464	142	842	485	825	1206	Average
GMC Acadia	1206	275	382	304	509	179	1150	466	617	1301	Poor
Honda Pilot	522	169	495	281	621	218	424	531	646	857	Good
Hyundai Santa Fe	972	177	303	255	563	224	1267	320	572	1108	Average
Hyundai Santa Fe Sport	972	174	294	282	442	245	538	302	590	1244	Good
Infiniti QX60	1089	173	482	407	479	350	1058	254	706	1492	Poor
Jeep Cherokee	432	224	514	187	665	304	958	419	894	542	Average
Jeep Grand Cherokee	630	224	475	233	459	244	931	292	831	614	Average
Kia Sorento	936	173	230	267	482	215	553	290	573	1018	Good
Land Rover Range Rover Sport	1278	242	660	642	631	413	1290	381	476	295	Poor
Lexus RX	900	225	719	310	465	133	1988	1119	692	2290	Vry. Pr.
Lincoln MKX	756	202	178	207	371	250	990	490	699	1170	Average
Mazda CX-9	792	186	308	227	568	313	1096	1060	609	897	Poor
Mercedes-Benz GLE	1053	322	666	572	556	465	370	855	862	1372	Vry. Pr.
Mitsubishi Outlander	981	173	402	297	620	242	510	443	405	774	Good
Nissan Murano	702	193	491	419	601	304	887	489	629	1196	Poor
Nissan Pathfinder	1440	193	608	419	588	213	947	504	676	823	Poor
Nissan Rogue	1053	173	430	417	499	162	925	337	587	1376	Poor
Porsche Macan	1080	380	540	424	523	576	1140	501	1211	1030	Vry. Pr.
Subaru Outback	1188	175	440	221	439	339	612	368	286	498	Vry. Gd.
Tesla Model X	702	212	0	0	0	306	0	1017	0	1422	Vry. Gd.
Toyota 4Runner	558	151	575	369	600	132	1646	605	549	503	Poor
Toyota Highlander	720	153	499	445	564	107	1745	268	259	546	Average
Volkswagen Atlas	1080	231	715	513	462	480	1383	751	912	1328	Vry. Pr.
Volvo XC60	909	279	597	451	848	274	350	487	498	648	Average
Volvo XC90	1044	242	615	416	700	324	536	966	575	1268	Vry. Pr.
Large SUV											
Buick Enclave	1206	284	404	415	583	156	782	678	634	1394	Poor
Cadillac Escalade ESV	1278	218	316	362	615	809	980	404	1230	1624	Vry. Pr.
Chevrolet Suburban	1278	218	325	368	618	211	1219	371	703	639	Average
Chevrolet Tahoe	1278	204	325	368	642	205	1219	512	1089	630	Poor
Chevrolet Traverse	1206	272	395	433	580	153	1215	561	528	731	Average
Ford Expedition	1098	166	227	152	371	191	716	199	470	975	Vry. Gd.
Infiniti QX80	1080	194	473	326	457	222	1268	304	513	1369	Poor
Land Rover Range Rover	873	242	660	642	631	491	1200	381	476	294	Poor
Lexus GX	819	151	762	423	591	120	1231	472	750	1346	Vry. Pr.
Lincoln Navigator	1125	166	200	233	389	290	923	283	497	1372	Average
Mercedes-Benz GLS	1062	305	686	565	556	484	379	804	789	1405	Vry. Pr.
Nissan Armada	1080	173	493	301	505	376	1095	296	626	937	Average
Toyota Sequoia	819	189	920	306	680	379	1331	455	350	391	Poor
Compact Pickup											
Chevrolet Colorado	1278	224	473	377	408	179	492	419	347	689	Good
Nissan Frontier	1080	193	524	374	669	163	878	360	444	447	Good
Toyota Tacoma	558	175	609	525	579	101	1430	500	506	567	Poor
Standard Pickup											
Chevrolet Silverado	1278	248	428	386	604	168	1232	371	716	643	Average
Ford F-150	612	166	209	504	393	114	817	512	369	622	Good
Nissan Titan	1116	169	555	300	543	199	1271	307	592	761	Average
Ram 1500	666	152	289	143	406	177	518	408	400	470	Vry. Gd.
Toyota Tundra	819	168	969	306	525	121	1232	419	620	425	Average
AVERAGE OF ALL VEHICLES	**$890**	**$206**	**$446**	**$346**	**$478**	**$309**	**$796**	**$471**	**$630**	**$953**	

SERVICE CONTRACTS

Service contracts are one of the most expensive options you can buy. In fact, service contracts are a major profit source for many dealers.

A service contract is not a warranty. It is more like an insurance plan that, in theory, covers repairs that are not covered by your warranty or that occur after the warranty runs out. They are often inaccurately referred to as "extended warranties."

Service contracts are generally a poor value. The companies who sell contracts are very sure that, on average, your repairs will cost considerably less than what you pay for the contract—if not, they wouldn't be in business.

Here are some important questions to ask before buying a service contract:

How reputable is the company responsible for the contract? If the company offering the contract goes out of business, you will be out of luck. The company may be required to be insured, but find out if they actually are and by whom. Check with your Better Business Bureau or office of consumer affairs if you are not sure of a company's reputation. Service contracts from car and insurance companies are more likely to remain in effect than those from independent companies.

Exactly what does the contract cover and for how long? Service contracts vary considerably—different items are covered and different time limits are offered. This is true even among service contracts offered by the same company. For example, one company has plans that range from 4 years/36,000 miles maximum coverage to 6 years/100,000 miles maximum coverage, with other options for only power train coverage. Make sure you know what components are covered because if a breakdown occurs on a part that is not covered, you are responsible for the repairs.

If you plan to resell your car in a few years, you won't want to purchase a long-running service contract. Some service contracts automatically cancel when you resell the car, while others require a hefty transfer fee before extending privileges to the new owner. Check out the transferability of the service contract.

Some automakers offer a "menu" format, which lets you pick the items you want covered in your service contract. Find out if the contract pays for preventive maintenance, towing, and rental car expenses. If not written into the contract, assume they are not covered.

Make sure the contract clearly specifies how you can reach the company. Knowing this before you purchase a service contract can save you time and aggravation in the future.

How will the repair bills be paid? It is best to have the service contractor pay bills directly. Some contracts require you to pay the repair bill, and reimburse you later. This can be a major hassle.

Where can the car be serviced? Can you take the car to any mechanic if you have trouble on the road? What if you move?

What other costs can be expected? Most service contracts will have a deductible expense, which means you will have to pay part of the repair cost. Compare deductibles on various plans. Also, some companies charge the deductible for each individual repair while other companies pay per visit, regardless of the number of repairs being made.

What are your responsibilities? Make sure you know what you have to do to uphold the contract. For example if you have to follow the manufacturer's recommended maintenance, keep detailed records or the contract could be voided. You will find your specific responsibilities in the contact. Be sure to have the seller point them out.

SERVICE CONTRACTS VS. SAVINGS ACCOUNT

One alternative to buying a service contract is to deposit the cost of the contract into a savings account. If the car needs a major repair not covered by your warranty, the money in your account is likely to cover the cost. Most likely, you'll be building up a down payment for your next car!

TIPS FOR DEALING WITH A MECHANIC

Call around. Don't choose a shop simply because it's nearby. Calling a few shops may turn up estimates cheaper by half.

Don't necessarily go for the lowest price. A good rule is to eliminate the highest and lowest estimates; the mechanic with the highest estimate is probably charging too much, and the lowest may be cutting too many corners.

Check the shop's reputation. While internet reviews need to be considered with some skepticism, see what others are saying about the shop. Your local consumer agency and the BBB may have unfavorable reports that would disqualify shops you may be considering.

Look for certification. Mechanics can be certified by the National Institute for Automotive Service Excellence, an industry yardstick for competence. Certification is offered in eight areas of repair and shops with certified mechanics are allowed to advertise this fact. However, make sure the mechanic working on your car is certified for the repair you need.

Take a look around. A well-kept shop reflects pride in workmanship. A skilled and efficient mechanic would probably not work in a messy shop.

Don't sign a blank check. The service order you sign should have specific instructions or describe your vehicle's symptoms. Avoid signing a vague work order. Be sure you are called for final approval before the shop does extra work. Many states require a written estimate signed by you and require that the shop get your permission for repairs that exceed the estimate by 10%.

Show interest. Ask about the repair. But don't act like an expert if you don't really understand what's wrong. Express your satisfaction. If you're happy with the work, compliment the mechanic and ask for him or her the next time you come in. You will get to know each other and the mechanic will get to know your vehicle.

Take a test-drive. Before you pay for a major repair, you should take the car for a test-drive. The few extra minutes you spend checking out the repair could save you a trip back to the mechanic. If you find that the problem still exists, there will be no question that the repair wasn't properly completed.

REPAIR PROTECTION BY CREDIT CARD

Paying your auto repair bills by credit card can provide a much needed recourse if you are having problems with an auto mechanic. According to federal law, you have the right to withhold payment for sloppy or incorrect repairs.

In order to use this right, you should first try to work out the problem with the mechanic. Also, unless the credit card company owns the repair shop (this might be the case with gasoline credit cards used at gas stations), two other conditions must be met. First, the repair shop must be in your home state (or within 100 miles of your current address), and second, the cost of repairs must be over $50. Until the problem is settled or resolved in court, the credit card company cannot charge you interest or penalties on the amount in dispute.

If you decide to take action, send a letter to the credit card company and a copy to the repair shop, explaining the details of the problem and what you want as settlement. Send the letter by certified mail with a return receipt requested.

Sometimes the credit card company or repair shop will attempt to put a "bad mark" on your credit record if you use this tactic. Legally, you can't be reported as delinquent if you've given the credit card company notice of your dispute, but a creditor can report that you are disputing your bill, which goes in your record. However, you have the right to challenge any incorrect information and add your side of the story to your file.

For more information, contact the Federal Trade Commission, Credit Practices Division, 601 Pennsylvania Avenue, NW, Washington, DC 20580 or at www.FTC.gov.

TIRE RATINGS

Buying tires has become an infrequent task because today's radial tires last much longer than the tires of the past. Surprisingly, a tire has to perform more functions simultaneously than any other part of the car (steering, bearing the load, cushioning the ride, and stopping).

Because comparing tires is difficult, many consumers mistakenly use price and brand name to determine quality. As there are hundreds of tire lines to choose from, and only a few tire manufacturers, the difference in many tires may only be the brand name.

But there is help. The government requires tires to be rated according to their safety and expected mileage.

Treadwear, traction, and heat resistance grades are printed on the sidewall and are attached to the tire on a paper label. Ask the dealer for the grades of the tires they sell. Using this rating system, a sampling of top rated tires follows on page 47.

Treadwear: The treadwear grade gives you an idea of the mileage you can expect from a tire. It is shown in numbers–720, 700, 680, 660, and so forth. Higher numbers mean longer tire life. A tire with a grade of 600 should give you twice as much mileage as one rated 300. Use the treadwear grade as a relative basis of comparison.

Traction: Traction grades of AA, A, B, and C describe the tire's ability to stop on wet surfaces. Tires graded AA will stop on a wet road in a shorter distance than tires graded B or C. Tires rated C have poor traction.

Heat Resistance: Heat resistance is graded A, B, and C. An A rating means the tire will run cooler than one rated B or C and be less likely to fail if driven over long distances at highway speeds. Tires that run cooler tend to have lower rolling resistance contributing to better fuel economy. Hot-running tires can result in blow-outs or tread separation.

TIRE CARE

Pump 'em Up: An estimated one-third of us are driving on underinflated tires. Because even good tires lose air, it is important to check your tire pressure monthly. Underinflated tires can be dangerous, use more fuel and cause premature tire failure. When checking your tires, be sure to use an accurate gauge and inflate to the pressure indicated in your owner's manual, not the maximum pressure printed on your tire. The good news is that cars now have built in tire monitoring due to the importance of proper inflation, but you should check tire pressure regularly even if the warning doesn't light up.

When to Replace: If all of Lincoln's head is visible when you insert the top of a penny into a tread groove, it's time to replace the tire. While this old rule of thumb is still valid, today's tires also have a built-in wear indicator. A series of horizontal bars appear across the surface when the tread depth reaches the danger zone.

GETTING THE BEST PRICE

The price of the same tire can vary depending on where you shop so shopping around is vital to finding a good buy. You are most likely to find the best prices at independent tire dealers who carry a variety of tire brands.

The price of a tire is based on its size, and tires come in as many as nine sizes. For example, the list price of the same tire can range from $74.20 to $134.35, depending on its size. To get the best buy:

1. Check to see which manufacturer makes the least expensive "off brand." Only a few manufacturers produce the over 1,800 types of tires sold in the U.S.

2. Don't forget to compare balancing and mounting costs. These extra charges can add up to more than $25 or be offered at no cost.

3. Never pay list price for a tire. A good rule of thumb is to pay at least 30-40 percent off the suggested list price.

4. Use the treadwear grade the same way you would the "unit price" in a supermarket. The tire with the lowest cost per grade point is the best value. For example, if tire A costs $100 and has a treadwear grade of 600, and tire B costs $80 and has a treadwear grade of 300, tire A is the better buy, even though its initial cost is more.

Tire A: $100÷600=$0.17 per point
Tire B: $80÷300=$0.27 per point

Where you live is a factor in how long your tires will last. Tire wear is affected by the level of abrasive material in the road surface. Generally, the road surfaces of the West Coast, Great Lakes region, and northern New England are easiest on tires. The Appalachian and Rocky Mountain areas are usually the hardest.

HOW TO READ A TIRE

Tire Type and Size: The most important information on a tire are the letters and the numbers indicating its type and size.

1. Tire Type: The P at the beginning of the tire size indicates that the tire is a passenger vehicle tire. LT indicates light truck tire, and T indicates a temporary or spare tire.

2. Tire Width is the first part of the number and is measured in millimeters, from side-wall to sidewall.

3. Tire Height is the next number and tells you the height of the tire from the bead to the tread. This is described as a percentage of the tire width. In our example, the tire's height is 65 percent of its width. The smaller the aspect ratio, the wider the tire in relation to its height.

4. Tire Construction designates how the tire was made. R indicates radial construction which is the most common type. Older tires were made using diagonal bias D or bias belted B construction, but these tire types are no longer used on passenger vehicles.

5. Wheel Diameter identifies the wheel rim diameter (in inches-15) needed for this tire.

6. Load Index: The load rating indicates the maximum load for that tire. A higher number indicates a higher load capacity. The rating 95, for example, corresponds to a load capacity of 1521 pounds. Larger vehicles, SUVs and pickups need tires with a higher load capacity.

7. Speed Rating indicates the maximum speed that the tire can sustain a ten minute endurance test without being in danger. All passenger car tires are rated at least S and pass the test at speeds up to 112 mph. Other ratings are as follows: T up to 118 mph, H up to 130 mph, V up to 149 mph and Z 150 mph or higher. Other types of tires, temporary spares and snow tires are lower on the rating scale.

8. Severe Conditions: M+S indicates the tire meets the Rubber Manufacturers Association's definition of a mud and snow tire. There are no performance tests for this standard. If the tire has an M+S and a "mountain and snowflake" symbol then the traction is at least 10% better than the regular version of the tire. These symbols are not in the above example.

9. Tire Identification Number
Example: DOT NJ HR 2AF 5212
The letters DOT certify compliance with all applicable safety standards established by the U.S. Department of Transportation. The next four characters is a code where the first two characters indicate the manufacturer and the second two characters indicate the plant where the tire was made.

For a guide to plant codes, go to www.tiresafetygroup.com.

Next you may see an optional string of three to four characters. Most manufacturers use these to record company specific information they use to identify their products or that can be used to identify tires in the market for recall purposes.

The last four digits determine the week and year the tire was made. The digits 5212 would signify that the tire was made during the 52nd week of 2012. Don't buy tires more than a year old. Tires naturally degrade with age, so you want the newest possible tires for the longest life (and safe operation.)

10. Tire Ply Composition and Material indicates the type of cord (polyester or steel) and number of plies in the tire, 4-ply, 6-ply, 8-ply, for both the tread and the sidewall.

11. Treadwear, Traction and Temperature Grades are three performance grades assigned to the tire and are the best way to truly evaluate the tires expected performance in these three critical areas. See page 45 for more information.

12. Max Load Limit tells you the cold inflation load limit in lbs. (pounds) and in kg (kilograms). The number corresponds to the load index.

13. Max Pressure is the maximum recommended pressure in psi (pounds per square inch) and in kPa (kilopascals). However, this is not the tire pressure for your car. You must check your owner's manual for the proper tire pressure for the tires on your car.

A Sampling of Top Rated Tires

Brand Name	Model	Description	Traction	Heat	Treadwear
Michelin	DEFENDER	All Sizes	A	B	820
Bridgestone	DUELER H/L ALENZA PLUS "H" & "V" Spd Rtd	All Sizes	A	A	800
Toyo	TOYO ULTRA Z900 (H-rated)	All sizes	A	A	800
Bridgestone	DUELER H/L ALENZA PLUS "T" Spd Rtd	All Sizes	A	B	800
Mastercraft	Avenger Touring LSR (TR)	15"-18"	A	A	780
Cooper	CS5 Grand Touring	All sizes	A	B	780
Big O	EURO TOUR (T RATED)	All sizes	A	A	740
Bridgestone	TURANZA SERENITY "H" Spd Rtd	All sizes	A	A	740
Cooper	Discoverer SRX (H)	All sizes	A	A	740
Goodyear	ASSURANCE COMFORTRED TOURING (T&H)	All sizes	A	B	740
Hankook	Optimo H725 (OE)	P235/60R17	A	B	740
Maxxis	MA-T1 Escapade	All sizes	A	A	720
Michelin	LTX M/S2	All Sizes	A	A	720
Big O	LEGACY TOUR PLUS (S & T RATED)	All sizes	A	B	720
Falken	SN211	All sizes	A	B	720
Michelin	LATITUDE TOUR	All Sizes except	A	B	720
Michelin	X RADIAL LT2	All Sizes	A	B	720
Vogue	CUSTOM BUILT IX (S)	P225/60R16	A	B	720
Vogue	WIDE TRAC TOURING II (S)	All sizes	A	B	720
Nokian	Nokian eNTYRE	All sizes	A	A	700
Big O	LEGACY TOUR PLUS	P205,215,225 & 235/70R15 T	A	B	700
Bridgestone	DUELER H/L ALENZA "T" Spd Rtd	All sizes	A	B	700
Bridgestone	TURANZA LS-T	All sizes	A	B	700
Co-op	GOLDENMARK LUXURY TOURING (T)	All sizes	A	B	700
Cooper	Discoverer CTS (T-rated)	All sizes	A	B	700
Cordovan	CENTURY	All sizes	A	B	700
Cordovan	GRAND SPIRIT TOURING LS	All sizes	A	B	700
Delta	ESTEEM XLE	P235/75R15	A	B	700
Goodyear	ASSURANCE COMFORTRED	All sizes	A	B	700
Hankook	DynaPro HT	All sizes	A	B	700
Hankook	Optimo H725	All sizes	A	B	700
Hankook	ROADHANDLER	All sizes	A	B	700
Hankook	Route Master UH70	All sizes	A	B	700
Laramie	GRANDEUR TOURING GT 60/65/70 ser.	14 -16	A	B	700
Mentor	VANTAGE TOURING LE	All sizes	A	B	700
Monarch	ULTRA TOUR LS	All sizes	A	B	700
Multi-Mile	EXCEL	All sizes	A	B	700
National	OVATION	P235/75R15	A	B	700
Spartan	AVISTA	P205/65R16 94T	A	B	700
Spartan	AVISTA (S & T)	ALL EXCEPT	A	B	700
Sumitomo	Enhance L/X (T-Rated)	All sizes	A	B	700
Sumitomo	TOURING LST	All sizes	A	B	700
Toyo	VERSADO LX	T	A	B	700
Toyo	TOUREVO LS	T	A	B	700
Toyo	800 ULTRA	ALL	A	B	700
Yokohama	AVID TRZ	P195/70R14 90T	A	B	700
Hankook	DynaPro HT (OE)	265/60R18, 265/60R18	B	A	700
Hankook	veNtus S1 noble2 (OE)	235/55R17, 235/55ZR17	B	A	700
Bridgestone	DUELER H/L ALENZA "S" Spd Rtd	All sizes	B	B	700
Cordovan	TOUR PLUS LST (T rated)	All sizes	A	A	680
Eldorado	LEGEND TOUR (T rated)	All sizes	A	A	680
Hercules	ROADTOUR XUV	235/60R17T, 235/65R18T, P255/65R18T	A	A	680
Jetzon	GENESIS LST (T rated)	All sizes	A	A	680
Multi-Mile	GRAND TOUR LS (T rated)	All sizes	A	A	680
Sigma	REGENT TOURING LS (T rated)	All sizes	A	A	680
Telstar	ECHELON ULTRA LST (T rated)	All sizes	A	A	680
Vanderbilt	TOURING LSE (T rated)	All sizes	A	A	680

For a complete listing of all the tires on the market, you can call the Auto Safety Hot Line toll free, at 888-327-4236 or 800-424-9153(TTY). Or, go to www.safercar.gov/tires

WARNING

As tires age, they naturally dry out and can become potentially dangerous. Some experts recommend getting rid of a six-year-old tire no matter what condition it is in. Recently, a national news organization went undercover and found 12 year old tires for sale, so be sure to check a tire's manufacture date listed as part of the tire identification number before purchasing. Ask for tires that are less than one year old.

INSURANCE

Insurance is a big part of ownership expenses, yet it's often forgotten in the showroom. As you shop, remember that the car's design and accident history may affect your insurance rates. Some cars cost less to insure because experience has shown that they are damaged less, less expensive to fix after a collision, or stolen less.

Auto insurance covers different aspects of damage and injury. The term "first party" means you and "third party" means someone else who was involved in a crash with your vehicle. The critical parts of your insurance are:

Liability (third party): This pays for damage or injury you or your vehicle may inflict on others. It is generally limited (in some cases to only $10,000 but may be several hundred thousand dollars) so that if you severely or fatally injure someone, the liability insurance will not be adequate to pay the costs. For minor or moderate damage or injury, insurance companies generally negotiate payments, but for major ones, there may be lawsuits.

Collision Damage (first party): This pays for crash damage to your own car when no other party is found to be at fault for the accident. If you lease your vehicle or have an outstanding loan on it, you will be required to have collision damage insurance.

Uninsured or Underinsured drivers: This pays your expenses when someone else is at fault, but lacks sufficient insurance or personal resources to pay for the damage or injury. The amount typically covers property damage, but may not cover serious injuries.

Comprehensive (first party): This covers the cost of some types of damage not related to crashes including theft.

Supplementary Insurance: Additional forms of insurance that may apply when auto insurance doesn't cover loss are health insurance, which may pay the cost of more serious injuries, life insurance which pays if you are killed in a crash and umbrella policy insurance which may pay liability costs beyond what is covered by your auto policy. An umbrella policy may be important if you want to protect assets such as savings, your house or business, or other major assets.

Shop Around: You can save hundreds of dollars by shopping around for insurance.

There are a number of factors that determine what coverage will cost you. A car's design can affect both the chances and severity of an accident. For example, a well-designed bumper, which few cars have, may escape damage in a low-speed crash. Some cars are easier to repair than others or may have less expensive parts. Cars with four doors tend to be damaged less than cars with two doors.

Other factors that affect your insurance costs include:

Your Annual Mileage: The more you drive, the more your vehicle will be "exposed" to a potential accident. Driving less

than 5,000 to 7,500 miles per year often gets a discount. Ask your insurer if they offer this option.

Where You Drive and Park: If you regularly drive and park in the city, you will most likely pay more than if you drive in rural areas. You may get a discount if you garage your car.

Youthful Drivers: Usually the highest premiums are paid by male drivers under the age of 25. Whether or not the under-25-year-old male is married also affects insurance rates. (Married males pay less.) As the driver gets older, and if he or she has good driving record, rates are lowered.

Insurance discounts and surcharges depend upon the way a vehicle is traditionally driven. Sports cars, for example, are usually surcharged due, in part, to the typical driving habits of their owners. Four-door sedans and station wagons generally merit discounts. Not all companies offer discounts or surcharges, and many cars receive neither. Some companies offer a discount or impose a surcharge on collision premiums only. Others apply discounts and surcharges on both collision and comprehensive coverage. Discounts and surcharges usually range from 10 to 30 percent. Remember that

REDUCING INSURANCE COSTS

one company may offer a discount on a particular car while another may not.

Major crashes are rare events for individuals, but more than 37,000 people are killed and double that number suffer serious injuries in crashes each year. In a very severe crash with major injury or death, the limits on first and third party auto insurance will be inadequate to cover the costs. NHTSA estimates that the economic cost of a fatality may range from several million to more than ten million dollars, and injuries such as quadriplegia and serious brain damage could easily have a lifetime cost of ten million dollars for each individual. If a crash is not deemed to be the fault of another motorist (such as with a single vehicle crash), your health insurance may cover the cost of your injuries, but is unlikely to cover such things as long-term rehabilitation and loss of income.

Get Your Discounts: After you have shopped around and found the best deal by comparing the costs of different coverages, be sure you get all the discounts you are entitled to.

Most insurance companies offer discounts of 5 to 30 percent on various parts of your insurance bill. Ask your insurance company for a complete list of the discounts that it offers. These can vary by company and from state to state.

Here are some of the most common insurance discounts:

Driver Education/Defensive Driving Courses: Discounts for completing a state-approved driver education course can mean a $40 reduction in the cost of coverage. Discounts of 5 to 15 percent are available in some states to those who complete a defensive driving course.

Good Student Discounts of up to 25 percent for full-time high school or college students who are in the upper 20 percent of their class, on the dean's list, or have a B or better grade point average.

Good Driver Discounts are available to drivers with an accident and violation-free record, (or no incidents in the past 3 years).

Mature Driver Credit: Drivers ages 50 and older may qualify for up to a 10 percent discount or a lower price bracket.

Sole Female Driver: Some companies offer discounts of 10 percent for females, ages 30 to 64, who are the only driver in a household.

Non-Drinkers and Non-Smokers: A few companies offer incentives ranging from 10–25 percent to those who abstain.

Farmer Discounts: Many companies offer farmers either a 10 to 30 percent discount or a lower price bracket.

Car Pooling: Commuters sharing driving may qualify for discounts of 5 to 25 percent or a lower price bracket.

Children away at school don't drive the family car very often, so if they're on your policy and they're at school, let your company know. If you insure them separately,

---

! DON'T SPEED !

Besides endangering the lives of your passengers and other drivers, speeding tickets will increase your insurance premium. It only takes one speeding ticket to lose your "preferred" or "good driver" discount, which requires a clean driving record. Two or more speeding tickets or accidents can increase your premium by 40% to 200%. Some insurers may simply drop your coverage. According to the Insurance Institute for Highway Safety (IIHS), you are 17% more likely to be in an accident if you have just one speeding ticket. Insurance companies know this and will charge you for it.

discounts of 10–40 percent or a lower price bracket are available.

Desirable Cars: Premiums are usually much higher for cars that are the favorite target of thieves.

Anti-Theft Device Credits: Discounts of 5-15 percent are offered in some states for cars equipped with a hood lock and an alarm or a disabling device (active or passive) that prevents the car from being started without a key.

Multi-policy and Multicar Policy Discount: Some companies offer discounts of up to 10–20 percent for insuring your home and auto with the same company, or more than one car.

First Accident Allowance: Some insurers offer a "first accident allowance," which guarantees that if a customer achieves a certain number of accident-free years, his or her rates won't go up after the first at-fault accident.

Deductibles: Opting for the largest deductible you're comfortable with will reduce your premiums. Increasing your deductible to $500 from $200 could cut your collision premium about 20 percent. Raising the deductible to $1,000 from $200 could lower your premium about 45 percent. The discounts may vary by company.

Collision Coverage: The older the car, the less the need for collision insurance. Consider dropping collision insurance entirely on an older car. Regardless of how much coverage you carry, the insurance company will only pay up to the car's "book value." For example, if your car requires $1,000 in repairs, but its "book value" is only $500, the insurance company is required to pay only $500.

Organizations: If you are a member of AARP, AAA, the military, a union, a professional group, an alumni association, or similar organization, you may be able to get lower cost insurance or a discount.

YOUNG DRIVERS

TIP

Each year, teenagers account for about 15 percent of highway deaths. According to the Insurance Institute for Highway Safety (IIHS), the highest driver death rate per 100,000 people is among 18-year-olds. Parents need to make sure their children are fully prepared to be competent, safe drivers before letting them out on the road. All states issue learner's permits. However, only 35 states and the District of Columbia require permits before getting a driver's license. It isn't difficult for teenagers to get a license and only 14 states prohibit teenagers from driving during night and early morning. Call your state's MVA for young driver laws.

Because of the challenges in learning how to drive safely, parents should not to let their teenagers drive an older SUV, very small car, or one without airbags.

CENTER FOR AUTO SAFETY

Every year, car manufacturers spend tens of millions of dollars to influence government decision making. General Motors, Ford, and all the other major automakers have large staffs in Washington to represent their interests. But who looks out for the consumer? Who works on behalf of safety and not shareholders?

For 47 years, the independent, non-profit Center for Auto Safety has been the voice for consumers before government agencies, in Congress, and in the courts. The Center was established in 1970 by Ralph Nader and Consumers Union, publishers of Consumer Reports. As consumer concerns about auto safety issues expanded, so did the work of the Center. Center accomplishments include:

Initiating Safety Recalls: Annually, the Center analyzes thousands of consumer complaints. Based on these complaints and other reports, the Center requests government investigations and pursues recalls by manufacturers of defective vehicles. Center advocacy has resulted in the recall of millions of vehicles, including the deadly GM faulty ignition switches, Jeep fuel tank fires, and exploding Takata airbags.

Representing the Consumer in Washington: The Center monitors the activities of our government to ensure it carries out its responsibilities to the American taxpayer. The Center's fulltime job is to see the consumer's point of view represented in vehicle safety policies and rules. Over the course of our history, the Center has submitted hundreds of comments on government safety standards, and testified repeatedly before Congress on auto safety, consumer protection, and fuel economy.

One major Center success was the fight to get airbags in every car. Another was working to change the practice of manufacturers using weak roofs that crush vehicle occupants in rollovers. Since 2013, vehicle roofs are more than twice as strong as before, and rollover deaths and injuries have been dramatically reduced.

Exposing Secret Warranties and Making Repair Bulletins Public: The Center played a prominent role in the disclosure of secret warranties — or "policy adjustments," as manufacturers call them. These occur when an automaker agrees to pay for certain repairs beyond the warranty period but refuses to notify consumers. More recently, the Center went to court to make Technical Service Bulletins sent by manufacturers to their dealers publicly available.

Lemon Laws: The Center's work on Lemon Laws aided in the enactment of laws in all 50 states making it easier to return a defective new car and get your money back. Before Lemon Laws, automakers would refuse to buy back vehicles. Today, it is your legal right in every state to have a bad car bought back by the manufacturer.

Tire Ratings: Thanks to a Center lawsuit overturning the Department of Transportation's revocation of a valuable tire information program, consumers have reliable treadwear ratings to help them get the most miles for their dollar.

Legal Action: When the Center has exhausted other means of obtaining relief for consumers, we go to court. Currently we are suing DOT seeking implementation of a rear seat belt warnings law and we have brought an action against the Federal Trade Commission to overturn its policy allowing used cars with unrepaired recalls to be sold as "safe." The Center has also challenged class action settlements that don't deliver for consumers.

CENTER FOR AUTO SAFETY ONLINE

The Center is your representative fighting for auto safety, quality, and fuel economy every day. We depend on public support to keep us running. Learn more at our website about what people are saying about the car you own, or new government policies that may affect you: www.autosafety.org. You can sign up for email updates, become a member, or make a tax-deductible contribution to auto safety, at: www.autosafety.org/make-donation/. To contribute by mail, send a check to: Center for Auto Safety, 1825 Connecticut Ave., NW #330, Washington, DC 20009-5708.

WWW.AUTOSAFETY.ORG

Will Self-Driving Cars Be Safe Driving Cars?

Everyone is talking about self-driving cars. The auto industry, journalists, and even some safety advocates believe these autonomous vehicles (a/k/a "robot-cars") can represent the greatest step towards automotive safety since universal installation of the airbag. Others say they will dramatically change our economy and how – and where – we live. At a moment when deaths from cars and trucks continue to dramatically increase, particularly for pedestrians, any steps that can reduce the carnage are worth exploring.

If the science works as promised by robot-car manufacturers, wide-spread adoption could deliver game-changing safety not only for drivers and passengers but pedestrians as well. Companies that have changed the world before – such as Google, Apple, Uber, and Tesla – are working to introduce this next generation technology in passenger and commercial vehicles. When matched with new vehicle designs and innovations from traditional auto manufacturers – like Ford, GM, and Audi – no one who cares about safety should ignore the promises of significant reductions in deaths, injuries, and crashes.

Americans in their wisdom, however, remain unconvinced. Seventy eight percent of respondents to one survey said they would not want to ride in a self-driving car. Only thirteen percent in a different study agreed they would be comfortable with vehicle "features that completely relieve the driver of all control for the entire drive."

This hesitation over new technology seems unusual for a country that invented the car, won the race to the Moon, and loves smartphones and video-camera doorbells. Yet, the idea of robot-cars is different than the change from 8-tracks to I-Tunes, or from toll-booths to EZ-Pass. Self-driving vehicles may change our 100-year relationship with cars, the way we work, and how our communities and infrastructure are built. Will you want to live closer to work and share a robot-car with your co-workers? Will you prefer to live further away because now your car will be driving that long commute instead of you? If your car is all software – do you own it or does the programmer? Unsurprisingly, it is hard to find substantive answers from those who stand to profit from the sale of new, very high-priced robot-cars.

Instead, we get positive press releases about self-driving cars and proposed laws giving freedom to the industry to write its own rules. Some publicly traded companies keep telling us (and their shareholders) they will have fully autonomous vehicles on the road by 2021 or sooner. Apparently, many in Washington are on board. When the Car Book went to press, two separate bills were moving through Congress which, if passed, would allow robot-cars to receive wide exemptions from existing federal motor vehicle safety standards and preempt state standards designed to protect consumers.

When an industry with a history of fighting safety features could receive broad exemptions from safety standards, including whether cars will have a steering wheel or brakes, it raises serious questions. When that same industry fights against making public crash data on self-driving cars, and in the absence of enforceable federal standards does not want states to control their own roads, there is legitimate reason for concern. After all, the auto industry has never been shy about rolling out new items to maximize profits, but has too often been slow to deal with defects or design flaws. The technology companies who are now in the car business have never been fond of federal regulations, or transparency.

The problem is that in the case of robot-cars a failure to disclose crash data or a quickly handle a cyber breach is not just bad for business it could be bad for life and limbs. If past is prologue, when it comes to category changing auto technology, we should all want to trust, but verify.

Even if verified, safety should never be a luxury. Available safety technology should always be standard, whether it is automatic emergency braking or supposedly safer robot-cars and only for the rich.

In 2018, we will continue to scrutinize claims of perfect robot-cars eliminating all dangers and hassles of driving, and push for answers about how robot-cars will interact with today's cars and infrastructure. The benefits of this technology may yet be realized, but the advertised utopia often ignores societal costs. The most important question may not be when robot-car technology *could* be on our roads and in our lives, but whether, and how, it *should* be.

Americans spend billions of dollars on vehicle repairs every year. While many of those repairs are satisfactory, there are times when getting your vehicle fixed can be a very difficult process. In fact, vehicle defects and repairs are the number one cause of consumer complaints, according to the Federal Trade Commission. This chapter is designed to help you if you have a complaint, whether it's for a new vehicle still under warranty or for one you've had for years. In addition, we offer a guide to arbitration, the names and addresses of consumer groups, federal agencies, and the manufacturers themselves. Finally, we tell you how to take the important step of registering your complaint, particularly if it involves safety, with the U.S. Department of Transportation.

No matter what your complaint, keep accurate records. Copies of the following items are indispensable in helping to resolve your problems:

☑ your original purchase papers

☑ your service invoices

☑ bills you have paid

☑ letters or emails you have written to the manufacturer or the repair facility owner

☑ written repair estimates from your independent mechanic.

☑ notes on discussion with company representatives including names and dates.

RESOLVING COMPLAINTS

Here are some basic steps to help you resolve your problem:

1 First, return your vehicle to the repair facility that did the work. Bring a written list of the problems and make sure that you keep a copy of the list. Give the repair facility a reasonable opportunity to examine your vehicle and attempt to fix it. Speak directly to the service manager (not to the service writer who wrote up your repair order), and ask him or her to test drive the vehicle with you so that you can point out the problem.

2 If that doesn't resolve the problem, take the vehicle to a diagnostic center or another mechanic for an independent examination. This may cost $45 to $60. Get a written statement defining the problem and outlining how it may be fixed. Give your repair shop a copy. If your vehicle is under warranty, do not allow any warranty repair by an independent mechanic; you may not be reimbursed by the manufacturer.

3 If your repair shop does not respond to the independent assessment, present your problem to an arbitration panel. These panels hear both sides of the story and try to come to a resolution.

If the problem is with a new vehicle dealer, or if you feel that the manufacturer is responsible, you may be able to use one of the manufacturer's arbitration programs.

If the problem is solely with an independent dealer, a local Better Business Bureau (BBB) may be able to mediate your complaint. It may also offer an arbitration hearing. In any case, the BBB should enter your complaint into its files on that establishment.

When contacting any arbitration program, determine how long the process takes, who makes the final decision, whether you are bound by that decision, and whether the program handles all problems or only warranty complaints.

Beware of "binding arbitration" because you give up your right to later pursue legal action.

4 If there are no arbitration programs in your area, contact private consumer groups, local government agencies, or your local "action line" newspaper columnist, newspaper editor, or radio/TV broadcaster. A phone call or letter from them may persuade a repair facility to take action. Send a copy of your letter to the repair shop.

5 One of your last resorts is to bring a lawsuit against the dealer, manufacturer, or repair facility in small claims court. The fee for filing such an action is usually small, and you generally act as your own attorney, saving attorney's fees. There is a monetary limit on the amount you can claim, which varies from state to state. Your local consumer affairs office, state attorney general's office, or the clerk of the court can tell you how to file such a suit.

6 Finally, talk with an attorney. It's best to select an attorney who is familiar with handling automotive problems and has no ties to the local business community. Lawyer referral services can provide names of attorneys who deal with automobile problems. If you can't afford an attorney, contact the Legal Aid Society.

WARRANTY COMPLAINTS

If your vehicle is under warranty or you are having problems with a factory-authorized dealership, here are some guidelines:

1 Have the warranty available to show the dealer. Make sure you call the problem to the dealer's attention before the end of the warranty period.

2 If you are still dissatisfied after giving the dealer a reasonable opportunity to fix your vehicle, contact the manufacturer's representative (also called the zone representative) in your area. This person can authorize the dealer to make repairs or take other steps to resolve the dispute. Your dealer will have your zone representative's name and telephone number. Explain the problem and ask for a meeting and a personal inspection of your vehicle.

3 If you can't get satisfaction from the zone representative, call or write the manufacturer's owner relations department. Your owner's manual contains this phone number and address. In each case, as you move up the chain, indicate the steps you have already taken and keep careful records of your efforts.

4 Your next option is to present your problem to a complaint handling arbitration program. Beware of "binding arbitration" because you give up your right to later pursue legal action and beware of arbitrators selected by a manufacturer, dealer or repair shop.

If you complain of a problem during the warranty period, you have a right to have the problem fixed even after the warranty runs out. If your warranty has not been honored, you may be able to "revoke acceptance," which means that you return the vehicle to the dealer. If you are successful, you may be entitled to a replacement vehicle or to a full refund of the purchase price and reimbursement of legal fees under the Magnuson-Moss Warranty Act. Or, if you are covered by one of the state lemon laws, you may be able to return the vehicle and receive a refund or replacement from the manufacturer.

NEED HELP?

If you need assistance with a vehicle safety issue or repair problem, the Center for Auto Safety is here to help! The Center collects consumer complaints in an effort to force automakers and the government to address safety defects and to prevent consumers from being ripped off on repairs. To file a complaint with the Center, visit www.autosafety.org/submit-complaint and provide as much detail as you can on your vehicle problem. To stay up to date on Center for Auto Safety vehicle safety activities, sign up by visiting www.autosafety.org and clicking on the "Stay Informed" button.

VEHICLE SAFETY HOT LINE: 800-424-9393
TTY FOR HEARING IMPAIRED: 800-424-9153
WWW.SAFERCAR.GOV

The toll-free Auto Safety Hot Line can provide information on recalls, record information about safety problems, and refer you to the appropriate government experts on other vehicle related problems. You can even have recall information mailed to you within 24 hours of your call at no charge. Most importantly, you can call the hot line to report safety problems which will become part of the National Highway - Traffic Safety Administration's complaint database. If you have access to the internet, www.safercar.gov is a more efficient way to register complaints and obtain recall and safety information. You can also look up the individual complaints about a particular vehicle.

Thanks to the efforts of the Center for Auto Safety, we are able to provide you with a car by car index of vehicle complaints on file with the National Highway Traffic Safety Administration (NHTSA). Each year, thousands of Americans file online, or call the government, to register complaints about their vehicles.

The Car Book Complaint Index is the result of our analysis of these complaints. It is based on a ratio of the number of complaints for each vehicle to the sales of that vehicle. In order to predict the expected complaint performance of the 2018 models, we have examined the complaint history of that car's series. The term series refers to the fact that when a manufacturer introduces a new model, that vehicle remains essentially unchanged, on average, for four to six years. For example, the Ford Explorer was redesigned in 2011 and remains essentially the same car for 2018. As such, we have compiled the complaint experience for that series in order to give you some information to use in deciding which car to buy. For vehicles introduced or significantly changed in 2018, we do not yet have enough data to develop a complaint index.

The following table presents the projected best and worst complaint ratings for the 2018 models for which we can develop ratings. Higher index numbers mean the vehicle generated a greater number of complaints. Lower numbers indicate fewer complaints.

2018 PROJECTED COMPLAINT INDEX

THE BEST	INDEX*
Lexus RC	406
Toyota Corolla iM	481
Genesis G80	625
Cadillac Escalade ESV	698
Infiniti QX50	736
BMW 2 Series	872
Chevrolet Cruze	957
Audi Q3	986
Mazda 3	1005
Toyota Corolla	1130
Toyota RAV4	1155
Lexus RX	1189
Toyota Highlander	1241
Lexus IS	1247
Porsche Macan	1273
Buick Encore	1274
Chevrolet Trax	1331
Ford F-150	1348
Chevrolet Malibu	1357
Nissan Rogue	1361
Mazda CX-9	1,412

THE WORST	INDEX*
Mercedes-Benz B	>20,000
Chevrolet Volt	>20,000
Hyundai Santa Fe Sport	>20,000
Chrysler Pacifica	>20,000
Tesla Model S	>20,000
Hyundai Tucson	15,728
Ford Fusion Energi	11,219
Jeep Cherokee	10,565
Dodge Journey	10,301
Mercedes-Benz CLA	9,724
Mercedes-Benz GLC	9,453
Dodge Durango	9,031
Volvo XC90	8,581
Jeep Grand Cherokee	8,487
Ford Focus	8,391
Ford Fiesta	8,267
Chevrolet Bolt	8,221
Jeep Renegade	7,232
Nissan Titan	7,187
Ford Explorer	7,141

*IMPORTANT NOTE: The numbers represent relative index scores, not the number of complaints received. The complaint index score considers sales volume and years on the road. Lower index numbers are better. We capped the complaint index at 20,000 for excessively high complaint indices.

Consumer Groups and Government Contacts

Advocates for Highway and Auto Safety
750 First St., NE, Suite 1130
Washington, DC 20002
(202) 408-1711/408-1699 fax
www.saferoads.org
An alliance of consumer, health and safety groups and insurance companies. A great resource for state laws governing auto safety. A leading organization fighting for safer cars before the U.S. Congress and the National Highway Traffic Safety Administration.

Consumer Action
1170 Market St., Suite 500
San Francisco, CA 94102
(415) 777-9635
www.consumer-action.org
Complaint handling and advocacy related to consumer rights. A great resource for non-English consumer information.

Consumers for Auto Reliability and Safety
1303 J St., Suite 270
Sacramento, CA 95814
(530) 759-9440
www.carconsumers.org
Auto safety, airbags, and lemon laws. A leader in exposing the sale and rental of cars with open safety recalls.

KIDS AND CARS
(816) 216-7085
www.kidsandcars.org
email@kidsandcars.org
Safety and advocacy related to protecting children in and around motor vehicles. They lead the effort to require already available technology to prevent the death of unattended children in hot cars or from tragic back over accidents.

SafetyBelt Safe, U.S.A.
P.O. Box 553
Altadena, CA 91003
(800) 745-SAFE
www.carseat.org
stombrella@carseat.org
Excellent information and training on child safety seats and safety belt usage. The majority of parents do not use child seats correctly.

National Highway Traffic Safety Administration
1200 New Jersey Ave., SE, West Bldg.
Washington, DC 20590
(888) 327-4236
www.nhtsa.gov
www.safercar.gov
NHTSA issues safety and fuel economy standards for new motor vehicles; investigates safety defects and enforces recall of defective vehicles and equipment; conducts research and demonstration programs on vehicle safety, fuel economy, driver safety, and automobile inspection and repair; provides grants for state highway safety programs in areas such as police traffic services, driver education and licensing, emergency medical services, pedestrian safety, and alcohol abuse.

In addition with the EPA, they are in charge of setting fuel economy standards. They have a huge job, are woefully underfunded and need consumers to support their efforts in Congress.

Environmental Protection Agency
1200 Pennsylvania Ave., NW
Washington, DC 20460
(202) 272-0167/www.epa.gov
www.fueleconomy.gov
EPA's responsibilities include setting and enforcing air and noise emission standards for motor vehicles and measuring fuel economy in new vehicles (EPA Fuel Economy Guide).

Federal Trade Commission
600 Pennsylvania Ave., NW
Washington, DC 20580
(202) 326-2222
www.ftc.gov
The FTC regulates advertising, credit practices, marketing abuses, and professional services and ensures that products are properly labeled (as in fuel economy ratings). The commission covers unfair or deceptive trade practices in motor vehicle sales and repairs, as well as non-safety defects.

U.S. Department of Justice
Civil Division
950 Pennsylvania Ave., NW
Washington, DC 20530
(202) 307-0066
www.justice.gov/civil
feedback@doj.gov
The DOJ enforces federal law that requires manufacturers to label new automobiles and forbids removal or alteration of labels before delivery to consumers. Labels must contain make, model, vehicle identification number, dealer's name, suggested base price, manufacturer option costs, and manufacturer's suggested retail price.

AUTOMOBILE MANUFACTURERS

Acura (Division of Honda)
John Ikeda, Vice President-General
Manager
See Honda for address
Customer Relations: 800-382-2238

Audi (Division of Volkswagen)
Scott Keogh, President
See Volkswagen for address
Customer Relations: 800-822-2834

BMW
Knudt Flor, President and CEO
300 Chestnut Ridge Road
Woodcliff Lake, NJ 07677-7731
Customer Relations: 800-831-1117

Buick (Division of General Motors)
P.O. Box 33136
Detroit, MI 48232-5136
Customer Relations: 800-521-7300

Cadillac (Division of General Motors)
P.O. Box 33169
Detroit, MI 48232-5169
Customer Relations: 800-458-8006

Chevrolet (Division of General Motors)
P.O. Box 33136
Detroit, MI 48323-5136
Customer Relations: 800-222-1020

Chrysler (Chrysler, Dodge, Fiat, Jeep, Ram)
Sergio Marchionne, CEO
1000 Chrysler Drive
Auburn Hills, MI 48326
Customer Relations: 800-247-9753

Dodge (Division of Chrysler)
P.O. Box 21-8004
Auburn Hills, MI 48321-8004
Customer Relations: 800-423-6343

Fiat (Division of Chrysler)
P.O. Box 21-8004
Auburn Hills, MI 48321-8004
Customer Relations: 888-242-6342

Ford (Ford, Lincoln)
Mark Fields, President and CEO
P.O. Box 6248
Dearborn, MI 48126
Customer Relations 800-392-3673

General Motors (Buick, Cadillac, Chev., GMC)
Mary Barra, Chairman and CEO
300 Renaisance Center
Detorit, MI 48265

Genesis (Division of Hyundai)
Erwin Raphael, General Manager
10550 Talbert Ave.
Fountain Valley, CA 92708
Customer Relations: 844-340-9741

GMC (Division of General Motors)
P.O. Box 33172
Detroit, MI 48232
Customer Relations: 800-462-8782

Honda (Honda, Acura)
Toshiaki Mikoshiba, President and CEO
1919 Torrance Blvd.
Torrance, CA 90501
Customer Relations: 800-999-1009

Hyundai (Hyundai, Genesis)
Jerry Flannery, President and CEO
P.O. Box 20850
Fountain Valley, CA 92728-0850
Customer Relations: 800-633-5151
Email: consumeraffairs@hmausa.com

Infiniti (Division of Nissan)
Roland Krueger, President
See Nissan for address
Customer Relations: 800-662-6200

Jaguar, Land Rover
Joachim Eberhardt, President
555 MacArthur Blvd.
Mahwah, NJ 07430
Jaguar Customer Relations: 800-452-4827
Land Rover Cust. Relations: 800-637-6837

Jeep (Division of Chrysler)
P.O. Box 21-8004
Auburn Hills, MI 48321-8004
Customer Relations: 877-426-5337

Kia
Jang Won Sohn, President and CEO
P.O. Box 52410
Irvine, CA 92619-2410
Customer Relations: 800-333-4542

Lexus (Division of Toyota)
Jeff Bracken, Vice President and General
Manager
P.O. Box 2991-Mail Drop L201
Torrance, CA 90509-2991
Customer Relations: 800-255-3987

Lincoln (Division of Ford)
Kumar Galhotra, President
See Ford for address
Customer Relations: 800-521-4140

Mazda
Masahiro Moro, President and CEO
P.O. Box 19734
Irvine, CA 92623-9734
Customer Relations: 800-222-5500

Mercedes-Benz
Jason Hoff, President and CEO
1 Mercedes Drive
Montvale, NJ 07645
Customer Relations 800-367-6372

Mini (Division of BMW)
Thomas Felbermair, Vice President
See BMW for address
Customer Relations: 866-275-6464

Mitsubishi
Ryujiro Kobashi, President and CEO
P.O. Box 6400
Cypress, CA 90630-9998
Customer Reloations: 800-648-7820

Nissan
Hiroto Saikawa, President and CEO
P.O. Box 685003
Franklin, TN 37068-5003
Customer Relations: 800-647-7261

Porsche
Klaus Zellmer, President and CEO
980 Hammond Dr., Suite 1000
Atlanta, GA 30328
Customer Relations: 800-767-7243

Ram (Division of Chrysler)
P.O. Box 21-8007
Auburn Hills, MI 48321-8004
Customer Relations: 866-726-4636

Smart (Division of Mercedes-Benz)
Bart Herring, General Manager
1 Mercedes Drive
Montvale, NJ 07645
Customer Relations 800-762-2466

Subaru
Tomomi Nakamura, Chairman and CEO
P.O. Box 6000
Cherry Hill, NJ 08034-6000
Customer Relations: 800-782-2783

Telsa
Elon Musk, Chairman and CEO
3500 Deer Creek
Palo Alto, CA 94304
Customer Relations: 877-798-3752

Toyota (Toyota, Lexus)
Jim Lentz, President and CEO
19001 South Western Ave. Dept. WC11
Torrance, CA 90501
Customer Relations: 800-331-4331

Volkswagen
Hinrich Woebcken, President and CEO
2200 Ferdinand Porsche Dr.
Herndon, VA 20171
Customer Relations: 800-822-8987

Volvo
Lex Kerssemakers, President and CEO
One Volvo Drive
P.O. Box 914
Rockleigh, NJ 07647
Customer Relations: 800-458-1552

LEMON LAWS

Sometimes, despite our best efforts, we buy a vehicle that just doesn't work right. There may be little problem after little problem, or perhaps one big problem that the dealer cannot seem to fix. Because of the "sour" taste that such vehicles leave in the mouths of consumers who buy them, these vehicles are known as "lemons."

In the past, it was difficult to obtain a refund or replacement if a vehicle was a lemon. The burden of proof was left to the consumer. Because it is hard to define exactly what constitutes a lemon, many lemon owners were unable to win a case against a manufacturer. And when they won, consumers had to pay for their attorneys giving them less than if they had traded in their lemon.

Thanks to "Lemon Laws" passed by all states, lemon-aide is available when consumers get stuck with a lemon. Although there are some important state-to-state variations, all of the laws have similarities: They establish a period of coverage, usually two years from delivery or the written warranty period, whichever is shorter; they may require some form of noncourt arbitration; and most importantly they define a lemon. In most states a new car, truck, or van is "presumed" to be a lemon when it has been taken back to the shop 3 to 4 times for the same problem or is out of service for a total of 30 days during the covered period. This time does not mean consecutive days and can be for different problems. 15 states have safety lemon provisions which presume a vehicle is a lemon after only 1 to 2 repairs of a defect likely to cause death or serious injury. Be sure to keep careful records of your repairs since some states now require only one of the repairs to be within the specified time period. Thirty-three states provide for the award of attorney fees with the other 17 relying on the Federal lemon law for fees. A vehicle may be covered by the lemon law even though it doesn't meet the specific state requirements.

Specific information about your state's law can be obtained from your state attorney general's office or at the Center for Auto Safety's website. The following table offers a general description of the Lemon Law in your state and what you need to do to set it in motion (Notification/Trigger). We indicate where state-run arbitration programs are available. State-run programs are the best type of arbitration. Be aware, a few state lemon laws are so bad consumers should only rely on the Federal lemon law (the Magnuson-Moss Warranty Act) and state contract law. We have marked these bad laws with a ☒ while the best laws have a ☑.

If you would like to see the complete law in your state, go to www.autosafety.org/lemon-laws-state.

☑ **The Best Lemon Laws**
☒ **The Worst Lemon Laws**

Alabama	Qualification: 3 unsuccessful repairs or 30 calendar days within shorter of 24 months or 24,000 miles, provided 1 repair attempt or 1 day out of service is within shorter of 1 year or 12,000 miles. Notice/Trigger: Certified mail to manufacturer + opportunity for final repair attempt within 14 calendar days.
Alaska	Qualification: 3 unsuccessful repairs or 30 business days out of service within shorter of 1 year or warranty. Notice/Trigger: Certified mail to manufacturer + dealer (or repair agent) that problem has not been corrected in reasonable number of attempts + refund or replacement demanded within 60 days. Manufacturer has 30 calendar days for final repair attempt.
Arizona	Qualification: 4 unsuccessful repairs or 30 calendar days out of service within warranty period or shorter of 2 years or 24,000 miles. Notice/Trigger: Written notice + opportunity to repair to manufacturer.
Arkansas ☑ BEST	Qualification: 3 unsuccessful repairs, 5 total repairs of any nonconformity, or 1 unsuccessful repair of problem likely to cause death or serious bodily injury within longer of 24 months or 24,000 miles. Notice/Trigger: Certified or registered mail to manufacturer who has 10 days to notify consumer of repair facility. Facility has 10 days to repair.

L—Law specifically applies to leased vehicles; S-C—State has certified guidelines for arbitration; S-R—State-run arbitration mechanism available

California

✓ BEST

Qualification: 4 repair attempts or 30 calendar days out of service or 2 repair attempts for defect likely to cause death or serious bodily injury within shorter of 18 months or 18,000 miles, or "reasonable" number of attempts during entire express warranty period. Notice/Trigger: Direct written notice to manufacturer at address clearly specified in owner's manual. Covers small businesses with up to 5 vehicles under 10,000 pounds GVWR.

Colorado

✗ WORST

Qualification: 4 unsuccessful repairs or 30 business days out of service within shorter of 1 year or warranty. Notice/Trigger: Prior certified mail notice + opportunity to repair for manufacturer.

Connecticut

Qualification: 4 unsuccessful repairs or 30 calendar days out of service within shorter of 2 years or 24,000 miles, or 2 unsuccessful repairs of problem likely to cause death or serious bodily injury within warranty period or 1 year. Notice/Trigger: Report to manufacturer, agent, or dealer. Written notice to manufacturer only if required in owner's manual or warranty. S-R

Delaware

Qualification: 4 unsuccessful repairs or 30 calendar days out of service within shorter of 1 year or warranty. Notice/Trigger: Written notice + opportunity to repair to manufacturer.

D.C.

Qualification: 4 unsuccessful repairs or 30 calendar days out of service or 1 unsuccessful repair of safety-related defect, within shorter of 2 years or 18,000 miles. Notice/Trigger: Report to manufacturer, agent, or dealer.

Florida

Qualification: 3 unsuccessful repairs or 15 calendar days within 24 months from delivery. Notice/Trigger: Certified or express mail notice to manufacturer who has 10 days to notify consumer of repair facility plus 10 more calendar days for final repair attempt after delivery to designated dealer. S-R

Georgia

Qualification: 1 unsuccessful repair of serious safety defect or 3 unsuccessful repair attempts or 30 calendar days out of service within shorter of 24,000 miles or 24 months. Notification/Trigger: Overnight or certified mail notice return receipt requested. Manufacturer has 7 days to notify consumer of repair facility & consumer has 14 days from manufacturer receipt of original notice to deliver vehicle to repair facility. Facility has 28 calendar days from manufacturer receipt of original notice to repair. State-run arbitration mechanism available. Law specifically applies to leased vehicles.

Hawaii

Qualification: 3 unsuccessful repair attempts, or 1 unsuccessful repair attempt of defect likely to cause death or serious bodily injury, or out of service for total of 30 days within shorter of 2 years or 24,000 miles. Notice/Trigger: Written notice + opportunity to repair to manufacturer. S-R

Idaho

Qualification: 4 repair attempts or 30 business days out of service within shorter of 2 years or 24,000 miles, or 1 repair of complete failure of braking or steering likely to cause death or serious bodily injury. Notice/Trigger: Written notice to manufacturer or dealer + one opportunity to repair to manufacturer. S-R.

Illinois

Qualification: 4 unsuccessful repairs or 30 business days out of service within shorter of 1 year or 12,000 miles. Notice/Trigger: Written notice + opportunity to repair to manufacturer.

Indiana

✗ WORST

Qualification: 4 unsuccessful repairs or 30 business days out of service within shorter of 18 months or 18,000 miles. Notice/Trigger: Written notice to manufacturer only if required in the warranty.

L—Law specifically applies to leased vehicles; S-C—State has certified guidelines for arbitration; S-R—State-run arbitration mechanism available

Iowa	Qualification: 3 unsuccessful repairs, or 1 unsuccessful repair of nonconformity likely to cause death or serious bodily injury, or 30 calendar days out of service within shorter of 2 years or 24,000 miles. Notice/Trigger: Certified registered mail + final opportunity to repair within 10 calendar days of receipt of notice to manufacturer.
Kansas	Qualification: 4 unsuccessful repairs or 30 calendar days out of service or 10 total repairs within shorter of 1 year or warranty. Notice/Trigger: Actual notice to manufacturer.
Kentucky	Qualification: 4 unsuccessful repairs or 30 calendar days out of service within shorter of 1 year or 12,000 miles. Notice/Trigger: Written notice to manufacturer.
Louisiana	Qualification: 4 unsuccessful repairs or 90 calendar days out of service within shorter of 1 year or warranty. Notice/Trigger: Report to manufacturer or dealer.
Maine	Qualification: 3 unsuccessful repairs (or 1 unsuccessful repair of serious failure of brakes or steering) or 15 business days out of service within shorter of warranty or 3 years or 18,000 miles. Applies to vehicles within first 18,000 miles or 3 years regardless of whether claimant is original owner. Notice/Trigger: Written notice to manufacturer or dealer. Manufacturer has 7 business days after receipt for final repair attempt. S-R
Maryland	Qualification: 4 unsuccessful repairs, 30 calendar days out of service or 1 unsuccessful repair of braking or steering system within shorter of 15 months or 15,000 miles. Notice/Trigger: Certified mail return receipt requested + opportunity to repair within 30 calendar days of receipt of notice to manufacturer or factory branch.
Massachusetts	Qualification: 3 unsuccessful repairs or 10 business days out of service within shorter of 1 year or 15,000 miles. Notice/Trigger: Notice to manufacturer or dealer who has 7 business days to attempt final repair. S-R
Michigan	Qualification: 4 unsuccessful repairs within 2 years from date of first unsuccessful repair or 30 calendar days within shorter of 1 year or warranty. Notice/Trigger: Certified mail return receipt requested to manufacturer who has 5 business days to repair after delivery. Consumer may notify manufacturer after third repair attempt.
Minnesota	Qualification: 4 unsuccessful repairs or 30 business days or 1 unsuccessful repair of total braking or steering loss likely to cause death or serious bodily injury within shorter of 2 years or warranty. Notice/Trigger: Written notice + opportunity to repair to manufacturer, agent, or dealer.
Mississippi	Qualification: 3 unsuccessful repairs or 15 business days out of service within shorter of 1 year or warranty. Notice/Trigger: Written notice to manufacturer who has 10 business days to repair after delivery to designated dealer.
Missouri	Qualification: 4 unsuccessful repairs or 30 business days out of service within shorter of 1 year or warranty. Notice/Trigger: Written notice to manufacturer who has 10 calendar days to repair after delivery to designated dealer.
Montana	Qualification: 4 unsuccessful repairs or 30 business days out of service after notice within shorter of 2 years or 18,000 miles. Notice/Trigger: Written notice + opportunity to repair to manufacturer. S-R
Nebraska	Qualification: 4 unsuccessful repairs or 40 calendar days out of service within shorter of 1 year or warranty. Notice/Trigger: Certified mail + opportunity to repair to manufacturer.

L—Law specifically applies to leased vehicles; S-C—State has certified guidelines for arbitration; S-R—State-run arbitration mechanism available

Nevada	Qualification: 4 unsuccessful repairs or 30 calendar days out of service within shorter of 1 year or warranty. Notice/Trigger: Written notice to manufacturer.
New Hampshire	Qualification: 3 unsuccessful repairs by same dealer or 30 business days out of service within warranty. Notice/Trigger: Report to manufacturer, distributor, agent, or dealer (on forms provided by manufacturer) + final opportunity to repair before arbitration. S-R
New Jersey ☑ BEST	Qualification: 3 Unsuccessful repairs or 20 calendar days out of service within shorter of 2 years or 24,000 miles; or 1 unsuccessful repair of a serious safety defect likely to cause death or serious bodily injury. Notice/Trigger: Certified mail notice, return receipt requested to manufacturer who has 10 days to repair. Consumer may notify manufacturer at any time after the second repair attempt, or after the first repair attempt in the case of a serious safety defect.
New Mexico ☒ WORST	Qualification: 4 unsuccessful repairs or 30 business days out of service within shorter of 1 year or warranty. Notice/Trigger: Written notice + opportunity to repair to manufacturer, agent, or dealer.
New York	Qualification: 4 unsuccessful repairs or 30 calendar days out of service within shorter of 2 years or 18,000 miles. Notice/Trigger: Notice to manufacturer, agent, or dealer.
North Carolina	Qualification: 4 unsuccessful repairs within shorter of 24 months, 24,000 miles or warranty or 20 business days out of service during any 12 month period of warranty. Notice/Trigger: Written notice to manufacturer + opportunity to repair within 15 calendar days of receipt only if required in warranty or owner's manual.
North Dakota ☒ WORST	Qualification: 3 unsuccessful repairs or 30 business days out of service within shorter of 1 year or warranty. Notice/Trigger: Direct written notice + opportunity to repair to manufacturer. (Manufacturer's informal arbitration process serves as prerequisite to consumer refund or replacement.)
Ohio ☑ BEST	Qualification: 3 unsuccessful repairs of same nonconformity, 30 calendar days out of service, 8 total repairs of any nonconformity, or 1 unsuccessful repair of problem likely to cause death or serious bodily injury within shorter of 1 year or 18,000 miles. Notice/Trigger: Report to manufacturer, its agent, or dealer.
Oklahoma	Qualification: 4 unsuccessful repairs or 30 calendar days out of service within shorter of 1 year or warranty. Notice/Trigger: Written notice + opportunity to repair to manufacturer.
Oregon	Qualification: 4 unsuccessful repairs or 30 business days within shorter of 1 year or 12,000 miles. Notice/Trigger: Direct written notice + opportunity to repair to manufacturer.
Pennsylvania	Qualification: 3 unsuccessful repairs or 30 calendar days within shorter of 1 year, 12,000 miles, or warranty. Notice/Trigger: Delivery to authorized service + repair facility. If delivery impossible, written notice to manufacturer or its repair facility obligates them to pay for delivery.
Rhode Island	Qualification: 4 unsuccessful repairs or 30 calendar days out of service within shorter of 1 year or 15,000 miles. Notice/Trigger: Report to dealer or manufacturer who has 7 days for final repair opportunity.

L—Law specifically applies to leased vehicles; S-C—State has certified guidelines for arbitration; S-R—State-run arbitration mechanism available

South Carolina	Qualification: 3 unsuccessful repairs or 30 calendar days out of service within shorter of 1 year or 12,000 miles. Notice/Trigger: Certified mail + opportunity to repair (not more than 10 business days) to manufacturer only if manufacturer informed consumer of such at time of sale.
South Dakota	Qualification: 4 unsuccessful repairs, 1 of which occurred during shorter of 1 year or 12,000 miles, or 30 calendar days out of service during shorter of 24 months or 24,000 miles. Notice/Trigger: Certified mail to manufacturer + final opportunity to repair + 7 calendar days to notify consumer of repair facility.
Tennessee	Qualification: 4 unsuccessful repairs or 30 calendar days out of service within shorter of 1 year or warranty. Notice/Trigger: Certified mail notice to manufacturer + final opportunity to repair within 10 calendar days.
Texas	Qualification: 4 unsuccessful repairs when 2 occurred within shorter of 1 year or 12,000 miles, + other 2 occur within shorter of 1 year or 12,000 miles immediately following second repair attempt; or 2 unsuccessful repairs of serious safety defect when 1 occurred within shorter of 1 year or 12,000 miles + other occurred within shorter of 1 year or 12,000 miles immediately following first repair; or 30 calendar days out of service within shorter of 2 years or 24,000 miles + at least 2 attempts were made within shorter of 1 year or 12,000 miles. Notice/Trigger: Written notice to manufacturer. S-R
Utah	Qualification: 4 unsuccessful repairs or 30 business days out of service within shorter of 1 year or warranty. Notice/Trigger: Report to manufacturer, agent, or dealer. S-R
Vermont	Qualification: 3 unsuccessful repairs when at least first repair was within warranty, or 30 calendar days out of service within warranty. Notice/Trigger: Written notice to manufacturer (on provided forms) after third repair attempt, or 30 days. Arbitration must be held within 45 days after notice, during which time manufacturer has 1 final repair. S-R Note: Repairs must been done by same authorized agent or dealer, unless consumer shows good cause for taking vehicle to different agent or dealer.
Virginia	Qualification: 3 unsuccessful repairs, or 1 repair attempt of serious safety defect, or 30 calendar days out of service within 18 months. Notice/Trigger: Written notice to manufacturer. If 3 unsuccessful repairs or 30 days already exhausted before notice, manufacturer has 1 more repair attempt not to exceed 15 days.
Washington	Qualification: 4 unsuccessful repairs, 30 calendar days out of service (15 during warranty period), or 2 repairs of serious safety defect, first reported within shorter of warranty or 24 months or 24,000 miles. One repair attempt + 15 of 30 days must fall within manufacturer's express warranty of at least 1 year of 12,000 miles. Notice/Trigger: Written notice to manufacturer. S-R Note: Consumer should receive replacement or refund within 40 calendar days of request.
West Virginia ☑ BEST	Qualification: 3 unsuccessful repairs or 30 calendar days out of service or 1 unsuccessful repair of problem likely to cause death or serious bodily injury within shorter of 1 year or warranty. Notice/Trigger: Written notice + opportunity to repair to manufacturer.
Wisconsin	Qualification: 4 unsuccessful repairs or 30 calendar days out of service within shorter of 1 year or warranty. Notice/Trigger: Report to manufacturer or dealer. Note: Consumer should receive replacement or refund within 30 calendar days after offer to return title.
Wyoming	Qualification: 3 unsuccessful repairs or 30 business days out of service within 1 year. Notice/Trigger: Direct written notice + opportunity to repair to manufacturer. S-R

L—Law specifically applies to leased vehicles; S-C—State has certified guidelines for arbitration; S-R—State-run arbitration mechanism available

5 BASIC STEPS TO CAR BUYING

Buying a car means matching wits with a seasoned professional. But if you know what to expect, you'll have a much better chance of getting a really good deal!

There's no question that buying a car can be an intimidating experience. But it doesn't have to be. First of all, you have in your hands all of the information you need to make an informed choice. Secondly, if you approach the purchase logically, you'll always maintain control of the decision. Start with the following basic steps:

1 Consider your needs and how you will use a vehicle, and based on that, narrow your choice down to a particular class of car—sports, station wagon, minivan, sedan, large luxury, SUV, truck, or economy car. These are general classifications and some cars may fit into more than one category. In most cases, The Car Book presents the vehicles by size class.

2 Determine what features are really important to you. Most buyers consider safety on the top of their list, which is why the "Safety Chapter" is right up front in The Car Book. Specifically items such as back up cameras, automatic braking, and lane keeping assist along with airbags, power options, the general size, fuel economy, number of passengers, as well as "hidden" elements such as maintenance and insurance costs, should be considered at this stage in your selection process.

3 Find three or four cars that meet the needs you outlined above and your pocketbook. It's important not to narrow your choice down to one car because then you lose all your bargaining power in the showroom. (Why? Because you might lose the psychological ability to walk away from a bad deal!) In fact, because cars today are more similar than dissimilar, it's not hard to keep three or four choices in mind. In the "Car Rating Pages" in the back of the book, we suggest some competitive choices for your consideration. For example, if you are interested in the Honda Accord, you should also consider the Toyota Camry, Ford Fusion, and Hyundai Sonata.

4 Make sure you take a good, long test drive. The biggest car buying mistake most of us make is to overlook those nagging problems that seem to surface only after we've brought the car home. Spend at least an hour driving the car and preferably without a salesperson. If a dealership won't allow you to test drive a car without a salesperson, go somewhere else. The test drive should include time on the highway, parking, taking the car in and out of your driveway or garage, sitting in the back seat, and using the trunk or storage area. Renting the car you're interested in for a day can be very insightful.

TIP: Whatever you do, don't talk price until you're ready to buy!

5 This is the stage most of us dread—negotiating the price. While price negotiation is a car buying tradition, a few dealers are trying to break tradition by offering so-called "no-haggle" or "posted" pricing. Since they're still in the minority and because it's very hard for an individual to establish true competition between dealers, we recommend avoiding negotiating altogether by using the nonprofit CarBargains pricing service described on page 67.

THE 180-DEGREE TURN

When buying a car, you have the most important tool in the bargaining process: the 180-degree turn. Be prepared to walk away from a deal, even at the risk of losing the "very best deal" your salesperson has ever offered, and you will be in the best position to get a real "best deal." Remember: Dealerships need you, the buyer, to survive.

IN THE SHOWROOM

Being prepared is the best way to turn a potentially intimidating showroom experience into a profitable one. Here's some advice on handling what you'll find in the showroom.

Beware of silence. Silence is often used to intimidate, so be prepared for long periods of time when the salesperson is "talking with the manager." This tactic is designed to make you want to "just get the negotiation over with." Instead of becoming a victim, do something that indicates you are serious about looking elsewhere. Bring the classified section of the newspaper and begin circling other cars or review brochures from other manufacturers. By sending the message that you have other options, you increase your bargaining power and speed up the process.

Don't fall in love with a car. Never look too interested in any particular car. Advise family members or friends who go with you against being too enthusiastic about any one car. Tip: Beat the dealers at their own game—bring along a friend who tells you that the price is "too much compared to the other deal," or "I really liked that other car much better," or "wasn't that other car much cheaper?"

Keep your wallet in your pocket. Don't leave a deposit, even if it's refundable. You'll feel pressure to rush your shopping, and you'll have to return and face the salesperson again before you are ready.

Shop at the end of the month. Salespeople anxious to meet sales goals are more willing to negotiate a lower price at this time.

Buy last year's model. The majority of new cars are the same as the previous year, with minor cosmetic changes. You can save considerably by buying in early fall when dealers are clearing space for "new" models. The important trade-off you make using this technique is that the carmaker may have added a new safety feature to an otherwise unchanged vehicle.

Buying from stock. You can often get a better deal on a car that the dealer has on the lot. However, these cars often have expensive options you may not want or need. Do not hesitate to ask the dealer to remove an option (and its accompanying charge) or sell you the car without charging for the option. The longer the car sits there, the more interest the dealer pays on the car, which increases the dealer's incentive to sell.

Ordering a car. Cars can be ordered from the manufacturer with exactly the options you want. Simply offering a fixed amount over invoice (see page 65 for more about the invoice price) may be attractive because it's a sure sale and the dealership has not invested in the car. All the salesperson has to do is take your order.

If you do order a car, make sure when it arrives that it includes only the options you requested. Don't fall for the trick where the dealer offers you unordered options at a "special price," because it was their mistake. If you didn't order an option, don't pay for it.

BEWARE OF MANDATORY ARBITRATION AGREEMENTS

More and more dealers are adding mandatory binding arbitration agreements, which they often call "dispute resolution mechanisms," to your purchase contract. What this means is that you waive the right to sue or appeal any problem you have with the vehicle. In addition, the dealer often gets to choose the arbitrator. Before you start negotiating the price, ask if the dealer requires Mandatory Binding Arbitration. If so, and they won't remove that requirement, you should buy elsewhere. Many dealers do not have this requirement.

GETTING THE BEST PRICE

One of the most difficult aspects of buying a new car is getting the best price. Most of us are at a disadvantage negotiating because we don't know how much the car actually cost the dealer. The difference between what the dealer paid and the sticker price represents the negotiable amount.

Beware, now that most savvy consumers know to check the so-called "dealer invoice," the industry has camouflaged this number. Special incentives, rebates, and kickbacks can account for $500 to $2,000 worth of extra profit to a dealer selling a car at "dealer invoice." The non-profit Center for the Study of Services recently discovered that in 37 percent of cases when dealers are forced to bid against each other, they offered the buyer a price below the "dealer invoice"—an unlikely event if the dealer was actually losing money. The bottom line is that "dealer invoice" doesn't really mean dealer cost.

You can't really negotiate with only one dealer, you need to get two or three bidding against each other. Introducing competition is the best way to get the lowest price on a new car. To do this you have to convince two or three dealers that you are, in fact, prepared to buy a car; that you have decided on the make, model, and features; and that your decision now rests solely on which dealer will give you the best price. You can try to do this by phone, but often dealers will not give you the best price, or will quote you a price over the phone that they will not honor later. Instead, you should try to do this in person. As anyone knows who has ventured into an auto showroom simply to get the best price, the process can be lengthy and terribly arduous. Nevertheless, if you can convince the dealer that you are serious and are willing to take the time to go to a number of dealers, it will pay off. Be sure the dealer knows that you simply want the best price for the particular make, model and options. Otherwise, we suggest you use the CarBargains service described on page 67.

Here are some other showroom strategies:

Shop away from home. If you find a big savings at a dealership far from your home or on the Internet, call a local dealer with the price. They may match it. If not, pick up the car from the distant dealer, knowing your trip has saved you hundreds of dollars. You can still bring it to your local dealer for warranty work and repairs.

Beware of misleading advertising. New car ads are meant to get you into the showroom. They usually promise low prices, big rebates, high trade-in, and spotless integrity—don't be deceived. Advertised prices are rarely the true selling price. They usually exclude transportation charges, service fees, or document fees. And always look out for the asterisk, both in advertisements and on invoices. It can be a signal that the advertiser has something to hide.

Don't talk price until you're ready to buy. On your first few trips to the showroom, simply look over the cars, decide what options you want, and do your test-driving.

Shop the corporate twins. Page 73 contains a list of corporate twins—nearly identical cars that carry different name plates. Check the price and options of the twins of the car you like. A higher-priced twin may have more options, so it may be a better deal than the lower-priced car with the added options you want.

Watch out for dealer preparation overcharges. Before paying the dealer to clean your car, make sure that preparation is not included in the basic price. The price sticker will state: "Manu-facturer's suggested retail price of this model includes dealer preparation."

If you must negotiate . . . negotiate up from the "invoice" price rather than down from the sticker price. Simply make an offer close to or at the "invoice" price. If the salesperson says that your offer is too low to make a profit, ask to see the factory invoice.

Don't trade in. Although it is more work, you can usually do better by selling your old car yourself than by trading it in. To determine what you'll gain by selling the car yourself, check the NADA Official Used Car Guide at your credit union or library. On the web, the Kelly Blue Book website at kbb.com is a good source for determining the value of your used car. The difference between the trade-in price (what the dealer will give you) and the retail price (what you typically can sell it for) is your extra payment for selling the car yourself. Another option is to get a bid for your car from one of the national used car chains, such as CarMax. They do buy used cars with no obligation for you to buy from them.

If you do decide to trade your car in at the dealership, keep the buying and selling separate. First, negotiate the best price for your new car, then find out how much the dealer will give you for your old car. Keeping the two deals separate ensures that you know what you're paying for your new car and simplifies the entire transaction.

Question everything the dealer writes down. Nothing is etched in stone. Because things are written down, we tend not to question them. This is wrong—always assume that anything written down, or printed, is negotiable.

BUYING FOR SAFETY

So how do you buy for safety? Many consumers mistakenly believe that handling and performance are the key elements in the safety of a car. While an extremely unresponsive car could cause an accident, most new cars have adequately safe handling. In fact, many people actually feel uncomfortable driving high performance cars because the highly responsive steering, acceleration, and suspension systems can be difficult to get used to. But the main reason handling is overrated as a safety measure is that automobile collisions are, by nature, accidents. Once they've begun, they are beyond human capacity to prevent, no matter how well your car handles. So the key to protecting yourself is to purchase a car that offers a high degree of crash protection and automatic crash avoidance features.

When it comes to crash protection there are amazing new features to look for which we describe in the Safety Chapter and in the Guide to the Ratings on pages 77-78.

Here's a general list of what you should look for:

Dynamic Head Restraints: They adjust to give better protection in an accident.

Air Belts: Belts that blow up like long, soft balloons in a crash. Just being introduced in rear seats on some Ford vehicles.

Lane Keeping Assist: Keeps you within the white lines.

Automatic Braking: Applies the brakes faster than you can.

Blind Spot Detection: Keeps you from hitting another vehicle that you may not see.

Rear View Camera: Keeps children behind your car safe and helps with parking.

Adaptive Cruise Control: Adjusts your speed based on surrounding highway traffic.

Roll Sensing Airbags: Offer extra protection in a rollover–standard in many new cars.

Bicycle Detection: Alerts you when a bicycle has been detected.

Left Turn Crash Avoidance: Prevents a crash if turning left into the path of another car.

Adaptive Headlights: Increases vision by turning headlights when steering wheel turns.

CarBargains' Best Price Service

Even with the information that we provide you in this chapter of *The Car Book*, many of us still will not be comfortable negotiating for a fair price. In fact, as we indicated on the previous page, we believe it's really very difficult to negotiate the best price with a single dealer. The key to getting the best price is to get dealers to compete with each other.

CarBargains is a service of the non-profit Consumers' CHECK-BOOK, a consumer group that provides comparative price and quality information for many products and services.

CarBargains will "shop" the dealerships in your area and obtain at least five price quotes for the make and model of the car that you want to buy. The dealers who submit quotes know that they are competing with other area dealerships and have agreed to honor the prices that they submit. It is important to note that CarBargains is not an auto broker or "car buying" service; they have no affiliation with dealers.

Here's how the service works:
1. You provide CarBargains with the specific make, model, and style of car you wish to buy (Toyota Camry XLE, for example).
2. Within two weeks, CarBargains will send you dealer quote sheets from at least five local dealers who have bid against one another to sell you that car. Each dealer's offer is actually a commitment to a dollar amount above (or below) "factory invoice cost" for that model. You get the name and phone number of the manager responsible for handling the quote.
You will also receive a printout that enables you to figure the exact cost for each available option you might want on the vehicle.
3. Determine which dealer offers the best price using the dealer quote sheets. Add up the cost including the specific options you want. Contact the sales manager of that dealership and arrange to purchase the car.

If a car with the options you want is not available on the dealer's lot, you can, in many cases, have the dealer order the car from the factory or from another dealer at the agreed price.

When you receive your quotes, you will also get some suggestions on low-cost sources of financing and a valuation of your used car (trade-in).

The price for this service ($250, or $225 if you become a member) may seem expensive, but when you consider the savings that will result by having dealers bid against each other, as well as the time and effort of trying to get these bids yourself, we believe it's a great value. The dealers know they have a bona fide buyer; they know they are bidding against 5-7 of their competitors; and, you have CarBargains' experts on your side.

To obtain CarBargains' competitive price quotes, call them at 800-475-7283 or visit their website at www.carbargains.org. Or, you can send a check for $250 to CarBargains, 1625 K St., NW, 8th Floor, Washington, DC 20006. Be sure to include your mailing address, phone number, and e-mail address (in case of questions), and the exact make, model, style, and year of the car you want to buy. You should receive your report within two weeks.

! AUTO BROKERS !

While CarBargains is a non-profit organization created to help you find the best price for the car you want to purchase, auto brokers are typically in the business to make money. As such, the price you end up paying for the car will include additional profit for the broker. There have been cases where the auto broker makes certain promises, takes your money, and you never hear from him again. While many brokers are legitimately trying to get their customers the best price, others have developed special relationships with certain dealers and may not do much shopping for you. As a consumer, it is difficult to tell which are which. This is why we recommend CarBargains. If CarBargains is not for you, then we suggest you consider using a buying service associated with your credit union or auto club. They can arrange for the purchase of a car at some fixed price over "dealer invoice."

FINANCING

You've done your test-drive, researched prices, studied crash tests, determined the options you want, and haggled to get the best price. Now you have to decide how to pay for the car.

If you have the cash, pay for the car right away. You avoid finance charges, you won't have a large debt haunting you, and the full value of the car is yours. You can then make the monthly payments to yourself to save up for your next car.

However, most of us cannot afford to pay cash for a car, which leaves two options: financing or leasing. While leasing may seem more affordable, financing will actually cost you less and give you flexibility. When you finance a car, you own it after you finish your payments. At the end of a lease, you have nothing. We don't recommend leasing, but if you want more information, see page 70.

Shop around for interest rates. Most banks and credit unions will knock off at least a quarter of a percent for their customers. Have these quotes handy when you talk financing with the dealer.

The higher your down payment, the less you'll have to finance. This will not only reduce your overall interest charges, but often qualifies you for a lower interest rate.

Avoid long car loans. The monthly payments are lower, but you'll pay far more in overall interest charges. For example, a two-year, $25,000 loan at 4 percent will cost you $1,055 in interest; the same amount at five years will cost you $2,625—well over twice as much!

Beware of manufacturer promotional rates—the 0 to 1 percent rates you see advertised. These low rates are usually only valid on two or three-year loans and only for the most credit-worthy customers.

Read everything you are asked to sign and ask questions about anything you don't fully understand.

Make sure that an extended warranty has not been added to the purchase price. Dealers will sometimes do this without telling you. Extended warranties are generally a bad value. See the "Warranties" chapter for more information.

Credit Unions vs. Banks: Credit unions generally charge fewer and lower fees and offer better rates than banks. In addition, credit unions offer counseling services where consumers can find pricing information on cars or compare monthly payments for financing. You can join a credit union either through your employer, an organization or club, or if you have a relative who is part of a credit union.

DON'T BE TONGUE-TIED

Beware of high-pressure phrases like "I've talked to the manager and this is really the best we can do. As it is, we're losing money on this deal." Rarely is this true. Dealers are in the business to make money and most do very well. Don't tolerate a take-it-or-leave-it attitude. Simply repeat that you will only buy when you see the deal you want and that you don't appreciate the dealer pressuring you. Threaten to leave if the dealer continues to pressure you to buy today.

Don't let the dealer answer your questions with a question. If you ask, "Can I get this same car with leather seats?" and the salesperson answers, "If I get you leather seats in this car, will you buy today?" this response tries to force you to decide to buy before you are ready. Ask the dealer to just answer your question and say that you'll buy when you're ready. It's the dealer's job to answer questions, not yours.

If you are having a difficult time getting what you want, ask the dealer: "Why won't you let me buy a car today?" Most salespeople will be thrown off by this phrase as they are often too busy trying to use it on you. If they respond in frustration, "OK, what do you want?" you can simply say "straightforward answers to simple questions."

Get a price; don't settle for: "If you're shopping price, go to the other dealers first and then come back." This technique ensures that they don't have to truly negotiate. Your best response is: "I only plan to come back if your price is the lowest, so that's what I need today, your lowest price."

TYPICAL OPERATING COSTS

Here are the annual operating costs for some popular vehicles. These costs include operating expenses (fuel, oil, maintenance, and tires) and ownership expenses (insurance, financing, taxes, depreciation, and licensing) and are based on keeping the vehicle for 3 years and driving 20,000 miles per year. This information is from Runzheimer International. Runzheimer evaluated thirty 2018 model cars, vans, SUVs, and light trucks and determined the most and least expensive to operate among those vehicles. (Source: www.runzheimer.com)

Projected Ownership and Operating Costs
Based on Driving 3 Years, 20,000 miles per Year

2018 Cars

Most Expensive

Genesis G90 Premium 6-cyl. 3.3L	$25,786
Cadillac CTS Luxury 6-cyl. 3.6L	$21,522
Mercedes-Benz E300 4-cyl. 2.0L	$21,176
Ford Taurus Limited AWD 6-cyl. 3.5L	$16,584
Buick Lacrosse Essence 6-cyl. 3.6L	$16,467

Least Expensive

Nissan Altima S 4-cyl. 2.5L	$11,497
Mazda 3 Touring 4-cyl. 2.5L	$11,050
Chevrolet Sonic LT 4-cyl. 1.8L	$10,462
Mazda 3 Sport 4-cyl. 2.0L	$9,994
Toyota Corolla LE 4-cyl. 1.8L	$9,843

Light Trucks, Vans, and SUVs

Most Expensive

Chevrolet Tahoe LS 8-cyl. 5.3L	$17,766
Ford F250 XL 2WD 8-cyl. 6.2L	$15,819
Dodge Grand Caravan SXT 6-cyl. 3.6L	$15,654
Chevrolet Silverado 1500 1LT 2WD 6FT 6-cyl. 4.3L	$14,091
Dodge Grand Caravan SE 6-cyl. 3.6L	$13,887

Least Expensive

Jeep Grand Cherokee Laredo 6-cyl. 3.6L	$13,431
Chevrolet Equinox Premier LZ 4-cyl. 1.5L	$12,958
Chevrolet Silverado 1500 LS 6-cyl. 4.3L	$12,931
Toyota Tundra SR 8-cyl. 4.6L	$12,852
Chevrolet Silverado 1500 Work 2WD 6FT 6-cyl. 4.3L	$12,519

Runzheimer is providing the attached information for reference only. Any direct reproduction or publication of this data in its entirety without prior consent from Runzheimer is strictly forbidden. Founded in 1933, Runzheimer connects people, companies and their vehicles in ways that drive superior productivity and impactful business intelligence. Runzheimer is the leader in workforce mobility programs, designing and delivering fair, accurate and defensible™ business vehicle programs, relocation information services and business expense solutions.

DO YOU NEED A SECOND CAR?

TIP

Rather than invest in a second vehicle more and more consumers are depending on alternatives such as transit, cabs, Uber, Lyft, and other ride or car sharing programs and various types of vehicle rental including car sharing such as Zipcar and Car2Go. While paying for rides may seem uneconomical, when you consider how much you use the second vehicle, it's overall ownership, maintenance, depreciation and operating costs, your monthly cost for alternative transportation will undoubtedly be far less. Many millennials are skipping even first car ownership, having determined that the responsibility, cost, and housing of their own car far outweighs the use of alternative rides and public transportation. Another choice people are making is selecting a smaller, less expensive, more fuel efficient car, even though there are occasions when a big vehicle would be very useful and convenient. Instead, they are renting a pickup for that occasional trip to the Home Depot or garden center or renting an SUV for picking up or dropping off kids at college or weekend furniture runs.

LEASING VS. BUYING

About 25% of new car transactions are actually leases. Unfortunately, most leasees don't realize that, in spite of the low monthly payments, leasing costs more than buying.

When you pay cash or finance a car, you own an asset; leasing leaves you with nothing except all the headaches and responsibilities of ownership with none of the benefits. When you lease you pay a monthly fee for a predetermined time in exchange for the use of a car. However, you also pay for maintenance, insurance, and repairs as if you owned the car. Finally, when it comes time to turn in the car, it has to be in top shape—otherwise, you'll have to pay for repairs, clean up, or body work. One of the most important things to remember about a lease is that it is very difficult and expensive to end it early.

If you are considering a lease, here are some leasing terms you need to know and some tips to get you through the process:

Capitalized Cost is the price of the car on which the lease is based. Negotiate this as if you were buying the car. Capitalized Cost Reduction is your down payment.

Know the make and model of the vehicle you want. Tell the agent exactly how you want the car equipped. You don't have to pay for options you don't request. Decide in advance how long you will keep the car.

Find out the price of the options on which the lease is based. Typically, they will be full retail price. Their cost can be negotiated (albeit with some difficulty) before you settle on the monthly payment.

Find out how much you are required to pay at delivery. Most leases require at least the first month's payment. Others have a security deposit, registration fees, or other "hidden costs." When shopping around, make sure price quotes include security deposit and taxes—sales tax, monthly use tax, or gross receipt tax. Ask how the length of the lease affects your monthly cost.

Find out how the lease price was determined. Lease prices are generally based on the manufacturer's suggested retail price, less the predetermined residual value. (Residual value is how much the seller expects the vehicle to be worth at the end of the lease.) The best lease values are cars with a high expected residual value. To protect themselves, leasers tend to underestimate residual value, but there is little you can do about this estimate.

Find out the annual mileage limit. Don't accept a contract with a lower limit than you need. Most standard contracts allow 15,000 to 18,000 miles per year. If you go under the allowance one year, you can go over it the next. Watch out for excess mileage fees. If you go over, you'll get charged per mile.

Avoid "capitalized cost reduction" or "equity leases." Here the leaser offers to lower the monthly payment by asking you for more money up front—in other words, a down payment.

Ask about early termination. Between 30 and 40 percent of two-year leases are terminated early and 40–60 percent of four-year leases terminate early—this means expensive early termination fees. If you terminate the lease before it is up, what are the financial penalties? Typically, they are very high so watch out. Ask the dealer exactly what you would owe at the end of each year if you wanted out of the lease. Remember, if your car is stolen, the lease will typically be terminated. While your insurance should cover the value of

LEASEWISE

TIP

If you must lease, why haggle when you can let someone else do it for you? LeaseWise, a service from the non-profit Center for the Study of Services, makes dealers bid for your lease. First, they get leasing bids from dealers on the vehicles you're interested in. Next, you'll receive a detailed report with all the bids, the dealer and invoice cost of the vehicle, and a complete explanation of the various bids. Then, you can lease from the lowest bidder or use the report as leverage with another dealer. The service costs $350. For more information, call 800-475-7283, or visit www.checkbook.org/auto/leasew.cfm

the car, you still may owe additional amounts per your lease contract.

Avoid maintenance contracts. Getting work done privately is cheaper in the long run. And don't forget, this is a new car with a standard warranty.

Arrange for your own insurance. By shopping around, you can generally find less expensive insurance than what's offered by the lessor.

Ask how quickly you can expect delivery. If your agent can't deliver in a reasonable time, maybe he or she can't meet the price quoted.

Retain your option to buy the car at the end of the lease at a predetermined price. The price should equal the residual value; if it is more then the leaser is trying to make an additional profit. Regardless of how the end-of-lease value is determined, if you want the car, make an offer based on the current "Blue Book" value of the car at the end of the lease.

Again, residual value is the value of your car at the end of the lease. The Automotive Lease Guide is often used by leasing companies to determine the residual value. Because determining the residual value means predicting what the car is going to be worth some time in the future, it is a very difficult thing to do. As such, leasing companies often underestimate the residual value which means you'll absorb more of the cost of the vehicle in the lease. On the other hand, if the residual value at the end of the lease is very low, consider buying the vehicle for that amount.

LEASING VS. BUYING

The following table compares the costs of leasing vs. buying the same car over three and six years. Your actual costs may vary, but you can use this format to compare the cars you are considering. Our example assumes the residual value of the purchased vehicle to be 55 percent after three years and 40 percent after six years.

After 3 Years	36 month Lease	5 Yr Loan–3.59% Sell in 3 Yrs
MSRP	$33,500	$33,500
Lease Value/Purchase Cost of Car[1]	$30,150	$30,150
Initial Payment/Down Payment[2]	$3,015	$3,015
Loan Amount	$–	$27,135
Monthly Payments[2]	$320	$495
Total Payments (first 3 years of loan)[3]	$11,520	$17,662
Amount Left on Loan	$–	$11,385
Excess miles and disposition fees[4]	$480	$–
Total Cost	$15,015	$32,062
Less Value of Vehicle .57 residual	$–	$19,095
Overall Cost, first 3 years	**$15,015**	**$12,967**
Savings over Leasing 3 Years		**$2,048**

After 6 Years	2nd 3 Yr Lease	5 Yr Loan–3.59% Keep Car 6 yrs.
MSRP - 2nd Car 5% increase in cost	$35,175	$33,500
Lease Value/Purchase Cost of Car(8)	$31,658	$30,150
Initial Payment/Down Payment[2]	$3,166	$3,015
Loan Amount	$–	$27,135
Monthly Payment[9]	$340	$495
Total Payments	$12,240	$29,700
Amount Left on Loan	$–	$–
Excess miles and disposition fees[4]	$480	$–
Total Cost of Second Lease	$15,886	$–
Total Cost	$30,901	$32,715
Less Value of Vehicle .41 residual 6 yrs[7]	$–	$13,735
Total Cost, 6 years[8]	**$30,901**	**$18,980**
Savings Over Leasing 6 Years		**$11,921**

1. Purchase price reflects that most buyer's pay about 90% of the MSRP.
2. Initial lease payment based on leases with 10% due at signing and loans with 10% down payment.
3. Monthly lease payments based on typical leases as reported by US News and World Report. Monthly finance payments based on a 5 year, 3.59% loan.
4. Total payments (lease and finance) paid for 3 years.
5. Average excess mileage fee of $480 based on a 12000 mile limit and averages 3 typical situations: 25% going 1500 mile over the limit at $0.15/mile; 50% pre-paying for 1500 in mile overages at $0.10/mile, and 25% not exceeding the mileage limit–plus a typical disposition fee of $350.
6. Total amount paid; includes down payment, monthly payments, and end of lease fees.
7. Three-year residual value of 55 percent based on average actual 36-month residual value for the top 10 selling vehicles for model year 2017.
8. Represents the expected 5% increase in the cost of a similar leased vehicle 3 years later.
9. Estimated increase in lease payment.
10. Total payments for the second 3 year lease and total payments for the 5 year loan at 3.59%.
11. Total cost of 2 3-year leases and total cost for 5 year loan purchase.
12. Six-year residual value of 40 percent based on average actual 72-month residual value for the top 10 selling vehicles for model year 2017.

DEPRECIATION

Over the past 20 years, new vehicle depreciation costs have steadily increased. A study conducted by Runzheimer International shows that depreciation and interest now account for just over 50 percent of the costs of owning and operating a vehicle. Recently, however, the increasing cost of depreciation has slowed down. This is due to the increased prices of new vehicles and the stabilization in finance rates.

While there is no foolproof method for predicting retained vehicle value, your best bet is to purchase a popular vehicle model. Chances are, though not always, it will also be a popular used vehicle, meaning that it will retain more of its value when you go to sell it.

Most new cars are traded in within four years and are then available on the used car market. The priciest used cars may not be the highest quality. Supply and demand, as well as appearance, are important factors in determining used car prices.

The table indicates which of the top-selling 2014 cars held their value the best and which did not.

2014 VEHICLES WITH THE BEST AND WORST RESALE VALUE

THE BEST				THE WORST			
Model	2014 Price	2017 Price	Retain. Value	Model	2014 Price	2017 Price	Retain. Value
Toyota Tacoma	$27,785	$26,950	97.0%	Chrysler 200	$21,700	$11,560	53.3%
Jeep Wrangler	$30,995	$29,650	95.7%	Ford Focus	$18,515	$9,950	53.7%
Toyota 4Runner	$32,820	$28,600	87.1%	Chevrolet Malibu	$23,510	$12,650	53.8%
Chevrolet Equinox	$26,190	$21,820	83.3%	Chevrolet Impala	$29,135	$15,850	54.4%
Toyota Tundra	$31,825	$26,500	83.3%	Volkswagen Passat	$23,945	$13,250	55.3%
Jeep Patriot	$18,295	$14,550	79.5%	Chevrolet Cruze	$23,805	$13,250	55.7%
Jeep Grand Cherokee	$29,195	$23,150	79.3%	Ford Fusion	$23,855	$13,465	56.5%
Nissan Murano	$30,230	$23,785	78.7%	Toyota Sienna	$30,490	$17,350	56.9%
Chevrolet Silverado	$31,310	$23,875	76.3%	Kia Forte	$16,100	$9,250	57.5%
GMC Acadia	$34,335	$25,650	74.7%	Ford Taurus	$28,900	$16,625	57.5%
Cadillac SRX	$42,880	$31,650	73.8%	Nissan Maxima	$31,200	$17,975	57.6%
Subaru Forester	$22,995	$16,820	73.2%	Cadillac CTS	$41,495	$24,150	58.2%
BMW 3 Series	$43,200	$31,600	73.2%	Mini Cooper	$19,950	$11,970	60.0%
Chevrolet Camaro	$23,555	$17,100	72.6%	Nissan Altima	$22,110	$13,450	60.8%
Ford F-150	$31,555	$22,750	72.1%	Volkswagen Jetta	$17,820	$10,865	61.0%
Hyundai Santa Fe	$29,800	$21,400	71.8%	Subaru Legacy	$23,295	$14,275	61.3%
Honda Accord	$21,955	$15,750	71.7%	Nissan Versa	$13,790	$8,550	62.0%
Honda CR-V	$24,195	$17,300	71.5%	Dodge Charger	$26,995	$16,750	62.1%
Toyota Highlander	$30,520	$21,650	70.9%	Buick LaCrosse	$33,135	$20,650	62.3%
Ram Pickup	$31,750	$22,500	70.9%	Hyundai Elantra	$19,600	$12,250	62.5%
Toyota Prius	$24,200	$17,150	70.9%	Hyundai Accent	$14,645	$9,175	62.7%
Nissan Frontier	$26,000	$18,300	70.4%	Fiat 500	$16,195	$10,155	62.7%
BMW X5	$52,800	$36,975	70.0%	Hyundai Sonata	$21,450	$13,550	63.2%
Mercedes-Benz E	$51,400	$35,980	70.0%	Volkswagen Golf	$19,995	$12,650	63.3%
Honda Odyssey	$28,825	$20,120	69.8%	Ford Fiesta	$14,600	$9,250	63.4%

CORPORATE TWINS

"Corporate twins" refers to vehicles that have different names but share the same mechanics, drivetrain, and chassis. In many cases the vehicles are identical. Sometimes the difference is in body style, price, or options as with the Chevrolet Tahoe and the Cadillac Escalade.

While corporate twins share the same basic structure and running gear, some will drive and feel different because of the tuning of the suspension, the standard equipment and options available, and the the comfort and convenience features. One twin may stress a soft ride and luxury while another a tighter, sportier feel.

Historically, corporate twins have been limited mainly to domestic car companies. Today, several Asian and European car companies have started the practice.

CORPORATE TWINS

Chrysler
Chrysler 300
Dodge Charger

Ford
Ford Escape
Lincoln MKC

Ford Expedition
Lincoln Navigator

Ford Fusion
Lincoln MKZ

General Motors
Buick Encore
Chevrolet Trax

Buick Enclave
Chevrolet Traverse

Buick Regal
Chevrolet Malibu

Cadillac Escalade
Chevrolet Tahoe
GMC Yukon

General Motors (cont.)
Cadillac Escalade ESV
Chevrolet Suburban
GMC Yukon XL

Cadillac XTS
Chevrolet Impala

Cadillac XT5
GMC Acadia

Chevrolet Colorado
GMC Canyon

Chevrolet Equinox
GMC Terrain

Chevrolet Silverado
GMC Sierra

Honda
Acura MDX
Honda Pilot

Hyundai–Kia
Hyundai Accent
Kia Rio

Hyundai–Kia (cont.)
Hyundai Elantra
Kia Forte

Nissan
Nissan Pathfinder
Infiniti QX60

Toyota
Lexus ES
Toyota Avalon

Lexus NX
Toyota RAV4

Lexus GX
Toyota 4Runner

Lexus RX
Toyota Highlander

Volkswagen-Audi
Audi A3
Volkswagen Golf

Cadillac Escalade

Chevrolet Tahoe

GMC Yukon

T his section provides an overview of the most important features of this year's new models. Nearly all the information you'll need to make a smart choice is concisely presented on one page. (The data are collected for the model expected to be the most popular.) Here's what you'll find and how to interpret the data we've provided:

The Ratings

These are the ratings in nine important categories, as well as an overall comparative rating. We have adopted the Olympic rating system with "10" being the best.

Overall Crash Test: This rating represents a combination of the front and side crash test ratings and provides a relative comparison of how this year's models did against each other. We give the best performers a 10 and the worst a 1. Remember to compare crash test results relative to other cars in the same size class. For details, see page 19.

Safety Features: This is an evaluation of how much extra safety is built into the car. We give credit for torso and pelvis side airbags, roll-sensing side airbags, a knee bolster bag, crash imminent braking, daytime running lamps, adjustable upper seat belt anchorages, lane keeping assist, pedestrian crash avoidance, automatic crash notification, lane departure warning, dynamic brake support, and frontal collision warning. We also include dynamic head restraints, backup cameras and blind spot detection among other important safety features. See the "Safety Checklist" descriptions on the following pages.

Rollover: Electronic Stability Control has dramatically

reduced the likelihood of rollovers (see page 30). Because of that, we've reduced the "weight" that the rollover rating has in the vehicle's overall rating. When ESC is not able to prevent the vehicle from getting into a position where a rollover is possible, the vehicle's center of gravity plays a major role in whether or not that vehicle will actually rollover. The government uses a formula which estimates the "risk of rollover" in percentages. (See page 31) Using those percentages, we rated the 2018 vehicles on a relative basis. Again, the good news is that ESC is often able to prevent a vehicle from getting into a position where it is likely to roll over.

Preventive Maintenance: Each manufacturer suggests a preventive maintenance schedule designed to keep the car in good shape and to protect your rights under the warranty. Those with the lowest estimated PM costs get a 10 and the highest a 1. See pages 39-43 for the estimated costs and more information.

Repair Costs: It is virtually impossible to predict exactly what any new car will cost you in repairs. As such, we take nine typical repairs that you are likely to experience after your warranty expires and compare those costs among this year's models. Those with the lowest cost get a 10 and the highest a 1. See pages 39-43 for specific part repair cost and more information.

Warranty: This is an overall assessment of the manufacturer's basic, powertrain, corrosion, and roadside assistance warranties compared to all other manufacturer warranties. We also give credit for perks like free scheduled maintenance. We give the highest-rated warranties a 10 and the lowest a 1. For details, see page 36.

Fuel Economy: Here we compare the EPA mileage ratings of each car. The misers get a 10 and the guzzlers get a 1. For the purposes of the overall rating we pick the fuel economy rating of what is expected to be the most popular engine and drive train configuration. See page 33 for more information.

Complaints: This is where you'll find how each vehicle stacks up against hundreds of others on the road, based on the U.S. government complaint data for that vehicle. If the car has not been around long enough to have developed a complaint history, it is given a 5 (average). The least complained about cars get a 10 and the most problematic a 1. See page 55 for details.

Insurance Costs: Insurance companies rate vehicles to determine how much they plan to charge for insurance. While each insurer may have slightly different methods of rating, vehicles typically get a discount (max and min), a surcharge (max and min) or neither (average or typical). We looked at data from the insurance rating program of the largest insurer in America. This rating can predict the cost of insuring that vehicle, however, your location, age, driving record, and other factors also play a significant role in your cost of insurance. (See The Insurance Section pages 48-50.) Vehicles with a low rating (1 or 3) are more expensive to insure than other vehicles in that class or category. On the other hand, vehicles with a high rating (8 or 10) would be less expensive to insure in that particular class of vehicles. Because insurance companies may rate vehicles differently, it's important to compare prices between companies before you buy the car.

Overall Rating: This is the "bottom line." Using a combination of all of the key ratings, this tells how this vehicle stacks up against the others on a scale of 1 to 10. Due to the importance of safety, the combined crash test rating is 20 percent of the overall rating while the other eight ratings are 10 percent each. Vehicles with no front or side crash test results, as of our publication date, cannot be given an overall rating. In other categories, if information is unavailable, an "average" is included in order to develop an overall rating.

At-a-Glance

Status: Here we tell you if a vehicle is all-new, unchanged, or has received appearance change. All-new vehicles (the minority) are brand new from the ground up. Unchanged vehicles are essentially the same, but could have some different color or feature options. Vehicles with an appearance change are those whose internal workings stayed essentially the same, but have updated body panels.

Year Series Started: Each year the model is made, the production usually improves and as a result there are fewer defects. Therefore, the longer a car has been made, the less likely you are to be plagued with manufacturing and design defects. On the other hand, the newer a car is, the more likely it is to have the latest in features and safety.

Twins: These are cars with different make and model names but share the same mechanics, drive train, and chassis. In some cases the vehicles are identical, in other cases the body style, pricing or options are different.

Body Styles: This is a listing of the various body styles available such as coupe, sedan, wagon, etc. SUVs and minivans are only offered in one body style. Data on the page are for the first style listed.

Seating: This is the number of seating positions in the most popular model. When more than one number is listed (for example, 5/6) it means that different seat configurations are available.

Anti-theft Device: This lists the anti-theft devices standard for the vehicle. An immobilizer is an electronic device fitted to an automobile which prevents the engine from running unless the correct key (or other token) is present. This prevents the car from being "hot-wired" and driven away. A car alarm is an electronic device that emits high-volume sound and can sometimes flash the vehicles headlights in an attempt to discourage theft of the vehicle itself, its contents, or both. Passive devices automatically enter an armed state after the ignition is turned off and doors are closed. Active devices require the user to perform some action like pressing a button to arm and disarm the system.

Parking Index Rating: Using the car's length, wheelbase, and turning circle, we have calculated how easy it will be to maneuver this car in tight spots. This rating of "very easy" to "very hard" is an indicator of how much difficulty you may have parking.

Where Made: Here we tell you where the car was assembled. You'll find that traditional domestic companies often build their vehicles in other countries. Also, many foreign companies build their cars in the U.S.

Fuel Factor

MPG Rating (city/hwy): This is the EPA-rated fuel economy for city and highway driving measured in miles per gallon. Most models have a variety of fuel economy ratings because of different engine and transmission options. We've selected the combination expected to be most popular.

Driving Range: Given the car's expected fuel economy and gas tank size, this value gives you an idea of the number of miles you can expect to go on a tank of gas.

Fuel: The type of fuel specified by the manufacturer: regular, premium, E85.

Annual Fuel Cost: This is an estimate based on driving 15,000 miles per year at $2.15/gallon for regular and $2.68/gallon for premium. If the vehicle takes E85 (85% ethanol and 15% gasoline) or gasoline we calculated the annual cost using regular gasoline.

Gas Guzzler Tax: Auto companies are required to pay a gas guzzler tax on the sale of cars with exceptionally low fuel economy. This tax does not apply to light trucks.

Greenhouse Gas Emissions: This shows the amount (in tons) of greenhouse gases (carbon dioxide, nitrous oxide, and methane) that a vehicle emits per year along with the CO2 emitted in producing and distributing the fuel.

Barrels of Oil Used Per Year: This is the number of barrels of petroleum the vehicle will likely use each year. One barrel, once refined, makes about 19.5 gallons of gas.

Competition

Here we tell you how the car stacks up with some of its key competitors. Use this information to broaden your choice of new car possibilities. This list is only a guideline, not an all-inclusive list of every possible alternative.

Price Range

This box contains information on the MSRP. When available, we offer a variety of prices between the base and the most luxurious version of the car. The difference is often substantial. Usually the more expensive versions have fancy trim, larger engines, and lots of automatic equipment. The least expensive versions usually have manual transmissions and few extra features. In addition to the price range, we provide the estimated dealer markup. Remember, prices and dealer costs can

change during the year. Use these figures for general reference and comparisons, not as a precise indication of exactly how much the car you are interested in will cost. See page 67 for a buying service designed to ensure that you get the very best price.

Safety Checklist

Crash Tests
Frontal and Side Crash Test Ratings: Here's where we tell you if the front or side crash test index was very good, good, average, poor or very poor when compared to 2018 cars tested to date. To provide this rating we use the crash test for the vehicles with the best available safety equipment among the models when multiple models were tested. Unfortunately, not all of the 2018 models have been crash tested. If the car has been previously tested and the 2018 model is unchanged, we can carry those results forward. For details about the crash test programs, see page 19.

Airbags
All vehicles have dual front airbags and head airbags that

TYPES OF AIRBAGS

Airbags were introduced over 40 years ago and have been so successful in saving lives that car makers now include a variety of types. Here's a rundown of the basic types of airbags you'll find in today's vehicles. Manufacturers have various marketing names for these airbags.

Front: These deploy toward the front occupants and are now standard in all vehicles.

Head: These deploy from above the doors and are often called curtain airbags. They can reduce head injuries, shield from spraying glass, and provide protection in rollovers. Some form of these are in all vehicles.

Side: These deploy from the side of the seat or door and protect both the front and rear passengers in a side impact. Bags mounted in seats offer protection in a wider range of seating positions. Not all vehicles have these.

Rollover Protection: These head curtain airbags remain inflated for five seconds to protect in a sustained rollover. Not all vehicles have these.

Knee Bolster: These fill space between the front occupant's knees and instrument panel protecting the knees and legs. Not all vehicles have these.

deploy across the side windows. We've identified three additional types of airbags that the vehicle may have. The Side Airbags have historically been two separate bag systems. Recently, most manufacturers have been combining torso and pelvis protection into one bag. When the two are combined, we list *Front Pelvis/Torso from Seat* after each airbag type. Otherwise we identify specific bag type (or not) that comes with the vehicle.

Torso Side Airbag: This airbag protects the chest from serious injury in a side impact crash.

Pelvis Side Airbag: Provides extra protection around the pelvis and hip area, the portion of the body is usually closest to the vehicles exterior.

Rollover Sensing Airbags: This is a special side airbag system which keeps the side airbags inflated longer in the event of a rollover. These are standard in many 2018 models.

Knee Bolster Airbag: This airbag fills the space between the front passenger's knees and the dashboard.

Crash Avoidance

Collision Avoidance: Great new technology is available that can react faster than you in the event of a frontal collision. There are three basic systems available: Crash Imminent Braking (CIB), Dynamic Brake Support (DBS), and Frontal Collision Warning (FCW). All of these systems use radar or laser sensors to either alert the driver (FCW) or actively intervene to apply the brakes prior to a crash. CIB will actually apply the brakes if you are about to experience a frontal crash. DBS will increase your braking force if the sensors determine that you are not applying enough force to stop in time. FCW will merely sound an alarm in the event of an imminent frontal collision. Whenever a vehicle has CIB or DBS, it will also have a Frontal Crash Warning. We believe that Crash Imminent Braking and Dynamic Brake Support are more useful than just a Frontal Collision Warning (and thus rated higher), however FCW is still a useful safety feature. The government has set standards for FCW and we've used a ^ to indicate which systems DON'T meet the FCW requirements.

Blind Spot Detection: This is a blind spot monitor that uses radar or other technologies to detect objects in the driver's blind spot. When switching lanes a visible, audible, or vibrating alert warns if a vehicle has entered your blind spot.

Lane Keeping Assist: Going one step beyond a Lane Departure Warning, cars with Lane Keeping Assist will actually apply pressure to the brakes or adjust the steering when it senses that a car is drifting out of its lane. Lane Departure Warning (LDW) will simply alert the driver. If the vehicle has Land Keeping Assist, it will also have LDW. We have combined the two since the technology for Lane Departure Warning is required for Lane Keeping Assist, which we believe to be a better technology. The government has set standards for LDW and we've used an ^ to indicate which systems DON'T meet the low requirements.

THE BEST SAFETY FEATURES

The good news: automatic crash avoidance features are becoming more available. The bad news: it is hard to determine which ones work the best. Currently, the National Highway Traffic Safety Administration has standards for three important safety features: Back up cameras, Lane Depature Warning, and Frontal Collision Warning. Compliance to these standards is voluntary. In the tradition of *The Car Book*, exposing differences to stimulate market changes, in 2016 we published for the first time which of these three safety features meets the government standards and we continue to do so this year. However, it is important to note that having one of these features that doesn't meet government standards is better than not having it at all. Unfortunately, in order to get some of these features you often have to buy expensive "option packages" or a more expensive model which may include things you don't necessarily need or want.

Backup Camera: This camera allows the driver to see what is behind them on a dashboard screen. This is a critically important safety feature if you have children or drive near or around children. It's also a great parking assist. For a backup camera system to meet NHTSA's voluntary standards it must meet requirements regarding image size, linger time, response time, durability and deactivation. On the safety check list we've indicated which back up cameras DON'T meet federal standards with an asterisk (*).

Pedestrian Crash Avoidance: These systems utilize a variety of technologies (infrared, camera, radar) to detect pedestrians and adjust the car's course to avoid a collision.

General

Automatic Crash Notification: Using cellular technology and global positioning systems, some vehicles have the ability to send a call for help in the event of airbag deployment or accident. Often free initially, you'll have to pay extra later for this feature. There are several different types of ACN systems. Some simply dial 911 in the event of a crash while others connect your car to a call center which can determine the severity of the crash and dispatch emergency services. Some systems even send information about the crash to the call center.

Daytime Running Lights: Some cars offer daytime running lights that can reduce your chances of being in a crash by up to 40 percent by increasing the visibility of your vehicle. We indicate whether daytime running lights are standard, optional, or not available.

Safety Belts/Restraints

Dynamic Head Restraints: Many people position their seat and head restraint according to their own body and comfort requirements. This may not be the best position to protect you in a crash. These adjustors, sensing a crash, will automatically move the seat and headrest to the optimal position to help reduce injury during a rear-end crash. The IIHS has rated the performance of many headrests.

Adjustable Belts: Proper positioning of the safety belt across your chest is critical to obtaining the benefits of buckling up. Some systems allow you to adjust the height of the belt so it crosses your chest properly.

Specifications

Drive: This indicates the type of drive the manufacturer offers. This could be two wheel drive in the front (FWD) or rear (RWD) or all or four wheel drive (AWD/4WD).

Engine: This is the engine size (liters) and type that is expected to be the most popular. The engine types specify V6 or V8 for six or eight cylinders and I3, I4 or I6 for engines with cylinders in-line. For electric vehicles, we indicate the type of auxiliary power offered.

Transmission: This is the type of transmission expected to be the most popular. Most drivers today prefer automatic transmissions. The number listed with the transmission (5-sp.) is the number of gears or speeds. Then we list whether it's automatic or manual and if the transmission is a continuously variable transmission (CVT). CVT changes smoothly and efficiently between ratios of engine to car speeds and can provide better fuel economy.

Tow Rating: Ratings of very low, low, average, high, and very high indicate the vehicle's relative ability to tow trailers or other loads. Some manufacturers do not provide a tow rating.

Head/Leg Room: This tells how roomy the front seat is. The values are given in inches and rated in comparison to all other vehicles.

Interior Space: This tells how roomy the car's passenger area should feel. This value is given in cubic feet and rated in comparison to all other vehicles. Many SUVs do not provide interior space specifications.

Cargo Space: This gives you the cubic feet available for cargo. For minivans, the volume is behind the last row of seats. In cars, it's the trunk space. We rate the roominess of the cargo space compared to all trucks, SUVs, and cars.

Wheelbase/Length: The distance between the centers of the front and rear wheels is the wheelbase and the length is the distance from front bumper to rear bumper. Wheelbase can affect the ride and length affects how big the car "feels."

Acura ILX
Compact

Acura ILX

Ratings—10 Best, 1 Worst

Rating	
Combo Crash Tests	—
Safety Features	7
Rollover	6
Preventive Maintenance	9
Repair Costs	7
Warranty	6
Fuel Economy	7
Complaints	—
Insurance Costs	10
OVERALL RATING	—

Acura ILX

At-a-Glance

Status/Year Series Started . . . . All New/2018
Twins . . . . —
Body Styles . . . . Sedan
Seating 5
Anti-Theft Device . . . . . . Std. Pass. Immobil. & Alarm
Parking Index Rating . . . . Easy
Where Made . . . . Marysville, OH
Fuel Factor:
MPG Rating (city/hwy) Good-25/35
Driving Range (mi.) Short-379
Fuel Type . . . . Premium
Annual Fuel Cost . . . . .Average-$1553
Gas Guzzler Tax . . . . .No
Greenhouse Gas Emissions (tons/yr.) Low-5.1
Barrels of Oil Used per year Average-11.4

How the Competition Rates

Competitors	Rating	Pg.
Audi A3	6	83
BMW 3 Series	7	91
Cadillac ATS	4	106

Price Range

	Retail	Markup
Base	$27,990	6%
Premium Package	$29,990	6%
Technology Package	$32,990	6%
Technology Pkg. w/A-SPEC	$34,980	6%

Safety Checklist

Crash Test:
Frontal . . . . —
Side . . . . —
Airbags:
Torso . . . Standard Front Pelvis/Torso from Seat
Roll Sensing . . . . .Yes
Knee Bolster . . . . None
Crash Avoidance:
Collision Avoidance . . . . . . Optional CIB & DBS
Blind Spot Detection . . . . Optional
Lane Keeping Assist . . . . Optional
Backup Camera . . . . Standard
Pedestrian Crash Avoidance . . . . Optional
General:
Auto. Crash Notification . . . Operator Assist.-Fee
Day Running Lamps . . . . Standard
Safety Belt/Restraint:
Dynamic Head Restraints . . . . None
Adjustable Belt . . . . .Standard Front

Note: As of May 2018, all vehicles are required to have a backup camera.
^Warning feature does not meet government standards.
*Backup camera does not meet government standards.

Acura ILX

Specifications

Drive . . . . .FWD
Engine 2.4-liter I4
Transmission . . . . 8-sp. Automatic
Tow Rating (lbs.) . . . . —
Head/Leg Room (in.) Cramped-38/42.3
Interior Space (cu. ft.) . . . . Very Cramped-89.3
Cargo Space (cu. ft.) . . . . Very Cramped-12.3
Wheelbase/Length (in.) 105.1/181.9

Ratings—10 Best, 1 Worst

Combo Crash Tests	8
Safety Features	10
Rollover	4
Preventive Maintenance	5
Repair Costs	2
Warranty	6
Fuel Economy	3
Complaints	4
Insurance Costs	10
OVERALL RATING	**7**

Acura MDX

Acura MDX

At-a-Glance

Status/Year Series Started	Unchanged/2014
Twins	Honda Pilot
Body Styles	SUV
Seating	7
Anti-Theft Device	Std. Pass. Immobil. & Alarm
Parking Index Rating	Hard
Where Made	Lincoln, AL

Fuel Factor:

MPG Rating (city/hwy)	Poor-18/27
Driving Range (mi.)	Average-413
Fuel Type	Premium
Annual Fuel Cost	Very High-$2104
Gas Guzzler Tax	No
Greenhouse Gas Emissions (tons/yr.)	High-8.6
Barrels of Oil Used per year	High-15.7

How the Competition Rates

Competitors	Rating	Pg.
BMW X5	5	98
Cadillac XT5	3	108
Infiniti QX60	5	170

Price Range

	Retail	Markup
Base	$44,050	7%
SH-AWD w/Tech. Package	$50,460	7%
Advance w/RES	$56,500	7%
SH-AWD Advance w/RES	$58,500	7%

Safety Checklist

Crash Test:
- Frontal . . . . Very Good
- Side . . . . Average

Airbags:
- Torso . . . Standard Front Pelvis/Torso from Seat
- Roll Sensing . . . . Yes
- Knee Bolster . . . . Standard Driver

Crash Avoidance:
- Collision Avoidance . . . . . Standard CIB & DBS
- Blind Spot Detection . . . . Optional
- Lane Keeping Assist . . . . Standard
- Backup Camera . . . . Standard*
- Pedestrian Crash Avoidance . . . . Optional

General:
- Auto. Crash Notification . . . Operator Assist.-Fee
- Day Running Lamps . . . . Standard

Safety Belt/Restraint:
- Dynamic Head Restraints . . . . None
- Adjustable Belt . . . . Standard Front

Note: As of May 2018, all vehicles are required to have a backup camera.
^Warning feature does not meet government standards.
*Backup camera does not meet government standards.

Acura MDX

Specifications

Drive	AWD
Engine	3.5-liter V6
Transmission	6-sp. Automatic
Tow Rating (lbs.)	Low-3500
Head/Leg Room (in.)	Very Cramped-38.1/41.4
Interior Space (cu. ft.)	Very Roomy-132.3
Cargo Space (cu. ft.)	Cramped-14.8
Wheelbase/Length (in.)	111/193.6

Ratings—10 Best, 1 Worst

Combo Crash Tests	9
Safety Features	8
Rollover	4
Preventive Maintenance	5
Repair Costs	5
Warranty	6
Fuel Economy	3
Complaints	7
Insurance Costs	10
OVERALL RATING	**9**

Acura RDX

Acura RDX

At-a-Glance

Status/Year Series Started........ Unchanged/2013
Twins .... –
Body Styles .... SUV
Seating 5
Anti-Theft Device ...... Std. Pass. Immobil. & Alarm
Parking Index Rating .... Hard
Where Made................... East Liberty, OH

Fuel Factor:
MPG Rating (city/hwy)................ Poor-19/27
Driving Range (mi.) .... Very Short-351
Fuel Type........................... Premium
Annual Fuel Cost .... Very High-$2032
Gas Guzzler Tax .... No
Greenhouse Gas Emissions (tons/yr.)..... High-8.2
Barrels of Oil Used per year High-15.0

How the Competition Rates

Competitors	Rating	Pg.
Buick Encore	10	102
Lexus NX	5	191
Lincoln MKC	6	195

Price Range	Retail	Markup
FWD	$35,670	5%
AWD	$37,170	5%
FWD w/Tech. Package	$39,370	5%
AWD w/Tech. Package	$40,870	5%

Safety Checklist

Crash Test:
Frontal......................... Very Good
Side............................... Good
Airbags:
Torso . . . Standard Front Pelvis/Torso from Seat
Roll Sensing............................ Yes
Knee Bolster .... Standard Driver
Crash Avoidance:
Collision Avoidance ...... Optional CIB & DBS
Blind Spot Detection .... Optional
Lane Keeping Assist .... Standard
Backup Camera................... Standard*
Pedestrian Crash Avoidance .... Optional
General:
Auto. Crash Notification.... Operator Assist.-Fee
Day Running Lamps .... Standard
Safety Belt/Restraint:
Dynamic Head Restraints .... None
Adjustable Belt............... Standard Front

Note: As of May 2018, all vehicles are required to have a backup camera.
^Warning feature does not meet government standards.
*Backup camera does not meet government standards.

Acura RDX

Specifications

Drive....................................... AWD
Engine 3.5-liter V6
Transmission .... 6-sp. Automatic
Tow Rating (lbs.) .... Very Low-1500
Head/Leg Room (in.) Cramped-38.7/42
Interior Space (cu. ft.)........... Average-103.5
Cargo Space (cu. ft.) Roomy-26.1
Wheelbase/Length (in.) 105.7/183.5

Ratings—10 Best, 1 Worst

Combo Crash Tests	10
Safety Features	9
Rollover	8
Preventive Maintenance	5
Repair Costs	3
Warranty	6
Fuel Economy	6
Complaints	3
Insurance Costs	10
OVERALL RATING	**9**

Acura TLX

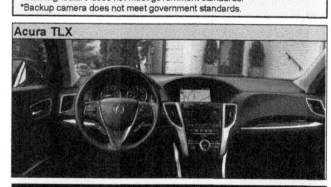

Acura TLX

At-a-Glance

Status/Year Series Started	Unchanged/2015
Twins	–
Body Styles	Sedan
Seating	5
Anti-Theft Device	Std. Pass. Immobil. & Alarm
Parking Index Rating	Hard
Where Made	Marysville, OH

Fuel Factor:

MPG Rating (city/hwy)	Average-23/33
Driving Range (mi.)	Very Long-458
Fuel Type	Premium
Annual Fuel Cost	High-$1673
Gas Guzzler Tax	No
Greenhouse Gas Emissions (tons/yr.)	Average-6.5
Barrels of Oil Used per year	Average-12.2

How the Competition Rates

Competitors	Rating	Pg.
Audi A6	7	86
BMW 5 Series	6	93
Lexus ES	5	187

Price Range	Retail	Markup
Base 2.4L	$33,000	5%
Base 3.5L	$36,200	5%
3.5L w/Tech. Package	$39,900	5%
SH-AWD w/Advance Package	$45,750	5%

Safety Checklist

Crash Test:

Frontal	Very Good
Side	Very Good

Airbags:

Torso	Standard Front Pelvis/Torso from Seat
Roll Sensing	Yes
Knee Bolster	Standard Driver

Crash Avoidance:

Collision Avoidance	Standard CIB & DBS
Blind Spot Detection	Optional
Lane Keeping Assist	Optional
Backup Camera	Standard
Pedestrian Crash Avoidance	Optional

General:

Auto. Crash Notification	Operator Assist.-Fee
Day Running Lamps	Standard

Safety Belt/Restraint:

Dynamic Head Restraints	None
Adjustable Belt	Standard Front

Note: As of May 2018, all vehicles are required to have a backup camera.
^Warning feature does not meet government standards.
*Backup camera does not meet government standards.

Specifications

Drive	FWD
Engine	2.4-liter I4
Transmission	8-sp. Automatic
Tow Rating (lbs.)	–
Head/Leg Room (in.)	Cramped-37.2/42.6
Interior Space (cu. ft.)	Cramped-93.3
Cargo Space (cu. ft.)	Very Cramped-13.2
Wheelbase/Length (in.)	109.3/190.3

Audi A3   Compact

Ratings—10 Best, 1 Worst

Combo Crash Tests	6
Safety Features	9
Rollover	7
Preventive Maintenance	1
Repair Costs	5
Warranty	7
Fuel Economy	6
Complaints	4
Insurance Costs	5
OVERALL RATING	**6**

Audi A3

Audi A3

At-a-Glance

Status/Year Series Started. Unchanged/2015
Twins . . . . Volkswagen Golf
Body Styles . . . . Sedan, Wagon
Seating. 5
Anti-Theft Device . . . . . . Std. Pass. Immobil. & Alarm
Parking Index Rating . . . . Easy
Where Made. . . . . Gyor, Hungary
Fuel Factor:
MPG Rating (city/hwy) Average-24/33
Driving Range (mi.) Short-397
Fuel Type. . . . . .Premium
Annual Fuel Cost . . . . .Average-$1628
Gas Guzzler Tax . . . . .No
Greenhouse Gas Emissions (tons/yr.). . Average-6.6
Barrels of Oil Used per year Average-12.2

How the Competition Rates

Competitors	Rating	Pg.
BMW 3 Series	7	91
Lexus IS	8	190
Mercedes-Benz C	1	206

Price Range	Retail	Markup
Premium Sedan	$31,950	8%
Premium Plus Sedan Quattro	$38,200	8%
Premium Cabrio	$38,350	8%
Prestige Cabriolet Quattro	$49,500	8%

Safety Checklist

Crash Test:
Frontal. . . . . Average
Side. . . . . Average
Airbags:
Torso Std. Fr. & Opt. Rr. Pelvis/Torso from Seat
Roll Sensing. . . . . .Yes
Knee Bolster . . . . .Standard Front
Crash Avoidance:
Collision Avoidance . . . . . . Standard CIB & DBS
Blind Spot Detection . . . . Optional
Lane Keeping Assist . . . . Optional
Backup Camera. . . . . .Standard*
Pedestrian Crash Avoidance . . . . None
General:
Auto. Crash Notification. . . . . None
Day Running Lamps . . . . Standard
Safety Belt/Restraint:
Dynamic Head Restraints . . . . None
Adjustable Belt. . . . . .Standard Front

Note: As of May 2018, all vehicles are required to have a backup camera.
^Warning feature does not meet government standards.
*Backup camera does not meet government standards.

Audi A3

Specifications

Drive. . . . . .AWD
Engine 2.0-liter I4
Transmission . . . . 6-sp. Automatic
Tow Rating (lbs.) . . . . —
Head/Leg Room (in.) . . . . Very Cramped-36.5/41.2
Interior Space (cu. ft.). . . . . Very Cramped-86
Cargo Space (cu. ft.) . . . . Very Cramped-10.03
Wheelbase/Length (in.) 103.8/175.4

Audi A4   Compact

Ratings—10 Best, 1 Worst

Combo Crash Tests	2
Safety Features	5
Rollover	8
Preventive Maintenance	4
Repair Costs	2
Warranty	7
Fuel Economy	7
Complaints	3
Insurance Costs	5
OVERALL RATING	**2**

Audi A4

Audi A4

At-a-Glance

Status/Year Series Started........ Unchanged/2017
Twins .... –
Body Styles .... Sedan
Seating 5
Anti-Theft Device ...... Std. Pass. Immobil. & Alarm
Parking Index Rating .... Average
Where Made.................. Ingolstadt, Germany
Fuel Factor:
  MPG Rating (city/hwy) Good-25/33
  Driving Range (mi.) Long-429
  Fuel Type........................ Premium
  Annual Fuel Cost .... Average-$1588
  Gas Guzzler Tax .... No
  Greenhouse Gas Emissions (tons/yr.)..... Low-5.2
  Barrels of Oil Used per year Average-11.8

How the Competition Rates

Competitors	Rating	Pg.
BMW 3 Series	7	91
Cadillac ATS	4	106
Mercedes-Benz C	1	206

Price Range	Retail	Markup
2.0T Premium Sedan	$36,000	8%
2.0T Premium Sedan Quattro	$40,500	8%
2.0T Premium Plus Sdn Quattro	$43,700	8%
2.0T Prestige Sedan Quattro	$50,000	8%

Safety Checklist

Crash Test:
  Frontal.......................... Very Poor
  Side............................... Average
Airbags:
  Torso Std. Fr. & Opt. Rr. Pelvis/Torso from Seat
  Roll Sensing........................ No
  Knee Bolster .... None
Crash Avoidance:
  Collision Avoidance ...... Standard CIB & DBS
  Blind Spot Detection .... Optional
  Lane Keeping Assist .... Optional^
  Backup Camera.................... Standard*
  Pedestrian Crash Avoidance .... Standard
General:
  Auto. Crash Notification........ Dial Assist-Fee
  Day Running Lamps .... Standard
Safety Belt/Restraint:
  Dynamic Head Restraints .... None
  Adjustable Belt................ Standard Front

Note: As of May 2018, all vehicles are required to have a backup camera.
^Warning feature does not meet government standards.
*Backup camera does not meet government standards.

Audi A4

Specifications

Drive.................................. AWD
Engine 2.0-liter I4
Transmission .... 8-sp. Automatic
Tow Rating (lbs.) .... –
Head/Leg Room (in.) Cramped-38.9/41.3
Interior Space (cu. ft.)............... Cramped-92
Cargo Space (cu. ft.) .... Very Cramped-13
Wheelbase/Length (in.) 111/186.1

Ratings—10 Best, 1 Worst

Combo Crash Tests	—
Safety Features	9
Rollover	8
Preventive Maintenance	4
Repair Costs	4
Warranty	7
Fuel Economy	7
Complaints	—
Insurance Costs	3
OVERALL RATING	—

Audi A5

At-a-Glance

Status/Year Series Started	All New/2018
Twins	—
Body Styles	Coupe
Seating	4
Anti-Theft Device	Std. Pass. Immobil. & Alarm
Parking Index Rating	Average
Where Made	Ingolstadt, Germany

Fuel Factor:

MPG Rating (city/hwy)	Good-24/34
Driving Range (mi.)	Long-423
Fuel Type	Premium
Annual Fuel Cost	Average-$1611
Gas Guzzler Tax	No
Greenhouse Gas Emissions (tons/yr.)	Low-5.4
Barrels of Oil Used per year	Average-12.2

How the Competition Rates

Competitors	Rating	Pg.
BMW 5 Series	6	93
Infiniti Q50	3	167
Lexus ES	5	187

Price Range	Retail	Markup
2.0T Premium Coupe Quattro	$42,800	8%
2.0T Premium Plus Cpe Quattro	$45,800	8%
2.0T Premium Cabrio Quattro	$49,600	8%
2.0T Premium Plus Cab. Quattro	$52,600	8%

Audi A5

Safety Checklist

Crash Test:

Frontal	—
Side	—

Airbags:

Torso	Standard Front Pelvis/Torso from Seat
Roll Sensing	Yes
Knee Bolster	Standard Front

Crash Avoidance:

Collision Avoidance	Standard CIB & DBS^
Blind Spot Detection	Optional
Lane Keeping Assist	Warning Only Optional
Backup Camera	Optional*
Pedestrian Crash Avoidance	Standard

General:

Auto. Crash Notification	Dial Assist-Fee
Day Running Lamps	Standard

Safety Belt/Restraint:

Dynamic Head Restraints	None
Adjustable Belt	Standard Front

Note: As of May 2018, all vehicles are required to have a backup camera.
^Warning feature does not meet government standards.
*Backup camera does not meet government standards.

Audi A5

Specifications

Drive	AWD
Engine	2.0-liter I4
Transmission	7-sp. Automatic
Tow Rating (lbs.)	—
Head/Leg Room (in.)	Cramped-39.4/41.3
Interior Space (cu. ft.)	Very Cramped-84
Cargo Space (cu. ft.)	Very Cramped-11.6
Wheelbase/Length (in.)	111.2/186.3

Ratings—10 Best, 1 Worst

Combo Crash Tests	8
Safety Features	7
Rollover	9
Preventive Maintenance	4
Repair Costs	1
Warranty	7
Fuel Economy	4
Complaints	9
Insurance Costs	3
OVERALL RATING	**7**

Audi A6

At-a-Glance

Status/Year Series Started........ Unchanged/2012
Twins .... –
Body Styles .... Sedan
Seating..5
Anti-Theft Device ..... Std. Pass. Immobil. & Alarm
Parking Index Rating .... Hard
Where Made................ Neckarsulm, Germany
Fuel Factor:
  MPG Rating (city/hwy)............ Poor-20/29
  Driving Range (mi.) .... Very Long-460
  Fuel Type............................Premium
  Annual Fuel Cost.................High-$1916
  Gas Guzzler Tax ....No
  Greenhouse Gas Emissions (tons/yr.)..... Low-5.1
  Barrels of Oil Used per year Average-11.8

How the Competition Rates

Competitors	Rating	Pg.
Acura TLX	9	82
Lincoln MKZ	4	197
Volvo S60	9	265

Price Range	Retail	Markup
2.0T Premium	$47,600	7%
2.0T Premium Plus Quattro	$53,800	8%
3.0 Premium Plus Quattro	$58,600	8%
3.0 Prestige Quattro	$61,600	8%

Safety Checklist

Crash Test:
  Frontal........................ Very Good
  Side.............................. Average
Airbags:
  Torso Std. Fr. & Opt. Rr. Pelvis/Torso from Seat
  Roll Sensing.........................Yes
  Knee Bolster .... Standard Front
Crash Avoidance:
  Collision Avoidance ...... Optional CIB & DBS
  Blind Spot Detection .... Optional
  Lane Keeping Assist .... Optional^
  Backup Camera...................Standard*
  Pedestrian Crash Avoidance .... None
General:
  Auto. Crash Notification............... None
  Day Running Lamps .... Standard
Safety Belt/Restraint:
  Dynamic Head Restraints .... None
  Adjustable Belt............... Standard Front

Note: As of May 2018, all vehicles are required to have a backup camera.
^Warning feature does not meet government standards.
*Backup camera does not meet government standards.

Audi A6

Specifications

Drive.......................................AWD
Engine 3.0-liter I4
Transmission .... 8-sp. Automatic
Tow Rating (lbs.) .... –
Head/Leg Room (in.) .... Very Cramped-37.2/41.3
Interior Space (cu. ft.)................Average-98
Cargo Space (cu. ft.) Cramped-14.1
Wheelbase/Length (in.) 114.7/194.2

Ratings—10 Best, 1 Worst

Combo Crash Tests	—
Safety Features	2
Rollover	4
Preventive Maintenance	4
Repair Costs	3
Warranty	7
Fuel Economy	4
Complaints	10
Insurance Costs	10

OVERALL RATING   —

Audi Q3

Audi Q3

At-a-Glance

Status/Year Series Started	Unchanged/2015
Twins	—
Body Styles	SUV
Seating	5
Anti-Theft Device	Std. Pass. Immobil. & Alarm
Parking Index Rating	Average
Where Made	Martorell, Spain

Fuel Factor:

MPG Rating (city/hwy)	Poor-20/28
Driving Range (mi.)	Short-388
Fuel Type	Premium
Annual Fuel Cost	High-$1941
Gas Guzzler Tax	No
Greenhouse Gas Emissions (tons/yr.)	High-7.8
Barrels of Oil Used per year	High-14.3

How the Competition Rates

Competitors	Rating	Pg.
Acura RDX	9	81
Buick Encore	10	102
Lexus NX	5	191

Price Range	Retail	Markup
2.0T Premium	$32,900	8%
2.0T Premium Quattro	$35,000	8%
2.0T Premium Plus	$35,800	8%
2.0T Premium Plus Quattro	$37,900	8%

Safety Checklist

Crash Test:

Frontal	—
Side	—

Airbags:

Torso	Standard Front Pelvis/Torso from Seat
Roll Sensing	Yes
Knee Bolster	None

Crash Avoidance:

Collision Avoidance	None
Blind Spot Detection	Optional
Lane Keeping Assist	None
Backup Camera	Standard*
Pedestrian Crash Avoidance	None

General:

Auto. Crash Notification	None
Day Running Lamps	Standard

Safety Belt/Restraint:

Dynamic Head Restraints	None
Adjustable Belt	Standard Front

Note: As of May 2018, all vehicles are required to have a backup camera.
^Warning feature does not meet government standards.
*Backup camera does not meet government standards.

Audi Q3

Specifications

Drive	AWD
Engine	2.0-liter I4
Transmission	6-sp. Automatic
Tow Rating (lbs.)	—
Head/Leg Room (in.)	Very Cramped-37/40
Interior Space (cu. ft.)	Very Cramped-84
Cargo Space (cu. ft.)	Cramped-16.7
Wheelbase/Length (in.)	102.5/172.6

Audi Q5   Medium SUV

Ratings—10 Best, 1 Worst

Combo Crash Tests	—
Safety Features	4
Rollover	4
Preventive Maintenance	4
Repair Costs	2
Warranty	7
Fuel Economy	5
Complaints	—
Insurance Costs	5
OVERALL RATING	—

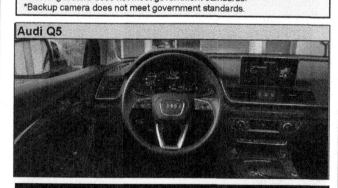

Audi Q5

At-a-Glance

Status/Year Series Started. . . . . All New/2018
Twins . . . . —
Body Styles . . . . SUV
Seating 5
Anti-Theft Device . . . . . Std. Pass. Immobil. & Alarm
Parking Index Rating . . . . Average
Where Made. . . . . Ingolstadt, Germany
Fuel Factor:
  MPG Rating (city/hwy) Average-23/27
  Driving Range (mi.) Long-456
  Fuel Type . . . . Premium
  Annual Fuel Cost . . . . High-$1808
  Gas Guzzler Tax . . . . No
  Greenhouse Gas Emissions (tons/yr.). . Average-6.0
  Barrels of Oil Used per year High-13.2

How the Competition Rates

Competitors	Rating	Pg.
Acura MDX	7	80
Lexus RX	4	193
Lincoln MKX	5	196

Price Range

Price Range	Retail	Markup
2.0T Premium	$41,500	8%
2.0T Premium Plus	$45,500	8%
2.0 Prestige	$50,800	8%

Audi Q5

Safety Checklist

Crash Test:
  Frontal. . . . . —
  Side. . . . . —
Airbags:
  Torso Std. Fr. & Opt. Rr. Pelvis/Torso from Seat
  Roll Sensing. . . . . Yes
  Knee Bolster . . . . None
Crash Avoidance:
  Collision Avoidance . . . . . Standard CIB & DBS
  Blind Spot Detection . . . . Optional
  Lane Keeping Assist . . . Warning Only Optional^
  Backup Camera. . . . . Optional*
  Pedestrian Crash Avoidance . . . . None
General:
  Auto. Crash Notification. . . . . None
  Day Running Lamps . . . . Standard
Safety Belt/Restraint:
  Dynamic Head Restraints . . . . Optional
  Adjustable Belt. . . . . Standard Front

Note: As of May 2018, all vehicles are required to have a backup camera.
^Warning feature does not meet government standards.
*Backup camera does not meet government standards.

Audi Q5

Specifications

Drive. . . . . AWD
Engine 2.0-liter I4
Transmission . . . . 7-sp. Automatic
Tow Rating (lbs.) . . . . —
Head/Leg Room (in.) Roomy-41.7/40.9
Interior Space (cu. ft.). . . . . —
Cargo Space (cu. ft.) Roomy-26.8
Wheelbase/Length (in.) 111/183.6

Ratings—10 Best, 1 Worst

Ratings	
Combo Crash Tests	6
Safety Features	8
Rollover	4
Preventive Maintenance	3
Repair Costs	1
Warranty	7
Fuel Economy	3
Complaints	4
Insurance Costs	5
OVERALL RATING	**3**

Audi Q7

Audi Q7

At-a-Glance

Status/Year Series Started	Unchanged/2016
Twins	–
Body Styles	SUV
Seating	7
Anti-Theft Device	Std. Pass. Immobil. & Alarm
Parking Index Rating	Very Hard
Where Made	Bratislava, Slovakia

Fuel Factor:

MPG Rating (city/hwy)	Poor-19/25
Driving Range (mi.)	Very Long-479
Fuel Type	Premium
Annual Fuel Cost	Very High-$2092
Gas Guzzler Tax	No
Greenhouse Gas Emissions (tons/yr.)	Average-6.9
Barrels of Oil Used per year	High-15.7

How the Competition Rates

Competitors	Rating	Pg.
BMW X5	5	98
Cadillac XT5	3	108
Lexus RX	4	193

Price Range	Retail	Markup
2.0T Premium	$49,900	8%
2.0T Premium Plus	$53,900	8%
3.0T Premium Plus	$60,400	8%
3.0T Prestige	$65,400	8%

Safety Checklist

Crash Test:

Frontal	Average
Side	Average

Airbags:

Torso	Std. Fr. & Opt. Rr. Pelvis/Torso from Seat
Roll Sensing	Yes
Knee Bolster	None

Crash Avoidance:

Collision Avoidance	Standard CIB & DBS
Blind Spot Detection	Optional
Lane Keeping Assist	Optional
Backup Camera	Standard*
Pedestrian Crash Avoidance	Standard

General:

Auto. Crash Notification	Dial Assist-Fee
Day Running Lamps	Standard

Safety Belt/Restraint:

Dynamic Head Restraints	None
Adjustable Belt	Standard Front

Note: As of May 2018, all vehicles are required to have a backup camera.
^Warning feature does not meet government standards.
*Backup camera does not meet government standards.

Audi Q7

Specifications

Drive	AWD
Engine	3.0-liter V6
Transmission	8-sp. Automatic
Tow Rating (lbs.)	High-7700
Head/Leg Room (in.)	Cramped-38.4/41.7
Interior Space (cu. ft.)	–
Cargo Space (cu. ft.)	Cramped-14.8
Wheelbase/Length (in.)	117.9/199.6

Ratings—10 Best, 1 Worst

Combo Crash Tests	—
Safety Features	6
Rollover	7
Preventive Maintenance	4
Repair Costs	3
Warranty	9
Fuel Economy	6
Complaints	10
Insurance Costs	1

OVERALL RATING   —

BMW 2 Series

At-a-Glance

Status/Year Series Started Appearance Change/2016
Twins . . . . —
Body Styles . . . . .Coupe
Seating. 4
Anti-Theft Device . Std. Pass. Immobil. & Active Alarm
Parking Index Rating . . . . Easy
Where Made. . . . . Leipzig, Germany
Fuel Factor:
  MPG Rating (city/hwy) Average-23/35
  Driving Range (mi.) . . . . .Very Short-373
  Fuel Type. . . . . .Premium
  Annual Fuel Cost . . . . .Average-$1638
  Gas Guzzler Tax . . . . .No
  Greenhouse Gas Emissions (tons/yr.) . . Average-6.4
  Barrels of Oil Used per year Average-12.2

How the Competition Rates

Competitors	Rating	Pg.
Audi A3	6	83
Cadillac ATS	4	106
Lexus IS	8	190

Price Range

Price Range	Retail	Markup
230i Coupe	$34,800	6%
230xi Convertible	$42,600	6%
M240i Coupe	$45,300	6%
M 240xi Coupe	$47,300	6%

BMW 2 Series

Safety Checklist

Crash Test:
  Frontal. . . . . —
  Side. . . . . —
Airbags:
  Torso . . . . Standard Front Torso from Seat
  Roll Sensing. . . . . .Yes
  Knee Bolster . . . . .Standard Front
Crash Avoidance:
  Collision Avoidance . . . . . . Optional CIB & DBS
  Blind Spot Detection . . . . None
  Lane Keeping Assist . . . .Warning Only Optional
  Backup Camera. . . . . Optional*
  Pedestrian Crash Avoidance . . . . Optional
General:
  Auto. Crash Notif. . Op. Assist. & Crash Info-Free
  Day Running Lamps . . . . Standard
Safety Belt/Restraint:
  Dynamic Head Restraints . . . . None
  Adjustable Belt. None

Note: As of May 2018, all vehicles are required to have a backup camera.
^Warning feature does not meet government standards.
*Backup camera does not meet government standards.

BMW 2 Series

Specifications

Drive. . . . . .RWD
Engine 2.0-liter I4
Transmission . . . . 8-sp. Automatic
Tow Rating (lbs.) . . . . —
Head/Leg Room (in.) Average-40.1/41.5
Interior Space (cu. ft.). . . . . .Very Cramped-90
Cargo Space (cu. ft.) Cramped-13.8
Wheelbase/Length (in.) 105.9/174.7

Ratings—10 Best, 1 Worst

Combo Crash Tests	6
Safety Features	7
Rollover	9
Preventive Maintenance	4
Repair Costs	2
Warranty	9
Fuel Economy	7
Complaints	8
Insurance Costs	3
OVERALL RATING	**7**

BMW 3 Series

BMW 3 Series

At-a-Glance

Status/Year Series Started........Unchanged/2013
Twins ....–
Body Styles ....Sedan, Wagon, Convertible
Seating 5
Anti-Theft Device .Std. Pass. Immobil. & Active Alarm
Parking Index Rating .... Average
Where Made..... Munich, Germany / Toluca, Mexico

Fuel Factor:
MPG Rating (city/hwy) Good-23/36
Driving Range (mi.) Long-434
Fuel Type...............................Premium
Annual Fuel Cost ....Average-$1622
Gas Guzzler Tax ....No
Greenhouse Gas Emissions (tons/yr.)..... Low-5.3
Barrels of Oil Used per year Average-11.8

How the Competition Rates

Competitors	Rating	Pg.
Audi A4	2	84
Audi A4	2	84
Mercedes-Benz C	1	206

Price Range	Retail	Markup
320i	$34,900	6%
328d	$41,750	6%
330xi	$42,250	6%
340i	$48,950	6%

Safety Checklist

Crash Test:
Frontal.......................... Average
Side.............................. Average

Airbags:
Torso .... Standard Front Torso from Seat
Roll Sensing.............................Yes
Knee Bolster ....Standard Front

Crash Avoidance:
Collision Avoidance ...... Optional CIB & DBS
Blind Spot Detection .... Optional
Lane Keeping Assist ....Warning Only Optional
Backup Camera................... Optional*
Pedestrian Crash Avoidance .... Optional

General:
Auto. Crash Notif. . Op. Assist. & Crash Info-Free
Day Running Lamps .... Standard

Safety Belt/Restraint:
Dynamic Head Restraints .... None
Adjustable Belt..................... None

Note: As of May 2018, all vehicles are required to have a backup camera.
^Warning feature does not meet government standards.
*Backup camera does not meet government standards.

BMW 3 Series

Specifications

Drive.....................................RWD
Engine 2.0-liter I4
Transmission .... 8-sp. Automatic
Tow Rating (lbs.) ....–
Head/Leg Room (in.) Average-40.3/42
Interior Space (cu. ft.)............Cramped-96
Cargo Space (cu. ft.) Average-17
Wheelbase/Length (in.) 110.6/182.4

Ratings—10 Best, 1 Worst

Combo Crash Tests	—
Safety Features	7
Rollover	9
Preventive Maintenance	4
Repair Costs	2
Warranty	9
Fuel Economy	6
Complaints	8
Insurance Costs	1

OVERALL RATING   —

BMW 4 Series

BMW 4 Series

At-a-Glance

Status/Year Series Started. Unchanged/2014
Twins . . . . —
Body Styles . . . . Coupe, Convertible
Seating 4
Anti-Theft Device . Std. Pass. Immobil. & Active Alarm
Parking Index Rating . . . . Average
Where Made. . . . . .Munich, Germany
Fuel Factor:
  MPG Rating (city/hwy) Average-23/35
  Driving Range (mi.) Long-430
  Fuel Type. . . . . .Premium
  Annual Fuel Cost . . . . .Average-$1638
  Gas Guzzler Tax . . . . .No
  Greenhouse Gas Emissions (tons/yr.). . Average-6.7
  Barrels of Oil Used per year Average-12.2

How the Competition Rates

Competitors	Rating	Pg.
Infiniti Q50	3	167
Lexus IS	8	190
Mercedes-Benz C	1	206

Price Range

	Retail	Markup
430i Coupe	$42,200	6%
430xi Gran Coupe	$44,200	6%
440i Convertible	$57,500	7%
440xi Convertible	$59,500	7%

Safety Checklist

Crash Test:
  Frontal. . . . . —
  Side. . . . . —
Airbags:
  Torso . . . . Standard Front Torso from Seat
  Roll Sensing. . . . . .Yes
  Knee Bolster . . . . .Standard Front
Crash Avoidance:
  Collision Avoidance . . . . . . Optional CIB & DBS
  Blind Spot Detection . . . . Optional
  Lane Keeping Assist . . . .Warning Only Optional
  Backup Camera. . . . . Optional*
  Pedestrian Crash Avoidance . . . . Optional
General:
  Auto. Crash Notif. . Op. Assist. & Crash Info-Free
  Day Running Lamps . . . . Standard
Safety Belt/Restraint:
  Dynamic Head Restraints . . . . None
  Adjustable Belt. . . . . None

Note: As of May 2018, all vehicles are required to have a backup camera.
^Warning feature does not meet government standards.
*Backup camera does not meet government standards.

BMW 4 Series

Specifications

Drive. . . . . .RWD
Engine 2.0-liter I4
Transmission . . . . 8-sp. Automatic
Tow Rating (lbs.) . . . . —
Head/Leg Room (in.) Average-39.8/42.2
Interior Space (cu. ft.). . . . . .Very Cramped-90
Cargo Space (cu. ft.) Cramped-15.7
Wheelbase/Length (in.) 110.6/182.6

BMW 5 Series Intermediate

BMW 5 Series

Ratings—10 Best, 1 Worst

Combo Crash Tests	4
Safety Features	7
Rollover	9
Preventive Maintenance	9
Repair Costs	1
Warranty	9
Fuel Economy	6
Complaints	7
Insurance Costs	1
OVERALL RATING	**6**

BMW 5 Series

At-a-Glance

Status/Year Series Started	Unchanged/2017
Twins	–
Body Styles	Sedan, Wagon
Seating	5
Anti-Theft Device	Std. Pass. Immobil. & Active Alarm
Parking Index Rating	Hard
Where Made	Dingolfing, Germany / Toluca, Mexico

Fuel Factor:

MPG Rating (city/hwy)	Average-23/34
Driving Range (mi.)	Very Long-498
Fuel Type	Premium
Annual Fuel Cost	Average-$1655
Gas Guzzler Tax	No
Greenhouse Gas Emissions (tons/yr.)	Average-6.6
Barrels of Oil Used per year	Average-12.2

How the Competition Rates

Competitors	Rating	Pg.
Infiniti Q50	3	167
Lexus ES	5	187
Volvo S60	9	265

Price Range

	Retail	Markup
530i	$52,400	6%
530xe	$54,700	6%
540xi	$60,000	7%
M550i	$73,400	7%

Safety Checklist

Crash Test:
- Frontal .... Very Poor
- Side .... Good

Airbags:
- Torso .... Standard Front Torso from Seat
- Roll Sensing .... Yes
- Knee Bolster .... None

Crash Avoidance:
- Collision Avoidance ...... Optional CIB & DBS^
- Blind Spot Detection .... Optional
- Lane Keeping Assist ... Warning Only Optional^
- Backup Camera .... Optional*
- Pedestrian Crash Avoidance .... Optional

General:
- Auto. Crash Notif. . Op. Assist. & Crash Info-Free
- Day Running Lamps .... Standard

Safety Belt/Restraint:
- Dynamic Head Restraints ...... Standard Front
- Adjustable Belt .... None

Note: As of May 2018, all vehicles are required to have a backup camera.
^Warning feature does not meet government standards.
*Backup camera does not meet government standards.

BMW 5 Series

Specifications

Drive	RWD
Engine	2.0-liter I4
Transmission	8-sp. Automatic
Tow Rating (lbs.)	–
Head/Leg Room (in.)	Average-40.5/41.4
Interior Space (cu. ft.)	Average-102
Cargo Space (cu. ft.)	Average-18.4
Wheelbase/Length (in.)	116.9/193.4

Ratings—10 Best, 1 Worst

Combo Crash Tests	—
Safety Features	10
Rollover	7
Preventive Maintenance	1
Repair Costs	1
Warranty	9
Fuel Economy	4
Complaints	5
Insurance Costs	1

OVERALL RATING   —

BMW 7 Series

BMW 7 Series

At-a-Glance

Status/Year Series Started. Unchanged/2016
Twins . . . . —
Body Styles . . . . Sedan
Seating 5
Anti-Theft Device . Std. Pass. Immobil. & Active Alarm
Parking Index Rating . . . . Very Hard
Where Made. . . Dingolfing, Germany / Toluca, Mexico
Fuel Factor:
  MPG Rating (city/hwy) Poor-21/29
  Driving Range (mi.) . . . . Very Long-494
  Fuel Type. . . . . Premium
  Annual Fuel Cost . . . . High-$1858
  Gas Guzzler Tax . . . . No
  Greenhouse Gas Emissions (tons/yr.). . Average-6.1
  Barrels of Oil Used per year High-13.7

How the Competition Rates

Competitors	Rating	Pg.
Buick LaCrosse	5	104
Mercedes-Benz E	3	208
Tesla Model S	10	239

Price Range	Retail	Markup
740i	$83,100	8%
740i xDrive	$86,100	8%
750i	$96,400	8%
750i xDrive	$99,400	8%

Safety Checklist

Crash Test:
  Frontal. . . . . —
  Side. . . . . —
Airbags:
  Torso . . . . Standard Front Torso from Seat
  Roll Sensing. . . . . .Yes
  Knee Bolster . . . . .Standard Front
Crash Avoidance:
  Collision Avoidance . . . . . .Optional CIB & DBS^
  Blind Spot Detection . . . . Optional
  Lane Keeping Assist . . . . Optional^
  Backup Camera. . . . . Standard
  Pedestrian Crash Avoidance . . . . Optional
General:
  Auto. Crash Notif. . Op. Assist. & Crash Info-Free
  Day Running Lamps . . . . Standard
Safety Belt/Restraint:
  Dynamic Head Restraints . . . . .Standard Front
  Adjustable Belt. . . . . None

Note: As of May 2018, all vehicles are required to have a backup camera.
^Warning feature does not meet government standards.
*Backup camera does not meet government standards.

BMW 7 Series

Specifications

Drive. . . . . .RWD
Engine 6.0-liter V8
Transmission . . . . 8-sp. Automatic
Tow Rating (lbs.) . . . . —
Head/Leg Room (in.) Average-39.9/41.4
Interior Space (cu. ft.). Roomy-107
Cargo Space (cu. ft.) Average-18.2
Wheelbase/Length (in.) 126.4/206.6

BMW i3   Subcompact

Ratings—10 Best, 1 Worst

Combo Crash Tests	—
Safety Features	6
Rollover	4
Preventive Maintenance	4
Repair Costs	10
Warranty	9
Fuel Economy	10
Complaints	4
Insurance Costs	10

OVERALL RATING —

BMW i3

BMW i3

At-a-Glance

Status/Year Series Started........Unchanged/2016
Twins.................................—
Body Styles............................Coupe
Seating................................4
Anti-Theft Device .Std. Pass. Immobil. & Active Alarm
Parking Index Rating..................Very Easy
Where Made...................Leipzig, Germany
Fuel Factor:
  MPG Rating (city/hwy).......Very Good-137/111
  Driving Range (mi.).....................180
  Fuel Type............................Premium
  Annual Fuel Cost.............Very Low-$650
  Gas Guzzler Tax........................No
  Greenhouse Gas Emissions (tons/yr.). Very Low-0.5
  Barrels of Oil Used per year........Very Low-1.2

How the Competition Rates

Competitors	Rating	Pg.
Chevrolet Bolt	—	110
Mercedes-Benz B	—	205
Tesla Model 3	—	238

Price Range

Price Range	Retail	Markup
60 Ah Hatchback	$42,400	6%
90 Ah Hatchback	$43,600	6%
90 Ah Hatchback w/Range Ext	$47,450	6%

Safety Checklist

Crash Test:
  Frontal.................................—
  Side...................................—
Airbags:
  Torso........Standard Front Torso from Seat
  Roll Sensing............................Yes
  Knee Bolster..............Standard Front
Crash Avoidance:
  Collision Avoidance......Optional CIB & DBS
  Blind Spot Detection..................None
  Lane Keeping Assist...Warning Only Optional^
  Backup Camera....................Optional*
  Pedestrian Crash Avoidance.........Optional
General:
  Auto. Crash Notif..Op. Assist. & Crash Info-Free
  Day Running Lamps..............Standard
Safety Belt/Restraint:
  Dynamic Head Restraints............None
  Adjustable Belt.....................None

Note: As of May 2018, all vehicles are required to have a backup camera.
^Warning feature does not meet government standards.
*Backup camera does not meet government standards.

BMW i3

Specifications

Drive.......................................RWD
Engine..................................Electric
Transmission..............................CVT
Tow Rating (lbs.)..........................—
Head/Leg Room (in.).........Cramped-39.6/40.5
Interior Space (cu. ft.)...........Very Cramped-83.1
Cargo Space (cu. ft.)........Very Cramped-11.8
Wheelbase/Length (in.)................101/157

95

Ratings—10 Best, 1 Worst

Combo Crash Tests	—
Safety Features	6
Rollover	4
Preventive Maintenance	7
Repair Costs	1
Warranty	9
Fuel Economy	6
Complaints	4
Insurance Costs	3
OVERALL RATING	**—**

BMW X1

BMW X1

At-a-Glance

Status/Year Series Started. Unchanged/2016
Twins . . . . —
Body Styles . . . . SUV
Seating 5
Anti-Theft Device . Std. Pass. Immobil. & Active Alarm
Parking Index Rating . . . . Easy
Where Made. . . . . Leipzig, Germany
Fuel Factor:
  MPG Rating (city/hwy) Average-22/32
  Driving Range (mi.) Average-412
  Fuel Type. . . . . .Premium
  Annual Fuel Cost . . . . .High-$1740
  Gas Guzzler Tax . . . . .No
  Greenhouse Gas Emissions (tons/yr.). Low-5.7
  Barrels of Oil Used per year Average-12.7

How the Competition Rates

Competitors	Rating	Pg.
Buick Encore	10	102
Lexus NX	5	191
Lincoln MKC	6	195

Price Range	Retail	Markup
sDrive28i	$33,900	6%
XDrive28i	$35,900	6%

Safety Checklist

Crash Test:
  Frontal. . . . . —
  Side. . . . . —
Airbags:
  Torso . . . . Standard Front Torso from Seat
  Roll Sensing. . . . . .Yes
  Knee Bolster . . . . .Standard Front
Crash Avoidance:
  Collision Avoidance . . . . . . Optional CIB & DBS
  Blind Spot Detection . . . . None
  Lane Keeping Assist . . . .Warning Only Optional
  Backup Camera. . . . . Optional*
  Pedestrian Crash Avoidance . . . . Optional
General:
  Auto. Crash Notif. . Op. Assist. & Crash Info-Free
  Day Running Lamps . . . . Standard
Safety Belt/Restraint:
  Dynamic Head Restraints . . . . None
  Adjustable Belt. . . . . None

Note: As of May 2018, all vehicles are required to have a backup camera.
^Warning feature does not meet government standards.
*Backup camera does not meet government standards.

BMW X1

Specifications

Drive. . . . . .RWD
Engine 2.0-liter I4
Transmission . . . . 8-sp. Automatic
Tow Rating (lbs.) Low-4400
Head/Leg Room (in.) Average-41.9/40.4
Interior Space (cu. ft.). Average-101
Cargo Space (cu. ft.) Roomy-27.1
Wheelbase/Length (in.) 105.1/174.8

Ratings—10 Best, 1 Worst

Combo Crash Tests	—
Safety Features	8
Rollover	—
Preventive Maintenance	1
Repair Costs	1
Warranty	9
Fuel Economy	5
Complaints	—
Insurance Costs	5
OVERALL RATING	—

BMW X3

BMW X3

At-a-Glance

Status/Year Series Started	All New/2018
Twins	—
Body Styles	SUV
Seating	5
Anti-Theft Device	Std. Pass. Immobil. & Active Alarm
Parking Index Rating	Hard
Where Made	—

Fuel Factor:

MPG Rating (city/hwy)	Average-22/29
Driving Range (mi.)	Long-425
Fuel Type	Premium
Annual Fuel Cost	High-$1805
Gas Guzzler Tax	No
Greenhouse Gas Emissions (tons/yr.)	Average-5.9
Barrels of Oil Used per year	High-13.2

How the Competition Rates

Competitors	Rating	Pg.
Acura MDX	7	80
Infiniti QX60	5	170
Lexus RX	4	193

Price Range	Retail	Markup
sDrive28i	$39,250	6%
XDrive28i	$41,250	6%
XDrive28d	$42,750	6%
XDrive35i	$47,950	6%

Safety Checklist

Crash Test:
- Frontal.................................. —
- Side.................................... —

Airbags:
- Torso .... Standard Front Torso from Seat
- Roll Sensing............................Yes
- Knee Bolster .... Standard Driver

Crash Avoidance:
- Collision Avoidance ...... Optional CIB & DBS
- Blind Spot Detection .... Optional
- Lane Keeping Assist ....Warning Only Optional
- Backup Camera.................... Optional
- Pedestrian Crash Avoidance .... Optional

General:
- Auto. Crash Notif. . Op. Assist. & Crash Info-Free
- Day Running Lamps .... Standard

Safety Belt/Restraint:
- Dynamic Head Restraints ......Standard Front
- Adjustable Belt..................... None

Note: As of May 2018, all vehicles are required to have a backup camera.
^Warning feature does not meet government standards.
*Backup camera does not meet government standards.

BMW X3

Specifications

Drive	AWD
Engine	2.0-liter I4
Transmission	5-sp. Automatic
Tow Rating (lbs.)	Very Low-1000
Head/Leg Room (in.)	Average-41.1/40.3
Interior Space (cu. ft.)	Cramped-93.7
Cargo Space (cu. ft.)	Roomy-28.7
Wheelbase/Length (in.)	112.8/185.9

BMW X5 — Medium SUV

Ratings—10 Best, 1 Worst

Combo Crash Tests	8
Safety Features	8
Rollover	3
Preventive Maintenance	3
Repair Costs	1
Warranty	9
Fuel Economy	3
Complaints	9
Insurance Costs	1
OVERALL RATING	**5**

BMW X5

BMW X5

At-a-Glance

Status/Year Series Started. Unchanged/2014
Twins . . . . –
Body Styles . . . . SUV
Seating 5
Anti-Theft Device . Std. Pass. Immobil. & Active Alarm
Parking Index Rating . . . . Very Hard
Where Made. . . . . . Spartanburg, SC / Toluca, Mexico
Fuel Factor:
  MPG Rating (city/hwy) Poor-18/27
  Driving Range (mi.) . . . . Very Long-474
  Fuel Type. . . . . Premium
  Annual Fuel Cost . . . . Very High-$2104
  Gas Guzzler Tax . . . . No
  Greenhouse Gas Emissions (tons/yr.). High-8.5
  Barrels of Oil Used per year High-15.7

How the Competition Rates

Competitors	Rating	Pg.
Acura MDX	7	80
Audi Q7	3	89
Cadillac XT5	3	108

Price Range	Retail	Markup
sDrive35i	$55,500	6%
XDrive35i	$57,800	7%
XDrive35d	$59,300	7%
XDrive50i	$72,300	7%

Safety Checklist

Crash Test:
  Frontal. . . . . Good
  Side. . . . . Average
Airbags:
  Torso . . . . Standard Front Torso from Seat
  Roll Sensing. . . . . .Yes
  Knee Bolster . . . . .Standard Front
Crash Avoidance:
  Collision Avoidance . . . . . . Optional CIB & DBS
  Blind Spot Detection . . . . None
  Lane Keeping Assist . . .Warning Only Optional
  Backup Camera. . . . . Optional*
  Pedestrian Crash Avoidance . . . . Optional
General:
  Auto. Crash Notif. . Op. Assist. & Crash Info-Free
  Day Running Lamps . . . . Standard
Safety Belt/Restraint:
  Dynamic Head Restraints . . . . . .Standard Front
  Adjustable Belt. . . . . None

Note: As of May 2018, all vehicles are required to have a backup camera.
^Warning feature does not meet government standards.
*Backup camera does not meet government standards.

BMW X5

Specifications

Drive. . . . . .AWD
Engine 3.0-liter V6
Transmission . . . . 8-sp. Automatic
Tow Rating (lbs.) Average-5950
Head/Leg Room (in.) Cramped-40.5/40.4
Interior Space (cu. ft.). . . . . –
Cargo Space (cu. ft.) Roomy-23
Wheelbase/Length (in.) 115.5/193.2

Ratings—10 Best, 1 Worst

Combo Crash Tests	—
Safety Features	6
Rollover	—
Preventive Maintenance	2
Repair Costs	1
Warranty	9
Fuel Economy	2
Complaints	3
Insurance Costs	1
OVERALL RATING	**—**

BMW X6

BMW X6

At-a-Glance

Status/Year Series Started	Unchanged/2010
Twins	–
Body Styles	SUV
Seating	5
Anti-Theft Device	Std. Pass. Immobil. & Active Alarm
Parking Index Rating	Very Hard
Where Made	Spartanburg, SC

Fuel Factor:

MPG Rating (city/hwy)	Very Poor-18/24
Driving Range (mi.)	Long-454
Fuel Type	Premium
Annual Fuel Cost	Very High-$2197
Gas Guzzler Tax	No
Greenhouse Gas Emissions (tons/yr.)	Average-7.0
Barrels of Oil Used per year	High-15.7

How the Competition Rates

Competitors	Rating	Pg.
Audi Q7	3	89
Cadillac XT5	3	108
Lincoln MKX	5	196

Price Range	Retail	Markup
XDrive35i	$60,500	7%
sDrive35i	$62,700	7%
XDrive50i	$77,450	7%
M	$104,100	7%

Safety Checklist

Crash Test:
Frontal.................................. —
Side.................................. —

Airbags:
Torso .... Standard Front Torso from Seat
Roll Sensing............................Yes
Knee Bolster .... None

Crash Avoidance:
Collision Avoidance ...... Optional CIB & DBS^
Blind Spot Detection .... None
Lane Keeping Assist ... Warning Only Optional^
Backup Camera.................... Optional*
Pedestrian Crash Avoidance .... Optional

General:
Auto. Crash Notif. . Op. Assist. & Crash Info-Free
Day Running Lamps .... Standard

Safety Belt/Restraint:
Dynamic Head Restraints ......Standard Front
Adjustable Belt.................... None

Note: As of May 2018, all vehicles are required to have a backup camera.
^Warning feature does not meet government standards.
*Backup camera does not meet government standards.

BMW X6

Specifications

Drive	AWD
Engine	3.0-liter V6
Transmission	8-sp. Automatic
Tow Rating (lbs.)	Average-6000
Head/Leg Room (in.)	Cramped-39.9/40.3
Interior Space (cu. ft.)	Average-101.4
Cargo Space (cu. ft.)	Roomy-26.6
Wheelbase/Length (in.)	115/193.8

Buick Cascada
Compact

Ratings—10 Best, 1 Worst

Combo Crash Tests	—
Safety Features	2
Rollover	7
Preventive Maintenance	1
Repair Costs	5
Warranty	8
Fuel Economy	4
Complaints	5
Insurance Costs	10

OVERALL RATING   —

Buick Cascada

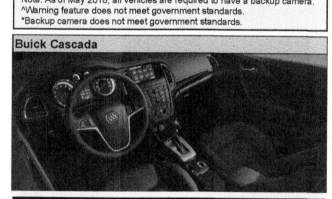

Buick Cascada

At-a-Glance

Status/Year Series Started Unchanged/2017
Twins . . . . —
Body Styles . . . . Convertible
Seating 4
Anti-Theft Device . Std. Pass. Immobil. & Active Alarm
Parking Index Rating . . . . Average
Where Made . . . . Gliwice, Poland

Fuel Factor:
MPG Rating (city/hwy) Poor-20/27
Driving Range (mi.) . . . . Very Short-324
Fuel Type . . . . Regular
Annual Fuel Cost . . . . Average-$1623
Gas Guzzler Tax . . . . No
Greenhouse Gas Emissions (tons/yr.) . . Average-6.5
Barrels of Oil Used per year High-14.3

How the Competition Rates

Competitors	Rating	Pg.
BMW 3 Series	7	91
Cadillac ATS	4	106
Lexus IS	8	190

Price Range

Price Range	Retail	Markup
Convertible	$33,065	1%
Convertible Premium	$36,065	4%
Convertible Sport Touring	$37,065	4%

Safety Checklist

Crash Test:
Frontal . . . . —
Side . . . . —

Airbags:
Torso . . . . Standard Front Torso from Seat
Roll Sensing . . . . No
Knee Bolster . . . . Standard Front

Crash Avoidance:
Collision Avoidance . . . . Warning Only Optional^
Blind Spot Detection . . . . None
Lane Keeping Assist . . . Warning Only Optional^
Backup Camera . . . . Standard*
Pedestrian Crash Avoidance . . . . None

General:
Auto. Crash Notif. . Op. Assist. & Crash Info-Free
Day Running Lamps . . . . Standard

Safety Belt/Restraint:
Dynamic Head Restraints . . . . None
Adjustable Belt . . . . Optional Rear

Note: As of May 2018, all vehicles are required to have a backup camera.
^Warning feature does not meet government standards.
*Backup camera does not meet government standards.

Specifications

Drive . . . . FWD
Engine 1.6-liter I4
Transmission . . . . 6-sp. Automatic
Tow Rating (lbs.) . . . . —
Head/Leg Room (in.) Cramped-37.8/42.2
Interior Space (cu. ft.) . . . . Very Cramped-82
Cargo Space (cu. ft.) . . . . Very Cramped-13.4
Wheelbase/Length (in.) 106.1/184.9

Ratings—10 Best, 1 Worst

Category	Rating
Combo Crash Tests	5
Safety Features	5
Rollover	4
Preventive Maintenance	2
Repair Costs	3
Warranty	8
Fuel Economy	3
Complaints	—
Insurance Costs	10
OVERALL RATING	**4**

Buick Enclave

Buick Enclave

At-a-Glance
Status/Year Series Started........... All New/2018
Twins ....Chevrolet Traverse
Body Styles .... SUV
Seating 7
Anti-Theft Device . Std. Pass. Immobil. & Active Alarm
Parking Index Rating ....Very Hard
Where Made.......................Lansing, MI
Fuel Factor:
 MPG Rating (city/hwy) Poor-18/26
 Driving Range (mi.) Average-405
 Fuel Type........................Regular
 Annual Fuel Cost..............High-$1759
 Gas Guzzler Tax ....No
 Greenhouse Gas Emissions (tons/yr.).. Average-7.0
 Barrels of Oil Used per year High-15.7

How the Competition Rates

Competitors	Rating	Pg.
Chevrolet Tahoe	4	122
Chevrolet Traverse	4	123
Volvo XC90	8	268

Price Range

Price Range	Retail	Markup
Base FWD	$39,995	1%
Essence FWD	$44,215	5%
Premium AWD	$50,315	5%
Avenir AWD	$55,715	5%

Safety Checklist
Crash Test:
 Frontal........................... Average
 Side............................Poor
Airbags:
 Torso . . . Standard Front Pelvis/Torso from Seat
 Roll Sensing........................Yes
 Knee Bolster .... None
Crash Avoidance:
 Collision Avoidance ...... Optional CIB & DBS
 Blind Spot Detection .... Optional
 Lane Keeping Assist ....Warning Only Optional
 Backup Camera.................Standard*
 Pedestrian Crash Avoidance......... Optional
General:
 Auto. Crash Notif. . Op. Assist. & Crash Info-Free
 Day Running Lamps .... Standard
Safety Belt/Restraint:
 Dynamic Head Restraints .... None
 Adjustable Belt................Optional Rear

Note: As of May 2018, all vehicles are required to have a backup camera.
^Warning feature does not meet government standards.
*Backup camera does not meet government standards.

Buick Enclave

Specifications
Drive.................................FWD
Engine 3.6-liter V6
Transmission .... 9-sp. Automatic
Tow Rating (lbs.) Low-5000
Head/Leg Room (in.) Average-41/41.2
Interior Space (cu. ft.).......................–
Cargo Space (cu. ft.) Roomy-23.6
Wheelbase/Length (in.) 120.9/204.3

Ratings—10 Best, 1 Worst

Combo Crash Tests	8
Safety Features	7
Rollover	3
Preventive Maintenance	7
Repair Costs	8
Warranty	8
Fuel Economy	6
Complaints	10
Insurance Costs	5
OVERALL RATING	**10**

Buick Encore

Buick Encore

At-a-Glance

Status/Year Series Started Unchanged/2013
Twins . . . . Chevrolet Trax
Body Styles . . . . SUV
Seating 5
Anti-Theft Device . Std. Pass. Immobil. & Active Alarm
Parking Index Rating . . . . Easy
Where Made . . . . Bupyeong, South Korea
Fuel Factor:
  MPG Rating (city/hwy) Average-23/30
  Driving Range (mi.) . . . . Very Short-360
  Fuel Type . . . . Regular
  Annual Fuel Cost . . . . Low-$1430
  Gas Guzzler Tax . . . . No
  Greenhouse Gas Emissions (tons/yr.) . . Average-6.9
  Barrels of Oil Used per year Average-12.7

How the Competition Rates

Competitors	Rating	Pg.
Acura RDX	9	81
Ford Escape	5	137
Lincoln MKC	6	195

Price Range	Retail	Markup
Preferred FWD	$24,365	4%
Sport Touring FWD	$25,565	4%
Essence AWD	$30,565	4%
Premium AWD	$32,015	4%

Safety Checklist

Crash Test:
  Frontal . . . . Very Good
  Side . . . . Average
Airbags:
  Torso . Std Front & Rear Pelvis/Torso from Seat
  Roll Sensing . . . . Yes
  Knee Bolster . . . . Standard Front
Crash Avoidance:
  Collision Avoidance . . . . . Warning Only Optional
  Blind Spot Detection . . . . Optional
  Lane Keeping Assist . . . Warning Only Optional
  Backup Camera . . . . Standard*
  Pedestrian Crash Avoidance . . . . None
General:
  Auto. Crash Notif. . Op. Assist. & Crash Info-Free
  Day Running Lamps . . . . Standard
Safety Belt/Restraint:
  Dynamic Head Restraints . . . . None
  Adjustable Belt . . . . Optional Front & Rear

Note: As of May 2018, all vehicles are required to have a backup camera.
^Warning feature does not meet government standards.
*Backup camera does not meet government standards.

Buick Encore

Specifications

Drive . . . . AWD
Engine 1.4-liter I4
Transmission . . . . 6-sp. Automatic
Tow Rating (lbs.) . . . . –
Head/Leg Room (in.) Cramped-39.6/40.8
Interior Space (cu. ft.) Cramped-92.8
Cargo Space (cu. ft.) Average-18.8
Wheelbase/Length (in.) 100.6/168.4

Ratings—10 Best, 1 Worst

Combo Crash Tests	—
Safety Features	10
Rollover	2
Preventive Maintenance	2
Repair Costs	4
Warranty	8
Fuel Economy	4
Complaints	4
Insurance Costs	8
OVERALL RATING	**—**

Buick Envision

Buick Envision

At-a-Glance

Status/Year Series Started. Unchanged/2016
Twins . . . . —
Body Styles . . . . SUV
Seating 5
Anti-Theft Device . Std. Pass. Immobil. & Active Alarm
Parking Index Rating . . . . Hard
Where Made. . . . . Yantai, Shandong
Fuel Factor:
  MPG Rating (city/hwy) Poor-21/27
  Driving Range (mi.) Average-404
  Fuel Type. . . . . Regular
  Annual Fuel Cost . . . . Average-$1575
  Gas Guzzler Tax . . . . No
  Greenhouse Gas Emissions (tons/yr.). . Average-6.2
  Barrels of Oil Used per year High-13.7

How the Competition Rates

Competitors	Rating	Pg.
Acura MDX	7	80
Audi Q7	3	89
BMW X5	5	98

Price Range

Price Range	Retail	Markup
Preferred FWD	$35,870	5%
Essence FWD	$37,720	5%
Premium I AWD	$42,320	5%
Premium II AWD	$44,960	5%

Safety Checklist

Crash Test:
  Frontal. . . . . —
  Side. . . . . —
Airbags:
  Torso . Std Front & Rear Pelvis/Torso from Seat
  Roll Sensing. . . . . Yes
  Knee Bolster . . . . Standard Front
Crash Avoidance:
  Collision Avoidance . . . . . . Optional CIB & DBS^
  Blind Spot Detection . . . . Optional
  Lane Keeping Assist . . . . Warning Only Optional
  Backup Camera. . . . . Standard
  Pedestrian Crash Avoidance . . . . Optional
General:
  Auto. Crash Notif. . Op. Assist. & Crash Info-Free
  Day Running Lamps . . . . Standard
Safety Belt/Restraint:
  Dynamic Head Restraints . . . . None
  Adjustable Belt. . . . . Optional Front & Rear

Note: As of May 2018, all vehicles are required to have a backup camera.
^Warning feature does not meet government standards.
*Backup camera does not meet government standards.

Buick Envision

Specifications

Drive. . . . . AWD
Engine 2.5-liter I4
Transmission . . . . 6-sp. Automatic
Tow Rating (lbs.) . . . . Very Low-1500
Head/Leg Room (in.) Cramped-40/40.9
Interior Space (cu. ft.). Average-100.6
Cargo Space (cu. ft.) Roomy-26.9
Wheelbase/Length (in.) 108.2/183.7

Buick LaCrosse

Ratings—10 Best, 1 Worst

Combo Crash Tests	5
Safety Features	9
Rollover	8
Preventive Maintenance	1
Repair Costs	2
Warranty	8
Fuel Economy	5
Complaints	8
Insurance Costs	5
OVERALL RATING	**5**

Buick LaCrosse

Buick LaCrosse

At-a-Glance

Status/Year Series Started Unchanged/2017
Twins . . . . –
Body Styles . . . . .Sedan
Seating 5
Anti-Theft Device . Std. Pass. Immobil. & Active Alarm
Parking Index Rating . . . . Hard
Where Made . . . . Fairfax, KS
Fuel Factor:
  MPG Rating (city/hwy) Average-21/31
  Driving Range (mi.) Short-388
  Fuel Type . . . . .Regular
  Annual Fuel Cost . . . . .Average-$1496
  Gas Guzzler Tax . . . . .No
  Greenhouse Gas Emissions (tons/yr.) . . Average-6.0
  Barrels of Oil Used per year High-13.2

How the Competition Rates

Competitors	Rating	Pg.
Cadillac XTS	8	109
Ford Taurus	3	147
Toyota Avalon	8	243

Price Range

Price Range	Retail	Markup
1SV	$29,565	1%
Preferred	$33,665	4%
Essence	$36,365	4%
Premium AWD	$43,425	4%

Safety Checklist

Crash Test:
  Frontal . . . . Good
  Side . . . . .Very Poor
Airbags:
  Torso Std. Fr. & Opt. Rr. Pelvis/Torso from Seat
  Roll Sensing . . . . .Yes
  Knee Bolster . . . . .Standard Front
Crash Avoidance:
  Collision Avoidance . . . . . . Optional CIB & DBS
  Blind Spot Detection . . . . Optional
  Lane Keeping Assist . . . . Optional
  Backup Camera . . . . .Standard*
  Pedestrian Crash Avoidance . . . . Optional
General:
  Auto. Crash Notif. . Op. Assist. & Crash Info-Free
  Day Running Lamps . . . . Standard
Safety Belt/Restraint:
  Dynamic Head Restraints . . . . None
  Adjustable Belt . . . . Optional Front & Rear

Note: As of May 2018, all vehicles are required to have a backup camera.
^Warning feature does not meet government standards.
*Backup camera does not meet government standards.

Buick LaCrosse

Specifications

Drive . . . . .FWD
Engine 3.6-liter V6
Transmission . . . . 8-sp. Automatic
Tow Rating (lbs.) . . . . –
Head/Leg Room (in.) Cramped-38.4/42
Interior Space (cu. ft.) Average-100
Cargo Space (cu. ft.) Cramped-15
Wheelbase/Length (in.) 114.4/197.5

Buick Regal

Ratings—10 Best, 1 Worst	
Combo Crash Tests	—
Safety Features	10
Rollover	7
Preventive Maintenance	1
Repair Costs	3
Warranty	8
Fuel Economy	6
Complaints	—
Insurance Costs	8
OVERALL RATING	—

Buick Regal

At-a-Glance

Status/Year Series Started	All New/2018
Twins	Chevrolet Malibu
Body Styles	Sedan, Wagon
Seating	5
Anti-Theft Device	Std. Pass. Immobil. & Active Alarm
Parking Index Rating	—
Where Made	Oshawa, Ontario

Fuel Factor:

MPG Rating (city/hwy)	Average-22/32
Driving Range (mi.)	Average-417
Fuel Type	Premium
Annual Fuel Cost	High-$1740
Gas Guzzler Tax	No
Greenhouse Gas Emissions (tons/yr.)	Average-6.7
Barrels of Oil Used per year	High-15.0

How the Competition Rates

Competitors	Rating	Pg.
Acura TLX	9	82
Lincoln MKZ	4	197
Mazda 6	5	203

Price Range	Retail	Markup
1SV	$27,065	1%
Sport Touring	$28,615	4%
Leather	$31,465	4%
GS AWD	$36,540	4%

Safety Checklist

Crash Test:

Frontal	—
Side	—

Airbags:

Torso	Std Front & Rear Pelvis/Torso from Seat
Roll Sensing	Yes
Knee Bolster	Standard Front

Crash Avoidance:

Collision Avoidance	Optional CIB & DBS
Blind Spot Detection	Optional
Lane Keeping Assist	Optional
Backup Camera	Standard*
Pedestrian Crash Avoidance	Optional

General:

Auto. Crash Notif.	Op. Assist. & Crash Info-Free
Day Running Lamps	Standard

Safety Belt/Restraint:

Dynamic Head Restraints	None
Adjustable Belt	Optional Rear

Note: As of May 2018, all vehicles are required to have a backup camera.
^Warning feature does not meet government standards.
*Backup camera does not meet government standards.

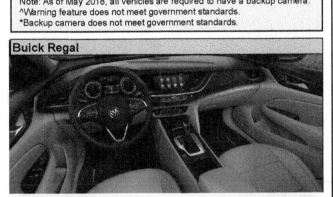

Buick Regal

Specifications

Drive	FWD
Engine	3.6-liter V6
Transmission	9-sp. Automatic
Tow Rating (lbs.)	—
Head/Leg Room (in.)	Cramped-38.8/42.1
Interior Space (cu. ft.)	Average-98
Cargo Space (cu. ft.)	Very Roomy-31.5
Wheelbase/Length (in.)	111.4/192.9

Cadillac ATS

Compact

Ratings—10 Best, 1 Worst

Combo Crash Tests	2
Safety Features	8
Rollover	8
Preventive Maintenance	2
Repair Costs	2
Warranty	10
Fuel Economy	5
Complaints	6
Insurance Costs	8
OVERALL RATING	**4**

Cadillac ATS

Cadillac ATS

At-a-Glance

Status/Year Series Started Unchanged/2013
Twins . . . . –
Body Styles . . . . Sedan, Coupe
Seating 5
Anti-Theft Device . Std. Pass. Immobil. & Active Alarm
Parking Index Rating . . . . Easy
Where Made . . . . Lansing, MI
Fuel Factor:
  MPG Rating (city/hwy) Average-21/33
  Driving Range (mi.) Average-402
  Fuel Type . . . . Regular
  Annual Fuel Cost . . . . Average-$1464
  Gas Guzzler Tax . . . . No
  Greenhouse Gas Emissions (tons/yr.) . . Average-7.2
  Barrels of Oil Used per year High-13.2

How the Competition Rates

Competitors	Rating	Pg.
Audi A3	6	83
Infiniti Q50	3	167
Lexus IS	8	190

Price Range	Retail	Markup
Base 2.0L Sedan RWD	$34,895	5%
Luxury 2.0L Sedan AWD	$40,695	5%
Performance 3.6L Sedan RWD	$47,295	5%
Premium 3.6L Coupe AWD	$49,295	5%

Safety Checklist

Crash Test:
  Frontal . . . . Very Poor
  Side . . . . Poor
Airbags:
  Torso Std. Fr. & Opt. Rr. Pelvis/Torso from Seat
  Roll Sensing . . . . Yes
  Knee Bolster . . . . Standard Front
Crash Avoidance:
  Collision Avoidance . . . . . . Optional CIB & DBS
  Blind Spot Detection . . . . Optional
  Lane Keeping Assist . . . . Optional
  Backup Camera . . . . Standard*
  Pedestrian Crash Avoidance . . . . None
General:
  Auto. Crash Notif. . Op. Assist. & Crash Info-Free
  Day Running Lamps . . . . Standard
Safety Belt/Restraint:
  Dynamic Head Restraints . . . . None
  Adjustable Belt . . . . Optional Rear

Note: As of May 2018, all vehicles are required to have a backup camera.
^Warning feature does not meet government standards.
*Backup camera does not meet government standards.

Cadillac ATS

Specifications

Drive . . . . RWD
Engine 2.0-liter I4
Transmission . . . . 6-sp. Automatic
Tow Rating (lbs.) . . . . –
Head/Leg Room (in.) Average-38.6/42.5
Interior Space (cu. ft.) Cramped-90.9
Cargo Space (cu. ft.) . . . . Very Cramped-10.4
Wheelbase/Length (in.) 109.3/182.8

Ratings—10 Best, 1 Worst

Combo Crash Tests	—
Safety Features	9
Rollover	7
Preventive Maintenance	2
Repair Costs	2
Warranty	10
Fuel Economy	3
Complaints	8
Insurance Costs	3
OVERALL RATING	**—**

Cadillac CT6

Cadillac CT6

At-a-Glance

Status/Year Series Started........ Unchanged/2016
Twins ....—
Body Styles ....Sedan
Seating..5
Anti-Theft Device . Std. Pass. Immobil. & Active Alarm
Parking Index Rating ....Very Hard
Where Made......................Hamtramck, MI

Fuel Factor:
MPG Rating (city/hwy) Poor-18/27
Driving Range (mi.) Average-413
Fuel Type........................Regular
Annual Fuel Cost ....High-$1735
Gas Guzzler Tax ....No
Greenhouse Gas Emissions (tons/yr.). . Average-6.9
Barrels of Oil Used per year High-15.7

How the Competition Rates

Competitors	Rating	Pg.
Lincoln Continental	6	194
Mercedes-Benz E	3	208
Tesla Model S	10	239

Price Range	Retail	Markup
Base 2.0L RWD	$54,095	5%
Luxury 3.6L AWD	$61,195	5%
Premium Luxury 3.6L AWD	$65,295	5%
Platinum 3.0L TT AWD	$88,295	5%

Safety Checklist

Crash Test:
Frontal.................................—
Side...................................—
Airbags:
Torso . . . Standard Front Pelvis/Torso from Seat
Roll Sensing...........................Yes
Knee Bolster ....Standard Front
Crash Avoidance:
Collision Avoidance ...... Optional CIB & DBS
Blind Spot Detection ....Optional
Lane Keeping Assist ....Optional
Backup Camera....................Standard
Pedestrian Crash Avoidance.........Optional
General:
Auto. Crash Notif. . Op. Assist. & Crash Info-Free
Day Running Lamps ....Standard
Safety Belt/Restraint:
Dynamic Head Restraints .... None
Adjustable Belt.........Optional Front & Rear

Note: As of May 2018, all vehicles are required to have a backup camera.
^Warning feature does not meet government standards.
*Backup camera does not meet government standards.

Specifications

Drive................................AWD
Engine 3.6-liter V6
Transmission ....5-sp. Automatic
Tow Rating (lbs.) ....—
Head/Leg Room (in.) Average-40.1/42.3
Interior Space (cu. ft.)...........Roomy-110
Cargo Space (cu. ft.) Cramped-15.3
Wheelbase/Length (in.) 122.4/204

Ratings—10 Best, 1 Worst

Combo Crash Tests	3
Safety Features	8
Rollover	3
Preventive Maintenance	1
Repair Costs	4
Warranty	10
Fuel Economy	3
Complaints	2
Insurance Costs	8
OVERALL RATING	**3**

Cadillac XT5

Cadillac XT5

At-a-Glance

Status/Year Series Started Unchanged/2017
Twins . . . . .GMC Acadia
Body Styles . . . . SUV
Seating 5
Anti-Theft Device . Std. Pass. Immobil. & Active Alarm
Parking Index Rating . . . . .Very Easy
Where Made . . . . Spring Hill, TN
Fuel Factor:
MPG Rating (city/hwy) Poor-19/25
Driving Range (mi.) Average-405
Fuel Type . . . . .Regular
Annual Fuel Cost . . . . .High-$1725
Gas Guzzler Tax . . . . .No
Greenhouse Gas Emissions (tons/yr.) . . Average-6.5
Barrels of Oil Used per year High-15.0

How the Competition Rates

Competitors	Rating	Pg.
Acura MDX	7	80
Audi Q7	3	89
Lexus RX	4	193

Price Range

	Retail	Markup
Base FWD	$39,995	5%
Luxury FWD	$45,995	5%
Premium Luxury AWD	$54,995	5%
Platinum AWD	$62,995	5%

Safety Checklist

Crash Test:
Frontal . . . . Average
Side . . . . .Very Poor
Airbags:
Torso . . . Standard Front Pelvis/Torso from Seat
Roll Sensing . . . . .Yes
Knee Bolster . . . . Standard Driver
Crash Avoidance:
Collision Avoidance . . . . . . Optional CIB & DBS
Blind Spot Detection . . . . Optional
Lane Keeping Assist . . . . Optional
Backup Camera . . . . .Standard*
Pedestrian Crash Avoidance . . . . Optional
General:
Auto. Crash Notif. . Op. Assist. & Crash Info-Free
Day Running Lamps . . . . Standard
Safety Belt/Restraint:
Dynamic Head Restraints . . . . None
Adjustable Belt . . . . Standard Front & Rear

Note: As of May 2018, all vehicles are required to have a backup camera.
^Warning feature does not meet government standards.
*Backup camera does not meet government standards.

Cadillac XT5

Specifications

Drive . . . . .FWD
Engine 3.6-liter V6
Transmission . . . . 8-sp. Automatic
Tow Rating (lbs.) Low-3500
Head/Leg Room (in.) Cramped-38.4/41.2
Interior Space (cu. ft.) Roomy-104.5
Cargo Space (cu. ft.) Roomy-30
Wheelbase/Length (in.) 112.5/189.5

Cadillac XTS

Cadillac XTS Large

Ratings—10 Best, 1 Worst

Combo Crash Tests	9
Safety Features	7
Rollover	6
Preventive Maintenance	1
Repair Costs	3
Warranty	10
Fuel Economy	3
Complaints	8
Insurance Costs	8
OVERALL RATING	**8**

Cadillac XTS

Cadillac XTS

At-a-Glance

Status/Year Series Started Appearance Change/2013
Twins . . . . Chevrolet Impala
Body Styles . . . . Sedan
Seating 5
Anti-Theft Device . Std. Pass. Immobil. & Active Alarm
Parking Index Rating . . . . Hard
Where Made . . . . Oshawa, Ontario

Fuel Factor:
MPG Rating (city/hwy) Poor-18/28
Driving Range (mi.) Average-407
Fuel Type . . . . Regular
Annual Fuel Cost . . . . High-$1714
Gas Guzzler Tax . . . . No
Greenhouse Gas Emissions (tons/yr.) High-8.6
Barrels of Oil Used per year High-15.7

How the Competition Rates

Competitors	Rating	Pg.
Buick LaCrosse	5	104
Chrysler 300	1	126
Ford Taurus	3	147

Price Range

Price Range	Retail	Markup
Base	$45,595	6%
Luxury AWD	$51,595	6%
Platinum	$64,895	7%
Platinum Vsport AWD	$72,695	7%

Safety Checklist

Crash Test:
Frontal . . . . Very Good
Side . . . . Good
Airbags:
Torso Std. Fr. & Opt. Rr. Pelvis/Torso from Seat
Roll Sensing . . . . Yes
Knee Bolster . . . . Standard Front
Crash Avoidance:
Collision Avoidance . . . . . . Optional CIB & DBS
Blind Spot Detection . . . . Optional
Lane Keeping Assist . . . . Optional
Backup Camera . . . . Optional*
Pedestrian Crash Avoidance . . . . None
General:
Auto. Crash Notif. . Op. Assist. & Crash Info-Free
Day Running Lamps . . . . Standard
Safety Belt/Restraint:
Dynamic Head Restraints . . . . None
Adjustable Belt . . . . Optional Front & Rear

Note: As of May 2018, all vehicles are required to have a backup camera.
^Warning feature does not meet government standards.
*Backup camera does not meet government standards.

Cadillac XTS

Specifications

Drive . . . . FWD
Engine 3.6-liter V6
Transmission . . . . 6-sp. Automatic
Tow Rating (lbs.) . . . . Very Low-1000
Head/Leg Room (in.) . . . . Very Roomy-39/45.8
Interior Space (cu. ft.) Average-104.2
Cargo Space (cu. ft.) Average-18
Wheelbase/Length (in.) 111.7/202

Chevrolet Bolt

Ratings—10 Best, 1 Worst

Combo Crash Tests	—
Safety Features	9
Rollover	3
Preventive Maintenance	6
Repair Costs	10
Warranty	6
Fuel Economy	10
Complaints	2
Insurance Costs	5

OVERALL RATING   —

Chevrolet Bolt EV

Chevrolet Bolt EV

At-a-Glance

Status/Year Series Started Unchanged/2017
Twins . . . . —
Body Styles . . . . Hatchback
Seating 5
Anti-Theft Device . . . . . Std. Pass. Immobil. & Alarm
Parking Index Rating . . . . Very Easy
Where Made . . . . Orion Township, MI
Fuel Factor:
  MPG Rating (city/hwy) . . . . Very Good-128/110
  Driving Range (mi.) . . . . Very Short-238
  Fuel Type . . . . Electricity
  Annual Fuel Cost . . . . Very Low-$550
  Gas Guzzler Tax . . . . No
  Greenhouse Gas Emissions (tons/yr.) . Very Low-0.0
  Barrels of Oil Used per year . . . . Very Low-0.0

How the Competition Rates

Competitors	Rating	Pg.
BMW i3	—	95
Nissan Leaf	—	223
Tesla Model 3	—	238

Price Range

Price Range	Retail	Markup
LT	$36,620	4%
Premier	$40,905	4%

Chevrolet Bolt EV

Safety Checklist

Crash Test:
  Frontal . . . . —
  Side . . . . —
Airbags:
  Torso . . . Standard Front Pelvis/Torso from Seat
  Roll Sensing . . . . Yes
  Knee Bolster . . . . Standard Front
Crash Avoidance:
  Collision Avoidance . . . . . Optional CIB & DBS
  Blind Spot Detection . . . . Optional
  Lane Keeping Assist . . . . Optional^
  Backup Camera . . . . Standard
  Pedestrian Crash Avoidance . . . . Optional
General:
  Auto. Crash Notif. . Op. Assist. & Crash Info-Free
  Day Running Lamps . . . . Standard
Safety Belt/Restraint:
  Dynamic Head Restraints . . . . None
  Adjustable Belt . . . . Optional Rear

Note: As of May 2018, all vehicles are required to have a backup camera.
^Warning feature does not meet government standards.
*Backup camera does not meet government standards.

Specifications

Drive . . . . FWD
Engine . . . . Electric
Transmission . . . . 1-sp. Automatic
Tow Rating (lbs.) . . . . Very Low-0
Head/Leg Room (in.) Average-39.7/41.6
Interior Space (cu. ft.) Cramped-95
Cargo Space (cu. ft.) Average-16.9
Wheelbase/Length (in.) 102.4/164

Ratings—10 Best, 1 Worst

Combo Crash Tests	7
Safety Features	4
Rollover	10
Preventive Maintenance	1
Repair Costs	5
Warranty	6
Fuel Economy	3
Complaints	8
Insurance Costs	1
OVERALL RATING	**4**

Chevrolet Camaro

Chevrolet Camaro

At-a-Glance

Status/Year Series Started........ Unchanged/2016
Twins .... –
Body Styles .... Coupe, Convertible
Seating 4
Anti-Theft Device . Std. Pass. Immobil. & Active Alarm
Parking Index Rating .... Hard
Where Made........................ Lansing, MI

Fuel Factor:
MPG Rating (city/hwy) Poor-19/28
Driving Range (mi.) Average-422
Fuel Type........................... Premium
Annual Fuel Cost .... Very High-$2006
Gas Guzzler Tax .... No
Greenhouse Gas Emissions (tons/yr.).. Average-6.5
Barrels of Oil Used per year High-14.3

How the Competition Rates

Competitors	Rating	Pg.
Chevrolet Corvette	–	113
Dodge Challenger	4	128
Ford Mustang	6	146

Price Range

Price Range	Retail	Markup
1LT Coupe	$26,700	4%
2LT Convertible	$35,700	4%
1SS Coupe	$37,000	4%
2SS Coupe	$42,000	4%

Safety Checklist

Crash Test:
Frontal........................... Average
Side......................... Very Good

Airbags:
Torso . . . Standard Front Pelvis/Torso from Seat
Roll Sensing........................... Yes
Knee Bolster .... Standard Front

Crash Avoidance:
Collision Avoidance .... None
Blind Spot Detection .... Optional
Lane Keeping Assist .... None
Backup Camera.................. Standard*
Pedestrian Crash Avoidance .... None

General:
Auto. Crash Notif. . Op. Assist. & Crash Info-Free
Day Running Lamps .... Standard

Safety Belt/Restraint:
Dynamic Head Restraints .... None
Adjustable Belt............... Optional Rear

Note: As of May 2018, all vehicles are required to have a backup camera.
^Warning feature does not meet government standards.
*Backup camera does not meet government standards.

Chevrolet Camaro

Specifications

Drive....................................... RWD
Engine 3.6-liter V6
Transmission .... 8-sp. Automatic
Tow Rating (lbs.) .... –
Head/Leg Room (in.) .... Very Cramped-36.6/42.6
Interior Space (cu. ft.).............. Very Cramped-77
Cargo Space (cu. ft.) .... Very Cramped-9.1
Wheelbase/Length (in.) 110.7/188.3

Ratings—10 Best, 1 Worst	Colorado	Canyon
Combo Crash Tests	3	3
Safety Features	2	2
Rollover	2	2
Preventive Maintenance	1	1
Repair Costs	8	8
Warranty	6	5
Fuel Economy	4	4
Complaints	5	3
Insurance Costs	10	8
OVERALL RATING	**2**	**1**

Chevrolet Colorado

GMC Canyon

Safety Checklist

Crash Test:
Frontal. . . . . Poor
Side. . . . . Poor
Airbags:
Torso . . . Standard Front Pelvis/Torso from Seat
Roll Sensing. . . . . .Yes
Knee Bolster . . . . None
Crash Avoidance:
Collision Avoidance . . . . .Warning Only Optional
Blind Spot Detection . . . . None
Lane Keeping Assist . . . .Warning Only Optional
Backup Camera. . . . . .Standard*
Pedestrian Crash Avoidance . . . . None
General:
Auto. Crash Notif. . Op. Assist. & Crash Info-Free
Day Running Lamps . . . . Standard
Safety Belt/Restraint:
Dynamic Head Restraints . . . . None
Adjustable Belt. . . . . Optional Front & Rear

Note: As of May 2018, all vehicles are required to have a backup camera.
^Warning feature does not meet government standards.
*Backup camera does not meet government standards.

At-a-Glance

Status/Year Series Started. Unchanged/2015
Twins . . . . GMC Canyon
Body Styles . . . . Pickup
Seating. 5
Anti-Theft Device . Std. Pass. Immobil. & Active Alarm
Parking Index Rating . . . . .Very Hard
Where Made. . . . . .Wentzville, MO
Fuel Factor:
MPG Rating (city/hwy) Poor-20/27
Driving Range (mi.) . . . . Very Long-475
Fuel Type. . . . . .Regular
Annual Fuel Cost . . . . .Average-$1623
Gas Guzzler Tax . . . . .No
Greenhouse Gas Emissions (tons/yr.). High-8.2
Barrels of Oil Used per year High-15.0

Chevrolet Colorado

How the Competition Rates

Competitors	Rating	Pg.
Nissan Frontier	1	221
Toyota Tacoma	2	255

Specifications

Drive. . . . . .RWD
Engine 2.5-liter I4
Transmission . . . . 6-sp. Automatic
Tow Rating (lbs.) Low-3500
Head/Leg Room (in.) . . . . Very Roomy-41.4/45
Interior Space (cu. ft.). . . . . –
Cargo Space (cu. ft.) . . . . Very Roomy-49.9
Wheelbase/Length (in.) 128.3/212.7

Price Range

Price Range	Retail	Markup
Base Ext. Cab 2WD	$20,000	1%
W/T Crew Cab 4WD	$31,220	5%
Z71 Crew Cab 4WD	$32,775	5%
LT Crew Cab 4WD	$33,775	5%

Ratings—10 Best, 1 Worst	
Combo Crash Tests	—
Safety Features	1
Rollover	10
Preventive Maintenance	1
Repair Costs	1
Warranty	6
Fuel Economy	2
Complaints	6
Insurance Costs	10
OVERALL RATING	**—**

Chevrolet Corvette

Chevrolet Corvette

At-a-Glance

Status/Year Series Started........	Unchanged/2014
Twins..................................	—
Body Styles.................	Coupe, Convertible
Seating...................................	2
Anti-Theft Device . Std. Pass. Immobil. & Active Alarm	
Parking Index Rating.................	Average
Where Made...................	Bowling Green, KY

Fuel Factor:

MPG Rating (city/hwy).........	Very Poor-15/25
Driving Range (mi.).............	Very Short-338
Fuel Type.......................	Premium
Annual Fuel Cost............	Very High-$2435
Gas Guzzler Tax................	No
Greenhouse Gas Emissions (tons/yr.).....	High-8.1
Barrels of Oil Used per year.......	Very High-18.3

How the Competition Rates

Competitors	Rating	Pg.
Chevrolet Camaro	4	111
Dodge Challenger	4	128
Ford Mustang	6	146

Price Range	Retail	Markup
Base Coupe	$55,495	8%
Z51 Convertible	$64,495	8%
Grand Sport Coupe	$65,495	8%
Z06 Convertible	$83,495	8%

Safety Checklist

Crash Test:
Frontal...............................	—
Side..................................	—

Airbags:
Torso.......	Standard Front Torso from Seat
Roll Sensing..........................	No
Knee Bolster.....................	None

Crash Avoidance:
Collision Avoidance..................	None
Blind Spot Detection...............	None
Lane Keeping Assist................	None
Backup Camera...................	Standard*
Pedestrian Crash Avoidance...........	None

General:
Auto. Crash Notif. . Op. Assist. & Crash Info-Free	
Day Running Lamps..............	Standard

Safety Belt/Restraint:
Dynamic Head Restraints..............	None
Adjustable Belt.....................	None

Note: As of May 2018, all vehicles are required to have a backup camera.
^Warning feature does not meet government standards.
*Backup camera does not meet government standards.

Chevrolet Corvette

Specifications

Drive.......................................	RWD
Engine..............................	6.2-liter V8
Transmission.....................	8-sp. Automatic
Tow Rating (lbs.)........................	—
Head/Leg Room (in.)...........	Average-38/43
Interior Space (cu. ft.)..............	Very Cramped-52
Cargo Space (cu. ft.)............	Cramped-15
Wheelbase/Length (in.)...........	106.7/176.9

Ratings—10 Best, 1 Worst

Combo Crash Tests	5
Safety Features	8
Rollover	7
Preventive Maintenance	4
Repair Costs	8
Warranty	6
Fuel Economy	9
Complaints	10
Insurance Costs	1
OVERALL RATING	**8**

Chevrolet Cruze

Chevrolet Cruze

At-a-Glance

Status/Year Series Started........ Unchanged/2016
Twins .... –
Body Styles .... Sedan, Hatchback
Seating....................................... 5
Anti-Theft Device . Std. Pass. Immobil. & Active Alarm
Parking Index Rating .... Average
Where Made.................... Lordstown, OH
Fuel Factor:
  MPG Rating (city/hwy) ...... Very Good-29/40
  Driving Range (mi.) Long-453
  Fuel Type....................... Regular
  Annual Fuel Cost .... Very Low-$1110
  Gas Guzzler Tax .... No
  Greenhouse Gas Emissions (tons/yr.). Very Low-4.4
  Barrels of Oil Used per year Low-10.0

How the Competition Rates

Competitors	Rating	Pg.
Ford Focus	5	143
Honda Civic	10	153
Toyota Corolla	8	245

Price Range	Retail	Markup
L MT	$16,975	1%
LS AT	$19,525	4%
LT AT	$21,450	4%
Premier Sedan AT	$23,475	4%

Safety Checklist

Crash Test:
  Frontal........................... Good
  Side...................... Very Poor
Airbags:
  Torso . Std Front & Rear Pelvis/Torso from Seat
  Roll Sensing....................... Yes
  Knee Bolster .... Standard Front
Crash Avoidance:
  Collision Avoidance .... Warning Only Optional
  Blind Spot Detection .... Optional
  Lane Keeping Assist .... Optional
  Backup Camera.................... Standard*
  Pedestrian Crash Avoidance .... None
General:
  Auto. Crash Notif. . Op. Assist. & Crash Info-Free
  Day Running Lamps .... Standard
Safety Belt/Restraint:
  Dynamic Head Restraints .... None
  Adjustable Belt................. Optional Rear

Note: As of May 2018, all vehicles are required to have a backup camera.
^Warning feature does not meet government standards.
*Backup camera does not meet government standards.

Chevrolet Cruze

Specifications

Drive....................................... FWD
Engine 1.4-liter I4
Transmission .... 6-sp. Autonatic
Tow Rating (lbs.) .... –
Head/Leg Room (in.) Cramped-38.9/42
Interior Space (cu. ft.)............. Cramped-94
Cargo Space (cu. ft.) Cramped-14.8
Wheelbase/Length (in.) 106.3/183.7

Chevrolet Equinox — Small SUV

Ratings—10 Best, 1 Worst

Combo Crash Tests	6
Safety Features	5
Rollover	2
Preventive Maintenance	1
Repair Costs	3
Warranty	6
Fuel Economy	7
Complaints	—
Insurance Costs	8
OVERALL RATING	**4**

Chevrolet Equinox

Chevrolet Equinox

At-a-Glance

Status/Year Series Started	All New/2018
Twins	GMC Terrain
Body Styles	SUV
Seating	5
Anti-Theft Device	Std. Pass. Immobil. & Active Alarm
Parking Index Rating	Average
Where Made	Oshawa, Ontario / Spring Hill, TN

Fuel Factor:

MPG Rating (city/hwy)	Good-26/32
Driving Range (mi.)	Average-417
Fuel Type	Regular
Annual Fuel Cost	Low-$1294
Gas Guzzler Tax	No
Greenhouse Gas Emissions (tons/yr.)	Low-5.2
Barrels of Oil Used per year	Average-11.8

How the Competition Rates

Competitors	Rating	Pg.
Dodge Journey	1	131
Ford Escape	5	137
Honda Pilot	8	158

Price Range

	Retail	Markup
L FWD	$23,580	1%
LS FWD	$25,510	5%
LT AWD 2.0	$32,840	5%
Premier AWD 2.0	$37,230	5%

Safety Checklist

Crash Test:
Frontal	Very Good
Side	Very Poor

Airbags:
Torso	Standard Front Pelvis/Torso from Seat
Roll Sensing	Yes
Knee Bolster	None

Crash Avoidance:
Collision Avoidance	Optional CIB
Blind Spot Detection	Optional
Lane Keeping Assist	Optional
Backup Camera	Standard
Pedestrian Crash Avoidance	None

General:
Auto. Crash Notif.	Op. Assist. & Crash Info-Free
Day Running Lamps	Standard

Safety Belt/Restraint:
Dynamic Head Restraints	None
Adjustable Belt	Optional Front & Rear

Note: As of May 2018, all vehicles are required to have a backup camera.
^Warning feature does not meet government standards.
*Backup camera does not meet government standards.

Chevrolet Equinox

Specifications

Drive	FWD
Engine	1.5-liter I4
Transmission	6-sp. Automatic
Tow Rating (lbs.)	Low-3500
Head/Leg Room (in.)	Cramped-40/40.9
Interior Space (cu. ft.)	Average-103.2
Cargo Space (cu. ft.)	Roomy-29.9
Wheelbase/Length (in.)	107.3/183.1

Chevrolet Impala

Ratings—10 Best, 1 Worst

Combo Crash Tests	6
Safety Features	7
Rollover	6
Preventive Maintenance	1
Repair Costs	6
Warranty	6
Fuel Economy	3
Complaints	8
Insurance Costs	3
OVERALL RATING	**4**

Chevrolet Impala

Chevrolet Impala

At-a-Glance

Status/Year Series Started	Unchanged/2014
Twins	Cadillac XTS
Body Styles	Sedan
Seating	5
Anti-Theft Device	Std. Pass. Immobil. & Active Alarm
Parking Index Rating	Hard
Where Made	Detroit, MI / Oshawa, Ontario

Fuel Factor:

MPG Rating (city/hwy)	Poor-18/28
Driving Range (mi.)	Short-397
Fuel Type	Regular
Annual Fuel Cost	High-$1714
Gas Guzzler Tax	No
Greenhouse Gas Emissions (tons/yr.)	High-8.6
Barrels of Oil Used per year	High-15.7

How the Competition Rates

Competitors	Rating	Pg.
Buick LaCrosse	5	104
Ford Taurus	3	147
Toyota Avalon	8	243

Price Range	Retail	Markup
LS	$27,985	5%
LT	$30,220	4%
Premier	$36,420	4%

Safety Checklist

Crash Test:

Frontal	Good
Side	Poor

Airbags:

Torso	Std. Fr. & Opt. Rr. Pelvis/Torso from Seat
Roll Sensing	Yes
Knee Bolster	Standard Front

Crash Avoidance:

Collision Avoidance	Optional CIB & DBS
Blind Spot Detection	Optional
Lane Keeping Assist	Warning Only Optional
Backup Camera	Optional*
Pedestrian Crash Avoidance	None

General:

Auto. Crash Notif.	Op. Assist. & Crash Info-Free
Day Running Lamps	Standard

Safety Belt/Restraint:

Dynamic Head Restraints	None
Adjustable Belt	Optional Front & Rear

Note: As of May 2018, all vehicles are required to have a backup camera.
^Warning feature does not meet government standards.
*Backup camera does not meet government standards.

Chevrolet Impala

Specifications

Drive	FWD
Engine	3.6-liter V6
Transmission	6-sp. Automatic
Tow Rating (lbs.)	Very Low-1000
Head/Leg Room (in.)	Very Roomy-39.9/45.8
Interior Space (cu. ft.)	Roomy-105
Cargo Space (cu. ft.)	Average-18.8
Wheelbase/Length (in.)	111.7/201.3

Chevrolet Malibu Intermediate

Ratings—10 Best, 1 Worst

Combo Crash Tests	5
Safety Features	9
Rollover	8
Preventive Maintenance	7
Repair Costs	8
Warranty	6
Fuel Economy	8
Complaints	10
Insurance Costs	3
OVERALL RATING	**9**

Chevrolet Malibu

Chevrolet Malibu

At-a-Glance

Status/Year Series Started. Unchanged/2016
Twins . . . . Buick Regal
Body Styles . . . . .Sedan
Seating 5
Anti-Theft Device . Std. Pass. Immobil. & Active Alarm
Parking Index Rating . . . . Average
Where Made. . . . . Fairfax, KS
Fuel Factor:
  MPG Rating (city/hwy) Good-27/36
  Driving Range (mi.) Short-395
  Fuel Type. . . . . .Regular
  Annual Fuel Cost . . . . Low-$1208
  Gas Guzzler Tax . . . . .No
  Greenhouse Gas Emissions (tons/yr.). Low-4.8
  Barrels of Oil Used per year Average-11.0

How the Competition Rates

Competitors	Rating	Pg.
Ford Fusion	4	144
Nissan Altima	4	219
Toyota Camry	8	244

Price Range	Retail	Markup
L	$21,680	1%
LS	$23,225	4%
LT	$25,125	4%
Hybrid	$27,875	4%

Safety Checklist

Crash Test:
  Frontal. . . . . .Poor
  Side. . . . . Very Good
Airbags:
  Torso . Std Front & Rear Pelvis/Torso from Seat
  Roll Sensing. . . . . .Yes
  Knee Bolster . . . . .Standard Front
Crash Avoidance:
  Collision Avoidance . . . . . . Optional CIB & DBS
  Blind Spot Detection . . . . Optional
  Lane Keeping Assist . . . . Optional
  Backup Camera. . . . . Optional*
  Pedestrian Crash Avoidance . . . . Optional
General:
  Auto. Crash Notif. . Op. Assist. & Crash Info-Free
  Day Running Lamps . . . . Standard
Safety Belt/Restraint:
  Dynamic Head Restraints . . . . None
  Adjustable Belt. . . . . .Optional Rear

Note: As of May 2018, all vehicles are required to have a backup camera.
^Warning feature does not meet government standards.
*Backup camera does not meet government standards.

Chevrolet Malibu

Specifications

Drive. . . . . .FWD
Engine 1.5-liter I4
Transmission . . . . 6-sp. Automatic
Tow Rating (lbs.) . . . . –
Head/Leg Room (in.) Average-39.1/42
Interior Space (cu. ft.). Average-102.9
Cargo Space (cu. ft.) Cramped-15.8
Wheelbase/Length (in.) 111.4/193.8

Chevrolet Silverado

Ratings—10 Best, 1 Worst	
Combo Crash Tests	9
Safety Features	3
Rollover	3
Preventive Maintenance	1
Repair Costs	5
Warranty	6
Fuel Economy	2
Complaints	9
Insurance Costs	10
OVERALL RATING	**7**

Chevrolet Silverado

At-a-Glance

Status/Year Series Started	Unchanged/2014
Twins	GMC Sierra
Body Styles	Pickup
Seating	5/6
Anti-Theft Device	Std. Pass. Immobil. & Active Alarm
Parking Index Rating	Very Hard
Where Made	Fort Wayne, IN

Fuel Factor:

MPG Rating (city/hwy)	Very Poor-16/22
Driving Range (mi.)	Very Long-474
Fuel Type	Regular
Annual Fuel Cost	Very High-$2015
Gas Guzzler Tax	No
Greenhouse Gas Emissions (tons/yr.)	High-8.1
Barrels of Oil Used per year	Very High-18.3

How the Competition Rates

Competitors	Rating	Pg.
Ford F-150	9	140
Ram 1500	2	232
Toyota Tundra	–	256

Price Range	Retail	Markup
W/T Reg. Cab 2WD	$28,475	5%
LT Dbl. Cab 4WD	$40,415	7%
LTZ Crew Cab 4WD	$47,925	7%
High Country Crew Cab 4WD	$55,375	7%

Safety Checklist

Crash Test:

Frontal	Good
Side	Good

Airbags:

Torso	Standard Front Pelvis/Torso from Seat
Roll Sensing	Yes
Knee Bolster	None

Crash Avoidance:

Collision Avoidance	Optional CIB
Blind Spot Detection	None
Lane Keeping Assist	Optional^
Backup Camera	Optional*
Pedestrian Crash Avoidance	None

General:

Auto. Crash Notif.	Op. Assist. & Crash Info-Free
Day Running Lamps	Standard

Safety Belt/Restraint:

Dynamic Head Restraints	None
Adjustable Belt	Optional Front & Rear

Note: As of May 2018, all vehicles are required to have a backup camera.
^Warning feature does not meet government standards.
*Backup camera does not meet government standards.

Chevrolet Silverado

Specifications

Drive	4WD
Engine	5.3-liter V8
Transmission	8-sp. Automatic
Tow Rating (lbs.)	Very High-9200
Head/Leg Room (in.)	Very Roomy-42.8/45.2
Interior Space (cu. ft.)	–
Cargo Space (cu. ft.)	Very Roomy-61
Wheelbase/Length (in.)	143.5/230

Chevrolet Sonic — Subcompact

Chevrolet Sonic

Ratings—10 Best, 1 Worst

Combo Crash Tests	7
Safety Features	7
Rollover	8
Preventive Maintenance	9
Repair Costs	9
Warranty	6
Fuel Economy	7
Complaints	6
Insurance Costs	1
OVERALL RATING	**9**

Chevrolet Sonic

At-a-Glance

Status/Year Series Started Unchanged/2012
Twins . . . . —
Body Styles . . . . Sedan, Hatchback
Seating 5
Anti-Theft Device . Std. Pass. Immobil. & Active Alarm
Parking Index Rating . . . . .Very Easy
Where Made. . . . . Orion Township, MI
Fuel Factor:
MPG Rating (city/hwy) Good-25/34
Driving Range (mi.) . . . . .Very Short-346
Fuel Type. . . . . .Regular
Annual Fuel Cost . . . . Low-$1295
Gas Guzzler Tax . . . . .No
Greenhouse Gas Emissions (tons/yr.). . Average-6.5
Barrels of Oil Used per year Average-11.8

How the Competition Rates

Competitors	Rating	Pg.
Ford Fiesta	2	141
Nissan Versa	1	230
Toyota Yaris	5	257

Price Range	Retail	Markup
LS Sedan MT	$15,295	4%
LT Sedan MT	$17,695	4%
LT Hatchback AT	$19,195	4%
Premier Hatchback AT	$21,295	4%

Safety Checklist

Crash Test:
Frontal. . . . . Very Good
Side. . . . . .Very Poor
Airbags:
Torso . Std Front & Rear Pelvis/Torso from Seat
Roll Sensing. . . . . .Yes
Knee Bolster . . . . .Standard Front
Crash Avoidance:
Collision Avoidance . . . . .Warning Only Optional
Blind Spot Detection . . . . None
Lane Keeping Assist . . . .Warning Only Optional
Backup Camera. . . . . .Standard*
Pedestrian Crash Avoidance . . . . None
General:
Auto. Crash Notif. . Op. Assist. & Crash Info-Free
Day Running Lamps . . . . Standard
Safety Belt/Restraint:
Dynamic Head Restraints . . . . None
Adjustable Belt. . . . . Optional Front & Rear

Note: As of May 2018, all vehicles are required to have a backup camera.
^Warning feature does not meet government standards.
*Backup camera does not meet government standards.

Chevrolet Sonic

Specifications

Drive. . . . . .FWD
Engine 1.8-liter I4
Transmission . . . . 6-sp. Automatic
Tow Rating (lbs.) . . . . —
Head/Leg Room (in.) Cramped-38.7/41.8
Interior Space (cu. ft.). Cramped-90.6
Cargo Space (cu. ft.) Average-19
Wheelbase/Length (in.) 99.4/159

Chevrolet Spark

Chevrolet Spark

Ratings—10 Best, 1 Worst

Combo Crash Tests	2
Safety Features	7
Rollover	3
Preventive Maintenance	9
Repair Costs	8
Warranty	6
Fuel Economy	9
Complaints	4
Insurance Costs	1
OVERALL RATING	**5**

Chevrolet Spark

At-a-Glance

Status/Year Series Started........ Unchanged/2016
Twins .... –
Body Styles .... Hatchback
Seating...4
Anti-Theft Device . Std. Pass. Immobil. & Active Alarm
Parking Index Rating ....Very Easy
Where Made............. Changwon, South Korea

Fuel Factor:
MPG Rating (city/hwy) .... Very Good-29/38
Driving Range (mi.) ....Very Short-292
Fuel Type.......................... Regular
Annual Fuel Cost .... Very Low-$1132
Gas Guzzler Tax ....No
Greenhouse Gas Emissions (tons/yr.). Very Low-4.2
Barrels of Oil Used per year Low-9.4

How the Competition Rates

Competitors	Rating	Pg.
Fiat 500	2	132
Honda Fit	10	155
Nissan Versa	1	230

Price Range	Retail	Markup
LS MT	$13,050	4%
1LT MT	$14,875	4%
1LT AT	$15,975	4%
2LT AT	$17,475	4%

Safety Checklist

Crash Test:
Frontal.......................... Very Poor
Side................................ Poor
Airbags:
Torso . Std Front & Rear Pelvis/Torso from Seat
Roll Sensing........................... Yes
Knee Bolster .... Standard Front
Crash Avoidance:
Collision Avoidance . . . . Warning Only Optional
Blind Spot Detection .... None
Lane Keeping Assist . . . . Warning Only Optional
Backup Camera.................... Standard*
Pedestrian Crash Avoidance .... None
General:
Auto. Crash Notif. . Op. Assist. & Crash Info-Free
Day Running Lamps .... Standard
Safety Belt/Restraint:
Dynamic Head Restraints .... None
Adjustable Belt................ Optional Rear

Note: As of May 2018, all vehicles are required to have a backup camera.
^Warning feature does not meet government standards.
*Backup camera does not meet government standards.

Chevrolet Spark

Specifications

Drive................................. FWD
Engine 1.4-liter I4
Transmission .... CVT
Tow Rating (lbs.) .... –
Head/Leg Room (in.) Cramped-39/41.7
Interior Space (cu. ft.)....... Very Cramped-83
Cargo Space (cu. ft.) ...... Very Cramped-11.1
Wheelbase/Length (in.) 93.9/143.1

Chevrolet Suburban/Yukon XL/Escalade ESV   Large SUV

Ratings—10 Best, 1 Worst	Suburban	Yukon XL	Escalade ESV
Combo Crash Tests	6	6	5
Safety Features	4	4	5
Rollover	2	2	2
Preventive Maintenance	1	5	1
Repair Costs	5	6	5
Warranty	6	5	10
Fuel Economy	1	1	1
Complaints	3	6	10
Insurance Costs	10	10	10
OVERALL RATING	**2**	**4**	**4**

Chevrolet Suburban

GMC Yukon XL

At-a-Glance

Status/Year Series Started Unchanged/2015
Twins . . . . . Cadillac Escalade ESV, GMC Yukon XL
Body Styles . . . . SUV
Seating 6/9
Anti-Theft Device . Std. Pass. Immobil. & Active Alarm
Parking Index Rating . . . . Very Hard
Where Made . . . . Arlington, TX
Fuel Factor:
  MPG Rating (city/hwy) . . . . Very Poor-15/22
  Driving Range (mi.) . . . . Very Long-543
  Fuel Type . . . . .Regular
  Annual Fuel Cost . . . . Very High-$2099
  Gas Guzzler Tax . . . . .No
  Greenhouse Gas Emissions (tons/yr.)Very High-10.0
  Barrels of Oil Used per year . . . . Very High-18.3

How the Competition Rates

Competitors	Rating	Pg.
Buick Enclave	4	101
Ford Expedition	–	138
Volvo XC90	8	268

Price Range	Retail	Markup
1500 LS RWD	$50,150	6%
1500 LT RWD	$55,280	6%
1500 LT 4WD	$58,280	6%
1500 Premier 4WD	$67,830	6%

Safety Checklist

Crash Test:
  Frontal . . . . Average
  Side . . . . Average
Airbags:
  Torso . . . Standard Front Pelvis/Torso from Seat
  Roll Sensing . . . . .Yes
  Knee Bolster . . . . None
Crash Avoidance:
  Collision Avoidance . . . . Optional CIB
  Blind Spot Detection . . . . Optional
  Lane Keeping Assist . . . . Optional
  Backup Camera . . . . .Standard*
  Pedestrian Crash Avoidance . . . . None
General:
  Auto. Crash Notif. . Op. Assist. & Crash Info-Free
  Day Running Lamps . . . . Standard
Safety Belt/Restraint:
  Dynamic Head Restraints . . . . None
  Adjustable Belt . . . . Optional Front & Rear

Note: As of May 2018, all vehicles are required to have a backup camera.
^Warning feature does not meet government standards.
*Backup camera does not meet government standards.

Cadillac Escalade ESV

Specifications

Drive 4WD
Engine 5.3-liter V8
Transmission . . . . 6-sp. Automatic
Tow Rating (lbs.) High-8000
Head/Leg Room (in.) . . . . Very Roomy-42.8/45.3
Interior Space (cu. ft.) Roomy-120.8
Cargo Space (cu. ft.) . . . . Very Roomy-39.3
Wheelbase/Length (in.) 130/224.4

Ratings—10 Best, 1 Worst

	Suburban	Yukon	Escalade
Combo Crash Tests	8	8	6
Safety Features	4	4	5
Rollover	2	2	2
Preventive Maintenance	1	5	1
Repair Costs	3	5	3
Warranty	6	5	10
Fuel Economy	2	1	2
Complaints	5	3	7
Insurance Costs	10	10	5
OVERALL RATING	**4**	**5**	**3**

GMC Yukon

At-a-Glance

Status/Year Series Started........ Unchanged/2015
Twins ....Cadillac Escalade, GMC Yukon
Body Styles .... SUV
Seating.................................... 6/9
Anti-Theft Device . Std. Pass. Immobil. & Active Alarm
Parking Index Rating .... Very Hard
Where Made...................... Arlington, TX
Fuel Factor:
  MPG Rating (city/hwy) ....Very Poor-16/22
  Driving Range (mi.) .... Very Long-474
  Fuel Type............................Regular
  Annual Fuel Cost .... Very High-$2015
  Gas Guzzler Tax ....No
  Greenhouse Gas Emissions (tons/yr.)..... High-8.2
  Barrels of Oil Used per year .... Very High-18.3

How the Competition Rates

Competitors	Rating	Pg.
Buick Enclave	4	101
Infiniti QX80	–	171
Volvo XC90	8	268

Price Range	Retail	Markup
LS RWD	$47,450	6%
LT RWD	$52,580	6%
LT4WD	$55,580	6%
Premier 4WD	$65,130	6%

Chevrolet Tahoe

Safety Checklist

Crash Test:
  Frontal........................... Good
  Side......................... Very Good
Airbags:
  Torso . . . Standard Front Pelvis/Torso from Seat
  Roll Sensing.........................Yes
  Knee Bolster .... None
Crash Avoidance:
  Collision Avoidance .... Optional CIB
  Blind Spot Detection .... Optional
  Lane Keeping Assist .... Optional
  Backup Camera....................Standard*
  Pedestrian Crash Avoidance........... None
General:
  Auto. Crash Notif. . Op. Assist. & Crash Info-Free
  Day Running Lamps .... Standard
Safety Belt/Restraint:
  Dynamic Head Restraints .... None
  Adjustable Belt......... Optional Front & Rear

Note: As of May 2018, all vehicles are required to have a backup camera.
^Warning feature does not meet government standards.
*Backup camera does not meet government standards.

Cadillac Escalade

Specifications

Drive....................................4WD
Engine 5.3-liter V8
Transmission .... 6-sp. Automatic
Tow Rating (lbs.) .... Very High-8400
Head/Leg Room (in.) .... Very Roomy-42.8/45.3
Interior Space (cu. ft.)............ Roomy-120.8
Cargo Space (cu. ft.) Cramped-15.3
Wheelbase/Length (in.) 116/204

Ratings—10 Best, 1 Worst	
Combo Crash Tests	5
Safety Features	6
Rollover	4
Preventive Maintenance	2
Repair Costs	5
Warranty	6
Fuel Economy	3
Complaints	—
Insurance Costs	10
OVERALL RATING	**4**

Chevrolet Traverse

At-a-Glance

Status/Year Series Started	All New/2018
Twins	Buick Enclave
Body Styles	SUV
Seating	7/8
Anti-Theft Device	Std. Pass. Immobil. & Active Alarm
Parking Index Rating	Very Hard
Where Made	Lansing, Michigan

Fuel Factor:

MPG Rating (city/hwy)	Poor-18/27
Driving Range (mi.)	Average-411
Fuel Type	Regular
Annual Fuel Cost	High-$1735
Gas Guzzler Tax	No
Greenhouse Gas Emissions (tons/yr.)	Average-6.9
Barrels of Oil Used per year	High-15.7

How the Competition Rates

Competitors	Rating	Pg.
Buick Enclave	4	101
Ford Flex	–	142
Volvo XC90	8	268

Price Range	Retail	Markup
LS FWD	$32,050	5%
LT FWD	$34,550	5%
Premier AWD	$47,350	5%
High Country AWD	$52,050	5%

Chevrolet Traverse

Safety Checklist

Crash Test:

Frontal	Average
Side	Poor

Airbags:

Torso	Standard Front Pelvis/Torso from Seat
Roll Sensing	Yes
Knee Bolster	None

Crash Avoidance:

Collision Avoidance	Optional CIB & DBS^
Blind Spot Detection	Optional
Lane Keeping Assist	Optional
Backup Camera	Standard*
Pedestrian Crash Avoidance	Optional

General:

Auto. Crash Notif.	Op. Assist. & Crash Info-Free
Day Running Lamps	Standard

Safety Belt/Restraint:

Dynamic Head Restraints	None
Adjustable Belt	Optional Rear

Note: As of May 2018, all vehicles are required to have a backup camera.
^Warning feature does not meet government standards.
*Backup camera does not meet government standards.

Chevrolet Traverse

Specifications

Drive	FWD
Engine	3.6-liter V6
Transmission	9-sp. Automatic
Tow Rating (lbs.)	Low-5000
Head/Leg Room (in.)	Average-41.3/41
Interior Space (cu. ft.)	Very Roomy-157.3
Cargo Space (cu. ft.)	Roomy-23
Wheelbase/Length (in.)	120.9/204.3

Chevrolet Trax

Small SUV

Ratings—10 Best, 1 Worst

Combo Crash Tests	8
Safety Features	7
Rollover	3
Preventive Maintenance	7
Repair Costs	5
Warranty	6
Fuel Economy	6
Complaints	10
Insurance Costs	10
OVERALL RATING	**10**

Chevrolet Trax

Chevrolet Trax

At-a-Glance

Status/Year Series Started. Unchanged/2015
Twins . . . . Buick Encore
Body Styles . . . . SUV
Seating. 5
Anti-Theft Device . Std. Pass. Immobil. & Active Alarm
Parking Index Rating . . . . Easy
Where Made. . South Korea / San Luis Potosi, Mexico
Fuel Factor:
  MPG Rating (city/hwy) Average-24/30
  Driving Range (mi.) . . . . Very Short-369
  Fuel Type. . . . . .Regular
  Annual Fuel Cost . . . . Low-$1393
  Gas Guzzler Tax . . . . .No
  Greenhouse Gas Emissions (tons/yr.) Low-5.5
  Barrels of Oil Used per year Average-12.2

How the Competition Rates

Competitors	Rating	Pg.
Ford Escape	5	137
Honda HR-V	5	156
Jeep Compass	4	173

Price Range

Price Range	Retail	Markup
LS FWD	$21,000	4%
LT FWD	$22,900	4%
LT AWD	$24,400	4%
Premier AWD	$28,795	4%

Safety Checklist

Crash Test:
  Frontal. . . . . Very Good
  Side. . . . . Average
Airbags:
  Torso . Std Front & Rear Pelvis/Torso from Seat
  Roll Sensing. . . . . .Yes
  Knee Bolster . . . . .Standard Front
Crash Avoidance:
  Collision Avoidance . . . . .Warning Only Optional
  Blind Spot Detection . . . . Optional
  Lane Keeping Assist . . . .Warning Only Optional
  Backup Camera. . . . . .Standard*
  Pedestrian Crash Avoidance . . . . None
General:
  Auto. Crash Notif. . Op. Assist. & Crash Info-Free
  Day Running Lamps . . . . Standard
Safety Belt/Restraint:
  Dynamic Head Restraints . . . . None
  Adjustable Belt. . . . . Optional Front & Rear

Note: As of May 2018, all vehicles are required to have a backup camera.
^Warning feature does not meet government standards.
*Backup camera does not meet government standards.

Chevrolet Trax

Specifications

Drive. . . . . .AWD
Engine 1.4-liter I4
Transmission . . . . 6-sp. Automatic
Tow Rating (lbs.) . . . . –
Head/Leg Room (in.) Cramped-39.6/40.8
Interior Space (cu. ft.). Cramped-92.8
Cargo Space (cu. ft.) Average-18.7
Wheelbase/Length (in.) 100.6/168.5

Ratings—10 Best, 1 Worst

Combo Crash Tests	4
Safety Features	8
Rollover	9
Preventive Maintenance	3
Repair Costs	7
Warranty	6
Fuel Economy	10
Complaints	1
Insurance Costs	10
OVERALL RATING	**7**

Chevrolet Volt

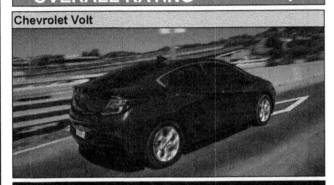
Chevrolet Volt

At-a-Glance

Status/Year Series Started........ Unchanged/2016
Twins .... –
Body Styles .... Sedan
Seating 5
Anti-Theft Device . Std. Pass. Immobil. & Active Alarm
Parking Index Rating .... Easy
Where Made........................ Detroit, MI

Fuel Factor:
MPG Rating (city/hwy) .... Very Good-43/42
Driving Range (mi.) Short-379
Fuel Type............................. Regular
Annual Fuel Cost .... Very Low-$864
Gas Guzzler Tax .... No
Greenhouse Gas Emissions (tons/yr.). Very Low-0.8
Barrels of Oil Used per year .... Very Low-2.0

How the Competition Rates

Competitors	Rating	Pg.
Audi A3	6	83
Ford Fusion Energi	8	145
Toyota Prius Prime	–	250

Price Range	Retail	Markup
LT	$33,220	4%
Premier	$37,570	4%

Safety Checklist

Crash Test:
Frontal............................... Poor
Side.................................. Good
Airbags:
Torso Std. Fr. & Opt. Rr. Pelvis/Torso from Seat
Roll Sensing............................ Yes
Knee Bolster .... Standard Front
Crash Avoidance:
Collision Avoidance ...... Optional CIB & DBS
Blind Spot Detection .... Optional
Lane Keeping Assist .... Optional
Backup Camera.................. Standard*
Pedestrian Crash Avoidance .... None
General:
Auto. Crash Notif. . Op. Assist. & Crash Info-Free
Day Running Lamps .... Standard
Safety Belt/Restraint:
Dynamic Head Restraints .... None
Adjustable Belt..................... None

Note: As of May 2018, all vehicles are required to have a backup camera.
^Warning feature does not meet government standards.
*Backup camera does not meet government standards.

Chevrolet Volt

Specifications

Drive....................................... FWD
Engine 1.5-liter I4
Transmission .... CVT
Tow Rating (lbs.) .... –
Head/Leg Room (in.) Cramped-37.8/42.1
Interior Space (cu. ft.).......... Very Cramped-90
Cargo Space (cu. ft.) .... Very Cramped-10.6
Wheelbase/Length (in.) 106.1/180.4

Chrysler 300

Ratings—10 Best, 1 Worst

Combo Crash Tests	2
Safety Features	5
Rollover	6
Preventive Maintenance	8
Repair Costs	2
Warranty	4
Fuel Economy	4
Complaints	3
Insurance Costs	1
OVERALL RATING	**1**

Chrysler 300

Chrysler 300

At-a-Glance

Status/Year Series Started. Unchanged/2011
Twins . . . . Dodge Charger
Body Styles . . . . Sedan
Seating. 5
Anti-Theft Device . . . . . . Std. Pass. Immobil. & Alarm
Parking Index Rating . . . . Very Hard
Where Made. . . . . Brampton, Ontario
Fuel Factor:
MPG Rating (city/hwy) Poor-19/30
Driving Range (mi.) Average-421
Fuel Type. . . . . Regular
Annual Fuel Cost . . . . Average-$1615
Gas Guzzler Tax . . . . No
Greenhouse Gas Emissions (tons/yr.) High-7.8
Barrels of Oil Used per year High-14.3

How the Competition Rates

Competitors	Rating	Pg.
Buick LaCrosse	5	104
Cadillac XT5	3	108
Toyota Avalon	8	243

Price Range	Retail	Markup
Touring RWD	$28,995	1%
Limited RWD	$36,595	3%
S V6 AWD	$38,295	4%
C V8	$40,995	4%

Safety Checklist

Crash Test:
Frontal. . . . . Very Poor
Side. . . . . Poor
Airbags:
Torso . . . Standard Front Pelvis/Torso from Seat
Roll Sensing. . . . . Yes
Knee Bolster . . . . Standard Driver
Crash Avoidance:
Collision Avoidance . . . . . . Optional CIB & DBS
Blind Spot Detection . . . . Optional
Lane Keeping Assist . . . . Optional^
Backup Camera. . . . . Optional
Pedestrian Crash Avoidance . . . . None
General:
Auto. Crash Notification . . . . None
Day Running Lamps . . . . Standard
Safety Belt/Restraint:
Dynamic Head Restraints . . . . None
Adjustable Belt. . . . . Standard Front

Note: As of May 2018, all vehicles are required to have a backup camera.
^Warning feature does not meet government standards.
*Backup camera does not meet government standards.

Chrysler 300

Specifications

Drive. . . . . RWD
Engine 3.6-liter V6
Transmission . . . . 8-sp. Automatic
Tow Rating (lbs.) . . . . –
Head/Leg Room (in.) Cramped-38.6/41.8
Interior Space (cu. ft.). Roomy-106.3
Cargo Space (cu. ft.) Cramped-16.3
Wheelbase/Length (in.) 120.2/198.6

Ratings—10 Best, 1 Worst

Combo Crash Tests	8
Safety Features	7
Rollover	6
Preventive Maintenance	10
Repair Costs	6
Warranty	4
Fuel Economy	3
Complaints	1
Insurance Costs	10
OVERALL RATING	**8**

Chrysler Pacifica

At-a-Glance

Status/Year Series Started Unchanged/2017
Twins . . . . –
Body Styles . . . . Minivan
Seating 7/8
Anti-Theft Device . . . . . . Std. Pass. Immobil. & Alarm
Parking Index Rating . . . . Very Hard
Where Made . . . . Windsor, Ontario

Fuel Factor:
MPG Rating (city/hwy) Poor-18/28
Driving Range (mi.) Average-407
Fuel Type . . . . .Regular
Annual Fuel Cost . . . . .High-$1714
Gas Guzzler Tax . . . . .No
Greenhouse Gas Emissions (tons/yr.) . . Average-6.9
Barrels of Oil Used per year High-15.0

How the Competition Rates

Competitors	Rating	Pg.
Honda Odyssey	9	157
Kia Sedona	–	180
Toyota Sienna	2	254

Price Range	Retail	Markup
LX	$26,995	0%
Touring L	$35,495	3%
Touring L Plus	$38,695	4%
Limited	$43,695	4%

Chrysler Pacifica

Safety Checklist

Crash Test:
Frontal . . . . Very Good
Side . . . . Poor
Airbags:
Torso . . . Standard Front Pelvis/Torso from Seat
Roll Sensing . . . . .Yes
Knee Bolster . . . . .Standard Front
Crash Avoidance:
Collision Avoidance . . . . . . Optional CIB & DBS
Blind Spot Detection . . . . Optional
Lane Keeping Assist . . . . Optional
Backup Camera . . . . Standard
Pedestrian Crash Avoidance . . . . None
General:
Auto. Crash Notification . . . . None
Day Running Lamps . . . . Standard
Safety Belt/Restraint:
Dynamic Head Restraints . . . . None
Adjustable Belt . . . . Standard Front & Rear

Note: As of May 2018, all vehicles are required to have a backup camera.
^Warning feature does not meet government standards.
*Backup camera does not meet government standards.

Chrysler Pacifica

Specifications

Drive . . . . .FWD
Engine 3.6-liter V6
Transmission . . . . 9-sp. Automatic
Tow Rating (lbs.) Low-3600
Head/Leg Room (in.) Average-40.1/41.1
Interior Space (cu. ft.) . . . . Very Roomy-165
Cargo Space (cu. ft.) . . . . Very Roomy-32.3
Wheelbase/Length (in.) 121.6/203.8

Dodge Challenger

Ratings—10 Best, 1 Worst

Combo Crash Tests	7
Safety Features	2
Rollover	7
Preventive Maintenance	8
Repair Costs	3
Warranty	4
Fuel Economy	4
Complaints	9
Insurance Costs	1
OVERALL RATING	**4**

Dodge Challenger

Dodge Challenger

At-a-Glance

Status/Year Series Started Unchanged/2015
Twins . . . . –
Body Styles . . . . .Coupe
Seating 5
Anti-Theft Device . . . . . Std. Pass. Immobil. & Alarm
Parking Index Rating . . . . Hard
Where Made. . . . . Brampton, Ontario
Fuel Factor:
MPG Rating (city/hwy) Poor-19/30
Driving Range (mi.) Average-421
Fuel Type. . . . . .Regular
Annual Fuel Cost . . . . .Average-$1615
Gas Guzzler Tax . . . . .No
Greenhouse Gas Emissions (tons/yr.) High-7.8
Barrels of Oil Used per year High-14.3

How the Competition Rates

Competitors	Rating	Pg.
Chevrolet Camaro	4	111
Chevrolet Corvette	–	113
Ford Mustang	6	146

Price Range

	Retail	Markup
SXT	$26,995	1%
R/T	$33,495	2%
R/T 392	$38,995	4%
SRT Hellcat	$63,795	3%

Safety Checklist

Crash Test:
  Frontal. . . . . Average
  Side. . . . . Very Good
Airbags:
  Torso . . . Standard Front Pelvis/Torso from Seat
  Roll Sensing. . . . . .Yes
  Knee Bolster . . . . None
Crash Avoidance:
  Collision Avoidance . . . . .Warning Only Optional
  Blind Spot Detection . . . . Optional
  Lane Keeping Assist . . . . None
  Backup Camera. . . . . Optional
  Pedestrian Crash Avoidance . . . . None
General:
  Auto. Crash Notification. . . . . None
  Day Running Lamps . . . . Standard
Safety Belt/Restraint:
  Dynamic Head Restraints . . . . None
  Adjustable Belt. . . . . None

Note: As of May 2018, all vehicles are required to have a backup camera.
^Warning feature does not meet government standards.
*Backup camera does not meet government standards.

Dodge Challenger

Specifications

Drive. . . . . .RWD
Engine 3.6-liter V6
Transmission . . . . 8-sp. Automatic
Tow Rating (lbs.) . . . . Very Low-1000
Head/Leg Room (in.) Average-39.3/42
Interior Space (cu. ft.). Cramped-93.9
Cargo Space (cu. ft.) Cramped-16.2
Wheelbase/Length (in.) 116.2/197.9

Ratings—10 Best, 1 Worst

Combo Crash Tests	3
Safety Features	5
Rollover	8
Preventive Maintenance	8
Repair Costs	7
Warranty	4
Fuel Economy	4
Complaints	3
Insurance Costs	1
OVERALL RATING	**2**

Dodge Charger

At-a-Glance

Status/Year Series Started	Unchanged/2011
Twins	Chrysler 300
Body Styles	Sedan
Seating	5
Anti-Theft Device	Std. Pass. Immobil. & Alarm
Parking Index Rating	Hard
Where Made	Brampton, Ontario

Fuel Factor:

MPG Rating (city/hwy)	Poor-19/31
Driving Range (mi.)	Long-426
Fuel Type	Regular
Annual Fuel Cost	Average-$1597
Gas Guzzler Tax	No
Greenhouse Gas Emissions (tons/yr.)	High-7.8
Barrels of Oil Used per year	High-14.3

How the Competition Rates

Competitors	Rating	Pg.
Buick LaCrosse	5	104
Chevrolet Impala	4	116
Ford Taurus	3	147

Price Range

Price Range	Retail	Markup
SXT	$28,495	1%
AWD GT	$32,495	3%
R/T	$34,995	3%
SRT Hellcat	$66,295	4%

Dodge Charger

Safety Checklist

Crash Test:

Frontal	Very Poor
Side	Average

Airbags:

Torso	Standard Front Pelvis/Torso from Seat
Roll Sensing	Yes
Knee Bolster	Standard Driver

Crash Avoidance:

Collision Avoidance	Optional CIB & DBS
Blind Spot Detection	Optional
Lane Keeping Assist	Optional
Backup Camera	Optional
Pedestrian Crash Avoidance	None

General:

Auto. Crash Notification	None
Day Running Lamps	Standard

Safety Belt/Restraint:

Dynamic Head Restraints	None
Adjustable Belt	Standard Front

Note: As of May 2018, all vehicles are required to have a backup camera.
^Warning feature does not meet government standards.
*Backup camera does not meet government standards.

Dodge Charger

Specifications

Drive	RWD
Engine	3.6-liter V6
Transmission	8-sp. Automatic
Tow Rating (lbs.)	Very Low-1000
Head/Leg Room (in.)	Cramped-38.6/41.8
Interior Space (cu. ft.)	Roomy-104.7
Cargo Space (cu. ft.)	Cramped-16.1
Wheelbase/Length (in.)	120.2/198.4

Dodge Durango

Ratings—10 Best, 1 Worst

Combo Crash Tests	3
Safety Features	7
Rollover	2
Preventive Maintenance	5
Repair Costs	6
Warranty	4
Fuel Economy	3
Complaints	1
Insurance Costs	10
OVERALL RATING	**2**

Dodge Durango

Dodge Durango

At-a-Glance

Status/Year Series Started Unchanged/2011
Twins . . . . –
Body Styles . . . . SUV
Seating 6/7
Anti-Theft Device .Std. Pass. Immob. & Opt. Pass. Alarm
Parking Index Rating . . . . Hard
Where Made . . . . .Detroit, MI

Fuel Factor:
MPG Rating (city/hwy) Poor-18/25
Driving Range (mi.) . . . . Very Long-507
Fuel Type . . . . .Regular
Annual Fuel Cost . . . . .High-$1784
Gas Guzzler Tax . . . . .No
Greenhouse Gas Emissions (tons/yr.) . . Average-7.1
Barrels of Oil Used per year High-15.7

How the Competition Rates

Competitors	Rating	Pg.
Ford Edge	9	136
GMC Acadia	2	149
Jeep Grand Cherokee	4	174

Price Range

	Retail	Markup
SXT RWD	$29,995	0%
GT RWD	$37,795	3%
R/T AWD	$46,295	4%
SRT AWD	$62,995	3%

Safety Checklist

Crash Test:
Frontal . . . . .Very Poor
Side . . . . Average
Airbags:
Torso . . . Standard Front Pelvis/Torso from Seat
Roll Sensing . . . . .Yes
Knee Bolster . . . . Standard Driver
Crash Avoidance:
Collision Avoidance . . . . .Optional CIB & DBS^
Blind Spot Detection . . . . Optional
Lane Keeping Assist . . .Warning Only Optional
Backup Camera . . . . Standard
Pedestrian Crash Avoidance . . . . None
General:
Auto. Crash Notification . . . . None
Day Running Lamps . . . . Standard
Safety Belt/Restraint:
Dynamic Head Restraints . . . . .Standard Front
Adjustable Belt . . . . .Standard Front

Note: As of May 2018, all vehicles are required to have a backup camera.
^Warning feature does not meet government standards.
*Backup camera does not meet government standards.

Dodge Durango

Specifications

Drive . . . . .AWD
Engine 3.6-liter V6
Transmission . . . . 8-sp. Automatic
Tow Rating (lbs.) . . . . Very Low-1350
Head/Leg Room (in.) Cramped-39.9/40.3
Interior Space (cu. ft.) . . . . Very Roomy-133.9
Cargo Space (cu. ft.) Average-17.2
Wheelbase/Length (in.) 119.8/201.2

Ratings—10 Best, 1 Worst

Combo Crash Tests	2
Safety Features	3
Rollover	2
Preventive Maintenance	9
Repair Costs	4
Warranty	4
Fuel Economy	3
Complaints	1
Insurance Costs	8
OVERALL RATING	**1**

Dodge Journey

Dodge Journey

At-a-Glance

Status/Year Series Started Unchanged/2009
Twins . . . . –
Body Styles . . . . SUV
Seating 5/7
Anti-Theft Device . . . . . Std. Pass. Immobil. & Alarm
Parking Index Rating . . . . Hard
Where Made. . . . . Toluca, Mexico
Fuel Factor:
MPG Rating (city/hwy) Poor-19/25
Driving Range (mi.) Long-437
Fuel Type. . . . . Regular
Annual Fuel Cost . . . . High-$1725
Gas Guzzler Tax . . . . No
Greenhouse Gas Emissions (tons/yr.) Very High-9.4
Barrels of Oil Used per year . . . . Very High-17.3

How the Competition Rates

Competitors	Rating	Pg.
Chevrolet Equinox	4	115
Ford Edge	9	136
GMC Acadia	2	149

Price Range	Retail	Markup
SE FWD	$22,495	1%
SXT FWD	$25,695	3%
Crossroad AWD	$31,395	4%
GT AWD	$34,395	4%

Safety Checklist

Crash Test:
Frontal. . . . . Poor
Side . . . . .Very Poor
Airbags:
Torso . . . Standard Front Pelvis/Torso from Seat
Roll Sensing. . . . . .Yes
Knee Bolster . . . . Standard Driver
Crash Avoidance:
Collision Avoidance . . . . None
Blind Spot Detection . . . . None
Lane Keeping Assist . . . . None
Backup Camera. . . . . Optional
Pedestrian Crash Avoidance . . . . None
General:
Auto. Crash Notification . . . . None
Day Running Lamps . . . . Standard
Safety Belt/Restraint:
Dynamic Head Restraints . . . . . .Standard Front
Adjustable Belt. . . . . .Standard Front

Note: As of May 2018, all vehicles are required to have a backup camera.
^Warning feature does not meet government standards.
*Backup camera does not meet government standards.

Dodge Journey

Specifications

Drive. . . . . .FWD
Engine 3.6-liter V6
Transmission . . . . 6-sp. Automatic
Tow Rating (lbs.) . . . . Very Low-2500
Head/Leg Room (in.) Average-40.8/40.8
Interior Space (cu. ft.). Roomy-123.7
Cargo Space (cu. ft.) . . . . Very Cramped-10.7
Wheelbase/Length (in.) 113.8/192.4

Fiat 500 Subcompact

Ratings—10 Best, 1 Worst

Combo Crash Tests	1
Safety Features	1
Rollover	4
Preventive Maintenance	8
Repair Costs	9
Warranty	5
Fuel Economy	7
Complaints	2
Insurance Costs	5
OVERALL RATING	**2**

Fiat 500

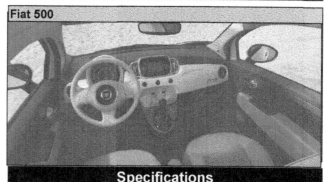

Fiat 500

Safety Checklist

Crash Test:
Frontal . . . . Very Poor
Side . . . . Poor
Airbags:
Torso . . . Standard Front Pelvis/Torso from Seat
Roll Sensing . . . . No
Knee Bolster . . . . Standard Driver
Crash Avoidance:
Collision Avoidance . . . . None
Blind Spot Detection . . . . None
Lane Keeping Assist . . . . None
Backup Camera . . . . None
Pedestrian Crash Avoidance . . . . None
General:
Auto. Crash Notification . . . . None
Day Running Lamps . . . . Standard
Safety Belt/Restraint:
Dynamic Head Restraints . . . . . . Standard Front
Adjustable Belt . . . . None

Note: As of May 2018, all vehicles are required to have a backup camera.
^Warning feature does not meet government standards.
*Backup camera does not meet government standards.

At-a-Glance

Status/Year Series Started Unchanged/2012
Twins . . . . –
Body Styles . . . . Hatchback
Seating 4
Anti-Theft Device . . . . . . Std. Pass. Immobil. & Alarm
Parking Index Rating . . . . Very Easy
Where Made . . . . Toluca, Mexico
Fuel Factor:
MPG Rating (city/hwy) Good-27/34
Driving Range (mi.) . . . . Very Short-312
Fuel Type . . . . Regular
Annual Fuel Cost . . . . Low-$1235
Gas Guzzler Tax . . . . No
Greenhouse Gas Emissions (tons/yr.) . . Average-6.0
Barrels of Oil Used per year Average-11.0

How the Competition Rates

Competitors	Rating	Pg.
Chevrolet Sonic	9	119
Mini Hardtop	6	215
Volkswagen Beetle	3	260

Price Range

Price Range	Retail	Markup
Pop Hatchback	$14,995	0%
Lounge Hatchback	$18,395	1%
Abarth Cabriolet	$21,490	2%
Electric	$31,800	2%

Specifications

Drive . . . . FWD
Engine 1.4-liter I4
Transmission . . . . 6-sp. Automatic
Tow Rating (lbs.) . . . . Very Low-0
Head/Leg Room (in.) Cramped-38.9/40.7
Interior Space (cu. ft.) . . . . Very Cramped-75.5
Cargo Space (cu. ft.) . . . . Very Cramped-9.5
Wheelbase/Length (in.) 90.6/139.6

Ratings—10 Best, 1 Worst

Combo Crash Tests	—
Safety Features	4
Rollover	4
Preventive Maintenance	8
Repair Costs	9
Warranty	5
Fuel Economy	5
Complaints	3
Insurance Costs	5
OVERALL RATING	—

Fiat 500X

Fiat 500X

At-a-Glance

Status/Year Series Started	Unchanged/2015
Twins	—
Body Styles	SUV
Seating	5
Anti-Theft Device	Std. Pass. Immobil. & Alarm
Parking Index Rating	Easy
Where Made	Melfi, Italy

Fuel Factor:

MPG Rating (city/hwy)	Average-22/31
Driving Range (mi.)	Very Short-321
Fuel Type	Regular
Annual Fuel Cost	Low-$1452
Gas Guzzler Tax	No
Greenhouse Gas Emissions (tons/yr.)	Low-5.8
Barrels of Oil Used per year	High-13.2

How the Competition Rates

Competitors	Rating	Pg.
Honda HR-V	5	156
Jeep Compass	4	173
Mazda CX-3	10	199

Price Range

Price Range	Retail	Markup
Pop FWD	$19,995	1%
Trekking FWD	$23,335	3%
Trekking AWD	$25,235	3%
Lounge AWD	$27,035	3%

Safety Checklist

Crash Test:
- Frontal ... —
- Side ... —

Airbags:
- Torso ... Standard Front Pelvis/Torso from Seat
- Roll Sensing ... Yes
- Knee Bolster ... Standard Driver

Crash Avoidance:
- Collision Avoidance ... Optional CIB & DBS[^]
- Blind Spot Detection ... Optional
- Lane Keeping Assist ... Optional[^]
- Backup Camera ... Optional[*]
- Pedestrian Crash Avoidance ... None

General:
- Auto. Crash Notification ... None
- Day Running Lamps ... Standard

Safety Belt/Restraint:
- Dynamic Head Restraints ... None
- Adjustable Belt ... Standard Front

Note: As of May 2018, all vehicles are required to have a backup camera.
^Warning feature does not meet government standards.
*Backup camera does not meet government standards.

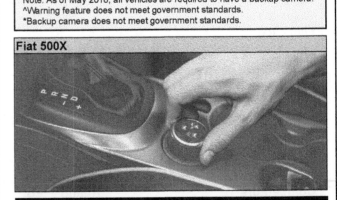

Fiat 500X

Specifications

Drive	FWD
Engine	2.4-liter I4
Transmission	9-sp. Automatic
Tow Rating (lbs.)	Very Low-1000
Head/Leg Room (in.)	Cramped-39.1/41.4
Interior Space (cu. ft.)	Cramped-91.7
Cargo Space (cu. ft.)	Very Cramped-12.2
Wheelbase/Length (in.)	101.2/167.2

Ratings—10 Best, 1 Worst

Combo Crash Tests	3
Safety Features	3
Rollover	4
Preventive Maintenance	9
Repair Costs	7
Warranty	4
Fuel Economy	9
Complaints	2
Insurance Costs	8
OVERALL RATING	**5**

Ford C-MAX

At-a-Glance

Status/Year Series Started	Unchanged/2013
Twins	—
Body Styles	Hatchback
Seating	5
Anti-Theft Device	Std. Pass. Immobil. & Alarm
Parking Index Rating	Average
Where Made	Wayne, MI
Fuel Factor:	
MPG Rating (city/hwy)	Very Good-42/37
Driving Range (mi.)	Very Long-534
Fuel Type	Regular
Annual Fuel Cost	Very Low-$928
Gas Guzzler Tax	No
Greenhouse Gas Emissions (tons/yr.)	Very Low-4.5
Barrels of Oil Used per year	Low-8.2

How the Competition Rates

Competitors	Rating	Pg.
BMW i3	—	95
Chevrolet Volt	7	125
Toyota Prius	7	248

Price Range

	Retail	Markup
SE Hybrid	$24,120	5%
Titanium Hybrid	$27,120	5%
SE Energi	$27,120	5%
Titanium Energi	$30,120	5%

Ford C-MAX

Safety Checklist

Crash Test:
Frontal . . . . Poor
Side . . . . Poor
Airbags:
Torso . . . Standard Front Pelvis/Torso from Seat
Roll Sensing . . . . Yes
Knee Bolster . . . . Standard Driver
Crash Avoidance:
Collision Avoidance . . . . None
Blind Spot Detection . . . . Standard
Lane Keeping Assist . . . . None
Backup Camera . . . . Optional
Pedestrian Crash Avoidance . . . . None
General:
Auto. Crash Notification . . . . . . Dial Assist.-Free
Day Running Lamps . . . . Standard
Safety Belt/Restraint:
Dynamic Head Restraints . . . . None
Adjustable Belt . . . . Standard Front

Note: As of May 2018, all vehicles are required to have a backup camera.
^Warning feature does not meet government standards.
*Backup camera does not meet government standards.

Ford C-MAX

Specifications

Drive	FWD
Engine	2.0-liter I4
Transmission	CVT
Tow Rating (lbs.)	Very Low-0
Head/Leg Room (in.)	Average-41/40.4
Interior Space (cu. ft.)	Average-99.7
Cargo Space (cu. ft.)	Roomy-24.5
Wheelbase/Length (in.)	104.3/173.6

Ratings—10 Best, 1 Worst

Combo Crash Tests	—
Safety Features	4
Rollover	2
Preventive Maintenance	7
Repair Costs	7
Warranty	4
Fuel Economy	7
Complaints	—
Insurance Costs	8
OVERALL RATING	—

Ford EcoSport

Ford EcoSport

At-a-Glance

Status/Year Series Started	All New/2018
Twins	—
Body Styles	SUV
Seating	5
Anti-Theft Device	Std. Pass. Immobil. & Alarm
Parking Index Rating	Very Easy
Where Made	Chennai, India

Fuel Factor:

MPG Rating (city/hwy)	Good-27/29
Driving Range (mi.)	Short-379
Fuel Type	Regular
Annual Fuel Cost	Low-$1319
Gas Guzzler Tax	No
Greenhouse Gas Emissions (tons/yr.)	Low-5.2
Barrels of Oil Used per year	Average-11.8

How the Competition Rates

Competitors	Rating	Pg.
Chevrolet Trax	10	124
Jeep Compass	4	173
Mazda CX-3	10	199

Price Range	Retail	Markup
S	$19,995	4%
SE	$22,905	4%
Titanium	$25,740	4%
SES	$26,740	4%

Safety Checklist

Crash Test:
- Frontal .... —
- Side .... —

Airbags:
- Torso . Std Front & Rear Pelvis/Torso from Seat
- Roll Sensing .... Yes
- Knee Bolster .... Standard Front

Crash Avoidance:
- Collision Avoidance .... None
- Blind Spot Detection .... Optional
- Lane Keeping Assist .... None
- Backup Camera .... *
- Pedestrian Crash Avoidance .... None

General:
- Auto. Crash Notification ...... Dial Assist.-Free
- Day Running Lamps .... Standard

Safety Belt/Restraint:
- Dynamic Head Restraints .... None
- Adjustable Belt .... Standard Front

Note: As of May 2018, all vehicles are required to have a backup camera.
^Warning feature does not meet government standards.
*Backup camera does not meet government standards.

Ford EcoSport

Specifications

Drive	FWD
Engine	2.0-liter I4
Transmission	6-sp. Automatic
Tow Rating (lbs.)	Very Low-1400
Head/Leg Room (in.)	Cramped-39.6/41.1
Interior Space (cu. ft.)	Cramped-91.1
Cargo Space (cu. ft.)	Average-20.9
Wheelbase/Length (in.)	99.2/161.3

Ford Edge

Ratings—10 Best, 1 Worst

Combo Crash Tests	10
Safety Features	8
Rollover	4
Preventive Maintenance	6
Repair Costs	6
Warranty	4
Fuel Economy	4
Complaints	4
Insurance Costs	10
OVERALL RATING	**9**

Ford Edge

At-a-Glance

Status/Year Series Started........ Unchanged/2015
Twins .... –
Body Styles .... SUV
Seating...5
Anti-Theft Device ...... Std. Pass. Immobil. & Alarm
Parking Index Rating .... Very Easy
Where Made..................... Oakville, Ontario
Fuel Factor:
MPG Rating (city/hwy) Poor-20/29
Driving Range (mi.) Long-425
Fuel Type........................... Regular
Annual Fuel Cost .... Average-$1562
Gas Guzzler Tax .... No
Greenhouse Gas Emissions (tons/yr.).. Average-7.1
Barrels of Oil Used per year High-15.7

How the Competition Rates

Competitors	Rating	Pg.
Chevrolet Equinox	4	115
Dodge Journey	1	131
Infiniti QX60	5	170

Price Range	Retail	Markup
SE FWD	$29,220	4%
SEL FWD	$31,955	5%
Titanium AWD	$37,925	5%
Sport AWD	$40,675	5%

Safety Checklist

Crash Test:
Frontal.......................... Very Good
Side.................................. Good
Airbags:
Torso . . . Standard Front Pelvis/Torso from Seat
Roll Sensing........................ Yes
Knee Bolster .... Standard Front
Crash Avoidance:
Collision Avoidance ...... Optional CIB & DBS
Blind Spot Detection .... Optional
Lane Keeping Assist .... Optional
Backup Camera................. Standard
Pedestrian Crash Avoidance.......... None
General:
Auto. Crash Notification...... Dial Assist.-Free
Day Running Lamps .... Standard
Safety Belt/Restraint:
Dynamic Head Restraints .... None
Adjustable Belt................ Standard Front

Note: As of May 2018, all vehicles are required to have a backup camera.
^Warning feature does not meet government standards.
*Backup camera does not meet government standards.

Ford Edge

Specifications

Drive............................... FWD
Engine 2.0-liter I4
Transmission .... 6-sp. Automatic
Tow Rating (lbs.) Low-3500
Head/Leg Room (in.) Roomy-40.2/42.6
Interior Space (cu. ft.).......... Roomy-113.9
Cargo Space (cu. ft.) ..... Very Roomy-39.2
Wheelbase/Length (in.) 112.2/188.1

Ratings—10 Best, 1 Worst

Combo Crash Tests	8
Safety Features	5
Rollover	2
Preventive Maintenance	7
Repair Costs	3
Warranty	4
Fuel Economy	5
Complaints	6
Insurance Costs	5
OVERALL RATING	**6**

Ford Escape

Ford Escape

At-a-Glance

Status/Year Series Started	Unchanged/2013
Twins	Lincoln MKC
Body Styles	SUV
Seating	5
Anti-Theft Device	Std. Pass. Immobil. & Alarm
Parking Index Rating	Average
Where Made	Louisville, Kentucky

Fuel Factor:

MPG Rating (city/hwy)	Average-22/31
Driving Range (mi.)	Short-390
Fuel Type	Regular
Annual Fuel Cost	Low-$1452
Gas Guzzler Tax	No
Greenhouse Gas Emissions (tons/yr.)	Average-7.2
Barrels of Oil Used per year	High-13.2

How the Competition Rates

Competitors	Rating	Pg.
Honda HR-V	5	156
Jeep Cherokee	5	172
Toyota RAV4	9	252

Price Range

	Retail	Markup
S FWD	$23,850	4%
SE FWD	$26,955	5%
SEL 4WD	$29,335	5%
Titanium 4WD	$33,395	5%

Safety Checklist

Crash Test:
- Frontal .... Good
- Side .... Good

Airbags:
- Torso ... Standard Front Pelvis/Torso from Seat
- Roll Sensing .... Yes
- Knee Bolster .... Standard Driver

Crash Avoidance:
- Collision Avoidance ..... Warning Only Optional
- Blind Spot Detection .... Optional
- Lane Keeping Assist .... Optional
- Backup Camera .... Standard
- Pedestrian Crash Avoidance .... None

General:
- Auto. Crash Notification ...... Dial Assist.-Free
- Day Running Lamps .... Standard

Safety Belt/Restraint:
- Dynamic Head Restraints .... None
- Adjustable Belt .... Standard Front

Note: As of May 2018, all vehicles are required to have a backup camera.
^Warning feature does not meet government standards.
*Backup camera does not meet government standards.

Ford Escape

Specifications

Drive	FWD
Engine	2.5-liter I4
Transmission	6-sp. Automatic
Tow Rating (lbs.)	Very Low-1500
Head/Leg Room (in.)	Roomy-39.9/43.1
Interior Space (cu. ft.)	Average-98.1
Cargo Space (cu. ft.)	Very Roomy-34.3
Wheelbase/Length (in.)	105.9/178.1

Ratings—10 Best, 1 Worst

Combo Crash Tests	—
Safety Features	7
Rollover	1
Preventive Maintenance	2
Repair Costs	9
Warranty	4
Fuel Economy	2
Complaints	7
Insurance Costs	10

OVERALL RATING —

Ford Expedition

Ford Expedition

At-a-Glance

Status/Year Series Started. . . . . All New/2003
Twins . . . . Lincoln Navigator
Body Styles . . . . SUV
Seating. 7/8
Anti-Theft Device . . . . . Std. Pass. Immobil. & Alarm
Parking Index Rating . . . . —'
Where Made. . . . . Louisville, Kentucky
Fuel Factor:
MPG Rating (city/hwy) . . . . Very Poor-17/22
Driving Range (mi.) . . . . Very Long-530
Fuel Type. . . . . .Regular
Annual Fuel Cost . . . . .High-$1941
Gas Guzzler Tax . . . . .No
Greenhouse Gas Emissions (tons/yr.) High-7.7
Barrels of Oil Used per year . . . . Very High-17.3

How the Competition Rates

Competitors	Rating	Pg.
Buick Enclave	4	101
Chevrolet Suburban	2	121
Toyota 4Runner	2	241

Price Range	Retail	Markup
XL RWD	$48,095	5%
XLT RWD	$54,705	5%
Limited 4WD	$65,705	5%
Platinum 4WD	$75,855	5%

Safety Checklist

Crash Test:
Frontal. . . . . —
Side. . . . . —
Airbags:
Torso . . . . Standard Front Torso from Seat
Roll Sensing. . . . . .Yes
Knee Bolster . . . . None
Crash Avoidance:
Collision Avoidance . . . . . Optional CIB & DBS
Blind Spot Detection . . . . Optional
Lane Keeping Assist . . . . Optional
Backup Camera. . . . . Standard
Pedestrian Crash Avoidance . . . . Optional
General:
Auto. Crash Notification. . . . . . Dial Assist.-Free
Day Running Lamps . . . . Standard
Safety Belt/Restraint:
Dynamic Head Restraints . . . . None
Adjustable Belt. . . . . .Standard Front

Note: As of May 2018, all vehicles are required to have a backup camera.
^Warning feature does not meet government standards.
*Backup camera does not meet government standards.

Specifications

Drive. 4WD
Engine 3.5-liter V6
Transmission . . . . 10-sp. Automatic
Tow Rating (lbs.) . . . . Very High-9300
Head/Leg Room (in.) . . . . Very Roomy-42/43.9
Interior Space (cu. ft.). . . . . Very Roomy-171.9
Cargo Space (cu. ft.) Average-20.9
Wheelbase/Length (in.) 122.5/210

Ratings—10 Best, 1 Worst	
Combo Crash Tests	5
Safety Features	5
Rollover	3
Preventive Maintenance	5
Repair Costs	6
Warranty	4
Fuel Economy	2
Complaints	2
Insurance Costs	10
OVERALL RATING	**3**

Ford Explorer

Ford Explorer

At-a-Glance

Status/Year Series Started	Unchanged/2011
Twins	–
Body Styles	SUV
Seating	6/7
Anti-Theft Device	Std. Pass. Immobil. & Alarm
Parking Index Rating	Hard
Where Made	Chicago, IL

Fuel Factor:

MPG Rating (city/hwy)	Very Poor-17/23
Driving Range (mi.)	Very Short-358
Fuel Type	Regular
Annual Fuel Cost	High-$1908
Gas Guzzler Tax	No
Greenhouse Gas Emissions (tons/yr.)	Very High-9.5
Barrels of Oil Used per year	Very High-17.3

How the Competition Rates

Competitors	Rating	Pg.
Dodge Journey	1	131
Honda Pilot	8	158
Toyota Highlander	9	247

Price Range	Retail	Markup
Base FWD	$31,660	4%
XLT FWD	$33,775	5%
Limited 4WD	$43,825	5%
Platinum 4WD	$53,235	5%

Safety Checklist

Crash Test:
Frontal . . . . Good
Side . . . . Poor

Airbags:
Torso . . . Standard Front Pelvis/Torso from Seat
Roll Sensing . . . . Yes
Knee Bolster . . . . Standard Passenger

Crash Avoidance:
Collision Avoidance . . . . . Warning Only Optional
Blind Spot Detection . . . . Optional
Lane Keeping Assist . . . . Optional
Backup Camera . . . . Standard
Pedestrian Crash Avoidance . . . . None

General:
Auto. Crash Notification . . . . . . Dial Assist.-Free
Day Running Lamps . . . . Standard

Safety Belt/Restraint:
Dynamic Head Restraints . . . . None
Adjustable Belt . . . . Standard Front

Note: As of May 2018, all vehicles are required to have a backup camera.
^Warning feature does not meet government standards.
*Backup camera does not meet government standards.

Ford Explorer

Specifications

Drive	AWD
Engine	3.5-liter V6
Transmission	6-sp. Automatic
Tow Rating (lbs.)	Low-5000
Head/Leg Room (in.)	Very Roomy-41.4/42.9
Interior Space (cu. ft.)	Very Roomy-151.5
Cargo Space (cu. ft.)	Roomy-21
Wheelbase/Length (in.)	112.8/198.3

Ratings—10 Best, 1 Worst

Combo Crash Tests	10
Safety Features	3
Rollover	2
Preventive Maintenance	8
Repair Costs	8
Warranty	4
Fuel Economy	2
Complaints	10
Insurance Costs	8
OVERALL RATING	**9**

Ford F-150

Ford F-150

At-a-Glance

Status/Year Series Started. Unchanged/2015
Twins . . . . –
Body Styles . . . . Pickup
Seating. 5/6
Anti-Theft Device . . . . . . Std. Pass. Immobil. & Alarm
Parking Index Rating . . . . Very Hard
Where Made. . . . . Dearborn, MI
Fuel Factor:
  MPG Rating (city/hwy) . . . . Very Poor-17/23
  Driving Range (mi.) . . . . Very Long-693
  Fuel Type. . . . . Regular
  Annual Fuel Cost . . . . High-$1908
  Gas Guzzler Tax . . . . No
  Greenhouse Gas Emissions (tons/yr.) Very High-9.5
  Barrels of Oil Used per year . . . . Very High-17.3

How the Competition Rates

Competitors	Rating	Pg.
Chevrolet Silverado	7	118
Ram 1500	2	232
Toyota Tundra	–	256

Price Range

	Retail	Markup
XL Reg. Cab 2WD	$27,680	5%
XLT Supercab 2WD	$37,185	8%
Lariat Supercrew 4WD	$48,220	8%
Platinum Supercrew 4WD	$57,880	8%

Safety Checklist

Crash Test:
  Frontal. . . . . Very Good
  Side. . . . . Very Good
Airbags:
  Torso . . . Standard Front Pelvis/Torso from Seat
  Roll Sensing. . . . . .Yes
  Knee Bolster . . . . None
Crash Avoidance:
  Collision Avoidance . . . . .Warning Only Optional
  Blind Spot Detection . . . . Optional
  Lane Keeping Assist . . . . Optional
  Backup Camera. . . . . Optional
  Pedestrian Crash Avoidance . . . . None
General:
  Auto. Crash Notification . . . . . . Dial Assist.-Free
  Day Running Lamps . . . . Standard
Safety Belt/Restraint:
  Dynamic Head Restraints . . . . None
  Adjustable Belt. . . . . .Standard Front

Note: As of May 2018, all vehicles are required to have a backup camera.
^Warning feature does not meet government standards.
*Backup camera does not meet government standards.

Ford F-150

Specifications

Drive. 4WD
Engine 3.5-liter V6
Transmission . . . . 6-sp. Automatic
Tow Rating (lbs.) . . . . Very High-10700
Head/Leg Room (in.) . . . . Very Roomy-40.8/43.9
Interior Space (cu. ft.). Roomy-116
Cargo Space (cu. ft.) . . . . Very Roomy-62.3
Wheelbase/Length (in.) 141.1/231.9

Ratings—10 Best, 1 Worst

Combo Crash Tests	3
Safety Features	2
Rollover	4
Preventive Maintenance	6
Repair Costs	10
Warranty	4
Fuel Economy	8
Complaints	2
Insurance Costs	3
OVERALL RATING	**2**

Ford Fiesta

Ford Fiesta

At-a-Glance

Status/Year Series Started	Unchanged/2011
Twins	–
Body Styles	Sedan, Hatchback
Seating	5
Anti-Theft Device	Std. Pass. Immobil. & Alarm
Parking Index Rating	Very Easy
Where Made	Cuautitlán, Mexico

Fuel Factor:

MPG Rating (city/hwy)	Good-27/37
Driving Range (mi.)	Short-381
Fuel Type	Regular
Annual Fuel Cost	Low-$1196
Gas Guzzler Tax	No
Greenhouse Gas Emissions (tons/yr.)	Low-5.8
Barrels of Oil Used per year	Average-10.6

How the Competition Rates

Competitors	Rating	Pg.
Chevrolet Sonic	9	119
Hyundai Veloster	6	166
Toyota Yaris	5	257

Price Range	Retail	Markup
S Sedan	$14,130	2%
SE Hatchback	$15,660	2%
Titanium Sedan	$19,120	2%
ST Hatchback	$21,610	2%

Safety Checklist

Crash Test:
- Frontal........................Average
- Side............................Very Poor

Airbags:
- Torso . . . Standard Front Pelvis/Torso from Seat
- Roll Sensing.........................Yes
- Knee Bolster . . . . Standard Driver

Crash Avoidance:
- Collision Avoidance . . . . None
- Blind Spot Detection . . . . None
- Lane Keeping Assist . . . . None
- Backup Camera....................Optional
- Pedestrian Crash Avoidance . . . . None

General:
- Auto. Crash Notification. . . . . . Dial Assist.-Free
- Day Running Lamps . . . . None

Safety Belt/Restraint:
- Dynamic Head Restraints . . . . None
- Adjustable Belt.................Standard Front

Note: As of May 2018, all vehicles are required to have a backup camera.
^Warning feature does not meet government standards.
*Backup camera does not meet government standards.

Ford Fiesta

Specifications

Drive	FWD
Engine	1.6-liter I4
Transmission	6-sp. Automatic
Tow Rating (lbs.)	Very Low-0
Head/Leg Room (in.)	Average-39.1/42.2
Interior Space (cu. ft.)	Very Cramped-85.1
Cargo Space (cu. ft.)	Cramped-14.9
Wheelbase/Length (in.)	98/159.7

Ratings—10 Best, 1 Worst

Combo Crash Tests	—
Safety Features	2
Rollover	3
Preventive Maintenance	6
Repair Costs	6
Warranty	4
Fuel Economy	2
Complaints	3
Insurance Costs	5
OVERALL RATING	**—**

Ford Flex

Ford Flex

At-a-Glance

Status/Year Series Started........Unchanged/2009
Twins..—
Body Styles ....SUV
Seating...6/7
Anti-Theft Device ...... Std. Pass. Immobil. & Alarm
Parking Index Rating ....Very Hard
Where Made..................Oakville, Ontario
Fuel Factor:
MPG Rating (city/hwy)...........Very Poor-16/23
Driving Range (mi.) ....Very Short-345
Fuel Type................................Regular
Annual Fuel Cost ....Very High-$1982
Gas Guzzler Tax ....No
Greenhouse Gas Emissions (tons/yr.).....High-7.7
Barrels of Oil Used per year ......Very High-17.3

How the Competition Rates

Competitors	Rating	Pg.
Buick Enclave	4	101
Chevrolet Tahoe	4	122
Volvo XC90	8	268

Price Range	Retail	Markup
SE FWD	$30,025	4%
SEL AWD	$34,680	5%
Limited FWD	$38,230	5%
Limited AWD	$40,180	5%

Safety Checklist

Crash Test:
Frontal................................—
Side..................................—
Airbags:
Torso .... Standard Front Torso from Seat
Roll Sensing............................Yes
Knee Bolster ....None
Crash Avoidance:
Collision Avoidance .....Warning Only Optional
Blind Spot Detection ....Optional
Lane Keeping Assist ....None
Backup Camera....................Standard
Pedestrian Crash Avoidance...........None
General:
Auto. Crash Notification...... Dial Assist.-Free
Day Running Lamps ....None
Safety Belt/Restraint:
Dynamic Head Restraints ....None
Adjustable Belt.................Standard Front

Note: As of May 2018, all vehicles are required to have a backup camera.
^Warning feature does not meet government standards.
*Backup camera does not meet government standards.

Specifications

Drive.......................................FWD
Engine 3.5-liter V6
Transmission ....6-sp. Automatic
Tow Rating (lbs.) Low-4500
Head/Leg Room (in.) Roomy-41.8/40.8
Interior Space (cu. ft.).......Very Roomy-155.8
Cargo Space (cu. ft.) Average-20
Wheelbase/Length (in.) 117.9/201.8

Ford Focus   Compact

Ratings—10 Best, 1 Worst

Combo Crash Tests	8
Safety Features	3
Rollover	6
Preventive Maintenance	5
Repair Costs	10
Warranty	4
Fuel Economy	8
Complaints	2
Insurance Costs	1
OVERALL RATING	**5**

Ford Focus

Ford Focus

At-a-Glance

Status/Year Series Started........ Unchanged/2012
Twins . . . . –
Body Styles . . . . Sedan, Hatchback
Seating 5
Anti-Theft Device . . . . . . Std. Pass. Immobil. & Alarm
Parking Index Rating . . . . Easy
Where Made. . . . . Wayne, MI

Fuel Factor:
MPG Rating (city/hwy) Good-26/38
Driving Range (mi.) Short-376
Fuel Type. . . . . Regular
Annual Fuel Cost . . . . Low-$1213
Gas Guzzler Tax . . . . No
Greenhouse Gas Emissions (tons/yr.) Low-4.8
Barrels of Oil Used per year Average-10.6

How the Competition Rates

Competitors	Rating	Pg.
Chevrolet Cruze	8	114
Honda Civic	10	153
Mazda Mazda3	6	202

Price Range	Retail	Markup
S Sedan	$16,775	4%
Titanium Sedan	$23,575	5%
ST Hatchback	$24,775	5%
Electric Hatchback	$29,120	5%

Safety Checklist

Crash Test:
Frontal. . . . . Good
Side. . . . . Good

Airbags:
Torso . . . Standard Front Pelvis/Torso from Seat
Roll Sensing. . . . . .Yes
Knee Bolster . . . . Standard Driver

Crash Avoidance:
Collision Avoidance . . . . None
Blind Spot Detection . . . . None
Lane Keeping Assist . . . . Optional
Backup Camera. . . . . Standard
Pedestrian Crash Avoidance . . . . None

General:
Auto. Crash Notification. . . . . . Dial Assist.-Free
Day Running Lamps . . . . None

Safety Belt/Restraint:
Dynamic Head Restraints . . . . None
Adjustable Belt. . . . . .Standard Front

Note: As of May 2018, all vehicles are required to have a backup camera.
^Warning feature does not meet government standards.
*Backup camera does not meet government standards.

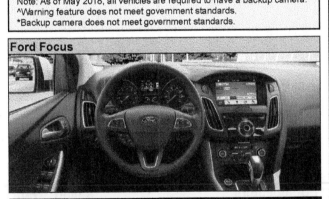

Ford Focus

Specifications

Drive. . . . . .FWD
Engine 2.0-liter I4
Transmission . . . . 6-sp. Automatic
Tow Rating (lbs.) . . . . –
Head/Leg Room (in.) Average-38.3/43.1
Interior Space (cu. ft.). . . . . .Very Cramped-90
Cargo Space (cu. ft.) . . . . Very Cramped-13.2
Wheelbase/Length (in.) 104.3/178.7

Ratings—10 Best, 1 Worst

Combo Crash Tests	3
Safety Features	8
Rollover	7
Preventive Maintenance	8
Repair Costs	9
Warranty	4
Fuel Economy	5
Complaints	4
Insurance Costs	1
OVERALL RATING	**4**

Ford Fusion

Ford Fusion

At-a-Glance

Status/Year Series Started. Unchanged/2013
Twins . . . . Lincoln MKZ
Body Styles . . . . Sedan
Seating. 5
Anti-Theft Device . . . . . . Std. Pass. Immobil. & Alarm
Parking Index Rating . . . . Average
Where Made. . . . . Hermosillo, Mexico
Fuel Factor:
  MPG Rating (city/hwy) Average-21/32
  Driving Range (mi.) Average-410
  Fuel Type. . . . . Regular
  Annual Fuel Cost . . . . .Average-$1479
  Gas Guzzler Tax . . . . No
  Greenhouse Gas Emissions (tons/yr.). . Average-6.9
  Barrels of Oil Used per year Average-12.7

How the Competition Rates

Competitors	Rating	Pg.
Chevrolet Malibu	9	117
Infiniti Q50	3	167
Toyota Camry	8	244

Price Range	Retail	Markup
S	$22,120	5%
SE AWD	$27,045	6%
Sport	$33,605	6%
Platinum	$36,750	6%

Safety Checklist

Crash Test:
  Frontal. . . . . .Very Poor
  Side. . . . . Average
Airbags:
  Torso . . . Standard Front Pelvis/Torso from Seat
  Roll Sensing. . . . . .Yes
  Knee Bolster . . . . .Standard Front
Crash Avoidance:
  Collision Avoidance . . . . . . Optional CIB & DBS
  Blind Spot Detection . . . . Optional
  Lane Keeping Assist . . . . Optional
  Backup Camera. . . . . Standard
  Pedestrian Crash Avoidance . . . . None
General:
  Auto. Crash Notification. . . . . . Dial Assist.-Free
  Day Running Lamps . . . . Standard
Safety Belt/Restraint:
  Dynamic Head Restraints . . . . None
  Adjustable Belt. . . . . Standard Front

Note: As of May 2018, all vehicles are required to have a backup camera.
^Warning feature does not meet government standards.
*Backup camera does not meet government standards.

Ford Fusion

Specifications

Drive. . . . . .FWD
Engine 2.5-liter I4
Transmission . . . . 6-sp. Automatic
Tow Rating (lbs.) . . . . –
Head/Leg Room (in.) Roomy-39.2/44.3
Interior Space (cu. ft.). Roomy-118.8
Cargo Space (cu. ft.) Cramped-16
Wheelbase/Length (in.) 112.2/191.8

Ford Fusion Energi

Ratings—10 Best, 1 Worst

Combo Crash Tests	7
Safety Features	8
Rollover	7
Preventive Maintenance	6
Repair Costs	10
Warranty	4
Fuel Economy	9
Complaints	1
Insurance Costs	5
OVERALL RATING	**8**

Ford Fusion Energi

Ford Fusion Energi

At-a-Glance

Status/Year Series Started. Unchanged/2016
Twins . . . . –
Body Styles . . . . Sedan
Seating 5
Anti-Theft Device . . . . . . Std. Pass. Immobil. & Alarm
Parking Index Rating . . . . Average
Where Made. . . . . Hermosillo, Mexico
Fuel Factor:
  MPG Rating (city/hwy) . . . . Very Good-40/36
  Driving Range (mi.) . . . . Very Long-533
  Fuel Type. . . . . Regular
  Annual Fuel Cost . . . . Very Low-$965
  Gas Guzzler Tax . . . . .No
  Greenhouse Gas Emissions (tons/yr.). Very Low-2.1
  Barrels of Oil Used per year . . . . Very Low-4.9

How the Competition Rates

Competitors	Rating	Pg.
Hyundai Sonata	9	164
Nissan Altima	4	219
Subaru Legacy	7	236

Price Range	Retail	Markup
SE Luxury Energi	$33,120	6%
Titanium Energi	$34,120	6%
Platinum Energi	$41,120	6%

Safety Checklist

Crash Test:
  Frontal. . . . . Very Good
  Side. . . . . .Very Poor
Airbags:
  Torso . . .Standard Front Pelvis/Torso from Seat
  Roll Sensing. . . . . .Yes
  Knee Bolster . . . . .Standard Front
Crash Avoidance:
  Collision Avoidance . . . . . . Optional CIB & DBS
  Blind Spot Detection . . . . Optional
  Lane Keeping Assist . . . . Optional
  Backup Camera. . . . . Standard
  Pedestrian Crash Avoidance . . . . None
General:
  Auto. Crash Notification. . . . . . Dial Assist.-Free
  Day Running Lamps . . . . Standard
Safety Belt/Restraint:
  Dynamic Head Restraints . . . . None
  Adjustable Belt. . . . . .Standard Front

Note: As of May 2018, all vehicles are required to have a backup camera.
^Warning feature does not meet government standards.
*Backup camera does not meet government standards.

Ford Fusion Energi

Specifications

Drive. . . . . .FWD
Engine 2.0-liter I4
Transmission . . . . CVT
Tow Rating (lbs.) . . . . –
Head/Leg Room (in.) Roomy-39.2/44.3
Interior Space (cu. ft.). Average-102.8
Cargo Space (cu. ft.) . . . . Very Cramped-8.2
Wheelbase/Length (in.) 112.2/191.8

Ratings—10 Best, 1 Worst	
Combo Crash Tests	8
Safety Features	3
Rollover	10
Preventive Maintenance	8
Repair Costs	6
Warranty	4
Fuel Economy	3
Complaints	6
Insurance Costs	3
OVERALL RATING	**6**

Ford Mustang

Ford Mustang

At-a-Glance

Status/Year Series Started Appearance Change/2015
Twins .... –
Body Styles .... Coupe, Convertible
Seating 4
Anti-Theft Device ...... Std. Pass. Immobil. & Alarm
Parking Index Rating .... Easy
Where Made........................ Flat Rock, MI
Fuel Factor:
MPG Rating (city/hwy)............... Poor-19/28
Driving Range (mi.) .... Very Short-355
Fuel Type............................. Regular
Annual Fuel Cost.............. Average-$1654
Gas Guzzler Tax .... No
Greenhouse Gas Emissions (tons/yr.)..... High-8.1
Barrels of Oil Used per year High-15.0

How the Competition Rates

Competitors	Rating	Pg.
Chevrolet Camaro	4	111
Chevrolet Corvette	–	113
Dodge Challenger	4	128

Price Range	Retail	Markup
Base Coupe	$24,645	4%
Eco Premium Coupe	$29,645	6%
GT Premium Convertible	$42,145	6%
Shelby GT350	$54,295	6%

Safety Checklist

Crash Test:
Frontal........................ Very Good
Side............................. Poor
Airbags:
Torso . . . Standard Front Pelvis/Torso from Seat
Roll Sensing........................ No
Knee Bolster .... Standard Front
Crash Avoidance:
Collision Avoidance .....Warning Only Optional
Blind Spot Detection .... Optional
Lane Keeping Assist .... None
Backup Camera.................... Standard
Pedestrian Crash Avoidance .... None
General:
Auto. Crash Notification...... Dial Assist.-Free
Day Running Lamps .... None
Safety Belt/Restraint:
Dynamic Head Restraints .... None
Adjustable Belt.................... None

Note: As of May 2018, all vehicles are required to have a backup camera.
^Warning feature does not meet government standards.
*Backup camera does not meet government standards.

Ford Mustang

Specifications

Drive.................................RWD
Engine 3.7-liter V6
Transmission .... 6-sp. Automatic
Tow Rating (lbs.) .... –
Head/Leg Room (in.) Average-37.6/44.5
Interior Space (cu. ft.)........... Very Cramped-84.5
Cargo Space (cu. ft.) .... Very Cramped-13.5
Wheelbase/Length (in.) 107.1/188.5

Ford Taurus — Large

Ratings—10 Best, 1 Worst

Combo Crash Tests	6
Safety Features	3
Rollover	6
Preventive Maintenance	5
Repair Costs	7
Warranty	4
Fuel Economy	3
Complaints	7
Insurance Costs	1
OVERALL RATING	**3**

Ford Taurus

Ford Taurus

At-a-Glance

Status/Year Series Started........Unchanged/2010
Twins ....–
Body Styles ....Sedan
Seating.....................................5
Anti-Theft Device ...... Std. Pass. Immobil. & Alarm
Parking Index Rating ....Very Hard
Where Made........................Chicago, IL
Fuel Factor:
MPG Rating (city/hwy)...............Poor-19/29
Driving Range (mi.) Long-427
Fuel Type...............................Regular
Annual Fuel Cost...............Average-$1634
Gas Guzzler Tax ....No
Greenhouse Gas Emissions (tons/yr.).....High-7.8
Barrels of Oil Used per year High-14.3

How the Competition Rates

Competitors	Rating	Pg.
Buick LaCrosse	5	104
Chevrolet Impala	4	116
Toyota Avalon	8	243

Price Range

Price Range	Retail	Markup
SE	$27,595	6%
SEL	$30,025	6%
Limited AWD	$38,955	6%
SHO AWD	$42,270	5%

Safety Checklist

Crash Test:
Frontal.........................Very Good
Side............................Very Poor
Airbags:
Torso .... Standard Front Torso from Seat
Roll Sensing........................Yes
Knee Bolster ....None
Crash Avoidance:
Collision Avoidance .....Warning Only Optional
Blind Spot Detection ....Optional
Lane Keeping Assist ....Optional
Backup Camera....................Standard
Pedestrian Crash Avoidance ....None
General:
Auto. Crash Notification...... Dial Assist.-Free
Day Running Lamps ....None
Safety Belt/Restraint:
Dynamic Head Restraints ....None
Adjustable Belt................Standard Front

Note: As of May 2018, all vehicles are required to have a backup camera.
^Warning feature does not meet government standards.
*Backup camera does not meet government standards.

Ford Taurus

Specifications

Drive.......................................FWD
Engine 3.5-liter V6
Transmission ....6-sp. Automatic
Tow Rating (lbs.) ....Very Low-1000
Head/Leg Room (in.).........Cramped-39/41.9
Interior Space (cu. ft.)............Average-102.2
Cargo Space (cu. ft.) Average-20.1
Wheelbase/Length (in.) 112.9/202.9

Genesis G80

Large

Ratings—10 Best, 1 Worst

Combo Crash Tests	—
Safety Features	10
Rollover	7
Preventive Maintenance	3
Repair Costs	4
Warranty	10
Fuel Economy	3
Complaints	10
Insurance Costs	—

OVERALL RATING —

Genesis G80

Genesis G80

At-a-Glance

Status/Year Series Started Appearance Change/2017
Twins . . . . —
Body Styles . . . . Sedan
Seating 5
Anti-Theft Device . Std. Pass. Immobil. & Active Alarm
Parking Index Rating . . . . Average
Where Made . . . . Ulsan, South Korea
Fuel Factor:
  MPG Rating (city/hwy) Poor-19/27
  Driving Range (mi.) Long-445
  Fuel Type . . . . Regular
  Annual Fuel Cost . . . . High-$1676
  Gas Guzzler Tax . . . . No
  Greenhouse Gas Emissions (tons/yr.) . . Average-6.8
  Barrels of Oil Used per year High-15.0

How the Competition Rates

Competitors	Rating	Pg.
Acura TLX	9	82
Lexus ES	5	187
Lincoln MKZ	4	197

Price Range

Price Range	Retail	Markup
3.8L V6	$41,750	6%
3.8L V6 AWD	$44,250	6%
3.3L Turbo V6 Sport	$55,250	7%
5.0L V8 AWD	$59,500	7%

Safety Checklist

Crash Test:
  Frontal . . . . —
  Side . . . . —
Airbags:
  Torso Std. Fr. & Opt. Rr. Pelvis/Torso from Seat
  Roll Sensing . . . . Yes
  Knee Bolster . . . . Standard Driver
Crash Avoidance:
  Collision Avoidance . . . . . . Standard CIB & DBS
  Blind Spot Detection . . . . Standard
  Lane Keeping Assist . . . . Standard
  Backup Camera . . . . Standard*
  Pedestrian Crash Avoidance . . . . None
General:
  Auto. Crash Notification . . . Operator Assist.-Fee
  Day Running Lamps . . . . Standard
Safety Belt/Restraint:
  Dynamic Head Restraints . . . . None
  Adjustable Belt . . . . Standard Front

Note: As of May 2018, all vehicles are required to have a backup camera.
^Warning feature does not meet government standards.
*Backup camera does not meet government standards.

Genesis G80

Specifications

Drive . . . . RWD
Engine 3.8-liter V6
Transmission . . . . 8-sp. Automatic
Tow Rating (lbs.) . . . . —
Head/Leg Room (in.) . . . . Very Roomy-41.1/45.7
Interior Space (cu. ft.) Roomy-107.7
Cargo Space (cu. ft.) Cramped-15.3
Wheelbase/Length (in.) 118.5/196.5

Ratings—10 Best, 1 Worst

Combo Crash Tests	3
Safety Features	7
Rollover	4
Preventive Maintenance	2
Repair Costs	3
Warranty	5
Fuel Economy	3
Complaints	2
Insurance Costs	10
OVERALL RATING	**2**

GMC Acadia

GMC Acadia

At-a-Glance

Status/Year Series Started	Unchanged/2017
Twins	Cadillac XT5
Body Styles	SUV
Seating	5/6/7
Anti-Theft Device	Std. Pass. Immobil. & Active Alarm
Parking Index Rating	Hard
Where Made	Lansing, MI

Fuel Factor:

MPG Rating (city/hwy)	Poor-18/25
Driving Range (mi.)	Short-391
Fuel Type	Regular
Annual Fuel Cost	High-$1784
Gas Guzzler Tax	No
Greenhouse Gas Emissions (tons/yr.)	Average-7.0
Barrels of Oil Used per year	High-15.7

How the Competition Rates

Competitors	Rating	Pg.
Lincoln MKX	5	196
Mitsubishi Outlander	4	217
Nissan Rogue	3	227

Price Range	Retail	Markup
SLE1 FWD	$32,560	5%
SLT1 FWD	$38,460	5%
SLT2 AWD	$43,860	5%
Denali AWD	$47,020	5%

Safety Checklist

Crash Test:

Frontal	Poor
Side	Very Poor

Airbags:

Torso	Standard Front Pelvis/Torso from Seat
Roll Sensing	Yes
Knee Bolster	Standard Driver

Crash Avoidance:

Collision Avoidance	Optional CIB & DBS
Blind Spot Detection	Optional
Lane Keeping Assist	Optional
Backup Camera	Standard*
Pedestrian Crash Avoidance	Optional

General:

Auto. Crash Notif.. Op. Assist. & Crash Info	Free
Day Running Lamps	Standard

Safety Belt/Restraint:

Dynamic Head Restraints	None
Adjustable Belt	Optional Front

Note: As of May 2018, all vehicles are required to have a backup camera.
^Warning feature does not meet government standards.
*Backup camera does not meet government standards.

GMC Acadia

Specifications

Drive	FWD
Engine	3.6-liter V6
Transmission	6-sp. Automatic
Tow Rating (lbs.)	Low-4000
Head/Leg Room (in.)	Average-40.3/41
Interior Space (cu. ft.)	Very Roomy-143.8
Cargo Space (cu. ft.)	Very Cramped-12.8
Wheelbase/Length (in.)	112.5/193.6

Ratings—10 Best, 1 Worst

Combo Crash Tests	9
Safety Features	3
Rollover	3
Preventive Maintenance	1
Repair Costs	5
Warranty	5
Fuel Economy	2
Complaints	6
Insurance Costs	10
OVERALL RATING	**5**

GMC Sierra

GMC Sierra

At-a-Glance

Status/Year Series Started........ Unchanged/2018
Twins .... Chevrolet Silverado
Body Styles .... Pickup
Seating.................................... 5/6
Anti-Theft Device . Std. Pass. Immobil. & Active Alarm
Parking Index Rating .... Very Hard
Where Made.................... Fort Wayne, IN
Fuel Factor:
  MPG Rating (city/hwy) .... Very Poor-16/22
  Driving Range (mi.) .... Very Long-474
  Fuel Type........................... Regular
  Annual Fuel Cost .... Very High-$2015
  Gas Guzzler Tax .... No
  Greenhouse Gas Emissions (tons/yr.)..... High-8.1
  Barrels of Oil Used per year .... Very High-18.3

How the Competition Rates

Competitors	Rating	Pg.
Chevrolet Silverado	7	118
Ford F-150	9	140
Toyota Tundra	–	256

Price Range	Retail	Markup
Base Reg. Cab 2WD	$29,095	5%
SLE Dbl. Cab 2WD	$38,010	7%
SLT Dbl. Cab 4WD	$45,780	7%
Denali Crew Cab 4WD	$56,055	7%

Safety Checklist

Crash Test:
  Frontal.......................... Good
  Side............................. Good
Airbags:
  Torso . . . Standard Front Pelvis/Torso from Seat
  Roll Sensing......................Yes
  Knee Bolster .... None
Crash Avoidance:
  Collision Avoidance .... Optional CIB
  Blind Spot Detection .... None
  Lane Keeping Assist .... Optional
  Backup Camera.................... Optional*
  Pedestrian Crash Avoidance .... None
General:
  Auto. Crash Notif.. Op. Assist. & Crash Info-Free
  Day Running Lamps .... Standard
Safety Belt/Restraint:
  Dynamic Head Restraints .... None
  Adjustable Belt......... Optional Front & Rear

^Warning feature does not meet government standards.
*Backup camera does not meet government standards.

GMC Sierra

Specifications

Drive.................................4WD
Engine 5.3-liter V8
Transmission .... 8-sp. Automatic
Tow Rating (lbs.) .... Very High-11800
Head/Leg Room (in.) .... Very Roomy-42.8/45.2
Interior Space (cu. ft.).................... –
Cargo Space (cu. ft.) .... Very Roomy-61
Wheelbase/Length (in.) 143.5/229.5

GMC Terrain

Small SUV

GMC Terrain

Ratings—10 Best, 1 Worst	
Combo Crash Tests	6
Safety Features	4
Rollover	4
Preventive Maintenance	1
Repair Costs	3
Warranty	5
Fuel Economy	7
Complaints	8
Insurance Costs	10
OVERALL RATING	**5**

GMC Terrain

Safety Checklist

Crash Test:
Frontal.........................Very Good
Side..............................Very Poor
Airbags:
Torso . . .Standard Front Pelvis/Torso from Seat
Roll Sensing............................Yes
Knee Bolster ....None
Crash Avoidance:
Collision Avoidance ....Optional CIB
Blind Spot Detection ....Optional
Lane Keeping Assist ....Optional
Backup Camera....................Standard*
Pedestrian Crash Avoidance ....None
General:
Auto. Crash Notif.. Op. Assist. & Crash Info-Free
Day Running Lamps ....Standard
Safety Belt/Restraint:
Dynamic Head Restraints ....None
Adjustable Belt................Standard Rear

^Warning feature does not meet government standards.
*Backup camera does not meet government standards.

At-a-Glance
Status/Year Series Started............All New/2010
Twins ....Chevrolet Equinox
Body Styles ....SUV
Seating 5
Anti-Theft Device .Std. Pass. Immobil. & Active Alarm
Parking Index Rating ....Average
Where Made...................Ingersoll, Ontario
Fuel Factor:
MPG Rating (city/hwy)............Good-26/30
Driving Range (mi.) Average-412
Fuel Type........................Regular
Annual Fuel Cost...............Low-$1329
Gas Guzzler Tax ....No
Greenhouse Gas Emissions (tons/yr.).....Low-5.2
Barrels of Oil Used per year Average-11.8

GMC Terrain

How the Competition Rates
Competitors	Rating	Pg.
Ford Escape	5	137
Honda CR-V	10	154
Hyundai Tucson	8	165

Price Range	Retail	Markup
SL FWD	$24,995	1%
SLE FWD	$27,820	5%
SLT AWD	$33,070	5%
Denali AWD	$39,270	5%

Specifications
Drive.......................................FWD
Engine 1.5-liter I4
Transmission ....9-sp. Automatic
Tow Rating (lbs.) ....Very Low-1500
Head/Leg Room (in.) Cramped-40/40.9
Interior Space (cu. ft.)...........Average-103.2
Cargo Space (cu. ft.) Roomy-29.6
Wheelbase/Length (in.) 107.3/182.3

Honda Accord

Ratings—10 Best, 1 Worst

Combo Crash Tests	—
Safety Features	9
Rollover	7
Preventive Maintenance	10
Repair Costs	6
Warranty	2
Fuel Economy	6
Complaints	—
Insurance Costs	8
OVERALL RATING	—

Honda Accord

Honda Accord

At-a-Glance

Status/Year Series Started. . . . . All New/2018
Twins . . . . —
Body Styles . . . . Sedan
Seating 5
Anti-Theft Device . . . . . . Std. Pass. Immobil. & Alarm
Parking Index Rating . . . . Hard
Where Made. Marysville, OH
Fuel Factor:
 MPG Rating (city/hwy) Average-23/34
 Driving Range (mi.) Short-398
 Fuel Type . . . . Regular
 Annual Fuel Cost . . . . Low-$1365
 Gas Guzzler Tax . . . . No
 Greenhouse Gas Emissions (tons/yr.) Low-5.5
 Barrels of Oil Used per year Average-12.2

How the Competition Rates

Competitors	Rating	Pg.
Ford Fusion	4	144
Nissan Altima	4	219
Toyota Camry	8	244

Price Range	Retail	Markup
LX Sedan MT	$22,335	9%
EX Sedan AT	$26,530	9%
EX-L Coupe V6 AT	$31,175	9%
Touring Sedan V6 AT	$34,830	9%

Safety Checklist

Crash Test:
 Frontal. . . . . —
 Side. . . . . —
Airbags:
 Torso . . . Standard Front Pelvis/Torso from Seat
 Roll Sensing. . . . . Yes
 Knee Bolster . . . . Standard Front
Crash Avoidance:
 Collision Avoidance . . . . . . Optional CIB & DBS^
 Blind Spot Detection . . . . Optional
 Lane Keeping Assist . . . . Optional
 Backup Camera. . . . . Standard
 Pedestrian Crash Avoidance . . . . Standard
General:
 Auto. Crash Notification. . . . . . Dial Assist.-Free
 Day Running Lamps . . . . Standard
Safety Belt/Restraint:
 Dynamic Head Restraints . . . . None
 Adjustable Belt. . . . . Standard Front

Note: As of May 2018, all vehicles are required to have a backup camera.
^Warning feature does not meet government standards.
*Backup camera does not meet government standards.

Honda Accord

Specifications

Drive. . . . . FWD
Engine 2.0-liter I4
Transmission . . . . CVT
Tow Rating (lbs.) . . . . —
Head/Leg Room (in.) Average-39.5/42.3
Interior Space (cu. ft.). Roomy-105.6
Cargo Space (cu. ft.) Cramped-16.7
Wheelbase/Length (in.) 111.4/192.2

Ratings—10 Best, 1 Worst	
Combo Crash Tests	5
Safety Features	6
Rollover	9
Preventive Maintenance	10
Repair Costs	8
Warranty	2
Fuel Economy	9
Complaints	8
Insurance Costs	10
OVERALL RATING	**10**

Honda Civic

At-a-Glance

Status/Year Series Started........ Unchanged/2016
Twins .... –
Body Styles .... Coupe
Seating................................. 5
Anti-Theft Device ...... Std. Pass. Immobil. & Alarm
Parking Index Rating .... Easy
Where Made...... Greensburg, IN / Alliston, Ontario
Fuel Factor:
  MPG Rating (city/hwy) .... Very Good-31/41
  Driving Range (mi.) Long-432
  Fuel Type........................... Regular
  Annual Fuel Cost............. Very Low-$1055
  Gas Guzzler Tax .... No
  Greenhouse Gas Emissions (tons/yr.). Very Low-4.2
  Barrels of Oil Used per year Low-9.4

How the Competition Rates

Competitors	Rating	Pg.
Nissan Sentra	5	228
Toyota Corolla	8	245
Volkswagen Jetta	7	262

Price Range	Retail	Markup
LX Coupe MT	$19,150	8%
EX Sedan AT	$21,140	8%
EX-L Sedan w/Sensing	$24,800	8%
Touring Sedan	$26,600	8%

Honda Civic

Safety Checklist

Crash Test:
  Frontal............................ Average
  Side.............................. Poor
Airbags:
  Torso . . . Standard Front Pelvis/Torso from Seat
  Roll Sensing........................ Yes
  Knee Bolster .... None
Crash Avoidance:
  Collision Avoidance ...... Optional CIB & DBS
  Blind Spot Detection .... None
  Lane Keeping Assist .... Optional
  Backup Camera.................. Standard
  Pedestrian Crash Avoidance .... Optional
General:
  Auto. Crash Notification...... Dial Assist.-Free
  Day Running Lamps .... Standard
Safety Belt/Restraint:
  Dynamic Head Restraints .... None
  Adjustable Belt.............. Standard Front

Note: As of May 2018, all vehicles are required to have a backup camera.
^Warning feature does not meet government standards.
*Backup camera does not meet government standards.

Honda Civic

Specifications

Drive................................. FWD
Engine 1.8-liter I4
Transmission .... CVT
Tow Rating (lbs.) .... –
Head/Leg Room (in.) Average-39.3/42.3
Interior Space (cu. ft.)............ Cramped-94.8
Cargo Space (cu. ft.) Cramped-15.1
Wheelbase/Length (in.) 106.3/179.4

Ratings—10 Best, 1 Worst

Combo Crash Tests	9
Safety Features	7
Rollover	4
Preventive Maintenance	10
Repair Costs	8
Warranty	2
Fuel Economy	7
Complaints	7
Insurance Costs	10
OVERALL RATING	**10**

Honda CR-V

Honda CR-V

Honda CR-V

At-a-Glance

Status/Year Series Started. Unchanged/2017
Twins . . . . –
Body Styles . . . . SUV
Seating. 5
Anti-Theft Device . . . . . . Std. Pass. Immobil. & Alarm
Parking Index Rating . . . . Easy
Where Made. . . . . East Liberty, OH
Fuel Factor:
  MPG Rating (city/hwy) Good-26/32
  Driving Range (mi.) Short-398
  Fuel Type. . . . . .Regular
  Annual Fuel Cost . . . . Low-$1294
  Gas Guzzler Tax . . . . .No
  Greenhouse Gas Emissions (tons/yr.). Low-5.2
  Barrels of Oil Used per year Average-11.8

How the Competition Rates

Competitors	Rating	Pg.
Ford Escape	5	137
Jeep Cherokee	5	172
Toyota RAV4	9	252

Price Range	Retail	Markup
LX 2WD	$24,045	6%
EX 2WD	$26,695	7%
EX-L AWD	$30,495	7%
Touring AWD	$33,695	7%

Safety Checklist

Crash Test:
  Frontal. . . . . Very Good
  Side. . . . . Good
Airbags:
  Torso . . . Standard Front Pelvis/Torso from Seat
  Roll Sensing. . . . . .Yes
  Knee Bolster . . . . None
Crash Avoidance:
  Collision Avoidance . . . . . . Optional CIB & DBS
  Blind Spot Detection . . . . Optional
  Lane Keeping Assist . . . . Optional
  Backup Camera. . . . . Standard
  Pedestrian Crash Avoidance . . . . Optional
General:
  Auto. Crash Notification. . . . . . Dial Assist.-Free
  Day Running Lamps . . . . Standard
Safety Belt/Restraint:
  Dynamic Head Restraints . . . . None
  Adjustable Belt. . . . . .Standard Front

Note: As of May 2018, all vehicles are required to have a backup camera.
^Warning feature does not meet government standards.
*Backup camera does not meet government standards.

Honda CR-V

Specifications

Drive. . . . . .FWD
Engine 2.4-liter I4
Transmission . . . . CVT
Tow Rating (lbs.) . . . . Very Low-1500
Head/Leg Room (in.) . . . . .Very Cramped-38/41.3
Interior Space (cu. ft.). Average-102.9
Cargo Space (cu. ft.) . . . . Very Roomy-39.2
Wheelbase/Length (in.) 104.7/180.6

Ratings—10 Best, 1 Worst	
Combo Crash Tests	9
Safety Features	4
Rollover	4
Preventive Maintenance	10
Repair Costs	9
Warranty	2
Fuel Economy	9
Complaints	8
Insurance Costs	5
OVERALL RATING	**10**

Honda Fit

Honda Fit

At-a-Glance

Status/Year Series Started Appearance Change/2015
Twins . . . . –
Body Styles . . . . Sedan, Hatchback
Seating 5
Anti-Theft Device . . . . . . Std. Pass. Immobil. & Alarm
Parking Index Rating . . . . .Very Easy
Where Made. . . . . .Celaya, Mexico
Fuel Factor:
MPG Rating (city/hwy) . . . . Very Good-33/41
Driving Range (mi.) Short-383
Fuel Type. . . . . .Regular
Annual Fuel Cost . . . . Very Low-$1016
Gas Guzzler Tax . . . . .No
Greenhouse Gas Emissions (tons/yr.) Low-5.0
Barrels of Oil Used per year Low-9.1

How the Competition Rates

Competitors	Rating	Pg.
Chevrolet Spark	5	120
Nissan Versa	1	230
Toyota Yaris	5	257

Price Range	Retail	Markup
LX MT	$16,190	3%
EX MT	$18,160	3%
EX AT	$18,960	3%
EX-L AT w/Nav	$21,520	3%

Safety Checklist

Crash Test:
Frontal. . . . . Good
Side. . . . . Good
Airbags:
Torso . . . Standard Front Pelvis/Torso from Seat
Roll Sensing. . . . . .Yes
Knee Bolster . . . . None
Crash Avoidance:
Collision Avoidance . . . . . . Optional CIB & DBS
Blind Spot Detection . . . . None
Lane Keeping Assist . . . . Optional
Backup Camera. . . . . Standard
Pedestrian Crash Avoidance . . . . None
General:
Auto. Crash Notification. . . . . . Dial Assist.-Free
Day Running Lamps . . . . None
Safety Belt/Restraint:
Dynamic Head Restraints . . . . None
Adjustable Belt. . . . . .Standard Front

Note: As of May 2018, all vehicles are required to have a backup camera.
^Warning feature does not meet government standards.
*Backup camera does not meet government standards.

Honda Fit

Specifications

Drive. . . . . .FWD
Engine 1.5-liter I4
Transmission . . . . CVT
Tow Rating (lbs.) . . . . –
Head/Leg Room (in.) Cramped-39.5/41.4
Interior Space (cu. ft.). Cramped-95.7
Cargo Space (cu. ft.) Cramped-16.6
Wheelbase/Length (in.) 99.6/160

Ratings—10 Best, 1 Worst

Combo Crash Tests	3
Safety Features	2
Rollover	4
Preventive Maintenance	7
Repair Costs	8
Warranty	2
Fuel Economy	8
Complaints	6
Insurance Costs	10
OVERALL RATING	**5**

Honda HR-V

Honda HR-V

At-a-Glance

Status/Year Series Started Unchanged/2016
Twins . . . . –
Body Styles . . . . SUV
Seating 5
Anti-Theft Device . . . . . . Std. Pass. Immobil. & Alarm
Parking Index Rating . . . . Easy
Where Made. .Celaya, Mexico
Fuel Factor:
  MPG Rating (city/hwy) Good-28/34
  Driving Range (mi.) Average-401
  Fuel Type. . . . . .Regular
  Annual Fuel Cost . . . . Low-$1208
  Gas Guzzler Tax . . . . .No
  Greenhouse Gas Emissions (tons/yr.) Low-4.7
  Barrels of Oil Used per year Average-10.6

How the Competition Rates

Competitors	Rating	Pg.
Chevrolet Trax	10	124
Jeep Renegade	1	175
Mazda CX-5	4	200

Price Range

Price Range	Retail	Markup
LX FWD MT	$19,570	3%
LX AWD AT	$21,670	3%
EX FWD AT	$22,420	3%
EX-L AWD w/Nav	$26,340	3%

Safety Checklist

Crash Test:
  Frontal. . . . . Poor
  Side. . . . . Average
Airbags:
  Torso . . . Standard Front Pelvis/Torso from Seat
  Roll Sensing. . . . . .Yes
  Knee Bolster . . . . None
Crash Avoidance:
  Collision Avoidance . . . . None
  Blind Spot Detection . . . . None
  Lane Keeping Assist . . . . None
  Backup Camera. . . . . Standard
  Pedestrian Crash Avoidance . . . . None
General:
  Auto. Crash Notification . . . . . . Dial Assist.-Free
  Day Running Lamps . . . . Standard
Safety Belt/Restraint:
  Dynamic Head Restraints . . . . None
  Adjustable Belt. . . . . .Standard Front

Note: As of May 2018, all vehicles are required to have a backup camera.
^Warning feature does not meet government standards.
*Backup camera does not meet government standards.

Honda HR-V

Specifications

Drive. . . . . .FWD
Engine 1.8-liter I4
Transmission . . . . CVT
Tow Rating (lbs.) . . . . –
Head/Leg Room (in.) Cramped-39.5/41.2
Interior Space (cu. ft.). Average-100.1
Cargo Space (cu. ft.) Roomy-24.3
Wheelbase/Length (in.) 102.8/169.1

Ratings—10 Best, 1 Worst

Combo Crash Tests	7
Safety Features	10
Rollover	5
Preventive Maintenance	9
Repair Costs	8
Warranty	2
Fuel Economy	3
Complaints	—
Insurance Costs	10
OVERALL RATING	**9**

Honda Odyssey

Honda Odyssey

At-a-Glance

Status/Year Series Started. . . . . All New/2018
Twins . . . . —
Body Styles . . . . Minivan
Seating. 7
Anti-Theft Device . . . . . Std. Pass. Immobil. & Alarm
Parking Index Rating . . . . Very Hard
Where Made. . . . . Lincoln, Alabama
Fuel Factor:
MPG Rating (city/hwy) Poor-19/28
Driving Range (mi.) Long-433
Fuel Type. . . . . .Regular
Annual Fuel Cost. . . . . .Average-$1654
Gas Guzzler Tax . . . . .No
Greenhouse Gas Emissions (tons/yr.). . Average-6.7
Barrels of Oil Used per year High-15.0

How the Competition Rates

Competitors	Rating	Pg.
Chrysler Pacifica	8	127
Kia Sedona	–	180
Toyota Sienna	2	254

Price Range	Retail	Markup
LX	$29,990	9%
EX	$33,860	9%
EX-L w/Nav	$39,360	9%
Touring	$44,510	9%

Safety Checklist

Crash Test:
Frontal. . . . . Good
Side. . . . . Good
Airbags:
Torso . . . Standard Front Pelvis/Torso from Seat
Roll Sensing. . . . . .Yes
Knee Bolster . . . . Standard Front
Crash Avoidance:
Collision Avoidance . . . . . . Optional CIB & DBS
Blind Spot Detection . . . . Optional
Lane Keeping Assist . . . . Optional
Backup Camera. . . . . Standard
Pedestrian Crash Avoidance . . . . Optional
General:
Auto. Crash Notification. . . . . Dial Assist.-Free
Day Running Lamps . . . . Standard
Safety Belt/Restraint:
Dynamic Head Restraints . . . . .Standard Front
Adjustable Belt. . . . . .Standard Front

Note: As of May 2018, all vehicles are required to have a backup camera.
^Warning feature does not meet government standards.
*Backup camera does not meet government standards.

Honda Odyssey

Specifications

Drive. . . . . .FWD
Engine 3.5-liter V6
Transmission . . . . 9-sp. Automatic
Tow Rating (lbs.) . . . . –
Head/Leg Room (in.) Average-40.7/40.9
Interior Space (cu. ft.). . . . . Very Roomy-163.6
Cargo Space (cu. ft.) . . . . Very Roomy-32.8
Wheelbase/Length (in.) 118.1/203.2

Honda Pilot   Medium SUV

Honda Pilot

Ratings—10 Best, 1 Worst

Combo Crash Tests	8
Safety Features	6
Rollover	4
Preventive Maintenance	10
Repair Costs	7
Warranty	2
Fuel Economy	3
Complaints	4
Insurance Costs	10
OVERALL RATING	**8**

Honda Pilot

At-a-Glance

Status/Year Series Started	Unchanged/2016
Twins	Acura MDX
Body Styles	SUV
Seating	8
Anti-Theft Device	Std. Pass. Immobil. & Alarm
Parking Index Rating	Hard
Where Made	Lincoln, AL

Fuel Factor:

MPG Rating (city/hwy)	Poor-19/27
Driving Range (mi.)	Long-428
Fuel Type	Regular
Annual Fuel Cost	High-$1676
Gas Guzzler Tax	No
Greenhouse Gas Emissions (tons/yr.)	Average-6.4
Barrels of Oil Used per year	High-14.3

How the Competition Rates

Competitors	Rating	Pg.
Ford Edge	9	136
Mitsubishi Outlander	4	217
Subaru Outback	8	237

Price Range

	Retail	Markup
LX 2WD	$30,595	9%
EX AWD	$34,830	9%
EX-L AWD	$38,255	9%
Touring AWD	$43,470	9%

Safety Checklist

Crash Test:
Frontal . . . . Good
Side . . . . Very Good

Airbags:
Torso . . . Standard Front Pelvis/Torso from Seat
Roll Sensing . . . . Yes
Knee Bolster . . . . None

Crash Avoidance:
Collision Avoidance . . . . . . Optional CIB & DBS
Blind Spot Detection . . . . Optional
Lane Keeping Assist . . . . Optional
Backup Camera . . . . Standard*
Pedestrian Crash Avoidance . . . . Optional

General:
Auto. Crash Notification . . . . . . Dial Assist.-Free
Day Running Lamps . . . . Standard

Safety Belt/Restraint:
Dynamic Head Restraints . . . . None
Adjustable Belt . . . . Standard Front

Note: As of May 2018, all vehicles are required to have a backup camera.
^Warning feature does not meet government standards.
*Backup camera does not meet government standards.

Honda Pilot

Specifications

Drive	AWD
Engine	3.5-liter V6
Transmission	6-sp. Automatic
Tow Rating (lbs.)	Low-3500
Head/Leg Room (in.)	Average-40.1/40.9
Interior Space (cu. ft.)	Very Roomy-152.9
Cargo Space (cu. ft.)	Cramped-16.5
Wheelbase/Length (in.)	111/194.5

Hyundai Accent

Hyundai Accent

Ratings—10 Best, 1 Worst

Combo Crash Tests	—
Safety Features	2
Rollover	—
Preventive Maintenance	6
Repair Costs	10
Warranty	10
Fuel Economy	8
Complaints	—
Insurance Costs	1
OVERALL RATING	**—**

Hyundai Accent

At-a-Glance

Status/Year Series Started. . . . . All New/2018
Twins . . . . Kia Rio
Body Styles . . . . Sedan, Hatchback
Seating 5
Anti-Theft Device . Std. Pass. Immobil. & Active Alarm
Parking Index Rating . . . . .Very Easy
Where Made. . . . . Ulsan, South Korea
Fuel Factor:
MPG Rating (city/hwy) Good-28/38
Driving Range (mi.) . . . . .Very Short-362
Fuel Type. . . . . .Regular
Annual Fuel Cost . . . . Very Low-$1157
Gas Guzzler Tax . . . . .No
Greenhouse Gas Emissions (tons/yr.). Very Low-4.6
Barrels of Oil Used per year Low-10.3

How the Competition Rates

Competitors	Rating	Pg.
Ford Fiesta	2	141
Nissan Versa	1	230
Toyota Yaris	5	257

Price Range	Retail	Markup
SE Sedan MT	$14,745	3%
SE Hatchback AT	$16,195	3%
Value Edition AT	$16,450	3%
Sport Hatchback AT	$17,495	3%

Safety Checklist

Crash Test:
Frontal. . . . . —
Side. . . . . —
Airbags:
Torso . . .Standard Front Pelvis/Torso from Seat
Roll Sensing. . . . . .Yes
Knee Bolster . . . . None
Crash Avoidance:
Collision Avoidance . . . . . . Optional CIB & DBS
Blind Spot Detection . . . . None
Lane Keeping Assist . . . . None
Backup Camera. . . . . Optional*
Pedestrian Crash Avoidance . . . . None
General:
Auto. Crash Notification . . . Operator Assist.-Fee
Day Running Lamps . . . . Optional
Safety Belt/Restraint:
Dynamic Head Restraints . . . . None
Adjustable Belt. . . . . .Standard Front

Note: As of May 2018, all vehicles are required to have a backup camera.
^Warning feature does not meet government standards.
*Backup camera does not meet government standards.

Hyundai Accent

Specifications

Drive. . . . . .FWD
Engine 1.6-liter I4
Transmission . . . . 6-sp. Automatic
Tow Rating (lbs.) . . . . —
Head/Leg Room (in.) Average-39.2/41.8
Interior Space (cu. ft.). . . . . Very Cramped-89.7
Cargo Space (cu. ft.) Cramped-13.7
Wheelbase/Length (in.) 101.6/172

Hyundai Elantra Compact

Ratings—10 Best, 1 Worst

Combo Crash Tests	—
Safety Features	7
Rollover	7
Preventive Maintenance	4
Repair Costs	10
Warranty	10
Fuel Economy	8
Complaints	6
Insurance Costs	1
OVERALL RATING	**—**

Hyundai Elantra

Hyundai Elantra

At-a-Glance

Status/Year Series Started. Unchanged/2017
Twins . . . . .Kia Forte
Body Styles . . . . .Sedan, Coupe, Hatchback
Seating. 5
Anti-Theft Device . Std. Pass. Immobil. & Active Alarm
Parking Index Rating . . . . Easy
Where Made. . . . . .Montgomery, AL
Fuel Factor:
  MPG Rating (city/hwy) Good-28/37
  Driving Range (mi.) Long-440
  Fuel Type. . . . . .Regular
  Annual Fuel Cost . . . . Very Low-$1169
  Gas Guzzler Tax . . . . .No
  Greenhouse Gas Emissions (tons/yr.). Low-4.7
  Barrels of Oil Used per year Low-10.3

How the Competition Rates

Competitors	Rating	Pg.
Honda Civic	10	153
Nissan Sentra	5	228
Toyota Corolla	8	245

Price Range

Price Range	Retail	Markup
SE MT	$16,950	3%
SEL AT	$18,850	3%
Eco AT	$20,550	4%
Limited AT	$22,100	5%

Safety Checklist

Crash Test:
  Frontal. . . . .—
  Side. . . . .—
Airbags:
  Torso . . . Standard Front Pelvis/Torso from Seat
  Roll Sensing. . . . . .Yes
  Knee Bolster . . . . Standard Driver
Crash Avoidance:
  Collision Avoidance . . . . . . Optional CIB & DBS
  Blind Spot Detection . . . . Optional
  Lane Keeping Assist . . . . Optional
  Backup Camera. . . . . Optional
  Pedestrian Crash Avoidance . . . . Optional
General:
  Auto. Crash Notification. . . Operator Assist.-Fee
  Day Running Lamps . . . . Standard
Safety Belt/Restraint:
  Dynamic Head Restraints . . . . None
  Adjustable Belt. . . . . .Standard Front

Note: As of May 2018, all vehicles are required to have a backup camera.
^Warning feature does not meet government standards.
*Backup camera does not meet government standards.

Hyundai Elantra

Specifications

Drive. . . . . .FWD
Engine 2.0-liter I4
Transmission . . . . 6-sp. Automatic
Tow Rating (lbs.) . . . . —
Head/Leg Room (in.) Average-38.8/42.2
Interior Space (cu. ft.). Cramped-95.8
Cargo Space (cu. ft.) Cramped-14.4
Wheelbase/Length (in.) 106.3/179.9

Hyundai Kona

Small SUV

Ratings—10 Best, 1 Worst

Combo Crash Tests	—
Safety Features	7
Rollover	—
Preventive Maintenance	6
Repair Costs	9
Warranty	10
Fuel Economy	—
Complaints	—
Insurance Costs	8
OVERALL RATING	**—**

Hyundai Kona

Hyundai Kona

Hyundai Kona

At-a-Glance

Status/Year Series Started . . . . All New/2018
Twins . . . . —
Body Styles . . . . SUV
Seating 5
Anti-Theft Device . Std. Pass. Immobil. & Active Alarm
Parking Index Rating . . . . .Very Easy
Where Made. . . . . Ulsan, South Korea
Fuel Factor:
  MPG Rating (city/hwy) . . . . .Very Poor-0/0
  Driving Range (mi.) . . . . —
  Fuel Type. . . . . —
  Annual Fuel Cost . . . . —
  Gas Guzzler Tax . . . . .No
  Greenhouse Gas Emissions (tons/yr.). . . . . —
  Barrels of Oil Used per year . . . . Very Low-0.0

How the Competition Rates

Competitors	Rating	Pg.
Buick Encore	10	102
Chevrolet Trax	10	124
Honda HR-V	5	156

Price Range

	Retail	Markup

Safety Checklist

Crash Test:
  Frontal. . . . . —
  Side. . . . . —
Airbags:
  Torso . . . Standard Front Pelvis/Torso from Seat
  Roll Sensing. . . . . .Yes
  Knee Bolster . . . . None
Crash Avoidance:
  Collision Avoidance . . . . . . .Optional CIB & DBS^
  Blind Spot Detection . . . . Optional
  Lane Keeping Assist . . . . Optional^
  Backup Camera. . . . . Standard
  Pedestrian Crash Avoidance . . . . Optional
General:
  Auto. Crash Notification. . . Operator Assist.-Fee
  Day Running Lamps . . . . Standard
Safety Belt/Restraint:
  Dynamic Head Restraints . . . . None
  Adjustable Belt. . . . . .Standard Front

Note: As of May 2018, all vehicles are required to have a backup camera.
^Warning feature does not meet government standards.
*Backup camera does not meet government standards.

Specifications

Drive. . . . . .FWD
Engine 1.6-liter I4
Transmission . . . . 7-sp. Automatic
Tow Rating (lbs.) . . . . .Very Low-2755
Head/Leg Room (in.) Average-39.6/41.5
Interior Space (cu. ft.). Cramped-94
Cargo Space (cu. ft.) Cramped-14.2
Wheelbase/Length (in.) 102.4/164

Hyundai Kona

Hyundai Santa Fe   Medium SUV

Ratings—10 Best, 1 Worst

Combo Crash Tests	—
Safety Features	7
Rollover	4
Preventive Maintenance	4
Repair Costs	5
Warranty	10
Fuel Economy	3
Complaints	2
Insurance Costs	8
OVERALL RATING	**—**

Hyundai Santa Fe

Hyundai Santa Fe

At-a-Glance

Status/Year Series Started. Unchanged/2013
Twins . . . . —
Body Styles . . . . SUV
Seating 6/7
Anti-Theft Device . Std. Pass. Immobil. & Active Alarm
Parking Index Rating . . . . Average
Where Made. . . . . West Point, GA
Fuel Factor:
MPG Rating (city/hwy) Poor-18/25
Driving Range (mi.) Short-387
Fuel Type . . . . Regular
Annual Fuel Cost . . . . High-$1784
Gas Guzzler Tax . . . . No
Greenhouse Gas Emissions (tons/yr.). High-8.5
Barrels of Oil Used per year High-15.7

How the Competition Rates

Competitors	Rating	Pg.
Acura MDX	7	80
Kia Sorento	6	181
Mitsubishi Outlander	4	217

Price Range	Retail	Markup
SE FWD	$30,800	5%
Limited FWD	$34,950	6%
SE Ultimate AWD	$40,450	5%
Limited Ultimate AWD	$41,150	6%

Safety Checklist

Crash Test:
  Frontal. . . . . —
  Side. . . . . —
Airbags:
  Torso . . . Standard Front Pelvis/Torso from Seat
  Roll Sensing. . . . . Yes
  Knee Bolster . . . . Standard Driver
Crash Avoidance:
  Collision Avoidance . . . . . . Optional CIB & DBS
  Blind Spot Detection . . . . Optional
  Lane Keeping Assist . . . .Warning Only Optional
  Backup Camera . . . . Standard
  Pedestrian Crash Avoidance . . . . Optional
General:
  Auto. Crash Notification. . . Operator Assist.-Fee
  Day Running Lamps . . . . Standard
Safety Belt/Restraint:
  Dynamic Head Restraints . . . . None
  Adjustable Belt. . . . . .Standard Front

Note: As of May 2018, all vehicles are required to have a backup camera.
^Warning feature does not meet government standards.
*Backup camera does not meet government standards.

Hyundai Santa Fe

Specifications

Drive. . . . . .FWD
Engine 3.3-liter V6
Transmission . . . . 6-sp. Automatic
Tow Rating (lbs.) Low-5000
Head/Leg Room (in.) Cramped-39.6/41.3
Interior Space (cu. ft.). . . . . Very Roomy-146.6
Cargo Space (cu. ft.) . . . . Very Cramped-13.5
Wheelbase/Length (in.) 110.2/193.1

Ratings—10 Best, 1 Worst

Combo Crash Tests	6
Safety Features	6
Rollover	4
Preventive Maintenance	4
Repair Costs	7
Warranty	10
Fuel Economy	4
Complaints	1
Insurance Costs	5
OVERALL RATING	**5**

Hyundai Santa Fe Sport

Hyundai Santa Fe Sport

At-a-Glance

Status/Year Series Started........ Unchanged/2014
Twins .... –
Body Styles .... SUV
Seating................................. 5
Anti-Theft Device . Std. Pass. Immobil. & Active Alarm
Parking Index Rating .... Easy
Where Made.................. West Point, GA

Fuel Factor:
MPG Rating (city/hwy)......... Poor-21/27
Driving Range (mi.) Average-406
Fuel Type........................Regular
Annual Fuel Cost..............Average-$1575
Gas Guzzler Tax ....No
Greenhouse Gas Emissions (tons/yr.)..... High-7.9
Barrels of Oil Used per year High-14.3

How the Competition Rates

Competitors	Rating	Pg.
Kia Sorento	6	181
Mazda CX-5	4	200
Mitsubishi Outlander Sport	4	218

Price Range	Retail	Markup
Base 2.4L FWD	$24,950	5%
Base 2.4L AWD	$26,500	5%
Ultimate 2.0T Turbo FWD	$35,650	5%
Ultimate 2.0T Turbo AWD	$37,200	5%

Safety Checklist

Crash Test:
Frontal............................. Good
Side.......................... Average
Airbags:
Torso ...Standard Front Pelvis/Torso from Seat
Roll Sensing.........................Yes
Knee Bolster .... Standard Driver
Crash Avoidance:
Collision Avoidance ...... Optional CIB & DBS
Blind Spot Detection .... Optional
Lane Keeping Assist ....Warning Only Optional
Backup Camera....................Standard*
Pedestrian Crash Avoidance .... Optional
General:
Auto. Crash Notification... Operator Assist.-Fee
Day Running Lamps .... Standard
Safety Belt/Restraint:
Dynamic Head Restraints .... None
Adjustable Belt................Standard Front

Note: As of May 2018, all vehicles are required to have a backup camera.
^Warning feature does not meet government standards.
*Backup camera does not meet government standards.

Hyundai Santa Fe Sport

Specifications

Drive..FWD
Engine 2.4-liter I4
Transmission .... 6-sp. Automatic
Tow Rating (lbs.) ....Very Low-2000
Head/Leg Room (in.) Cramped-39.6/41.3
Interior Space (cu. ft.)................Roomy-108
Cargo Space (cu. ft.) .... Very Roomy-35.4
Wheelbase/Length (in.) 106.3/184.6

Hyundai Sonata

Hyundai Sonata

Ratings—10 Best, 1 Worst

Combo Crash Tests	9
Safety Features	6
Rollover	7
Preventive Maintenance	5
Repair Costs	8
Warranty	10
Fuel Economy	7
Complaints	5
Insurance Costs	5
OVERALL RATING	**9**

Hyundai Sonata

At-a-Glance

Status/Year Series Started Appearance Change/2015
Twins . . . . –
Body Styles . . . . Sedan
Seating 5
Anti-Theft Device . Std. Pass. Immobil. & Active Alarm
Parking Index Rating . . . . Easy
Where Made. . . . . Montgomery, AL
Fuel Factor:
  MPG Rating (city/hwy) Good-25/35
  Driving Range (mi.) . . . . Very Long-531
  Fuel Type. . . . . .Regular
  Annual Fuel Cost . . . . Low-$1281
  Gas Guzzler Tax . . . . .No
  Greenhouse Gas Emissions (tons/yr.). Low-5.2
  Barrels of Oil Used per year Average-11.8

How the Competition Rates

Competitors	Rating	Pg.
Mazda 6	5	203
Toyota Camry	8	244
Volkswagen Passat	4	263

Price Range

	Retail	Markup
SE 2.4L	$22,050	4%
SEL 2.4L	$23,700	6%
Sport 2.0L Turbo	$26,600	2%
Limited 2.0L Turbo	$32,450	6%

Safety Checklist

Crash Test:
  Frontal. . . . . Very Good
  Side. . . . . Average
Airbags:
  Torso . . . Standard Front Pelvis/Torso from Seat
  Roll Sensing. . . . . .Yes
  Knee Bolster . . . . Standard Driver
Crash Avoidance:
  Collision Avoidance . . . . . . Optional CIB & DBS
  Blind Spot Detection . . . . Optional
  Lane Keeping Assist . . . .Warning Only Optional
  Backup Camera. . . . . Optional*
  Pedestrian Crash Avoidance. . . . . Optional
General:
  Auto. Crash Notification. . . Operator Assist.-Fee
  Day Running Lamps . . . . Standard
Safety Belt/Restraint:
  Dynamic Head Restraints . . . . None
  Adjustable Belt. . . . . .Standard Front

Note: As of May 2018, all vehicles are required to have a backup camera.
^Warning feature does not meet government standards.
*Backup camera does not meet government standards.

Hyundai Sonata

Specifications

Drive. . . . . .FWD
Engine 2.4-liter I4
Transmission . . . . 6-sp. Automatic
Tow Rating (lbs.) . . . . Very Low-0
Head/Leg Room (in.) . . . . Very Roomy-40.4/45.5
Interior Space (cu. ft.). Roomy-106.1
Cargo Space (cu. ft.) Cramped-16.3
Wheelbase/Length (in.) 110.4/191.1

Ratings—10 Best, 1 Worst

Combo Crash Tests	4
Safety Features	8
Rollover	4
Preventive Maintenance	4
Repair Costs	10
Warranty	10
Fuel Economy	6
Complaints	1
Insurance Costs	10
OVERALL RATING	**8**

Hyundai Tucson

Hyundai Tucson

At-a-Glance

Status/Year Series Started. Unchanged/2016
Twins . . . . –
Body Styles . . . . SUV
Seating. 5
Anti-Theft Device . Std. Pass. Immobil. & Active Alarm
Parking Index Rating . . . . .Very Easy
Where Made. . . . . Ulsan, South Korea

Fuel Factor:
MPG Rating (city/hwy) Average-24/28
Driving Range (mi.) Average-421
Fuel Type. . . . . .Regular
Annual Fuel Cost . . . . Low-$1433
Gas Guzzler Tax . . . . .No
Greenhouse Gas Emissions (tons/yr.) Low-5.8
Barrels of Oil Used per year Average-12.7

How the Competition Rates

Competitors	Rating	Pg.
Ford Escape	5	137
Honda HR-V	5	156
Toyota RAV4	9	252

Price Range

Price Range	Retail	Markup
SE FWD	$22,700	4%
Eco AWD	$25,550	5%
Sport AWD	$27,300	5%
Limited AWD	$31,175	5%

Safety Checklist

Crash Test:
Frontal. . . . . .Poor
Side. . . . . Average
Airbags:
Torso . . . Standard Front Pelvis/Torso from Seat
Roll Sensing. . . . . .Yes
Knee Bolster . . . . None
Crash Avoidance:
Collision Avoidance . . . . . . Optional CIB & DBS
Blind Spot Detection . . . . Optional
Lane Keeping Assist . . . .Warning Only Optional
Backup Camera. . . . . Standard
Pedestrian Crash Avoidance . . . . Optional
General:
Auto. Crash Notification . . . Operator Assist.-Fee
Day Running Lamps . . . . Optional
Safety Belt/Restraint:
Dynamic Head Restraints . . . . . .Standard Front
Adjustable Belt. . . . . .Standard Front

Note: As of May 2018, all vehicles are required to have a backup camera.
^Warning feature does not meet government standards.
*Backup camera does not meet government standards.

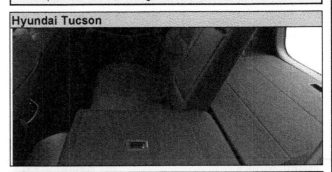

Hyundai Tucson

Specifications

Drive. . . . . .FWD
Engine 2.0-liter I4
Transmission . . . . 6-sp. Automatic
Tow Rating (lbs.) . . . . –
Head/Leg Room (in.) Average-39.6/41.5
Interior Space (cu. ft.). Average-102.2
Cargo Space (cu. ft.) . . . . Very Roomy-31
Wheelbase/Length (in.) 105.1/176.2

Ratings—10 Best, 1 Worst

Combo Crash Tests	4
Safety Features	3
Rollover	7
Preventive Maintenance	5
Repair Costs	9
Warranty	10
Fuel Economy	8
Complaints	3
Insurance Costs	3
OVERALL RATING	**6**

Hyundai Veloster

Hyundai Veloster

At-a-Glance

Status/Year Series Started Appearance Change/2016
Twins . . . . –
Body Styles . . . . .Coupe
Seating 5
Anti-Theft Device .Std. Pass. Immobil. & Active Alarm
Parking Index Rating . . . . .Very Easy
Where Made. . . . . Ulsan, South Korea
Fuel Factor:
MPG Rating (city/hwy) Good-28/36
Driving Range (mi.) Average-411
Fuel Type. . . . . .Regular
Annual Fuel Cost . . . . Low-$1181
Gas Guzzler Tax . . . . .No
Greenhouse Gas Emissions (tons/yr.)Very High-10.6
Barrels of Oil Used per year . . . . Very Low-4.7

How the Competition Rates

Competitors	Rating	Pg.
Chevrolet Sonic	9	119
Mini Hardtop	6	215
Toyota Yaris	5	257

Price Range

Price Range	Retail	Markup
Base MT	$18,100	4%
Base AT	$19,200	4%
Turbo MT	$22,600	5%
Turbo AT	$23,800	5%

Safety Checklist

Crash Test:
Frontal. . . . . .Poor
Side. . . . . .Poor
Airbags:
Torso . . . Standard Front Pelvis/Torso from Seat
Roll Sensing. . . . . .Yes
Knee Bolster . . . . None
Crash Avoidance:
Collision Avoidance . . . . None
Blind Spot Detection . . . . None
Lane Keeping Assist . . . . None
Backup Camera. . . . . .Standard*
Pedestrian Crash Avoidance . . . . None
General:
Auto. Crash Notification . . . Operator Assist.-Fee
Day Running Lamps . . . . Standard
Safety Belt/Restraint:
Dynamic Head Restraints . . . . . .Standard Front
Adjustable Belt. . . . . .Standard Front

Note: As of May 2018, all vehicles are required to have a backup camera.
^Warning feature does not meet government standards.
*Backup camera does not meet government standards.

Hyundai Veloster

Specifications

Drive. . . . . .FWD
Engine 1.6-liter I4
Transmission . . . . 6-dp. Automatic
Tow Rating (lbs.) . . . . –
Head/Leg Room (in.) Roomy-39/43.9
Interior Space (cu. ft.). . . . . Very Cramped-89.8
Cargo Space (cu. ft.) Cramped-15.5
Wheelbase/Length (in.) 104.3/166.1

Ratings—10 Best, 1 Worst

Combo Crash Tests	4
Safety Features	5
Rollover	8
Preventive Maintenance	5
Repair Costs	3
Warranty	9
Fuel Economy	4
Complaints	8
Insurance Costs	1
OVERALL RATING	**3**

Infiniti Q50

Infiniti Q50

At-a-Glance

Status/Year Series Started Appearance Change/2014
Twins . . . . –
Body Styles . . . . .Sedan
Seating 5
Anti-Theft Device . . . . . . Std. Pass. Immobil. & Alarm
Parking Index Rating . . . . Average
Where Made . . . . Tochigi, Japan

Fuel Factor:
MPG Rating (city/hwy) Poor-20/29
Driving Range (mi.) . . . . Very Long-465
Fuel Type . . . . Premium
Annual Fuel Cost . . . . .High-$1916
Gas Guzzler Tax . . . . .No
Greenhouse Gas Emissions (tons/yr.) High-7.8
Barrels of Oil Used per year High-14.3

How the Competition Rates

Competitors	Rating	Pg.
BMW 3 Series	7	91
Lexus IS	8	190
Lincoln MKZ	4	197

Price Range

	Retail	Markup
Base RWD 2.0T	$34,200	8%
Luxe RWD 3.0T	$38,950	8%
Sport AWD 3.0T	$42,650	8%
Hybrid Luxe AWD	$52,600	8%

Safety Checklist

Crash Test:
Frontal . . . . .Very Poor
Side . . . . Very Good

Airbags:
Torso Std. Fr. & Opt. Rr. Pelvis/Torso from Seat
Roll Sensing . . . . .Yes
Knee Bolster . . . . None

Crash Avoidance:
Collision Avoidance . . . . . . Optional CIB & DBS
Blind Spot Detection . . . . Optional
Lane Keeping Assist . . . .Warning Only Optional
Backup Camera . . . . .Standard*
Pedestrian Crash Avoidance . . . . None

General:
Auto. Crash Notification . . . . Operator Assist.-Fee
Day Running Lamps . . . . Standard

Safety Belt/Restraint:
Dynamic Head Restraints . . . . None
Adjustable Belt . . . . .Standard Front

Note: As of May 2018, all vehicles are required to have a backup camera.
^Warning feature does not meet government standards.
*Backup camera does not meet government standards.

Infiniti Q50

Specifications

Drive . . . . .RWD
Engine 3.0-liter V6
Transmission . . . . 7-sp. Automatic
Tow Rating (lbs.) . . . . –
Head/Leg Room (in.) . . . . Very Roomy-39.5/44.5
Interior Space (cu. ft.) Average-100
Cargo Space (cu. ft.) . . . . Very Cramped-13.5
Wheelbase/Length (in.) 112.2/189.6

Ratings—10 Best, 1 Worst

Combo Crash Tests	—
Safety Features	7
Rollover	6
Preventive Maintenance	7
Repair Costs	2
Warranty	9
Fuel Economy	6
Complaints	2
Insurance Costs	5
OVERALL RATING	**—**

Infiniti QX30

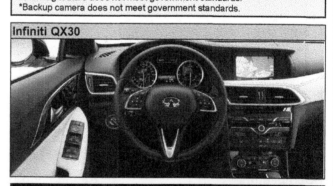
Infiniti QX30

At-a-Glance

Status/Year Series Started. Unchanged/2017
Twins . . . . —
Body Styles . . . . SUV
Seating 5
Anti-Theft Device . . . . Standard Pass. Immobil.
Parking Index Rating . . . . Easy
Where Made" . . . . Sunderland, England
Fuel Factor:
  MPG Rating (city/hwy) Average-24/33
  Driving Range (mi.) . . . . Very Short-361
  Fuel Type . . . . Premium
  Annual Fuel Cost . . . . .Average-$1628
  Gas Guzzler Tax . . . . .No
  Greenhouse Gas Emissions (tons/yr.). Low-5.4
  Barrels of Oil Used per year Average-12.2

How the Competition Rates

Competitors	Rating	Pg.
Acura RDX	9	81
Buick Encore	10	102
Lexus NX	5	191

Price Range	Retail	Markup
Base FWD	$29,950	7%
Luxury FWD	$32,600	8%
Premium AWD	$37,700	8%
Sport FWD	$38,500	8%

Safety Checklist

Crash Test:
  Frontal. . . . . —
  Side. . . . . —
Airbags:
  Torso . . . Standard Front Pelvis/Torso from Seat
  Roll Sensing. . . . . .Yes
  Knee Bolster . . . . .Standard Front
Crash Avoidance:
  Collision Avoidance . . . . . . Optional CIB & DBS
  Blind Spot Detection . . . . Optional
  Lane Keeping Assist . . . .Warning Only Optional
  Backup Camera. . . . . Standard
  Pedestrian Crash Avoidance . . . . None
General:
  Auto. Crash Notification. . . Operator Assist.-Fee
  Day Running Lamps . . . . Standard
Safety Belt/Restraint:
  Dynamic Head Restraints . . . . None
  Adjustable Belt. . . . . .Standard Front

Note: As of May 2018, all vehicles are required to have a backup camera.
^Warning feature does not meet government standards.
*Backup camera does not meet government standards.

Specifications

Drive. . . . . .FWD
Engine 2.0-liter I4
Transmission . . . . 7-sp. Automatic
Tow Rating (lbs.) . . . .—
Head/Leg Room (in.) Cramped-38.4/41.3
Interior Space (cu. ft.). . . . . Very Cramped-88.8
Cargo Space (cu. ft.) Average-19.2
Wheelbase/Length (in.) 106.3/174.2

Infiniti QX50 — Small SUV

Infiniti QX50

Ratings—10 Best, 1 Worst

Combo Crash Tests	—
Safety Features	3
Rollover	4
Preventive Maintenance	9
Repair Costs	2
Warranty	9
Fuel Economy	2
Complaints	10
Insurance Costs	10

OVERALL RATING —

Infiniti QX50

At-a-Glance

Status/Year Series Started........ Unchanged/2014
Twins .... —
Body Styles .... SUV
Seating 5
Anti-Theft Device ...... Std. Pass. Immobil. & Alarm
Parking Index Rating .... Average
Where Made..................... Tochigi, Japan
Fuel Factor:
  MPG Rating (city/hwy) .... Very Poor-17/24
  Driving Range (mi.) Short-391
  Fuel Type........................... Premium
  Annual Fuel Cost .... Very High-$2277
  Gas Guzzler Tax ....No
  Greenhouse Gas Emissions (tons/yr.)..... High-7.4
  Barrels of Oil Used per year High-16.5

How the Competition Rates

Competitors	Rating	Pg.
Buick Encore	10	102
Mazda CX-5	4	200
Subaru Forester	4	234

Price Range

	Retail	Markup
RWD	$34,650	8%
AWD	$36,450	8%

Safety Checklist

Crash Test:
  Frontal................................. —
  Side................................... —
Airbags:
  Torso . . . Standard Front Pelvis/Torso from Seat
  Roll Sensing........................... No
  Knee Bolster .... None
Crash Avoidance:
  Collision Avoidance .... Optional CIB
  Blind Spot Detection .... Optional
  Lane Keeping Assist ....Warning Only Optional
  Backup Camera.................Standard*
  Pedestrian Crash Avoidance........... None
General:
  Auto. Crash Notification... Operator Assist.-Fee
  Day Running Lamps .... Standard
Safety Belt/Restraint:
  Dynamic Head Restraints ......Standard Front
  Adjustable Belt................Standard Front

Note: As of May 2018, all vehicles are required to have a backup camera.
^Warning feature does not meet government standards.
*Backup camera does not meet government standards.

Infiniti QX50

Specifications

Drive.......................................RWD
Engine 3.7-liter V6
Transmission .... 7-sp. Automatic
Tow Rating (lbs.) .... —
Head/Leg Room (in.) Roomy-38.7/44.3
Interior Space (cu. ft.)............ Roomy-115.4
Cargo Space (cu. ft.) Average-18.6
Wheelbase/Length (in.) 113.4/186.8

Ratings—10 Best, 1 Worst

Combo Crash Tests	6
Safety Features	5
Rollover	3
Preventive Maintenance	3
Repair Costs	3
Warranty	9
Fuel Economy	3
Complaints	5
Insurance Costs	8
OVERALL RATING	**5**

Infiniti QX60

Infiniti QX60

At-a-Glance

Status/Year Series Started. Unchanged/2013
Twins . . . . Nissan Pathfinder
Body Styles . . . . SUV
Seating. 7
Anti-Theft Device . . . . . . Std. Pass. Immobil. & Alarm
Parking Index Rating . . . . Hard
Where Made. . . . . Smyrna, TN
Fuel Factor:
  MPG Rating (city/hwy). Poor-19/26
  Driving Range (mi.) Average-422
  Fuel Type. . . . . Premium
  Annual Fuel Cost . . . . Very High-$2061
  Gas Guzzler Tax . . . . No
  Greenhouse Gas Emissions (tons/yr.). High-8.2
  Barrels of Oil Used per year High-15.0

How the Competition Rates

Competitors	Rating	Pg.
Acura MDX	7	80
Audi Q7	3	89
BMW X5	5	98

Price Range	Retail	Markup
RWD	$43,100	8%
AWD	$44,900	8%

Safety Checklist

Crash Test:
  Frontal. . . . . Average
  Side. . . . . Average
Airbags:
  Torso . . . Standard Front Pelvis/Torso from Seat
  Roll Sensing. . . . . Yes
  Knee Bolster . . . . None
Crash Avoidance:
  Collision Avoidance . . . . . . Optional CIB & DBS
  Blind Spot Detection . . . . Optional
  Lane Keeping Assist . . . .Warning Only Optional
  Backup Camera. . . . . .Standard*
  Pedestrian Crash Avoidance . . . . Optional
General:
  Auto. Crash Notification. . . Operator Assist.-Fee
  Day Running Lamps . . . . Standard
Safety Belt/Restraint:
  Dynamic Head Restraints . . . . None
  Adjustable Belt. . . . . . . Standard Front and Rear

Note: As of May 2018, all vehicles are required to have a backup camera.
^Warning feature does not meet government standards.
*Backup camera does not meet government standards.

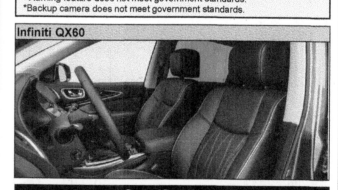

Infiniti QX60

Specifications

Drive. . . . . AWD
Engine 3.5-liter V6
Transmission . . . . 7-sp. Automatic
Tow Rating (lbs.) Low-5000
Head/Leg Room (in.) Roomy-40.7/42.3
Interior Space (cu. ft.). . . . . Very Roomy-149.8
Cargo Space (cu. ft.) Cramped-15.8
Wheelbase/Length (in.) 114.2/196.4

Ratings—10 Best, 1 Worst

Combo Crash Tests	—
Safety Features	7
Rollover	2
Preventive Maintenance	3
Repair Costs	4
Warranty	9
Fuel Economy	1
Complaints	7
Insurance Costs	5
OVERALL RATING	—

Infiniti QX80

Infiniti QX80

At-a-Glance

Status/Year Series Started Appearance Change/2011
Twins . . . . —
Body Styles . . . . SUV
Seating 7/8
Anti-Theft Device . . . . . . Std. Pass. Immobil. & Alarm
Parking Index Rating . . . . Very Hard
Where Made. . . . . Kyushu, Japan
Fuel Factor:
  MPG Rating (city/hwy) . . . . Very Poor-14/20
  Driving Range (mi.) Average-421
  Fuel Type. . . . . .Premium
  Annual Fuel Cost . . . . Very High-$2753
  Gas Guzzler Tax . . . . .No
  Greenhouse Gas Emissions (tons/yr.)Very High-11.2
  Barrels of Oil Used per year . . . . Very High-20.6

How the Competition Rates

Competitors	Rating	Pg.
Buick Enclave	4	101
Chevrolet Tahoe	4	122
Volvo XC90	8	268

Price Range	Retail	Markup
Base RWD	$63,850	8%
Base AWD	$66,950	8%
Signature AWD	$70,435	8%
Limited AWD	$89,450	8%

Safety Checklist

Crash Test:
  Frontal. . . . . —
  Side. . . . . —
Airbags:
  Torso . . .Standard Front Pelvis/Torso from Seat
  Roll Sensing. . . . . .Yes
  Knee Bolster . . . . None
Crash Avoidance:
  Collision Avoidance . . . . . . Optional CIB & DBS
  Blind Spot Detection . . . . Optional
  Lane Keeping Assist . . . .Warning Only Optional
  Backup Camera. . . . . .Standard*
  Pedestrian Crash Avoidance . . . . Optional
General:
  Auto. Crash Notification. . . Operator Assist.-Fee
  Day Running Lamps . . . . Standard
Safety Belt/Restraint:
  Dynamic Head Restraints . . . . . .Standard Front
  Adjustable Belt. . . . . Standard Front & Rear

Note: As of May 2018, all vehicles are required to have a backup camera.
^Warning feature does not meet government standards.
*Backup camera does not meet government standards.

Infiniti QX80

Specifications

Drive. . . . . .AWD
Engine 5.6-liter V8
Transmission . . . . 7-sp. Automatic
Tow Rating (lbs.) . . . . Very High-8500
Head/Leg Room (in.) . . . . Very Cramped-39.9/39.6
Interior Space (cu. ft.). . . . . Very Roomy-151.3
Cargo Space (cu. ft.) Cramped-16.6
Wheelbase/Length (in.) 121.1/208.9

Jeep Cherokee

Jeep Cherokee

Ratings—10 Best, 1 Worst

Combo Crash Tests	5
Safety Features	7
Rollover	3
Preventive Maintenance	10
Repair Costs	5
Warranty	3
Fuel Economy	4
Complaints	1
Insurance Costs	10
OVERALL RATING	**5**

Jeep Cherokee

At-a-Glance

Status/Year Series Started Appearance Change/2014
Twins .... –
Body Styles .... SUV
Seating 5
Anti-Theft Device .Std. Pass. Immobil. & Opt. Pass. Alarm
Parking Index Rating .... Average
Where Made........................Toldeo, OH
Fuel Factor:
MPG Rating (city/hwy) Poor-21/28
Driving Range (mi.) Short-376
Fuel Type................................Regular
Annual Fuel Cost ....Average-$1553
Gas Guzzler Tax ....No
Greenhouse Gas Emissions (tons/yr.). . Average-6.3
Barrels of Oil Used per year High-14.3

How the Competition Rates

Competitors	Rating	Pg.
Ford Escape	5	137
Mazda CX-5	4	200
Toyota RAV4	9	252

Price Range

	Retail	Markup
Latitude FWD	$24,395	1%
Trailhawk 4WD	$30,995	2%
Limited 4WD	$31,295	2%
Overland 4WD	$37,340	3%

Safety Checklist

Crash Test:
Frontal.........................Very Poor
Side.......................... Very Good
Airbags:
Torso Std. Fr. & Opt. Rr. Pelvis/Torso from Seat
Roll Sensing.........................Yes
Knee Bolster ....Standard Front
Crash Avoidance:
Collision Avoidance ...... Optional CIB & DBS
Blind Spot Detection .... Optional
Lane Keeping Assist .... Optional^
Backup Camera.................... Optional
Pedestrian Crash Avoidance........... None
General:
Auto. Crash Notification.............. None
Day Running Lamps .... Standard
Safety Belt/Restraint:
Dynamic Head Restraints .... None
Adjustable Belt.............Standard Front

Note: As of May 2018, all vehicles are required to have a backup camera.
^Warning feature does not meet government standards.
*Backup camera does not meet government standards.

Jeep Cherokee

Specifications

Drive............................AWD
Engine 2.4-liter I4
Transmission .... 9-sp. Automatic
Tow Rating (lbs.) .... Very Low-2000
Head/Leg Room (in.) Cramped-39.4/41.1
Interior Space (cu. ft.)........ Average-103.4
Cargo Space (cu. ft.) Roomy-24.6
Wheelbase/Length (in.) 106.2/182

Ratings—10 Best, 1 Worst	
Combo Crash Tests	2
Safety Features	2
Rollover	2
Preventive Maintenance	10
Repair Costs	10
Warranty	3
Fuel Economy	5
Complaints	3
Insurance Costs	10
OVERALL RATING	**4**

Jeep Compass

Jeep Compass

At-a-Glance

Status/Year Series Started. Unchanged/2017
Twins . . . . –
Body Styles . . . . SUV
Seating. 5
Anti-Theft Device .Std. Pass. Immobil. & Opt. Pass. Alarm
Parking Index Rating . . . . Easy
Where Made. . . . . .Toluca, Mexico
Fuel Factor:
MPG Rating (city/hwy) Average-22/30
Driving Range (mi.) . . . . .Very Short-338
Fuel Type. . . . . Regular
Annual Fuel Cost . . . . .Average-$1470
Gas Guzzler Tax . . . . .No
Greenhouse Gas Emissions (tons/yr.). . Average-5.9
Barrels of Oil Used per year High-13.2

How the Competition Rates

Competitors	Rating	Pg.
Acura RDX	9	81
GMC Terrain	5	150
Honda HR-V	5	156

Price Range	Retail	Markup
Sport FWD	$20,995	1%
Latitude FWD	$24,295	2%
Trailhawk 4WD	$28,695	2%
Limited 4WD	$29,095	3%

Safety Checklist

Crash Test:
Frontal. . . . . Poor
Side. . . . . .Very Poor
Airbags:
Torso . . .Standard Front Pelvis/Torso from Seat
Roll Sensing. . . . . .Yes
Knee Bolster . . . . None
Crash Avoidance:
Collision Avoidance . . . . None
Blind Spot Detection . . . . None
Lane Keeping Assist . . . . None
Backup Camera. . . . . Optional*
Pedestrian Crash Avoidance . . . . None
General:
Auto. Crash Notification . . . . None
Day Running Lamps . . . . Optional
Safety Belt/Restraint:
Dynamic Head Restraints . . . . . .Standard Front
Adjustable Belt. . . . . .Standard Front

Note: As of May 2018, all vehicles are required to have a backup camera.
^Warning feature does not meet government standards.
*Backup camera does not meet government standards.

Jeep Compass

Specifications

Drive. . . . . .AWD
Engine 2.4-liter I4
Transmission . . . . 6-sp. Automatic
Tow Rating (lbs.) . . . . .Very Low-2000
Head/Leg Room (in.) Average-39.2/41.8
Interior Space (cu. ft.). Roomy-126.7
Cargo Space (cu. ft.) Roomy-27.2
Wheelbase/Length (in.) 103.8/173

Ratings—10 Best, 1 Worst

Combo Crash Tests	6
Safety Features	7
Rollover	3
Preventive Maintenance	8
Repair Costs	6
Warranty	3
Fuel Economy	1
Complaints	2
Insurance Costs	8
OVERALL RATING	**4**

Jeep Grand Cherokee

At-a-Glance

Status/Year Series Started. Unchanged/2011
Twins . . . . –
Body Styles . . . . SUV
Seating 5
Anti-Theft Device . Std. Pass. Immobil. & Opt. Pass. Alarm
Parking Index Rating . . . . Average
Where Made. . . . . .Detroit, MI

Fuel Factor:
MPG Rating (city/hwy) . . . . . . .Very Poor-14/22
Driving Range (mi.) Average-412
Fuel Type. . . . . .Regular
Annual Fuel Cost . . . . Very High-$2195
Gas Guzzler Tax . . . . .No
Greenhouse Gas Emissions (tons/yr.) Very High-8.8
Barrels of Oil Used per year . . . . . . .Very High-19.4

How the Competition Rates

Competitors	Rating	Pg.
Chevrolet Equinox	4	115
Honda CR-V	10	154
Lexus NX	5	191

Price Range

Price Range	Retail	Markup
Laredo RWD	$30,595	0%
Limited RWD	$38,195	3%
Trailhawk 4WD	$43,295	4%
Overland 4WD	$47,995	4%

Jeep Grand Cherokee

Safety Checklist

Crash Test:
Frontal. . . . . Good
Side. . . . . Poor
Airbags:
Torso . . . Standard Front Pelvis/Torso from Seat
Roll Sensing. . . . . .Yes
Knee Bolster . . . . Standard Driver
Crash Avoidance:
Collision Avoidance . . . . . . Optional CIB & DBS
Blind Spot Detection . . . . Optional
Lane Keeping Assist . . . . Optional^
Backup Camera . . . . Optional
Pedestrian Crash Avoidance. . . . . None
General:
Auto. Crash Notification. . . . . None
Day Running Lamps . . . . Standard
Safety Belt/Restraint:
Dynamic Head Restraints . . . . . .Standard Front
Adjustable Belt. . . . . .Standard Front

^Warning feature does not meet government standards.
*Backup camera does not meet government standards.

Jeep Grand Cherokee

Specifications

Drive. 4WD
Engine 5.7-liter V8
Transmission . . . . 8-sp. Automatic
Tow Rating (lbs.) High-7200
Head/Leg Room (in.) Cramped-39.9/40.3
Interior Space (cu. ft.). Average-103.9
Cargo Space (cu. ft.) . . . . Very Roomy-36.3
Wheelbase/Length (in.) 114.8/189.8

Jeep Renegade

Ratings—10 Best, 1 Worst	
Combo Crash Tests	2
Safety Features	4
Rollover	3
Preventive Maintenance	4
Repair Costs	7
Warranty	3
Fuel Economy	5
Complaints	2
Insurance Costs	5
OVERALL RATING	**1**

Jeep Renegade

Jeep Renegade

At-a-Glance

Status/Year Series Started Unchanged/2015
Twins . . . . —
Body Styles . . . . SUV
Seating 5
Anti-Theft Device . Std. Pass. Immobil. & Opt. Pass. Alarm
Parking Index Rating . . . . Easy
Where Made . . . . Melfi, Italy
Fuel Factor:
  MPG Rating (city/hwy) Average-22/31
  Driving Range (mi.) . . . . Very Short-321
  Fuel Type . . . . Premium
  Annual Fuel Cost . . . . High-$1760
  Gas Guzzler Tax . . . . No
  Greenhouse Gas Emissions (tons/yr.) . . Average-6.1
  Barrels of Oil Used per year Average-12.9

How the Competition Rates

Competitors	Rating	Pg.
Chevrolet Equinox	4	115
Ford Edge	9	136
Hyundai Tucson	8	165

Price Range	Retail	Markup
Sport FWD	$17,995	1%
Latitude FWD	$21,495	2%
Trailhawk 4WD	$26,645	2%
Limited 4WD	$27,195	2%

Safety Checklist

Crash Test:
  Frontal . . . . Poor
  Side . . . . Very Poor
Airbags:
  Torso . . . Standard Front Pelvis/Torso from Seat
  Roll Sensing . . . . Yes
  Knee Bolster . . . . Standard Driver
Crash Avoidance:
  Collision Avoidance . . . . . . Optional CIB & DBS^
  Blind Spot Detection . . . . Optional
  Lane Keeping Assist . . . . Optional^
  Backup Camera . . . . Optional*
  Pedestrian Crash Avoidance . . . . None
General:
  Auto. Crash Notification . . . . None
  Day Running Lamps . . . . Optional
Safety Belt/Restraint:
  Dynamic Head Restraints . . . . None
  Adjustable Belt . . . . Standard Front

Note: As of May 2018, all vehicles are required to have a backup camera.
^Warning feature does not meet government standards.
*Backup camera does not meet government standards.

Jeep Renegade

Specifications

Drive . . . . FWD
Engine 1.4-liter I4
Transmission . . . . 9-sp. Automatic
Tow Rating (lbs.) . . . . Very Low-2000
Head/Leg Room (in.) Average-41.1/41.2
Interior Space (cu. ft.) Average-100.1
Cargo Space (cu. ft.) Average-18.5
Wheelbase/Length (in.) 101.2/166.6

Jeep Wrangler Small SUV

Ratings—10 Best, 1 Worst

Category	Rating
Combo Crash Tests	—
Safety Features	1
Rollover	1
Preventive Maintenance	10
Repair Costs	9
Warranty	3
Fuel Economy	2
Complaints	—
Insurance Costs	3

OVERALL RATING —

Jeep Wrangler

At-a-Glance

Status/Year Series Started . . . . All New/2018
Twins . . . . —
Body Styles . . . . SUV
Seating 5
Anti-Theft Device .Std. Pass. Immobil. & Opt. Pass. Alarm
Parking Index Rating . . . . Hard
Where Made . . . . Toledo, Ohio
Fuel Factor:
 MPG Rating (city/hwy) . . . . Very Poor-17/21
 Driving Range (mi.) Average-418
 Fuel Type . . . . Regular
 Annual Fuel Cost . . . . Very High-$1976
 Gas Guzzler Tax . . . . No
 Greenhouse Gas Emissions (tons/yr.) High-8.0
 Barrels of Oil Used per year . . . . Very High-18.3

How the Competition Rates

Competitors	Rating	Pg.
Mazda CX-5	4	200
Mitsubishi Outlander Sport	4	218
Subaru Forester	4	234

Price Range	Retail	Markup
Sport	$23,995	1%
Rubicon	$33,645	5%
Unlimited Sahara	$34,245	5%
Unlimited Rubicon	$37,445	5%

Jeep Wrangler

Safety Checklist

Crash Test:
 Frontal . . . . —
 Side . . . . —
Airbags:
 Torso . . . . None
 Roll Sensing . . . . No
 Knee Bolster . . . . None
Crash Avoidance:
 Collision Avoidance . . . . None
 Blind Spot Detection . . . . None
 Lane Keeping Assist . . . . None
 Backup Camera . . . . Optional
 Pedestrian Crash Avoidance . . . . None
General:
 Auto. Crash Notification . . . . None
 Day Running Lamps . . . . Standard
Safety Belt/Restraint:
 Dynamic Head Restraints . . . . None
 Adjustable Belt . . . . Standard Front

Note: As of May 2018, all vehicles are required to have a backup camera.
^Warning feature does not meet government standards.
*Backup camera does not meet government standards.

Jeep Wrangler

Specifications

Drive 4WD
Engine 3.6-liter V6
Transmission . . . . 8-sp. Automatic
Tow Rating (lbs.) . . . . Very Low-1000
Head/Leg Room (in.) Average-41.3/41
Interior Space (cu. ft.) Average-104
Cargo Space (cu. ft.) . . . . Very Roomy-31.5
Wheelbase/Length (in.) 95.4/184.9

Ratings—10 Best, 1 Worst

Combo Crash Tests	—
Safety Features	2
Rollover	7
Preventive Maintenance	9
Repair Costs	10
Warranty	9
Fuel Economy	8
Complaints	5
Insurance Costs	3
OVERALL RATING	**—**

Kia Forte

Kia Forte

At-a-Glance

Status/Year Series Started Unchanged/2014
Twins . . . . Hyundai Elantra
Body Styles . . . . Sedan, Hatchback
Seating 5
Anti-Theft Device . Std. Pass. Immobil. & Active Alarm
Parking Index Rating . . . . Easy
Where Made . . . . Pesquería, Mexico
Fuel Factor:
MPG Rating (city/hwy) Good-29/37
Driving Range (mi.) Long-424
Fuel Type . . . . Regular
Annual Fuel Cost . . . . Very Low-$1144
Gas Guzzler Tax . . . . No
Greenhouse Gas Emissions (tons/yr.) . Very Low-4.6
Barrels of Oil Used per year Low-10.3

How the Competition Rates

Competitors	Rating	Pg.
Ford Focus	5	143
Honda Civic	10	153
Toyota Corolla	8	245

Price Range

	Retail	Markup
LX Sedan MT	$16,600	2%
LX Sedan AT	$18,200	4%
S Sedan	$19,300	5%
EX Hatchback AT	$22,100	5%

Safety Checklist

Crash Test:
Frontal . . . . —
Side . . . . —
Airbags:
Torso . . . Standard Front Pelvis/Torso from Seat
Roll Sensing . . . . Yes
Knee Bolster . . . . None
Crash Avoidance:
Collision Avoidance . . . . None
Blind Spot Detection . . . . Optional
Lane Keeping Assist . . . Warning Only Optional^
Backup Camera . . . . Optional*
Pedestrian Crash Avoidance . . . . Optional
General:
Auto. Crash Notification . . . . . . Dial Assist.-Free
Day Running Lamps . . . . None
Safety Belt/Restraint:
Dynamic Head Restraints . . . . None
Adjustable Belt . . . . Standard Front

Note: As of May 2018, all vehicles are required to have a backup camera.
^Warning feature does not meet government standards.
*Backup camera does not meet government standards.

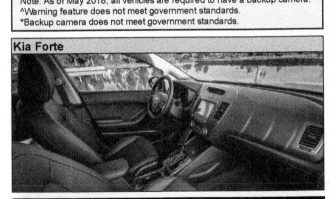
Kia Forte

Specifications

Drive . . . . FWD
Engine 2.0-liter I4
Transmission . . . . 6-sp. Automatic
Tow Rating (lbs.) . . . . —
Head/Leg Room (in.) Average-39.1/42.2
Interior Space (cu. ft.) Cramped-96.2
Cargo Space (cu. ft.) Cramped-14.9
Wheelbase/Length (in.) 106.3/179.5

Ratings—10 Best, 1 Worst

Combo Crash Tests	7
Safety Features	7
Rollover	8
Preventive Maintenance	6
Repair Costs	10
Warranty	9
Fuel Economy	7
Complaints	6
Insurance Costs	1
OVERALL RATING	**9**

Kia Optima

Kia Optima

At-a-Glance

Status/Year Series Started Unchanged/2011
Twins . . . . –
Body Styles . . . . Sedan
Seating 5
Anti-Theft Device . Std. Pass. Immobil. & Active Alarm
Parking Index Rating . . . . Easy
Where Made . . . . West Point, GA
Fuel Factor:
  MPG Rating (city/hwy) Good-24/34
  Driving Range (mi.) . . . . Very Long-512
  Fuel Type . . . . Regular
  Annual Fuel Cost . . . . Low-$1329
  Gas Guzzler Tax . . . . No
  Greenhouse Gas Emissions (tons/yr.) Low-5.3
  Barrels of Oil Used per year Average-11.8

How the Competition Rates

Competitors	Rating	Pg.
Mazda 6	5	203
Nissan Altima	4	219
Toyota Camry	8	244

Price Range	Retail	Markup
LX	$22,500	4%
S	$23,500	4%
LX Turbo	$24,300	6%
SX Turbo	$30,500	7%

Safety Checklist

Crash Test:
  Frontal . . . . Good
  Side . . . . Poor
Airbags:
  Torso . . . Standard Front Pelvis/Torso from Seat
  Roll Sensing . . . . Yes
  Knee Bolster . . . . Standard Driver
Crash Avoidance:
  Collision Avoidance . . . . . . Optional CIB & DBS
  Blind Spot Detection . . . . Optional
  Lane Keeping Assist . . . Warning Only Optional
  Backup Camera . . . . Standard
  Pedestrian Crash Avoidance . . . . Optional
General:
  Auto. Crash Notification . . . . . . Dial Assist.-Free
  Day Running Lamps . . . . Optional
Safety Belt/Restraint:
  Dynamic Head Restraints . . . . None
  Adjustable Belt . . . . Standard Front

Note: As of May 2018, all vehicles are required to have a backup camera.
^Warning feature does not meet government standards.
*Backup camera does not meet government standards.

Kia Optima

Specifications

Drive . . . . FWD
Engine 2.4-liter I4
Transmission . . . . 6-sp. Automatic
Tow Rating (lbs.) . . . . –
Head/Leg Room (in.) . . . . Very Roomy-40/45.5
Interior Space (cu. ft.) Roomy-117.6
Cargo Space (cu. ft.) Cramped-15.4
Wheelbase/Length (in.) 110/190.7

Ratings—10 Best, 1 Worst

Combo Crash Tests	—
Safety Features	3
Rollover	6
Preventive Maintenance	7
Repair Costs	10
Warranty	9
Fuel Economy	8
Complaints	—
Insurance Costs	1
OVERALL RATING	—

Kia Rio

Kia Rio

At-a-Glance

Status/Year Series Started. . . . . All New/2018
Twins . . . . Hyundai Accent
Body Styles . . . . Sedan, Hatchback
Seating 5
Anti-Theft Device . Std. Pass. Immobil. & Active Alarm
Parking Index Rating . . . . Very Easy
Where Made. . . . . Gwanmyeong, South Korea
Fuel Factor:
  MPG Rating (city/hwy) Good-28/37
  Driving Range (mi.) . . . . Very Short-374
  Fuel Type . . . . Regular
  Annual Fuel Cost . . . . Very Low-$1169
  Gas Guzzler Tax . . . . No
  Greenhouse Gas Emissions (tons/yr.). Very Low-4.6
  Barrels of Oil Used per year Low-10.3

How the Competition Rates

Competitors	Rating	Pg.
Chevrolet Sonic	9	119
Ford Focus	5	143
Nissan Versa	1	230

Price Range

Price Range	Retail	Markup
LX Sedan MT	$14,165	2%
LX Hatchback AT	$15,495	3%
EX Sedan AT	$17,755	5%
SX Hatchback AT	$20,905	6%

Safety Checklist

Crash Test:
  Frontal. . . . . —
  Side. . . . . —
Airbags:
  Torso . . . Standard Front Pelvis/Torso from Seat
  Roll Sensing. . . . . Yes
  Knee Bolster . . . . None
Crash Avoidance:
  Collision Avoidance . . . . . . Optional CIB & DBS
  Blind Spot Detection . . . . None
  Lane Keeping Assist . . . . None
  Backup Camera. . . . . Standard
  Pedestrian Crash Avoidance . . . . None
General:
  Auto. Crash Notification. . . . . . Dial Assist.-Free
  Day Running Lamps . . . . Optional
Safety Belt/Restraint:
  Dynamic Head Restraints . . . . None
  Adjustable Belt. . . . . Standard Front

Note: As of May 2018, all vehicles are required to have a backup camera.
^Warning feature does not meet government standards.
*Backup camera does not meet government standards.

Kia Rio

Specifications

Drive. . . . . FWD
Engine 1.6-liter I4
Transmission . . . . 6-sp. Automatic
Tow Rating (lbs.) . . . . —
Head/Leg Room (in.) Average-38.9/42.1
Interior Space (cu. ft.). . . . . Very Cramped-89.9
Cargo Space (cu. ft.) Cramped-13.7
Wheelbase/Length (in.) 101.6/172.6

Kia Sedona

Ratings—10 Best, 1 Worst

Combo Crash Tests	—
Safety Features	4
Rollover	5
Preventive Maintenance	4
Repair Costs	9
Warranty	9
Fuel Economy	3
Complaints	7
Insurance Costs	5

OVERALL RATING   —

Kia Sedona

Kia Sedona

At-a-Glance

Status/Year Series Started	Unchanged/2015
Twins	—
Body Styles	Minivan
Seating	7/8
Anti-Theft Device	Std. Pass. Immobil. & Active Alarm
Parking Index Rating	Hard
Where Made	West Point, GA

Fuel Factor:

MPG Rating (city/hwy)	Poor-18/25
Driving Range (mi.)	Long-435
Fuel Type	Regular
Annual Fuel Cost	High-$1784
Gas Guzzler Tax	No
Greenhouse Gas Emissions (tons/yr.)	Average-7.2
Barrels of Oil Used per year	High-15.7

How the Competition Rates

Competitors	Rating	Pg.
Chrysler Pacifica	8	127
Honda Odyssey	9	157
Toyota Sienna	2	254

Price Range

	Retail	Markup
L	$26,900	3%
EX	$33,600	6%
SX	$36,900	7%
SXL	$41,900	7%

Safety Checklist

Crash Test:

Frontal	—
Side	—

Airbags:

Torso	Standard Front Pelvis/Torso from Seat
Roll Sensing	Yes
Knee Bolster	None

Crash Avoidance:

Collision Avoidance	Optional CIB & DBS
Blind Spot Detection	Optional
Lane Keeping Assist	Warning Only Optional
Backup Camera	Optional*
Pedestrian Crash Avoidance	Optional

General:

Auto. Crash Notification	Dial Assist.-Free
Day Running Lamps	None

Safety Belt/Restraint:

Dynamic Head Restraints	None
Adjustable Belt	Standard Front & Rear

Note: As of May 2018, all vehicles are required to have a backup camera.
^Warning feature does not meet government standards.
*Backup camera does not meet government standards.

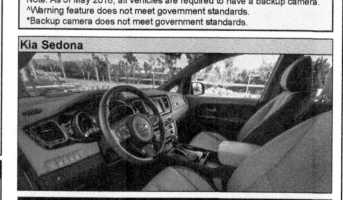

Kia Sedona

Specifications

Drive	FWD
Engine	3.3-liter V6
Transmission	6-sp. Automatic
Tow Rating (lbs.)	Low-3500
Head/Leg Room (in.)	Roomy-39.8/43.1
Interior Space (cu. ft.)	Very Roomy-172.3
Cargo Space (cu. ft.)	Very Roomy-33.9
Wheelbase/Length (in.)	120.5/201.4

Ratings—10 Best, 1 Worst

Combo Crash Tests	7
Safety Features	4
Rollover	4
Preventive Maintenance	5
Repair Costs	8
Warranty	9
Fuel Economy	4
Complaints	4
Insurance Costs	5
OVERALL RATING	**6**

Kia Sorento

Kia Sorento

At-a-Glance

Status/Year Series Started	Unchanged/2016
Twins	–
Body Styles	SUV
Seating	5
Anti-Theft Device	Std. Pass. Immobil. & Active Alarm
Parking Index Rating	Very Easy
Where Made	West Point, GA

Fuel Factor:

MPG Rating (city/hwy)	Poor-21/28
Driving Range (mi.)	Long-445
Fuel Type	Regular
Annual Fuel Cost	Average-$1553
Gas Guzzler Tax	No
Greenhouse Gas Emissions (tons/yr.)	Average-6.2
Barrels of Oil Used per year	High-13.7

How the Competition Rates

Competitors	Rating	Pg.
Dodge Durango	2	130
Ford Edge	9	136
Nissan Rogue	3	227

Price Range	Retail	Markup
L FWD	$25,800	4%
LX AWD V6	$31,300	4%
SX AWD	$40,400	5%
SXL AWD	$45,700	7%

Safety Checklist

Crash Test:
- Frontal . . . . Good
- Side . . . . Poor

Airbags:
- Torso . . . Standard Front Pelvis/Torso from Seat
- Roll Sensing . . . . Yes
- Knee Bolster . . . . None

Crash Avoidance:
- Collision Avoidance . . . . . . Optional CIB & DBS
- Blind Spot Detection . . . . Optional
- Lane Keeping Assist . . . . Warning Only Optional
- Backup Camera . . . . Standard*
- Pedestrian Crash Avoidance . . . . Optional

General:
- Auto. Crash Notification . . . . . . Dial Assist.-Free
- Day Running Lamps . . . . None

Safety Belt/Restraint:
- Dynamic Head Restraints . . . . None
- Adjustable Belt . . . . Standard Front

Note: As of May 2018, all vehicles are required to have a backup camera.
^Warning feature does not meet government standards.
*Backup camera does not meet government standards.

Kia Sorento

Specifications

Drive	FWD
Engine	2.4-liter I4
Transmission	6-sp. Automatic
Tow Rating (lbs.)	Very Low-2000
Head/Leg Room (in.)	Roomy-39.5/44.1
Interior Space (cu. ft.)	Very Roomy-146.4
Cargo Space (cu. ft.)	Very Roomy-38.8
Wheelbase/Length (in.)	109.4/187.4

Kia Soul

Compact

Kia Soul

Ratings—10 Best, 1 Worst	
Combo Crash Tests	8
Safety Features	5
Rollover	4
Preventive Maintenance	4
Repair Costs	8
Warranty	9
Fuel Economy	6
Complaints	6
Insurance Costs	1
OVERALL RATING	**7**

Kia Soul

At-a-Glance

Status/Year Series Started	Unchanged/2014
Twins	–
Body Styles	Wagon
Seating	5
Anti-Theft Device	Std. Pass. Immobil
Parking Index Rating	Very Easy
Where Made	Gwangju, South Korea

Fuel Factor:

MPG Rating (city/hwy)	Average-25/30
Driving Range (mi.)	Short-384
Fuel Type	Regular
Annual Fuel Cost	Low-$1360
Gas Guzzler Tax	No
Greenhouse Gas Emissions (tons/yr.)	Low-5.5
Barrels of Oil Used per year	Average-12.2

How the Competition Rates

Competitors	Rating	Pg.
Chevrolet Spark	5	120
Mini Hardtop	6	215
Toyota Yaris iA	6	258

Price Range	Retail	Markup
Base MT	$16,100	2%
!	$22,800	6%
EV e	$32,250	7%
EV +	$35,950	8%

Safety Checklist

Crash Test:
Frontal	Good
Side	Good

Airbags:
Torso	Standard Front Pelvis/Torso from Seat
Roll Sensing	Yes
Knee Bolster	None

Crash Avoidance:
Collision Avoidance	Optional CIB & DBS
Blind Spot Detection	Optional
Lane Keeping Assist	Warning Only Optional
Backup Camera	Optional
Pedestrian Crash Avoidance	Optional

General:
Auto. Crash Notification	Dial Assist.-Free
Day Running Lamps	Optional

Safety Belt/Restraint:
Dynamic Head Restraints	None
Adjustable Belt	Standard Front

Note: As of May 2018, all vehicles are required to have a backup camera.
^Warning feature does not meet government standards.
*Backup camera does not meet government standards.

Kia Soul

Specifications

Drive	FWD
Engine	2.0-liter I4
Transmission	6-sp. Automatic
Tow Rating (lbs.)	–
Head/Leg Room (in.)	Cramped-39.6/40.9
Interior Space (cu. ft.)	Average-101
Cargo Space (cu. ft.)	Roomy-24.2
Wheelbase/Length (in.)	101.2/163

Kia Sportage

Small SUV

Ratings—10 Best, 1 Worst

Combo Crash Tests	7
Safety Features	6
Rollover	4
Preventive Maintenance	5
Repair Costs	7
Warranty	9
Fuel Economy	5
Complaints	8
Insurance Costs	8
OVERALL RATING	**9**

Kia Sportage

Kia Sportage

At-a-Glance

Status/Year Series Started........ Unchanged/2011
Twins .... –
Body Styles .... SUV
Seating..5
Anti-Theft Device . Std. Pass. Immobil. & Active Alarm
Parking Index Rating .... Very Easy
Where Made............... Gwangju, South Korea

Fuel Factor:
MPG Rating (city/hwy) Average-22/29
Driving Range (mi.) .... Very Short-358
Fuel Type................................Regular
Annual Fuel Cost .... Average-$1489
Gas Guzzler Tax ....No
Greenhouse Gas Emissions (tons/yr.). . Average-5.9
Barrels of Oil Used per year High-13.2

How the Competition Rates

Competitors	Rating	Pg.
Ford Escape	5	137
Honda HR-V	5	156
Toyota RAV4	9	252

Price Range	Retail	Markup
LX FWD	$23,500	4%
EX FWD	$26,300	5%
EX AWD	$27,800	5%
SX AWD	$34,300	6%

Safety Checklist

Crash Test:
Frontal........................... Average
Side............................. Good
Airbags:
Torso . . .Standard Front Pelvis/Torso from Seat
Roll Sensing...........................Yes
Knee Bolster .... None
Crash Avoidance:
Collision Avoidance ...... Optional CIB & DBS
Blind Spot Detection .... Optional
Lane Keeping Assist ....Warning Only Optional
Backup Camera................... Standard
Pedestrian Crash Avoidance .... Optional
General:
Auto. Crash Notification...... Dial Assist.-Free
Day Running Lamps .... Standard
Safety Belt/Restraint:
Dynamic Head Restraints .... None
Adjustable Belt.............. Standard Front

Note: As of May 2018, all vehicles are required to have a backup camera.
^Warning feature does not meet government standards.
*Backup camera does not meet government standards.

Kia Sportage

Specifications

Drive..FWD
Engine 2.4-liter I4
Transmission .... 6-sp. Automaitc
Tow Rating (lbs.) .... Very Low-2000
Head/Leg Room (in.) Cramped-39.1/41.4
Interior Space (cu. ft.)................Average-100
Cargo Space (cu. ft.) Roomy-26.1
Wheelbase/Length (in.) 103.9/174.8

Land Rover Range Rover

Land Rover Range Rover

Ratings—10 Best, 1 Worst

Combo Crash Tests	—
Safety Features	5
Rollover	2
Preventive Maintenance	6
Repair Costs	4
Warranty	7
Fuel Economy	1
Complaints	7
Insurance Costs	5
OVERALL RATING	**—**

Land Rover Range Rover

At-a-Glance

Status/Year Series Started Unchanged/2013
Twins . . . . —
Body Styles . . . . SUV
Seating 5
Anti-Theft Device . . . . . Std. Pass. Immobil. & Alarm
Parking Index Rating . . . . Very Hard
Where Made . . . . Solihull, England
Fuel Factor:
MPG Rating (city/hwy) . . . . Very Poor-14/19
Driving Range (mi.) Long-440
Fuel Type . . . . Premium
Annual Fuel Cost . . . . Very High-$2805
Gas Guzzler Tax . . . . No
Greenhouse Gas Emissions (tons/yr.) Very High-11.3
Barrels of Oil Used per year . . . . Very High-20.6

How the Competition Rates

Competitors	Rating	Pg.
Buick Enclave	4	101
Chevrolet Suburban	2	121
Toyota 4Runner	2	241

Price Range

Price Range	Retail	Markup
Base	$85,650	6%
HSE	$92,650	6%
Supercharged	$103,895	6%
Autobiography	$140,995	6%

Safety Checklist

Crash Test:
    Frontal . . . . —
    Side . . . . —
Airbags:
    Torso . . . Standard Front Pelvis/Torso from Seat
    Roll Sensing . . . . Yes
    Knee Bolster . . . . None
Crash Avoidance:
    Collision Avoidance . . . . . Std. CIB & Opt. DBS^
    Blind Spot Detection . . . . Optional
    Lane Keeping Assist . . . . Optional^
    Backup Camera . . . . Standard*
    Pedestrian Crash Avoidance . . . . None
General:
    Auto. Crash Notification . . . Operator Assist.-Fee
    Day Running Lamps . . . . Standard
Safety Belt/Restraint:
    Dynamic Head Restraints . . . . None
    Adjustable Belt . . . . Standard Front

Note: As of May 2018, all vehicles are required to have a backup camera.
^Warning feature does not meet government standards.
*Backup camera does not meet government standards.

Land Rover Range Rover

Specifications

Drive 4WD
Engine 5.0-liter V8
Transmission . . . . 6-sp. Automatic
Tow Rating (lbs.) High-7716
Head/Leg Room (in.) Average-42.5/39.1
Interior Space (cu. ft.) . . . . —
Cargo Space (cu. ft.) . . . . Very Roomy-32.1
Wheelbase/Length (in.) 115/196.8

Land Rover Range Rover Evoque — Small SUV

Ratings—10 Best, 1 Worst

Combo Crash Tests	—
Safety Features	6
Rollover	4
Preventive Maintenance	6
Repair Costs	5
Warranty	7
Fuel Economy	5
Complaints	6
Insurance Costs	3
OVERALL RATING	—

Land Rover Range Rover Evoque

Land Rover Range Rover Evoque

At-a-Glance

Status/Year Series Started Unchanged/2012
Twins . . . . —
Body Styles . . . . SUV
Seating 5
Anti-Theft Device . . . . . . Std. Pass. Immobil. & Alarm
Parking Index Rating . . . . Easy
Where Made . . . . Halewood, England
Fuel Factor:
MPG Rating (city/hwy) Average-21/30
Driving Range (mi.) Long-449
Fuel Type . . . . Premium
Annual Fuel Cost . . . . High-$1835
Gas Guzzler Tax . . . . No
Greenhouse Gas Emissions (tons/yr.) High-7.5
Barrels of Oil Used per year High-13.7

How the Competition Rates

Competitors	Rating	Pg.
Lexus NX	5	191
Mazda CX-5	4	200
Subaru Crosstrek	5	233

Price Range	Retail	Markup
SE	$41,800	6%
SE Premium	$45,700	6%
HSE	$51,000	6%
HSE Dynamic	$54,200	6%

Safety Checklist

Crash Test:
Frontal . . . . —
Side . . . . —
Airbags:
Torso . . . Standard Front Pelvis/Torso from Seat
Roll Sensing . . . . Yes
Knee Bolster . . . . Standard Driver
Crash Avoidance:
Collision Avoidance . . . . . Std. CIB & Opt. DBS^
Blind Spot Detection . . . . Optional
Lane Keeping Assist . . . . Optional^
Backup Camera . . . . Standard*
Pedestrian Crash Avoidance . . . . None
General:
Auto. Crash Notification . . . Operator Assist.-Fee
Day Running Lamps . . . . Standard
Safety Belt/Restraint:
Dynamic Head Restraints . . . . None
Adjustable Belt . . . . Standard Front

Note: As of May 2018, all vehicles are required to have a backup camera.
^Warning feature does not meet government standards.
*Backup camera does not meet government standards.

Land Rover Range Rover Evoque

Specifications

Drive 4WD
Engine 2.0-liter I4
Transmission . . . . 9-sp. Automatic
Tow Rating (lbs.) . . . . —
Head/Leg Room (in.) Cramped-40.3/40.1
Interior Space (cu. ft.) . . . . —
Cargo Space (cu. ft.) Average-20.3
Wheelbase/Length (in.) 104.8/171.5

Land Rover Range Rover Sport

Ratings—10 Best, 1 Worst

Combo Crash Tests	—
Safety Features	5
Rollover	3
Preventive Maintenance	1
Repair Costs	4
Warranty	7
Fuel Economy	1
Complaints	9
Insurance Costs	1
OVERALL RATING	**—**

Land Rover Range Rover Sport

At-a-Glance

Status/Year Series Started	Unchanged/2014
Twins	—
Body Styles	SUV
Seating	5
Anti-Theft Device	Std. Pass. Immobil. & Alarm
Parking Index Rating	Hard
Where Made	Solihull, England

Fuel Factor:

MPG Rating (city/hwy)	Very Poor-14/19
Driving Range (mi.)	Long-440
Fuel Type	Premium
Annual Fuel Cost	Very High-$2805
Gas Guzzler Tax	No
Greenhouse Gas Emissions (tons/yr.)	Very High-11.2
Barrels of Oil Used per year	Very High-20.6

How the Competition Rates

Competitors	Rating	Pg.
Acura MDX	7	80
Audi Q7	3	89
BMW X5	5	98

Price Range	Retail	Markup
SE	$65,650	6%
HSE	$70,650	6%
Supercharged	$80,650	6%
Autobiography	$94,450	6%

Land Rover Range Rover Sport

Safety Checklist

Crash Test:
- Frontal . . . . —
- Side . . . . —

Airbags:
- Torso . . . Standard Front Pelvis/Torso from Seat
- Roll Sensing . . . . Yes
- Knee Bolster . . . . None

Crash Avoidance:
- Collision Avoidance . . . . . Std. CIB & Opt. DBS^
- Blind Spot Detection . . . . Optional
- Lane Keeping Assist . . . . Optional^
- Backup Camera . . . . Standard*
- Pedestrian Crash Avoidance . . . . None

General:
- Auto. Crash Notification . . . Operator Assist.-Fee
- Day Running Lamps . . . . Standard

Safety Belt/Restraint:
- Dynamic Head Restraints . . . . None
- Adjustable Belt . . . . Standard Front

Note: As of May 2018, all vehicles are required to have a backup camera.
^Warning feature does not meet government standards.
*Backup camera does not meet government standards.

Land Rover Range Rover Sport

Specifications

Drive	4WD
Engine	5.0-liter V8
Transmission	8-sp. Automatic
Tow Rating (lbs.)	High-7716
Head/Leg Room (in.)	Average-39.4/42.2
Interior Space (cu. ft.)	—
Cargo Space (cu. ft.)	Roomy-27.7
Wheelbase/Length (in.)	115.1/191.8

Ratings—10 Best, 1 Worst

Combo Crash Tests	7
Safety Features	9
Rollover	7
Preventive Maintenance	6
Repair Costs	2
Warranty	7
Fuel Economy	5
Complaints	4
Insurance Costs	1
OVERALL RATING	**5**

Lexus ES

At-a-Glance

Status/Year Series Started Appearance Change/2012
Twins . . . . Toyota Avalon
Body Styles . . . . Sedan
Seating 5
Anti-Theft Device . . . . . . Std. Pass. Immobil. & Alarm
Parking Index Rating . . . . Average
Where Made. Kyushu, Japan
Fuel Factor:
MPG Rating (city/hwy) Average-21/31
Driving Range (mi.) Average-423
Fuel Type. . . . . .Regular
Annual Fuel Cost . . . . .Average-$1496
Gas Guzzler Tax . . . . .No
Greenhouse Gas Emissions (tons/yr.) High-7.5
Barrels of Oil Used per year High-13.7

How the Competition Rates

Competitors	Rating	Pg.
Acura TLX	9	82
Audi A6	7	86
Volkswagen Passat	4	263

Price Range	Retail	Markup
350	$38,900	7%
300h	$41,820	7%

Lexus ES

Safety Checklist

Crash Test:
Frontal. . . . . Good
Side. . . . . Good
Airbags:
Torso . Std Front & Rear Pelvis/Torso from Seat
Roll Sensing. . . . . .Yes
Knee Bolster . . . . .Standard Front
Crash Avoidance:
Collision Avoidance . . . . . . Standard CIB & DBS
Blind Spot Detection . . . . Optional
Lane Keeping Assist . . . . Optional
Backup Camera. . . . . Standard
Pedestrian Crash Avoidance . . . . None
General:
Auto. Crash Notification . . . Operator Assist.-Fee
Day Running Lamps . . . . Standard
Safety Belt/Restraint:
Dynamic Head Restraints . . . . None
Adjustable Belt. . . . . .Standard Front

Note: As of May 2018, all vehicles are required to have a backup camera.
^Warning feature does not meet government standards.
*Backup camera does not meet government standards.

Lexus ES

Specifications

Drive. . . . . .FWD
Engine 3.5-liter V6
Transmission . . . . 6-sp. Automatic
Tow Rating (lbs.) . . . . –
Head/Leg Room (in.) . . . . Very Cramped-37.5/41.9
Interior Space (cu. ft.). Average-100.1
Cargo Space (cu. ft.) Cramped-15.2
Wheelbase/Length (in.) 111/192.7

Ratings—10 Best, 1 Worst	
Combo Crash Tests	—
Safety Features	9
Rollover	7
Preventive Maintenance	8
Repair Costs	1
Warranty	7
Fuel Economy	3
Complaints	4
Insurance Costs	1
OVERALL RATING	—

Lexus GS

At-a-Glance

Status/Year Series Started.......	Unchanged/2012
Twins....................................	—
Body Styles	Sedan
Seating..................................	5
Anti-Theft Device	Std. Pass. Immobil. & Alarm
Parking Index Rating	Average
Where Made............................	Tahara, Japan

Fuel Factor:

MPG Rating (city/hwy)	Poor-19/29
Driving Range (mi.)	Short-391
Fuel Type...............................	Premium
Annual Fuel Cost	Very High-$1981
Gas Guzzler Tax	No
Greenhouse Gas Emissions (tons/yr.).....	High-7.8
Barrels of Oil Used per year	High-14.3

How the Competition Rates

Competitors	Rating	Pg.
Cadillac XTS	8	109
Lincoln MKZ	4	197
Volvo S60	9	265

Price Range	Retail	Markup
200t	$46,310	8%
350	$50,695	8%
200t F Sport	$53,980	8%
350 F Sport AWD	$56,555	8%

Lexus GS

Safety Checklist

Crash Test:
- Frontal............................. —
- Side............................... —

Airbags:
- Torso . Std Front & Rear Pelvis/Torso from Seat
- Roll Sensing......................Yes
- Knee Bolster ....Standard Front

Crash Avoidance:
- Collision Avoidance ...... Optional CIB & DBS
- Blind Spot Detection .... Optional
- Lane Keeping Assist .... Optional
- Backup Camera.................. Standard
- Pedestrian Crash Avoidance .... None

General:
- Auto. Crash Notification... Operator Assist.-Fee
- Day Running Lamps .... Standard

Safety Belt/Restraint:
- Dynamic Head Restraints .... None
- Adjustable Belt................Standard Front

Note: As of May 2018, all vehicles are required to have a backup camera.
^Warning feature does not meet government standards.
*Backup camera does not meet government standards.

Lexus GS

Specifications

Drive...............................	RWD
Engine	3.5-liter V6
Transmission	8-sp. Automatic
Tow Rating (lbs.)	—
Head/Leg Room (in.)	Cramped-38/42.3
Interior Space (cu. ft.)............	Average-99
Cargo Space (cu. ft.)	Cramped-14.1
Wheelbase/Length (in.)	112.2/190.7

Ratings—10 Best, 1 Worst

Combo Crash Tests	—
Safety Features	9
Rollover	1
Preventive Maintenance	6
Repair Costs	2
Warranty	7
Fuel Economy	1
Complaints	9
Insurance Costs	10

OVERALL RATING   —

Lexus GX

Lexus GX

At-a-Glance

Status/Year Series Started. Unchanged/2010
Twins Lexus RX, Toyota 4Runner, Toyota Highlander
Body Styles . . . . SUV
Seating 7
Anti-Theft Device . . . . . . Std. Pass. Immobil. & Alarm
Parking Index Rating . . . . Very Hard
Where Made. Tahara, Japan

Fuel Factor:
MPG Rating (city/hwy) . . . . Very Poor-15/20
Driving Range (mi.) Short-389
Fuel Type. . . . . Premium
Annual Fuel Cost . . . . Very High-$2636
Gas Guzzler Tax . . . . .No
Greenhouse Gas Emissions (tons/yr.)Very High-10.6
Barrels of Oil Used per year . . . . Very High-19.4

How the Competition Rates

Competitors	Rating	Pg.
Buick Enclave	4	101
Chevrolet Suburban	2	121
Volvo XC90	8	268

Price Range	Retail	Markup
460	$51,680	9%
460 Luxury	$63,380	9%

Lexus GX

Safety Checklist

Crash Test:
Frontal. . . . . —
Side. . . . . —
Airbags:
Torso Std. Fr. & Opt. Rr. Pelvis/Torso from Seat
Roll Sensing. . . . . .Yes
Knee Bolster . . . . Standard Front
Crash Avoidance:
Collision Avoidance . . . . . . Optional CIB & DBS
Blind Spot Detection . . . . Optional
Lane Keeping Assist . . . .Warning Only Optional
Backup Camera. . . . . .Standard*
Pedestrian Crash Avoidance . . . . None
General:
Auto. Crash Notification. . . Operator Assist.-Fee
Day Running Lamps . . . . Standard
Safety Belt/Restraint:
Dynamic Head Restraints . . . . . .Standard Front
Adjustable Belt. . . . . Standard Front & Rear

Note: As of May 2018, all vehicles are required to have a backup camera.
^Warning feature does not meet government standards.
*Backup camera does not meet government standards.

Lexus GX

Specifications

Drive. 4WD
Engine 4.6-liter V8
Transmission . . . . 6-sp. Automatic
Tow Rating (lbs.) Average-6500
Head/Leg Room (in.) Cramped-38/41.7
Interior Space (cu. ft.). . . . . Very Roomy-129.7
Cargo Space (cu. ft.) . . . . Very Cramped-11.6
Wheelbase/Length (in.) 109.8/192.1

Ratings—10 Best, 1 Worst

Combo Crash Tests	5
Safety Features	9
Rollover	9
Preventive Maintenance	7
Repair Costs	1
Warranty	7
Fuel Economy	5
Complaints	10
Insurance Costs	5
OVERALL RATING	**8**

Lexus IS

At-a-Glance

Status/Year Series Started Unchanged/2014
Twins . . . . –
Body Styles . . . . .Sedan, Convertible
Seating 5
Anti-Theft Device . . . . . . Std. Pass. Immobil. & Alarm
Parking Index Rating . . . . Easy
Where Made . . . . Kyushu, Japan / Tahara, Japan
Fuel Factor:
  MPG Rating (city/hwy) Average-21/30
  Driving Range (mi.) Average-422
  Fuel Type . . . . Premium
  Annual Fuel Cost . . . . .High-$1835
  Gas Guzzler Tax . . . . .No
  Greenhouse Gas Emissions (tons/yr.) High-7.5
  Barrels of Oil Used per year High-13.7

How the Competition Rates

Competitors	Rating	Pg.
Audi A3	6	83
BMW 3 Series	7	91
Infiniti Q50	3	167

Price Range	Retail	Markup
200t	$37,825	8%
300 AWD	$40,200	8%
350	$41,370	8%
350 AWD	$43,535	8%

Lexus IS

Safety Checklist

Crash Test:
  Frontal . . . . .Poor
  Side . . . . Good
Airbags:
  Torso . Std Front & Rear Pelvis/Torso from Seat
  Roll Sensing . . . . .Yes
  Knee Bolster . . . . .Standard Front
Crash Avoidance:
  Collision Avoidance . . . . . .Optional CIB & DBS^
  Blind Spot Detection . . . . Optional
  Lane Keeping Assist . . . . Standard
  Backup Camera . . . . Optional
  Pedestrian Crash Avoidance . . . . None
General:
  Auto. Crash Notification . . . Operator Assist.-Fee
  Day Running Lamps . . . . Standard
Safety Belt/Restraint:
  Dynamic Head Restraints . . . . None
  Adjustable Belt . . . . .Standard Front

Note: As of May 2018, all vehicles are required to have a backup camera.
^Warning feature does not meet government standards.
*Backup camera does not meet government standards.

Lexus IS

Specifications

Drive . . . . .RWD
Engine 2.5-liter V6
Transmission . . . . 6-sp. Automatic
Tow Rating (lbs.) . . . . –
Head/Leg Room (in.) Roomy-38.2/44.8
Interior Space (cu. ft.) . . . . Very Cramped-90.2
Cargo Space (cu. ft.) Cramped-13.8
Wheelbase/Length (in.) 110.2/183.7

Ratings—10 Best, 1 Worst

Combo Crash Tests	7
Safety Features	8
Rollover	4
Preventive Maintenance	1
Repair Costs	3
Warranty	7
Fuel Economy	5
Complaints	7
Insurance Costs	5
OVERALL RATING	**5**

Lexus NX

Lexus NX

At-a-Glance

Status/Year Series Started Appearance Change/2015
Twins . . . . –
Body Styles . . . . SUV
Seating 5
Anti-Theft Device . . . . . . Std. Pass. Immobil. & Alarm
Parking Index Rating . . . . .Very Easy
Where Made. . . . . Kyushu, Japan
Fuel Factor:
  MPG Rating (city/hwy) Average-22/28
  Driving Range (mi.) Short-387
  Fuel Type. . . . . .Premium
  Annual Fuel Cost . . . . .High-$1830
  Gas Guzzler Tax . . . . .No
  Greenhouse Gas Emissions (tons/yr.). Very Low-3.5
  Barrels of Oil Used per year High-13.7

How the Competition Rates

Competitors	Rating	Pg.
Buick Enclave	4	101
Lincoln MKC	6	195
Mazda CX-5	4	200

Price Range

	Retail	Markup
200t FWD	$35,285	7%
200t AWD	$36,685	7%
200t F Sport AWD	$38,785	7%
300h	$39,720	6%

Safety Checklist

Crash Test:
  Frontal. . . . . Very Good
  Side. . . . . .Very Poor
Airbags:
  Torso . . .Standard Front Pelvis/Torso from Seat
  Roll Sensing. . . . . .Yes
  Knee Bolster . . . . .Standard Front
Crash Avoidance:
  Collision Avoidance . . . . . . Optional CIB & DBS
  Blind Spot Detection . . . . Optional
  Lane Keeping Assist . . . . Optional
  Backup Camera . . . . Standard
  Pedestrian Crash Avoidance . . . . None
General:
  Auto. Crash Notification. . . Operator Assist.-Fee
  Day Running Lamps . . . . Standard
Safety Belt/Restraint:
  Dynamic Head Restraints . . . . None
  Adjustable Belt. . . . . .Standard Front

Note: As of May 2018, all vehicles are required to have a backup camera.
^Warning feature does not meet government standards.
*Backup camera does not meet government standards.

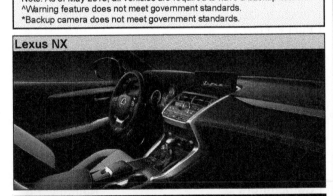

Lexus NX

Specifications

Drive. . . . . .AWD
Engine 2.0-liter I4
Transmission . . . . 6-sp. Automatic
Tow Rating (lbs.) . . . . .Very Low-2000
Head/Leg Room (in.) Average-38.2/42.8
Interior Space (cu. ft.). . . . . Very Cramped-71.6
Cargo Space (cu. ft.) Average-17.7
Wheelbase/Length (in.) 104.7/182.3

Ratings—10 Best, 1 Worst

Combo Crash Tests	—
Safety Features	8
Rollover	8
Preventive Maintenance	6
Repair Costs	1
Warranty	7
Fuel Economy	6
Complaints	10
Insurance Costs	3
OVERALL RATING	**—**

Lexus RC

Lexus RC

At-a-Glance

Status/Year Series Started	Unchanged/2016
Twins	—
Body Styles	Coupe
Seating	4
Anti-Theft Device	Std. Pass. Immobil. & Alarm
Parking Index Rating	Easy
Where Made	Tahara, Japan

Fuel Factor:

MPG Rating (city/hwy)	Average-22/32
Driving Range (mi.)	Long-445
Fuel Type	Premium
Annual Fuel Cost	High-$1740
Gas Guzzler Tax	No
Greenhouse Gas Emissions (tons/yr.)	Low-5.7
Barrels of Oil Used per year	Average-12.7

How the Competition Rates

Competitors	Rating	Pg.
Audi A3	6	83
Cadillac ATS	4	106
Mercedes-Benz C	1	206

Price Range	Retail	Markup
200T	$40,155	8%
300 AWD	$42,770	8%
350	$43,010	8%
350 AWD	$45,175	8%

Safety Checklist

Crash Test:
- Frontal . . . . —
- Side . . . . —

Airbags:
- Torso . . . Standard Front Pelvis/Torso from Seat
- Roll Sensing . . . . Yes
- Knee Bolster . . . . Standard Front

Crash Avoidance:
- Collision Avoidance . . . . . . Optional CIB & DBS
- Blind Spot Detection . . . . Standard
- Lane Keeping Assist . . . . Warning Only Optional
- Backup Camera . . . . Standard
- Pedestrian Crash Avoidance . . . . None

General:
- Auto. Crash Notification . . . Operator Assist.-Fee
- Day Running Lamps . . . . Standard

Safety Belt/Restraint:
- Dynamic Head Restraints . . . . None
- Adjustable Belt . . . . None

^Warning feature does not meet government standards.
*Backup camera does not meet government standards.

Lexus RC

Specifications

Drive	RWD
Engine	2.0-liter I4
Transmission	8-sp. Automatic
Tow Rating (lbs.)	—
Head/Leg Room (in.)	Roomy-37.8/45.4
Interior Space (cu. ft.)	Very Cramped-82
Cargo Space (cu. ft.)	Very Cramped-10.4
Wheelbase/Length (in.)	107.5/184.8

Ratings—10 Best, 1 Worst

Combo Crash Tests	3
Safety Features	8
Rollover	4
Preventive Maintenance	5
Repair Costs	1
Warranty	7
Fuel Economy	4
Complaints	10
Insurance Costs	5
OVERALL RATING	**4**

Lexus RX

Lexus RX

At-a-Glance

Status/Year Series Started........ Unchanged/2016
Twins Lexus GX, Toyota 4Runner, Toyota Highlander
Body Styles .... SUV
Seating 5
Anti-Theft Device ...... Std. Pass. Immobil. & Alarm
Parking Index Rating .... Hard
Where Made.... Kyushu, Japan / Cambridge, Ontario
Fuel Factor:
MPG Rating (city/hwy) Poor-20/28
Driving Range (mi.) Long-441
Fuel Type....................... Regular
Annual Fuel Cost .... Average-$1601
Gas Guzzler Tax .... No
Greenhouse Gas Emissions (tons/yr.).. Average-6.4
Barrels of Oil Used per year High-14.3

How the Competition Rates

Competitors	Rating	Pg.
Audi Q7	3	89
BMW X5	5	98
Lincoln MKC	6	195

Price Range

Price Range	Retail	Markup
350 Base FWD	$43,120	7%
350 Base AWD	$44,520	7%
350 F Sport	$50,420	7%
450 Hybrid AWD	$53,035	6%

Safety Checklist

Crash Test:
Frontal.......................... Very Poor
Side............................... Good
Airbags:
Torso Std. Fr. & Opt. Rr. Pelvis/Torso from Seat
Roll Sensing........................... Yes
Knee Bolster .... Standard Driver
Crash Avoidance:
Collision Avoidance ...... Optional CIB & DBS
Blind Spot Detection .... Standard
Lane Keeping Assist .... Optional
Backup Camera.................... Standard
Pedestrian Crash Avoidance .... None
General:
Auto. Crash Notification... Operator Assist.-Fee
Day Running Lamps .... Standard
Safety Belt/Restraint:
Dynamic Head Restraints .... None
Adjustable Belt............... Standard Front

Note: As of May 2018, all vehicles are required to have a backup camera.
^Warning feature does not meet government standards.
*Backup camera does not meet government standards.

Lexus RX

Specifications

Drive....................................... FWD
Engine 3.5-liter V6
Transmission .... 8-sp. Automatic
Tow Rating (lbs.) .... –
Head/Leg Room (in.) Roomy-39.4/44.4
Interior Space (cu. ft.)........... Very Roomy-139.7
Cargo Space (cu. ft.) Average-18.4
Wheelbase/Length (in.) 109.8/192.5

Lincoln Continental   Large

Ratings—10 Best, 1 Worst

Combo Crash Tests	10
Safety Features	8
Rollover	7
Preventive Maintenance	5
Repair Costs	2
Warranty	9
Fuel Economy	2
Complaints	2
Insurance Costs	3
OVERALL RATING	**6**

Lincoln Continental

Lincoln Continental

At-a-Glance

Status/Year Series Started. Unchanged/2017
Twins . . . . –
Body Styles . . . . .Sedan
Seating. 5
Anti-Theft Device . . . . . . Std. Pass. Immobil. & Alarm
Parking Index Rating . . . . Very Hard
Where Made. .Chicago, IL
Fuel Factor:
  MPG Rating (city/hwy) . . . . .Very Poor-17/26
  Driving Range (mi.) . . . . .Very Short-362
  Fuel Type. . . . . .Regular
  Annual Fuel Cost . . . . .High-$1825
  Gas Guzzler Tax . . . . .No
  Greenhouse Gas Emissions (tons/yr.). High-7.3
  Barrels of Oil Used per year High-16.5

How the Competition Rates

Competitors	Rating	Pg.
Buick LaCrosse	5	104
Cadillac XTS	8	109
Mercedes-Benz E	3	208

Price Range	Retail	Markup
Premiere FWD	$44,560	5%
Select FWD	$47,515	5%
Reserve AWD	$55,915	6%
Black Label AWD	$64,915	6%

Safety Checklist

Crash Test:
  Frontal. . . . . Very Good
  Side. . . . . Very Good
Airbags:
  Torso . . . Standard Front Pelvis/Torso from Seat
  Roll Sensing. . . . . .Yes
  Knee Bolster . . . . .Standard Front
Crash Avoidance:
  Collision Avoidance . . . . . . Optional CIB & DBS
  Blind Spot Detection . . . . Optional
  Lane Keeping Assist . . . . Optional
  Backup Camera. . . . . Standard
  Pedestrian Crash Avoidance . . . . None
General:
  Auto. Crash Notification . . . . . . Dial Assist.-Free
  Day Running Lamps . . . . Standard
Safety Belt/Restraint:
  Dynamic Head Restraints . . . . None
  Adjustable Belt. . . . . .Standard Front

Note: As of May 2018, all vehicles are required to have a backup camera.
^Warning feature does not meet government standards.
*Backup camera does not meet government standards.

Lincoln Continental

Specifications

Drive. . . . . .FWD
Engine 3.7-liter V6
Transmission . . . . 6-sp. Automatic
Tow Rating (lbs.) . . . . –
Head/Leg Room (in.) Roomy-39.3/44.4
Interior Space (cu. ft.). Roomy-106.4
Cargo Space (cu. ft.) Cramped-16.7
Wheelbase/Length (in.) 117.9/201.4

Lincoln MKC
Small SUV

Ratings—10 Best, 1 Worst

Combo Crash Tests	3
Safety Features	5
Rollover	3
Preventive Maintenance	6
Repair Costs	4
Warranty	9
Fuel Economy	3
Complaints	8
Insurance Costs	10
OVERALL RATING	**6**

Lincoln MKC

Lincoln MKC

At-a-Glance

Status/Year Series Started....... Unchanged/2015
Twins ....Ford Escape
Body Styles .... SUV
Seating...5
Anti-Theft Device ...... Std. Pass. Immobil. & Alarm
Parking Index Rating .... Average
Where Made.................. Louisville, Kentucky

Fuel Factor:
MPG Rating (city/hwy)............... Poor-19/26
Driving Range (mi.) .... Very Short-335
Fuel Type................................Regular
Annual Fuel Cost................... High-$1700
Gas Guzzler Tax ....No
Greenhouse Gas Emissions (tons/yr.)..... High-8.2
Barrels of Oil Used per year High-15.0

How the Competition Rates

Competitors	Rating	Pg.
Buick Encore	10	102
Lexus NX	5	191
Mitsubishi Outlander Sport	4	218

Price Range

Price Range	Retail	Markup
Premiere FWD	$33,355	5%
Select FWD	$36,110	6%
Reserve AWD	$42,395	6%
Black Label AWD	$48,380	7%

Safety Checklist

Crash Test:
Frontal............................. Poor
Side.............................. Poor
Airbags:
Torso . . . Standard Front Pelvis/Torso from Seat
Roll Sensing...........................Yes
Knee Bolster .... Standard Driver
Crash Avoidance:
Collision Avoidance ..... Warning Only Optional
Blind Spot Detection .... Optional
Lane Keeping Assist .... Optional
Backup Camera.................. Standard
Pedestrian Crash Avoidance .... None
General:
Auto. Crash Notification...... Dial Assist.-Free
Day Running Lamps .... Optional
Safety Belt/Restraint:
Dynamic Head Restraints .... None
Adjustable Belt...............Standard Front

Note: As of May 2018, all vehicles are required to have a backup camera.
^Warning feature does not meet government standards.
*Backup camera does not meet government standards.

Lincoln MKC

Specifications

Drive.......................................AWD
Engine 2.0-liter I5
Transmission .... 6-sp. Automatic
Tow Rating (lbs.) .... Very Low-2000
Head/Leg Room (in.) Average-39.6/42.8
Interior Space (cu. ft.)........... Average-97.9
Cargo Space (cu. ft.) Roomy-25.2
Wheelbase/Length (in.) 105.9/179.2

Ratings—10 Best, 1 Worst

Combo Crash Tests	2
Safety Features	6
Rollover	5
Preventive Maintenance	7
Repair Costs	6
Warranty	9
Fuel Economy	2
Complaints	3
Insurance Costs	10
OVERALL RATING	**5**

Lincoln MKX

Lincoln MKX

At-a-Glance

Status/Year Series Started........ Unchanged/2016
Twins ....–
Body Styles .... SUV
Seating..5
Anti-Theft Device ...... Std. Pass. Immobil. & Alarm
Parking Index Rating ....–
Where Made..................... Oakville, Ontario
Fuel Factor:
  MPG Rating (city/hwy) .... Very Poor-17/25
  Driving Range (mi.) .... Very Short-357
  Fuel Type.............................. Regular
  Annual Fuel Cost .... High-$1850
  Gas Guzzler Tax .... No
  Greenhouse Gas Emissions (tons/yr.)..... High-7.5
  Barrels of Oil Used per year High-16.5

How the Competition Rates

Competitors	Rating	Pg.
Acura MDX	7	80
Audi Q7	3	89
Lexus RX	4	193

Price Range	Retail	Markup
Premiere FWD	$39,035	5%
Select FWD	$42,550	6%
Reserve AWD	$49,055	6%
Black Label AWD	$56,725	7%

Safety Checklist

Crash Test:
  Frontal......................... Very Poor
  Side............................... Poor
Airbags:
  Torso . . . Standard Front Pelvis/Torso from Seat
  Roll Sensing........................... Yes
  Knee Bolster .... Standard Front
Crash Avoidance:
  Collision Avoidance .... Optional CIB
  Blind Spot Detection .... Optional
  Lane Keeping Assist ....Warning Only Optional
  Backup Camera.................... Standard*
  Pedestrian Crash Avoidance .... Optional
General:
  Auto. Crash Notification...... Dial Assist.-Free
  Day Running Lamps .... Optional
Safety Belt/Restraint:
  Dynamic Head Restraints .... None
  Adjustable Belt.............. Standard Front

^Warning feature does not meet government standards.
*Backup camera does not meet government standards.

Lincoln MKX

Specifications

Drive... FWD
Engine 3.7-liter V6
Transmission .... 6-sp. Automatic
Tow Rating (lbs.) ....–
Head/Leg Room (in.) Roomy-39.9/42.8
Interior Space (cu. ft.)...........................–
Cargo Space (cu. ft.) ...... Very Roomy-37.2
Wheelbase/Length (in.) 112.2/190

Lincoln MKZ

Ratings—10 Best, 1 Worst

Combo Crash Tests	3
Safety Features	6
Rollover	7
Preventive Maintenance	8
Repair Costs	2
Warranty	9
Fuel Economy	3
Complaints	6
Insurance Costs	5
OVERALL RATING	**4**

Lincoln MKZ

Lincoln MKZ

At-a-Glance

Status/Year Series Started	Unchanged/2013
Twins	Ford Fusion
Body Styles	Sedan
Seating	5
Anti-Theft Device	Std. Pass. Immobil. & Alarm
Parking Index Rating	Hard
Where Made	Hermosillo, Mexico

Fuel Factor:

MPG Rating (city/hwy)	Poor-18/27
Driving Range (mi.)	Very Short-349
Fuel Type	Regular
Annual Fuel Cost	High-$1735
Gas Guzzler Tax	No
Greenhouse Gas Emissions (tons/yr.)	High-8.1
Barrels of Oil Used per year	High-15.0

How the Competition Rates

Competitors	Rating	Pg.
Acura TLX	9	82
Audi A6	7	86
Infiniti Q50	3	167

Price Range	Retail	Markup
Base FWD	$35,010	5%
Hybrid Select	$36,760	5%
Select AWD	$38,650	5%
Black Label Hybrid FWD	$47,670	6%

Safety Checklist

Crash Test:

Frontal	Very Poor
Side	Average

Airbags:

Torso	Standard Front Pelvis/Torso from Seat
Roll Sensing	Yes
Knee Bolster	None

Crash Avoidance:

Collision Avoidance	Optional CIB & DBS
Blind Spot Detection	Optional
Lane Keeping Assist	Optional
Backup Camera	Standard
Pedestrian Crash Avoidance	None

General:

Auto. Crash Notification	Dial Assist.-Free
Day Running Lamps	Standard

Safety Belt/Restraint:

Dynamic Head Restraints	None
Adjustable Belt	Standard Front

^Warning feature does not meet government standards.
*Backup camera does not meet government standards.

Lincoln MKZ

Specifications

Drive	FWD
Engine	3.7-liter V6
Transmission	6-sp. Automatic
Tow Rating (lbs.)	Very Low-1000
Head/Leg Room (in.)	Average-37.9/44.3
Interior Space (cu. ft.)	Cramped-96.5
Cargo Space (cu. ft.)	Cramped-15.4
Wheelbase/Length (in.)	112.2/194.1

Lincoln Navigator

Ratings—10 Best, 1 Worst

Combo Crash Tests	—
Safety Features	5
Rollover	1
Preventive Maintenance	2
Repair Costs	6
Warranty	9
Fuel Economy	1
Complaints	—
Insurance Costs	10
OVERALL RATING	**—**

Lincoln Navigator

Lincoln Navigator

At-a-Glance

Status/Year Series Started. . . . . All New/2018
Twins . . . . Ford Expedition
Body Styles . . . . SUV
Seating. 7/8
Anti-Theft Device . . . . . . Std. Pass. Immobil. & Alarm
Parking Index Rating . . . . —
Where Made. . . . . Louisville, Kentucky
Fuel Factor:
MPG Rating (city/hwy) . . . . Very Poor-16/21
Driving Range (mi.) Average-412
Fuel Type. . . . . .Regular
Annual Fuel Cost . . . . Very High-$2051
Gas Guzzler Tax . . . . .No
Greenhouse Gas Emissions (tons/yr.). High-8.3
Barrels of Oil Used per year . . . . . . Very High-18.3

How the Competition Rates

Competitors	Rating	Pg.
Buick Enclave	4	101
Chevrolet Suburban	2	121
Volvo XC90	8	268

Price Range

Price Range	Retail	Markup
Premier RWD	$72,055	5%
Select 4WD	$78,710	6%
Select L 4WD	$83,905	6%
Black Label 4WD	$93,205	6%

Safety Checklist

Crash Test:
Frontal. . . . . —
Side. . . . . —
Airbags:
Torso . . . . Standard Front Torso from Seat
Roll Sensing. . . . . .Yes
Knee Bolster . . . . None
Crash Avoidance:
Collision Avoidance . . . . . . Optional CIB & DBS
Blind Spot Detection . . . . Standard
Lane Keeping Assist . . . . Optional
Backup Camera . . . . *
Pedestrian Crash Avoidance . . . . Optional
General:
Auto. Crash Notification. . . . . . Dial Assist.-Free
Day Running Lamps . . . . Standard
Safety Belt/Restraint:
Dynamic Head Restraints . . . . None
Adjustable Belt. . . . . .Standard Front

Note: As of May 2018, all vehicles are required to have a backup camera.
^Warning feature does not meet government standards.
*Backup camera does not meet government standards.

Specifications

Drive. 4WD
Engine 3.5-liter V6
Transmission . . . . 10-sp. Automatic
Tow Rating (lbs.) . . . . Very High-8400
Head/Leg Room (in.) . . . . Very Roomy-41.8/43.9
Interior Space (cu. ft.). . . . . Very Roomy-172
Cargo Space (cu. ft.) Average-19.3
Wheelbase/Length (in.) 122.5/210

Ratings—10 Best, 1 Worst

Combo Crash Tests	9
Safety Features	5
Rollover	5
Preventive Maintenance	7
Repair Costs	9
Warranty	1
Fuel Economy	8
Complaints	9
Insurance Costs	8
OVERALL RATING	**10**

Mazda CX-3

Mazda CX-3

At-a-Glance

Status/Year Series Started	Unchanged/2016
Twins	–
Body Styles	SUV
Seating	5
Anti-Theft Device	Std. Passive Immobil. Only
Parking Index Rating	Very Easy
Where Made	Hiroshima, Japan / Hofu, Japan

Fuel Factor:

MPG Rating (city/hwy)	Good-29/34
Driving Range (mi.)	Short-394
Fuel Type	Regular
Annual Fuel Cost	Low-$1183
Gas Guzzler Tax	No
Greenhouse Gas Emissions (tons/yr.)	Low-4.8
Barrels of Oil Used per year	Average-10.6

How the Competition Rates

Competitors	Rating	Pg.
Buick Encore	10	102
Chevrolet Trax	10	124
Honda HR-V	5	156

Price Range

	Retail	Markup
Sport FWD	$19,960	3%
Sport AWD	$21,210	3%
Touring AWD	$23,210	3%
Grand Touring AWD	$26,240	3%

Safety Checklist

Crash Test:
Frontal . . . . Very Good
Side . . . . Good

Airbags:
Torso . . . Standard Front Pelvis/Torso from Seat
Roll Sensing . . . . Yes
Knee Bolster . . . . None

Crash Avoidance:
Collision Avoidance . . . . . . Optional CIB & DBS^
Blind Spot Detection . . . . Optional
Lane Keeping Assist . . . . Optional^
Backup Camera . . . . Standard
Pedestrian Crash Avoidance . . . . None

General:
Auto. Crash Notification . . . . . . Dial Assist.-Free
Day Running Lamps . . . . Standard

Safety Belt/Restraint:
Dynamic Head Restraints . . . . None
Adjustable Belt . . . . Standard Front

Note: As of May 2018, all vehicles are required to have a backup camera.
^Warning feature does not meet government standards.
*Backup camera does not meet government standards.

Mazda CX-3

Specifications

Drive	FWD
Engine	2.0-liter I4
Transmission	6-sp. Automatic
Tow Rating (lbs.)	–
Head/Leg Room (in.)	Cramped-38.4/41.7
Interior Space (cu. ft.)	Very Cramped-87.6
Cargo Space (cu. ft.)	Very Cramped-12.4
Wheelbase/Length (in.)	101.2/168.3

Ratings—10 Best, 1 Worst

Combo Crash Tests	6
Safety Features	4
Rollover	3
Preventive Maintenance	7
Repair Costs	10
Warranty	1
Fuel Economy	7
Complaints	8
Insurance Costs	1
OVERALL RATING	**4**

Mazda CX-5

Mazda CX-5

At-a-Glance

Status/Year Series Started........ Unchanged/2013
Twins .... –
Body Styles .... SUV
Seating.. 5
Anti-Theft Device .... Std. Passive Immobil. Only
Parking Index Rating .... Average
Where Made.................... Hiroshima, Japan
Fuel Factor:
  MPG Rating (city/hwy)............... Good-26/32
  Driving Range (mi.) Average-420
  Fuel Type........................Regular
  Annual Fuel Cost .... Low-$1294
  Gas Guzzler Tax ....No
  Greenhouse Gas Emissions (tons/yr.).. Average-6.2
  Barrels of Oil Used per year Average-11.4

How the Competition Rates

Competitors	Rating	Pg.
Buick Enclave	4	101
Honda CR-V	10	154
Mitsubishi Outlander Sport	4	218

Price Range	Retail	Markup
Sport FWD	$24,045	3%
Touring FWD	$25,915	3%
Grand Select AWD	$30,195	3%
Grand Touring AWD	$30,695	3%

Safety Checklist

Crash Test:
  Frontal.............................. Good
  Side.......................Very Poor
Airbags:
  Torso . . . Standard Front Pelvis/Torso from Seat
  Roll Sensing.........................Yes
  Knee Bolster .... None
Crash Avoidance:
  Collision Avoidance ......Optional CIB & DBS^
  Blind Spot Detection .... Optional
  Lane Keeping Assist .... Optional^
  Backup Camera.................... Standard
  Pedestrian Crash Avoidance .... None
General:
  Auto. Crash Notification...... Dial Assist.-Free
  Day Running Lamps .... Standard
Safety Belt/Restraint:
  Dynamic Head Restraints .... None
  Adjustable Belt.................Standard Front

Note: As of May 2018, all vehicles are required to have a backup camera.
^Warning feature does not meet government standards.
*Backup camera does not meet government standards.

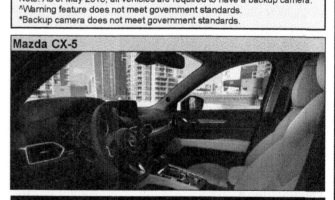
Mazda CX-5

Specifications

Drive..FWD
Engine 2.0-liter I4
Transmission .... 6-sp. Automatic
Tow Rating (lbs.) .... Very Low-2000
Head/Leg Room (in.) Average-40.1/41
Interior Space (cu. ft.)............. Average-103.8
Cargo Space (cu. ft.) .... Very Roomy-34.1
Wheelbase/Length (in.) 106.3/178.7

Mazda CX-9

Ratings—10 Best, 1 Worst

Combo Crash Tests	—
Safety Features	5
Rollover	3
Preventive Maintenance	7
Repair Costs	3
Warranty	1
Fuel Economy	3
Complaints	9
Insurance Costs	10
OVERALL RATING	—

Mazda CX-9

At-a-Glance

Status/Year Series Started........ Unchanged/2016
Twins .... —
Body Styles .... SUV
Seating 7
Anti-Theft Device ...... Std. Passive Immobil. Only
Parking Index Rating .... Hard
Where Made................... Hiroshima, Japan
Fuel Factor:
  MPG Rating (city/hwy)............... Poor-20/26
  Driving Range (mi.) Long-424
  Fuel Type........................Regular
  Annual Fuel Cost............. Average-$1647
  Gas Guzzler Tax ....No
  Greenhouse Gas Emissions (tons/yr.) Very High-10.0
  Barrels of Oil Used per year .... Very High-18.3

How the Competition Rates

Competitors	Rating	Pg.
Infiniti QX60	5	170
Kia Sorento	6	181
Lexus RX	4	193

Price Range	Retail	Markup
Sport FWD	$31,520	6%
Touring FWD	$35,970	6%
Grand Touring AWD	$42,270	6%
Signature AWD	$44,315	6%

Safety Checklist

Crash Test:
  Frontal................................ —
  Side.................................. —
Airbags:
  Torso . . .Standard Front Pelvis/Torso from Seat
  Roll Sensing...........................Yes
  Knee Bolster .... None
Crash Avoidance:
  Collision Avoidance ......Optional CIB & DBS^
  Blind Spot Detection .... Optional
  Lane Keeping Assist .... Optional^
  Backup Camera.................... Standard
  Pedestrian Crash Avoidance .... None
General:
  Auto. Crash Notification...... Dial Assist.-Free
  Day Running Lamps .... Standard
Safety Belt/Restraint:
  Dynamic Head Restraints .... None
  Adjustable Belt...............Standard Front

Note: As of May 2018, all vehicles are required to have a backup camera.
^Warning feature does not meet government standards.
*Backup camera does not meet government standards.

Mazda CX-9

Specifications

Drive.......................................AWD
Engine 3.7-liter I4
Transmission .... 6-sp. Automatic
Tow Rating (lbs.) Low-3500
Head/Leg Room (in.) Cramped-39.3/40.9
Interior Space (cu. ft.)............ Very Roomy-135.1
Cargo Space (cu. ft.) Cramped-14.4
Wheelbase/Length (in.) 115.3/199.4

Mazda 3 Compact

Ratings—10 Best, 1 Worst

Combo Crash Tests	4
Safety Features	5
Rollover	7
Preventive Maintenance	7
Repair Costs	9
Warranty	1
Fuel Economy	8
Complaints	10
Insurance Costs	3
OVERALL RATING	**6**

Mazda Mazda3

Mazda Mazda3

At-a-Glance

Status/Year Series Started. Unchanged/2014
Twins . . . . –
Body Styles . . . . Sedan, Hatchback
Seating 5
Anti-Theft Device . . . . . . Std. Passive Immobil. Only
Parking Index Rating . . . . Easy
Where Made. Hofu, Japan
Fuel Factor:
  MPG Rating (city/hwy) Good-28/37
  Driving Range (mi.) Average-415
  Fuel Type. . . . . .Regular
  Annual Fuel Cost . . . . Very Low-$1169
  Gas Guzzler Tax . . . . .No
  Greenhouse Gas Emissions (tons/yr.). Low-4.7
  Barrels of Oil Used per year Average-10.6

How the Competition Rates

Competitors	Rating	Pg.
Ford Focus	5	143
Nissan Sentra	5	228
Volkswagen Jetta	7	262

Price Range	Retail	Markup
Sport Sedan MT	$18,095	4%
Touring Sedan AT	$21,140	4%
Touring Hatchback AT	$21,890	5%
Grand Touring Hatchback AT	$24,945	5%

Safety Checklist

Crash Test:
  Frontal. . . . . Poor
  Side. . . . . Poor
Airbags:
  Torso . . . Standard Front Pelvis/Torso from Seat
  Roll Sensing. . . . . .Yes
  Knee Bolster . . . . None
Crash Avoidance:
  Collision Avoidance . . . . . .Optional CIB & DBS^
  Blind Spot Detection . . . . Optional
  Lane Keeping Assist . . . . Optional
  Backup Camera. . . . . Standard
  Pedestrian Crash Avoidance . . . . None
General:
  Auto. Crash Notification. . . . . . Dial Assist.-Free
  Day Running Lamps . . . . Standard
Safety Belt/Restraint:
  Dynamic Head Restraints . . . . None
  Adjustable Belt. . . . . .Standard Front

Note: As of May 2018, all vehicles are required to have a backup camera.
^Warning feature does not meet government standards.
*Backup camera does not meet government standards.

Mazda Mazda3

Specifications

Drive. . . . . .FWD
Engine 2.0-liter I4
Transmission . . . . 6-sp. Automatic
Tow Rating (lbs.) . . . . –
Head/Leg Room (in.) Cramped-38.6/42.2
Interior Space (cu. ft.). Cramped-96.3
Cargo Space (cu. ft.) . . . . Very Cramped-12.4
Wheelbase/Length (in.) 106.3/180.3

Ratings—10 Best, 1 Worst

Combo Crash Tests	7
Safety Features	5
Rollover	8
Preventive Maintenance	6
Repair Costs	8
Warranty	1
Fuel Economy	8
Complaints	7
Insurance Costs	1
OVERALL RATING	**6**

Mazda Mazda6

At-a-Glance

Status/Year Series Started Unchanged/2014
Twins . . . . —
Body Styles . . . . .Sedan
Seating 5
Anti-Theft Device . . . . Std. Passive Immobil. Only
Parking Index Rating . . . . Average
Where Made. Flat Rock, MI
Fuel Factor:
MPG Rating (city/hwy) Good-26/38
Driving Range (mi.) . . . . Very Long-497
Fuel Type. . . . . .Regular
Annual Fuel Cost . . . . Low-$1213
Gas Guzzler Tax . . . . .No
Greenhouse Gas Emissions (tons/yr.) . . Average-6.0
Barrels of Oil Used per year Average-11.0

How the Competition Rates

Competitors	Rating	Pg.
Kia Optima	9	178
Nissan Altima	4	219
Toyota Camry	8	244

Price Range	Retail	Markup
Sport MT	$21,945	5%
Sport AT	$22,995	5%
Touring AT	$25,245	6%
Grand Touring AT	$30,695	6%

Mazda Mazda6

Safety Checklist

Crash Test:
Frontal. . . . . Good
Side. . . . . Good
Airbags:
Torso . . . Standard Front Pelvis/Torso from Seat
Roll Sensing. . . . . .Yes
Knee Bolster . . . . None
Crash Avoidance:
Collision Avoidance . . . . . . Optional CIB & DBS
Blind Spot Detection . . . . Optional
Lane Keeping Assist . . . .Warning Only Optional
Backup Camera. . . . . Standard
Pedestrian Crash Avoidance . . . . None
General:
Auto. Crash Notification . . . . . . Dial Assist.-Free
Day Running Lamps . . . . Standard
Safety Belt/Restraint:
Dynamic Head Restraints . . . . None
Adjustable Belt. . . . . .Standard Front

Note: As of May 2018, all vehicles are required to have a backup camera.
^Warning feature does not meet government standards.
*Backup camera does not meet government standards.

Mazda Mazda6

Specifications

Drive. . . . . .FWD
Engine 2.5-liter I4
Transmission . . . . 6-sp. Automatic
Tow Rating (lbs.) . . . . —
Head/Leg Room (in.) Cramped-38.4/42.2
Interior Space (cu. ft.). Average-99.7
Cargo Space (cu. ft.) Cramped-14.8
Wheelbase/Length (in.) 111.4/191.5

Ratings—10 Best, 1 Worst

Combo Crash Tests	—
Safety Features	1
Rollover	10
Preventive Maintenance	6
Repair Costs	6
Warranty	1
Fuel Economy	8
Complaints	5
Insurance Costs	10
OVERALL RATING	—

Mazda MX-5 Miata

Mazda MX-5 Miata

At-a-Glance

Status/Year Series Started........ Unchanged/2016
Twins .... —
Body Styles .... Coupe, Convertible
Seating 2
Anti-Theft Device .... Std. Passive Immobil. Only
Parking Index Rating ....Very Easy
Where Made.................. Hiroshima, Japan
Fuel Factor:
  MPG Rating (city/hwy)........... Good-27/36
  Driving Range (mi.) ....Very Short-362
  Fuel Type........................Premium
  Annual Fuel Cost ....Average-$1464
  Gas Guzzler Tax ....No
  Greenhouse Gas Emissions (tons/yr.)..... Low-4.9
  Barrels of Oil Used per year Average-11.0

How the Competition Rates

Competitors	Rating	Pg.
Buick Cascada	–	100
Toyota 86	–	242

Price Range

Price Range	Retail	Markup
Sport MT	$24,915	6%
Club AT	$29,530	6%
Grand Touring AT	$31,270	6%
Launch Edition AT	$34,925	6%

Safety Checklist

Crash Test:
  Frontal. . . . . —
  Side. . . . . —
Airbags:
  Torso . . . Standard Front Pelvis/Torso from Seat
  Roll Sensing. . . . . No
  Knee Bolster . . . . None
Crash Avoidance:
  Collision Avoidance . . . . None
  Blind Spot Detection . . . . Optional
  Lane Keeping Assist . . . .Warning Only Optional
  Backup Camera. . . . . None
  Pedestrian Crash Avoidance. . . . . None
General:
  Auto. Crash Notification. . . . . None
  Day Running Lamps . . . . Standard
Safety Belt/Restraint:
  Dynamic Head Restraints . . . . None
  Adjustable Belt. . . . . None

Note: As of May 2018, all vehicles are required to have a backup camera.
^Warning feature does not meet government standards.
*Backup camera does not meet government standards.

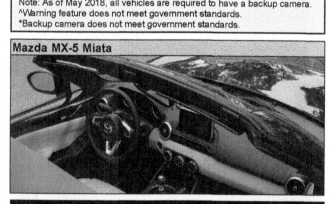
Mazda MX-5 Miata

Specifications

Drive. . . . . .RWD
Engine 2.0-liter I4
Transmission . . . . 6-sp. Manual
Tow Rating (lbs.) . . . . —
Head/Leg Room (in.) Cramped-37.4/43.1
Interior Space (cu. ft.). . . . . —
Cargo Space (cu. ft.) . . . . Very Cramped-4.6
Wheelbase/Length (in.) 90.9/154.1

Ratings—10 Best, 1 Worst

Combo Crash Tests	—
Safety Features	4
Rollover	4
Preventive Maintenance	6
Repair Costs	10
Warranty	3
Fuel Economy	10
Complaints	1
Insurance Costs	5
OVERALL RATING	—

Mercedes-Benz B

Mercedes-Benz B

At-a-Glance

Status/Year Series Started Unchanged/2012
Twins . . . . —
Body Styles . . . . Hatchback
Seating 5
Anti-Theft Device . Std. Active Immobil. & Pass. Alarm
Parking Index Rating . . . . Easy
Where Made Rastatt, Germany / Kecskemet, Hungary
Fuel Factor:
MPG Rating (city/hwy) . . . . Very Good-85/82
Driving Range (mi.) . . . . Very Short-87
Fuel Type . . . . Electricity
Annual Fuel Cost . . . . Very Low-$800
Gas Guzzler Tax . . . . No
Greenhouse Gas Emissions (tons/yr.) . Very Low-0.0
Barrels of Oil Used per year . . . . Very Low-0.0

How the Competition Rates

Competitors	Rating	Pg.
BMW i3	—	95
Chevrolet Bolt	—	110
Toyota Prius Prime	—	250

Price Range

Price Range	Retail	Markup
B250e	$39,900	8%

Safety Checklist

Crash Test:
Frontal . . . . —
Side . . . . —
Airbags:
Torso Std. Fr. & Opt. Rr. Pelvis/Torso from Seat
Roll Sensing . . . . No
Knee Bolster . . . . Standard Driver
Crash Avoidance:
Collision Avoidance . . . . . . Standard CIB & DBS
Blind Spot Detection . . . . Optional
Lane Keeping Assist . . . .Warning Only Optional
Backup Camera . . . . Optional*
Pedestrian Crash Avoidance . . . . None
General:
Auto. Crash Notif.. Op. Assist. & Crash Info-Free
Day Running Lamps . . . . None
Safety Belt/Restraint:
Dynamic Head Restraints . . . . None
Adjustable Belt . . . . Standard Front

Note: As of May 2018, all vehicles are required to have a backup camera.
^Warning feature does not meet government standards.
*Backup camera does not meet government standards.

Mercedes-Benz B

Specifications

Drive . . . . FWD
Engine . . . . Electric
Transmission . . . . CVT
Tow Rating (lbs.) . . . . —
Head/Leg Room (in.) . . . . —
Interior Space (cu. ft.) Cramped-90.5
Cargo Space (cu. ft.) Roomy-21.6
Wheelbase/Length (in.) 106.3/171.5

Ratings—10 Best, 1 Worst

Combo Crash Tests	3
Safety Features	9
Rollover	7
Preventive Maintenance	1
Repair Costs	3
Warranty	3
Fuel Economy	5
Complaints	5
Insurance Costs	3
OVERALL RATING	**1**

Mercedes-Benz C

Mercedes-Benz C

At-a-Glance

Status/Year Series Started. Unchanged/2015
Twins . . . . –
Body Styles . . . . .Sedan, Coupe, Wagon
Seating 5
Anti-Theft Device . Std. Active Immobil. & Pass. Alarm
Parking Index Rating . . . . Average
Where Made. . . . . Tuscaloosa, AL
Fuel Factor:
  MPG Rating (city/hwy) Average-22/30
  Driving Range (mi.) Long-450
  Fuel Type . . . . .Premium
  Annual Fuel Cost . . . . .High-$1782
  Gas Guzzler Tax . . . . .No
  Greenhouse Gas Emissions (tons/yr.) . . Average-7.2
  Barrels of Oil Used per year High-13.2

How the Competition Rates

Competitors	Rating	Pg.
BMW 3 Series	7	91
Cadillac ATS	4	106
Lexus IS	8	190

Price Range	Retail	Markup
C300 Sedan	$39,500	8%
C300 Coupe	$42,650	8%
C300 Coupe 4Matic	$44,650	8%
AMG C63 Coupe	$67,000	8%

Safety Checklist

Crash Test:
  Frontal. . . . . Average
  Side. . . . . .Very Poor
Airbags:
  Torso Std. Fr. & Opt. Rr. Pelvis/Torso from Seat
  Roll Sensing. . . . . No
  Knee Bolster . . . . Standard Driver
Crash Avoidance:
  Collision Avoidance . . . . . . Standard CIB & DBS
  Blind Spot Detection . . . . Optional
  Lane Keeping Assist . . . . Optional
  Backup Camera . . . . Standard
  Pedestrian Crash Avoidance . . . . Optional
General:
  Auto. Crash Notif.. Op. Assist. & Crash Info-Free
  Day Running Lamps . . . . None
Safety Belt/Restraint:
  Dynamic Head Restraints . . . . . .Standard Front
  Adjustable Belt. . . . . .Standard Front

Note: As of May 2018, all vehicles are required to have a backup camera.
^Warning feature does not meet government standards.
*Backup camera does not meet government standards.

Mercedes-Benz C

Specifications

Drive. . . . . .RWD
Engine 2.0-liter I4
Transmission . . . . 9-sp. Automatic
Tow Rating (lbs.) . . . . –
Head/Leg Room (in.) . . . . Very Cramped-37.1/41.7
Interior Space (cu. ft.). . . . . .Very Cramped-81
Cargo Space (cu. ft.) . . . . Very Cramped-12.8
Wheelbase/Length (in.) 111.8/184.5

Ratings—10 Best, 1 Worst

Combo Crash Tests	—
Safety Features	8
Rollover	6
Preventive Maintenance	1
Repair Costs	3
Warranty	3
Fuel Economy	7
Complaints	1
Insurance Costs	1
OVERALL RATING	—

Mercedes-Benz CLA

Mercedes-Benz CLA

At-a-Glance

Status/Year Series Started........ Unchanged/2014
Twins .... —
Body Styles ....Coupe
Seating.....................................5
Anti-Theft Device . Std. Active Immobil. & Pass. Alarm
Parking Index Rating .... Easy
Where Made................ Kecskemet, Hungary
Fuel Factor:
MPG Rating (city/hwy) Good-24/37
Driving Range (mi.) Short-376
Fuel Type................................Premium
Annual Fuel Cost.............Average-$1563
Gas Guzzler Tax ....No
Greenhouse Gas Emissions (tons/yr.)..... Low-5.1
Barrels of Oil Used per year Average-11.4

How the Competition Rates

Competitors	Rating	Pg.
Audi A4	2	84
Cadillac ATS	4	106
Infiniti Q50	3	167

Price Range

Price Range	Retail	Markup
Coupe 4Matic	$3,440	-89%
Coupe	$32,400	8%
AMG 4Matic	$49,950	8%

Safety Checklist

Crash Test:
Frontal................................. —
Side.................................. —
Airbags:
Torso Std. Fr. & Opt. Rr. Pelvis/Torso from Seat
Roll Sensing...........................Yes
Knee Bolster ....Standard Front
Crash Avoidance:
Collision Avoidance ...... Standard CIB & DBS
Blind Spot Detection .... Optional
Lane Keeping Assist ....Warning Only Optional
Backup Camera................... Optional*
Pedestrian Crash Avoidance .... None
General:
Auto. Crash Notif.. Op. Assist. & Crash Info-Free
Day Running Lamps .... None
Safety Belt/Restraint:
Dynamic Head Restraints .... None
Adjustable Belt...............Standard Front

Note: As of May 2018, all vehicles are required to have a backup camera.
^Warning feature does not meet government standards.
*Backup camera does not meet government standards.

Mercedes-Benz CLA

Specifications

Drive.....................................FWD
Engine 2.0-liter I4
Transmission .... 7-sp. Automatic
Tow Rating (lbs.) .... —
Head/Leg Room (in.) .... Very Cramped-38.2/40.2
Interior Space (cu. ft.)............Very Cramped-88
Cargo Space (cu. ft.) ....Very Cramped-13
Wheelbase/Length (in.) 106.3/182.3

Ratings—10 Best, 1 Worst

Combo Crash Tests	5
Safety Features	10
Rollover	8
Preventive Maintenance	3
Repair Costs	1
Warranty	3
Fuel Economy	5
Complaints	5
Insurance Costs	5
OVERALL RATING	**3**

Mercedes-Benz E

Mercedes-Benz E

Mercedes-Benz E

At-a-Glance

Status/Year Series Started. Unchanged/2017
Twins . . . . –
Body Styles . . . . Sedan
Seating. 5
Anti-Theft Device . Std. Active Immobil. & Pass. Alarm
Parking Index Rating . . . . Average
Where Made. . . . . .Sindelfingen, Germany
Fuel Factor:
  MPG Rating (city/hwy) Average-22/30
  Driving Range (mi.) Long-435
  Fuel Type. . . . . .Premium
  Annual Fuel Cost . . . . .High-$1782
  Gas Guzzler Tax . . . . .No
  Greenhouse Gas Emissions (tons/yr.). Low-5.8
  Barrels of Oil Used per year High-13.2

How the Competition Rates

Competitors	Rating	Pg.
Buick LaCrosse	5	104
Lincoln Continental	6	194
Tesla Model S	10	239

Price Range	Retail	Markup
E300 Sedan	$52,150	8%
E400 Coupe	$54,550	8%
E400 Cabriolet	$62,600	8%
E550 Cabriolet	$69,100	8%

Safety Checklist

Crash Test:
  Frontal. . . . . .Poor
  Side. . . . . Good
Airbags:
  Torso Std. Fr. & Opt. Rr. Pelvis/Torso from Seat
  Roll Sensing. . . . . .Yes
  Knee Bolster . . . . Standard Driver
Crash Avoidance:
  Collision Avoidance . . . . . Standard CIB & DBS
  Blind Spot Detection . . . . Optional
  Lane Keeping Assist . . . . Optional
  Backup Camera. . . . . Optional*
  Pedestrian Crash Avoidance . . . . Optional
General:
  Auto. Crash Notif.. Op. Assist. & Crash Info-Free
  Day Running Lamps . . . . None
Safety Belt/Restraint:
  Dynamic Head Restraints . . . . .Standard Front
  Adjustable Belt. . . . . .Standard Front

Note: As of May 2018, all vehicles are required to have a backup camera.
^Warning feature does not meet government standards.
*Backup camera does not meet government standards.

Specifications

Drive. . . . . .RWD
Engine 2.0-liter V6
Transmission . . . . 9-sp. Automatic
Tow Rating (lbs.) . . . . –
Head/Leg Room (in.) . . . . Very Cramped-37.9/41.3
Interior Space (cu. ft.). Average-98
Cargo Space (cu. ft.) . . . . Very Cramped-13.1
Wheelbase/Length (in.) 115.7/193.8

Ratings—10 Best, 1 Worst

Combo Crash Tests	—
Safety Features	8
Rollover	5
Preventive Maintenance	10
Repair Costs	2
Warranty	3
Fuel Economy	6
Complaints	6
Insurance Costs	10
OVERALL RATING	—

Mercedes-Benz GLA

Mercedes-Benz GLA

At-a-Glance

Status/Year Series Started Unchanged/2015
Twins . . . . —
Body Styles . . . . SUV
Seating 5
Anti-Theft Device . Std. Active Immobil. & Pass. Alarm
Parking Index Rating . . . . Average
Where Made. . . . . Rastatt, Germany

Fuel Factor:
MPG Rating (city/hwy) Average-23/31
Driving Range (mi.) Short-385
Fuel Type. . . . . Premium
Annual Fuel Cost . . . . High-$1712
Gas Guzzler Tax . . . . .No
Greenhouse Gas Emissions (tons/yr.) Low-5.6
Barrels of Oil Used per year Average-12.7

How the Competition Rates

Competitors	Rating	Pg.
Acura RDX	9	81
Lexus NX	5	191
Lincoln MKC	6	195

Price Range	Retail	Markup
GLA250	$32,850	8%
GLA250 4Matic	$34,850	8%
AMG GLA45 4Matic	$49,900	8%

Safety Checklist

Crash Test:
Frontal. . . . .
Side. . . . .
Airbags:
Torso Std. Fr. & Opt. Rr. Pelvis/Torso from Seat
Roll Sensing. . . . . .Yes
Knee Bolster . . . . .Standard Front
Crash Avoidance:
Collision Avoidance . . . . . . Standard CIB & DBS
Blind Spot Detection . . . . Optional
Lane Keeping Assist . . . .Warning Only Optional
Backup Camera. . . . . Optional
Pedestrian Crash Avoidance . . . . None
General:
Auto. Crash Notif.. Op. Assist. & Crash Info-Free
Day Running Lamps . . . . None
Safety Belt/Restraint:
Dynamic Head Restraints . . . . None
Adjustable Belt. None

Note: As of May 2018, all vehicles are required to have a backup camera.
^Warning feature does not meet government standards.
*Backup camera does not meet government standards.

Mercedes-Benz GLA

Specifications

Drive. . . . . .AWD
Engine 2.0-liter I4
Transmission . . . . 7-sp. Automatic
Tow Rating (lbs.) . . . . —
Head/Leg Room (in.) Cramped-38.3/41.9
Interior Space (cu. ft.). Cramped-91
Cargo Space (cu. ft.) Average-17.2
Wheelbase/Length (in.) 106.3/173.9

Ratings—10 Best, 1 Worst

Combo Crash Tests	—
Safety Features	10
Rollover	—
Preventive Maintenance	3
Repair Costs	2
Warranty	3
Fuel Economy	4
Complaints	1
Insurance Costs	10

OVERALL RATING   —

Mercedes-Benz GLC

Mercedes-Benz GLC

At-a-Glance

Status/Year Series Started Unchanged/2016
Twins . . . . —
Body Styles . . . . SUV
Seating 5
Anti-Theft Device . Std. Active Immobil. & Pass. Alarm
Parking Index Rating . . . . Average
Where Made . . . . Tuscaloosa, AL

Fuel Factor:
MPG Rating (city/hwy) Poor-21/28
Driving Range (mi.) Average-412
Fuel Type . . . . Premium
Annual Fuel Cost . . . . High-$1883
Gas Guzzler Tax . . . . No
Greenhouse Gas Emissions (tons/yr.) High-8.6
Barrels of Oil Used per year High-13.7

How the Competition Rates

Competitors	Rating	Pg.
Audi Q7	3	89
BMW X5	5	98
Volkswagen Atlas	6	259

Price Range	Retail	Markup
GLC300	$39,150	8%
GLC300 4Matic	$41,150	8%
AMG GLC43	$54,900	8%

Safety Checklist

Crash Test:
  Frontal . . . .
  Side . . . .
Airbags:
  Torso Std. Fr. & Opt. Rr. Pelvis/Torso from Seat
  Roll Sensing . . . . Yes
  Knee Bolster . . . . Standard Driver
Crash Avoidance:
  Collision Avoidance . . . . . . Standard CIB & DBS
  Blind Spot Detection . . . . Optional
  Lane Keeping Assist . . . . Optional
  Backup Camera . . . . Standard
  Pedestrian Crash Avoidance . . . . Optional
General:
  Auto. Crash Notif.. Op. Assist. & Crash Info-Free
  Day Running Lamps . . . . None
Safety Belt/Restraint:
  Dynamic Head Restraints . . . . . . Standard Front
  Adjustable Belt . . . . Standard Front

Note: As of May 2018, all vehicles are required to have a backup camera.
^Warning feature does not meet government standards.
*Backup camera does not meet government standards.

Mercedes-Benz GLC

Specifications

Drive 4WD
Engine 2.0-liter I4
Transmission . . . . 9-sp. Automatic
Tow Rating (lbs.) Low-3500
Head/Leg Room (in.) . . . . Very Cramped-37.8/40.8
Interior Space (cu. ft.) . . . . Very Cramped-79.5
Cargo Space (cu. ft.) Cramped-16.5
Wheelbase/Length (in.) 113.1/183.3

Ratings—10 Best, 1 Worst

Combo Crash Tests	—
Safety Features	9
Rollover	2
Preventive Maintenance	3
Repair Costs	2
Warranty	3
Fuel Economy	2
Complaints	6
Insurance Costs	8
OVERALL RATING	—

Mercedes-Benz GLE

At-a-Glance

Status/Year Series Started........ Unchanged/2012
Twins .... –
Body Styles .... SUV
Seating.................................... 5
Anti-Theft Device . Std. Active Immobil. & Pass. Alarm
Parking Index Rating .... Hard
Where Made................... Bremen, Germany
Fuel Factor:
MPG Rating (city/hwy) .... Very Poor-18/23
Driving Range (mi.) .... Very Long-491
Fuel Type........................... Premium
Annual Fuel Cost .... Very High-$2233
Gas Guzzler Tax .... No
Greenhouse Gas Emissions (tons/yr.)..... High-7.3
Barrels of Oil Used per year High-16.5

How the Competition Rates

Competitors	Rating	Pg.
Buick Encore	10	102
Lexus NX	5	191
Lincoln MKC	6	195

Price Range	Retail	Markup
GLS350	$67,050	8%
GLS450	$68,700	8%
GLS550	$93,850	8%
GLS63 AMG	$124,100	8%

Mercedes-Benz GLE

Safety Checklist

Crash Test:
Frontal.................................
Side..................................
Airbags:
Torso Std. Fr. & Opt. Rr. Pelvis/Torso from Seat
Roll Sensing........................... Yes
Knee Bolster .... Standard Driver
Crash Avoidance:
Collision Avoidance ...... Std. DBS & Opt. CIB
Blind Spot Detection .... Optional
Lane Keeping Assist .... Optional
Backup Camera................... Standard
Pedestrian Crash Avoidance .... Optional
General:
Auto. Crash Notif.. Op. Assist. & Crash Info-Free
Day Running Lamps .... None
Safety Belt/Restraint:
Dynamic Head Restraints .... None
Adjustable Belt............... Standard Front

Note: As of May 2018, all vehicles are required to have a backup camera.
^Warning feature does not meet government standards.
*Backup camera does not meet government standards.

Mercedes-Benz GLE

Specifications

Drive........................... RWD
Engine 3.5-liter V6
Transmission .... 7-sp. Automatic
Tow Rating (lbs.) Average-6600
Head/Leg Room (in.) .... Very Cramped-38.9/40.3
Interior Space (cu. ft.).................. –
Cargo Space (cu. ft.) .... Very Roomy-38.2
Wheelbase/Length (in.) 114.8/189.1

Ratings—10 Best, 1 Worst

Combo Crash Tests	—
Safety Features	9
Rollover	2
Preventive Maintenance	3
Repair Costs	2
Warranty	3
Fuel Economy	2
Complaints	7
Insurance Costs	10

OVERALL RATING —

Mercedes-Benz GLS

Mercedes-Benz GLS

At-a-Glance

Status/Year Series Started........ Unchanged/2016
Twins .... —
Body Styles .... SUV
Seating.......................................5
Anti-Theft Device . Std. Active Immobil. & Pass. Alarm
Parking Index Rating .... Very Hard
Where Made.................... Tuscaloosa, AL
Fuel Factor:
  MPG Rating (city/hwy) .... Very Poor-17/22
  Driving Range (mi.) .... Very Long-500
  Fuel Type........................Premium
  Annual Fuel Cost .... Very High-$2353
  Gas Guzzler Tax ....No
  Greenhouse Gas Emissions (tons/yr.)..... Low-5.1
  Barrels of Oil Used per year .... Very Low-0.0

How the Competition Rates

Competitors	Rating	Pg.
Buick Enclave	4	101
Chevrolet Suburban	2	121
Volvo XC90	8	268

Price Range	Retail	Markup
GLE300d 4Matic	$53,400	8%
GLE350 4Matic	$54,500	8%
GLE550e 4Matic	$66,300	8%
GLE63 AMG 4Matic	$101,690	8%

Safety Checklist

Crash Test:
  Frontal. . . . .
  Side. . . . .
Airbags:
  Torso Std. Fr. & Opt. Rr. Pelvis/Torso from Seat
  Roll Sensing. . . . . .Yes
  Knee Bolster . . . . Standard Driver
Crash Avoidance:
  Collision Avoidance . . . . . . Standard CIB & DBS
  Blind Spot Detection . . . . Optional
  Lane Keeping Assist . . . . Optional
  Backup Camera. . . . . .Standard*
  Pedestrian Crash Avoidance . . . . Optional
General:
  Auto. Crash Notif.. Op. Assist. & Crash Info-Free
  Day Running Lamps . . . . None
Safety Belt/Restraint:
  Dynamic Head Restraints . . . . None
  Adjustable Belt. . . . . .Standard Front

Note: As of May 2018, all vehicles are required to have a backup camera.
^Warning feature does not meet government standards.
*Backup camera does not meet government standards.

Mercedes-Benz GLS

Specifications

Drive. 4WD
Engine 3.0-liter V6
Transmission . . . . 9-sp. Automatic
Tow Rating (lbs.) High-7500
Head/Leg Room (in.) Average-41.2/40.3
Interior Space (cu. ft.). . . . . —
Cargo Space (cu. ft.) Cramped-16
Wheelbase/Length (in.) 121.1/201.6

Ratings—10 Best, 1 Worst	
Combo Crash Tests	—
Safety Features	10
Rollover	7
Preventive Maintenance	3
Repair Costs	1
Warranty	3
Fuel Economy	3
Complaints	7
Insurance Costs	1
OVERALL RATING	—

Mercedes-Benz S

Mercedes-Benz S

At-a-Glance

Status/Year Series Started Appearance Change/2014
Twins .... —
Body Styles .... Sedan, Coupe
Seating 5
Anti-Theft Device . Std. Active Immobil. & Pass. Alarm
Parking Index Rating .... Very Hard
Where Made............... Sindelfingen, Germany

Fuel Factor:
MPG Rating (city/hwy) Poor-19/28
Driving Range (mi.) .... Very Long-511
Fuel Type....................................Premium
Annual Fuel Cost .... Very High-$2006
Gas Guzzler Tax .... No
Greenhouse Gas Emissions (tons/yr.)..... Low-5.7
Barrels of Oil Used per year High-15.0

How the Competition Rates

Competitors	Rating	Pg.
Cadillac XTS	8	109
Lincoln Continental	6	194
Tesla Model S	10	239

Price Range	Retail	Markup
S450	$89,900	8%
S560	$99,900	8%
S560 4Matic	$102,900	8%
S63 AMG	$147,500	8%

Safety Checklist

Crash Test:
Frontal.....................................
Side.......................................
Airbags:
Torso Std. Fr. & Opt. Rr. Pelvis/Torso from Seat
Roll Sensing...........................Yes
Knee Bolster ....Standard Front
Crash Avoidance:
Collision Avoidance ...... Standard CIB & DBS
Blind Spot Detection .... Optional
Lane Keeping Assist .... Optional
Backup Camera..................Standard*
Pedestrian Crash Avoidance .... Optional
General:
Auto. Crash Notif.. Op. Assist. & Crash Info-Free
Day Running Lamps .... None
Safety Belt/Restraint:
Dynamic Head Restraints ......Standard Front
Adjustable Belt...............Standard Front

Note: As of May 2018, all vehicles are required to have a backup camera.
^Warning feature does not meet government standards.
*Backup camera does not meet government standards.

Mercedes-Benz S

Specifications

Drive..RWD
Engine 3.0-liter V6
Transmission .... 9-sp. Automatic
Tow Rating (lbs.) .... —
Head/Leg Room (in.) Average-39.7/41.4
Interior Space (cu. ft.)................Roomy-112
Cargo Space (cu. ft.) Cramped-16.3
Wheelbase/Length (in.) 124.6/206.5

Ratings—10 Best, 1 Worst

Combo Crash Tests	—
Safety Features	4
Rollover	7
Preventive Maintenance	5
Repair Costs	6
Warranty	9
Fuel Economy	6
Complaints	—
Insurance Costs	5
OVERALL RATING	**—**

Mini Countryman

Mini Countryman

At-a-Glance

Status/Year Series Started. Unchanged/2017
Twins . . . . —
Body Styles . . . . Hatchback
Seating 5
Anti-Theft Device . Std. Pass. Immobil. & Active Alarm
Parking Index Rating . . . . Very Easy
Where Made. . . . . Oxford, England
Fuel Factor:
  MPG Rating (city/hwy) Average-24/32
  Driving Range (mi.) Long-435
  Fuel Type . . . . Premium
  Annual Fuel Cost . . . . Average-$1647
  Gas Guzzler Tax . . . . No
  Greenhouse Gas Emissions (tons/yr.) Low-5.3
  Barrels of Oil Used per year Average-12.2

How the Competition Rates

Competitors	Rating	Pg.
Chevrolet Cruze	8	114
Ford C-MAX	5	134
Toyota Yaris iA	6	258

Price Range

Price Range	Retail	Markup
Base	$26,100	8%
ALL4	$28,100	8%
S	$29,100	8%
S ALL4	$31,100	8%

Mini Countryman

Safety Checklist

Crash Test:
  Frontal. . . . .
  Side. . . . .
Airbags:
  Torso . . . . Standard Front Torso from Seat
  Roll Sensing. . . . . Yes
  Knee Bolster . . . . Standard Front
Crash Avoidance:
  Collision Avoidance . . . . . . Optional CIB & DBS^
  Blind Spot Detection . . . . None
  Lane Keeping Assist . . . . None
  Backup Camera . . . . Optional*
  Pedestrian Crash Avoidance . . . . None
General:
  Auto. Crash Notif.. Op. Assist. & Crash Info-Free
  Day Running Lamps . . . . Standard
Safety Belt/Restraint:
  Dynamic Head Restraints . . . . None
  Adjustable Belt. None

Note: As of May 2018, all vehicles are required to have a backup camera.
^Warning feature does not meet government standards.
*Backup camera does not meet government standards.

Specifications

Drive . . . . FWD
Engine 1.5-liter I3
Transmission . . . . 6-sp. Automatic
Tow Rating (lbs.) . . . . —
Head/Leg Room (in.) Cramped-39.9/40.4
Interior Space (cu. ft.). Average-97
Cargo Space (cu. ft.) Average-17.6
Wheelbase/Length (in.) 105.1/169.8

Ratings—10 Best, 1 Worst

Combo Crash Tests	4
Safety Features	4
Rollover	7
Preventive Maintenance	5
Repair Costs	4
Warranty	9
Fuel Economy	8
Complaints	7
Insurance Costs	5
OVERALL RATING	**6**

Mini Hardtop

Mini Hardtop

At-a-Glance

Status/Year Series Started........ Unchanged/2016
Twins .... –
Body Styles .... Sedan
Seating 4
Anti-Theft Device . Std. Pass. Immobil. & Active Alarm
Parking Index Rating .... Very Easy
Where Made.................... Oxford, England

Fuel Factor:
MPG Rating (city/hwy) Good-27/35
Driving Range (mi.) .... Very Short-349
Fuel Type........................... Premium
Annual Fuel Cost................ Average-$1480
Gas Guzzler Tax ....No
Greenhouse Gas Emissions (tons/yr.)..... Low-4.9
Barrels of Oil Used per year Average-11.0

How the Competition Rates

Competitors	Rating	Pg.
Chevrolet Sonic	9	119
Honda Fit	10	155
Toyota Yaris	5	257

Price Range

	Retail	Markup
Base Hatchback	$20,950	5%
S Hatchback	$25,400	9%
S Convertible	$29,600	9%
John Cooper Works Hatchback	$30,900	12%

Safety Checklist

Crash Test:
Frontal........................... Average
Side........................... Very Poor
Airbags:
Torso .... Standard Front Torso from Seat
Roll Sensing........................... Yes
Knee Bolster .... Standard Front
Crash Avoidance:
Collision Avoidance ..... Optional CIB & DBS^
Blind Spot Detection .... None
Lane Keeping Assist .... None
Backup Camera................. Optional*
Pedestrian Crash Avoidance .... None
General:
Auto. Crash Notif.. Op. Assist. & Crash Info-Free
Day Running Lamps .... Standard
Safety Belt/Restraint:
Dynamic Head Restraints .... None
Adjustable Belt................... None

Note: As of May 2018, all vehicles are required to have a backup camera.
^Warning feature does not meet government standards.
*Backup camera does not meet government standards.

Mini Hardtop

Specifications

Drive................................... FWD
Engine 1.5-liter I3
Transmission .... 6-sp. Automatic
Tow Rating (lbs.) .... –
Head/Leg Room (in.) Average-39.9/41.4
Interior Space (cu. ft.)........... Very Cramped-84
Cargo Space (cu. ft.) .... Very Cramped-9
Wheelbase/Length (in.) 101.1/157.4

Ratings—10 Best, 1 Worst

Combo Crash Tests	2
Safety Features	1
Rollover	4
Preventive Maintenance	8
Repair Costs	7
Warranty	10
Fuel Economy	9
Complaints	4
Insurance Costs	1
OVERALL RATING	**3**

Mitsubishi Mirage

Mitsubishi Mirage

Mitsubishi Mirage

At-a-Glance

Status/Year Series Started. Unchanged/2014
Twins . . . . –
Body Styles . . . . Hatchback
Seating. 5
Anti-Theft Device . Std. Pass. Immobil. & Active Alarm
Parking Index Rating . . . . .Very Easy
Where Made. . . . . .Laem Chabang, Thailand
Fuel Factor:
MPG Rating (city/hwy) . . . . Very Good-37/43
Driving Range (mi.) . . . . Very Short-363
Fuel Type. . . . . .Regular
Annual Fuel Cost . . . . Very Low-$931
Gas Guzzler Tax . . . . .No
Greenhouse Gas Emissions (tons/yr.). Very Low-3.7
Barrels of Oil Used per year Low-8.5

How the Competition Rates

Competitors	Rating	Pg.
Ford Fiesta	2	141
Nissan Versa	1	230
Toyota Yaris	5	257

Price Range	Retail	Markup
ES MT	$13,395	2%
ES AT	$14,595	2%
SE AT	$16,095	2%
GT AT	$16,595	2%

Safety Checklist

Crash Test:
Frontal. . . . . .Poor
Side. . . . . .Very Poor
Airbags:
Torso . . . Standard Front Pelvis/Torso from Seat
Roll Sensing. . . . . .Yes
Knee Bolster . . . . Standard Driver
Crash Avoidance:
Collision Avoidance . . . . None
Blind Spot Detection . . . . None
Lane Keeping Assist . . . . None
Backup Camera. None
Pedestrian Crash Avoidance . . . . None
General:
Auto. Crash Notification. . . . . None
Day Running Lamps . . . . None
Safety Belt/Restraint:
Dynamic Head Restraints . . . . None
Adjustable Belt. . . . . .Standard Front

Note: As of May 2018, all vehicles are required to have a backup camera.
^Warning feature does not meet government standards.
*Backup camera does not meet government standards.

Mitsubishi Mirage

Specifications

Drive. . . . . .FWD
Engine 1.2-liter I3
Transmission . . . . CVT
Tow Rating (lbs.) . . . . –
Head/Leg Room (in.) Cramped-39.1/41.7
Interior Space (cu. ft.). . . . . Very Cramped-86.1
Cargo Space (cu. ft.) Average-17.2
Wheelbase/Length (in.) 96.5/148.8

Mitsubishi Outlander

Ratings—10 Best, 1 Worst

Combo Crash Tests	5
Safety Features	5
Rollover	4
Preventive Maintenance	4
Repair Costs	8
Warranty	10
Fuel Economy	6
Complaints	3
Insurance Costs	1
OVERALL RATING	**4**

Mitsubishi Outlander

Mitsubishi Outlander

At-a-Glance

Status/Year Series Started Unchanged/2014
Twins . . . . –
Body Styles . . . . SUV
Seating 7
Anti-Theft Device . Std. Pass. Immobil. & Active Alarm
Parking Index Rating . . . . Easy
Where Made . . . . Okazaki, Japan
Fuel Factor:
MPG Rating (city/hwy) Average-24/29
Driving Range (mi.) Average-411
Fuel Type . . . . .Regular
Annual Fuel Cost . . . . Low-$1412
Gas Guzzler Tax . . . . .No
Greenhouse Gas Emissions (tons/yr.) Low-5.6
Barrels of Oil Used per year Average-12.7

How the Competition Rates

Competitors	Rating	Pg.
Ford Edge	9	136
Kia Sorento	6	181
Nissan Rogue	3	227

Price Range	Retail	Markup
ES FWD	$23,495	3%
SE FWD	$24,495	3%
SEL AWD	$27,495	3%
GT AWD	$31,695	3%

Safety Checklist

Crash Test:
Frontal . . . . Average
Side . . . . Poor
Airbags:
Torso . . . Standard Front Pelvis/Torso from Seat
Roll Sensing . . . . .Yes
Knee Bolster . . . . Standard Driver
Crash Avoidance:
Collision Avoidance . . . . . . Optional CIB & DBS
Blind Spot Detection . . . . Optional
Lane Keeping Assist . . . .Warning Only Optional
Backup Camera . . . . Optional*
Pedestrian Crash Avoidance . . . . Optional
General:
Auto. Crash Notification . . . . None
Day Running Lamps . . . . Standard
Safety Belt/Restraint:
Dynamic Head Restraints . . . . None
Adjustable Belt . . . . .Standard Front

Note: As of May 2018, all vehicles are required to have a backup camera.
^Warning feature does not meet government standards.
*Backup camera does not meet government standards.

Mitsubishi Outlander

Specifications

Drive 4WD
Engine 2.4-liter I4
Transmission . . . . CVT
Tow Rating (lbs.) . . . . Very Low-1500
Head/Leg Room (in.) Average-40.6/40.9
Interior Space (cu. ft.) . . . . Very Roomy-128.2
Cargo Space (cu. ft.) . . . . Very Cramped-10.3
Wheelbase/Length (in.) 105.1/183.3

Mitsubishi Outlander Sport

Ratings—10 Best, 1 Worst

Combo Crash Tests	4
Safety Features	5
Rollover	2
Preventive Maintenance	7
Repair Costs	5
Warranty	10
Fuel Economy	5
Complaints	7
Insurance Costs	1
OVERALL RATING	**4**

Mitsubishi Outlander Sport

Mitsubishi Outlander Sport

At-a-Glance

Status/Year Series Started Unchanged/2013
Twins . . . . –
Body Styles . . . . SUV
Seating 5
Anti-Theft Device . Std. Pass. Immobil. & Active Alarm
Parking Index Rating . . . . .Very Easy
Where Made . . . . Okazaki, Japan
Fuel Factor:
  MPG Rating (city/hwy) Average-23/29
  Driving Range (mi.) Short-388
  Fuel Type . . . . Regular
  Annual Fuel Cost . . . . Low-$1449
  Gas Guzzler Tax . . . . No
  Greenhouse Gas Emissions (tons/yr.) Low-5.8
  Barrels of Oil Used per year High-13.2

How the Competition Rates

Competitors	Rating	Pg.
Acura RDX	9	81
Hyundai Santa Fe Sport	5	163
Jeep Cherokee	5	172

Price Range	Retail	Markup
ES 2.0L FWD MT	$19,795	3%
ES 2.0L AWD AT	$22,495	3%
SEL 2.4L FWD AT	$24,195	3%
GT 2.4L 4WD	$27,695	3%

Safety Checklist

Crash Test:
  Frontal . . . . Average
  Side . . . . Poor
Airbags:
  Torso . . . Standard Front Pelvis/Torso from Seat
  Roll Sensing . . . . Yes
  Knee Bolster . . . . Standard Driver
Crash Avoidance:
  Collision Avoidance . . . . . . Optional CIB & DBS
  Blind Spot Detection . . . . Optional
  Lane Keeping Assist . . . .Warning Only Optional
  Backup Camera . . . . Optional*
  Pedestrian Crash Avoidance . . . . Optional
General:
  Auto. Crash Notification . . . . None
  Day Running Lamps . . . . Standard
Safety Belt/Restraint:
  Dynamic Head Restraints . . . . None
  Adjustable Belt . . . . .Standard Front

Note: As of May 2018, all vehicles are required to have a backup camera.
^Warning feature does not meet government standards.
*Backup camera does not meet government standards.

Mitsubishi Outlander Sport

Specifications

Drive . . . . FWD
Engine 2.0-liter I4
Transmission . . . . CVT
Tow Rating (lbs.) . . . . –
Head/Leg Room (in.) Average-39.4/41.6
Interior Space (cu. ft.) Average-97.5
Cargo Space (cu. ft.) Roomy-21.7
Wheelbase/Length (in.) 105.1/169.1

Nissan Altima

Ratings—10 Best, 1 Worst

Combo Crash Tests	6
Safety Features	3
Rollover	8
Preventive Maintenance	4
Repair Costs	9
Warranty	1
Fuel Economy	8
Complaints	7
Insurance Costs	1
OVERALL RATING	**4**

Nissan Altima

Nissan Altima

At-a-Glance

Status/Year Series Started Unchanged/2013
Twins . . . . –
Body Styles . . . . Sedan, Coupe
Seating 5
Anti-Theft Device . . . . . . Std. Pass. Immobil. & Alarm
Parking Index Rating . . . . Easy
Where Made . . . . Smyrna, TN / Canton, MS
Fuel Factor:
MPG Rating (city/hwy) Good-27/38
Driving Range (mi.) . . . . Very Long-559
Fuel Type . . . . Regular
Annual Fuel Cost . . . . Low-$1184
Gas Guzzler Tax . . . . No
Greenhouse Gas Emissions (tons/yr.) Low-5.8
Barrels of Oil Used per year Average-10.6

How the Competition Rates

Competitors	Rating	Pg.
Chevrolet Malibu	9	117
Ford Fusion	4	144
Kia Optima	9	178

Price Range	Retail	Markup
S 2.5L	$22,900	7%
SV 2.5L	$25,760	7%
SR 3.5L	$27,990	7%
SL 3.5L	$32,990	7%

Safety Checklist

Crash Test:
Frontal . . . . Very Good
Side . . . . Very Poor
Airbags:
Torso . . . Standard Front Pelvis/Torso from Seat
Roll Sensing . . . . Yes
Knee Bolster . . . . None
Crash Avoidance:
Collision Avoidance . . . . . . Optional CIB & DBS
Blind Spot Detection . . . . Optional
Lane Keeping Assist . . . . None
Backup Camera . . . . Optional*
Pedestrian Crash Avoidance . . . . None
General:
Auto. Crash Notification . . . Operator Assist.-Fee
Day Running Lamps . . . . Optional
Safety Belt/Restraint:
Dynamic Head Restraints . . . . None
Adjustable Belt . . . . Standard Front

Note: As of May 2018, all vehicles are required to have a backup camera.
^Warning feature does not meet government standards.
*Backup camera does not meet government standards.

Nissan Altima

Specifications

Drive . . . . FWD
Engine 2.5-liter I4
Transmission . . . . 6-sp. Automatic
Tow Rating (lbs.) . . . . –
Head/Leg Room (in.) . . . . Very Roomy-40/45
Interior Space (cu. ft.) Average-101.9
Cargo Space (cu. ft.) Cramped-15.4
Wheelbase/Length (in.) 109.3/191.5

Ratings—10 Best, 1 Worst

Combo Crash Tests	—
Safety Features	7
Rollover	2
Preventive Maintenance	3
Repair Costs	5
Warranty	1
Fuel Economy	1
Complaints	7
Insurance Costs	10

OVERALL RATING   —

Nissan Armada

Nissan Armada

At-a-Glance

Status/Year Series Started. Unchanged/2017
Twins . . . . —
Body Styles . . . . SUV
Seating. 7/8
Anti-Theft Device . . . . . . Std. Pass. Immobil. & Alarm
Parking Index Rating . . . . Very Hard
Where Made. . . . . Canton, MS
Fuel Factor:
  MPG Rating (city/hwy) . . . . Very Poor-14/19
  Driving Range (mi.) Average-413
  Fuel Type. . . . . .Regular
  Annual Fuel Cost . . . . Very High-$2314
  Gas Guzzler Tax . . . . .No
  Greenhouse Gas Emissions (tons/yr.) Very High-9.2
  Barrels of Oil Used per year . . . . Very High-20.6

How the Competition Rates

Competitors	Rating	Pg.
Buick Enclave	4	101
Chevrolet Suburban	2	121
Volvo XC90	8	268

Price Range	Retail	Markup
SV 2WD	$44,900	8%
SL 2WD	$49,650	8%
SL 4WD	$52,550	8%
Platinum 4WD	$60,490	8%

Safety Checklist

Crash Test:
  Frontal. . . . .
  Side. . . . .
Airbags:
  Torso . . . Standard Front Pelvis/Torso from Seat
  Roll Sensing. . . . . .Yes
  Knee Bolster . . . . None
Crash Avoidance:
  Collision Avoidance . . . . . . Optional CIB & DBS
  Blind Spot Detection . . . . Optional
  Lane Keeping Assist . . .Warning Only Optional
  Backup Camera. . . . . .Standard*
  Pedestrian Crash Avoidance . . . . None
General:
  Auto. Crash Notification. . . Operator Assist.-Fee
  Day Running Lamps . . . . Standard
Safety Belt/Restraint:
  Dynamic Head Restraints . . . . . .Standard Front
  Adjustable Belt. . . . . . .Standard Front and Rear

Note: As of May 2018, all vehicles are required to have a backup camera.
^Warning feature does not meet government standards.
*Backup camera does not meet government standards.

Nissan Armada

Specifications

Drive. . . . . .RWD
Engine 5.6-liter V8
Transmission . . . . 7-sp. Automatic
Tow Rating (lbs.) . . . . Very High-8500
Head/Leg Room (in.) Roomy-40.9/41.9
Interior Space (cu. ft.). . . . . Very Roomy-154.5
Cargo Space (cu. ft.) Cramped-16.2
Wheelbase/Length (in.) 121.1/208.9

Ratings—10 Best, 1 Worst	
Combo Crash Tests	4
Safety Features	2
Rollover	2
Preventive Maintenance	3
Repair Costs	7
Warranty	1
Fuel Economy	1
Complaints	6
Insurance Costs	5
OVERALL RATING	**1**

Nissan Frontier

Nissan Frontier

At-a-Glance

Status/Year Series Started	Unchanged/2005
Twins	–
Body Styles	Pickup
Seating	5
Anti-Theft Device	Std. Pass. Immobil. & Alarm
Parking Index Rating	Very Hard
Where Made	Canton, MS

Fuel Factor:

MPG Rating (city/hwy)	Very Poor-15/21
Driving Range (mi.)	Very Short-363
Fuel Type	Regular
Annual Fuel Cost	Very High-$2135
Gas Guzzler Tax	No
Greenhouse Gas Emissions (tons/yr.)	Very High-10.5
Barrels of Oil Used per year	Very High-19.4

How the Competition Rates

Competitors	Rating	Pg.
Chevrolet Colorado	2	112
Toyota Tacoma	2	255

Price Range	Retail	Markup
S King Cab I4 2WD MT	$18,390	3%
SV Crew Cab V6 2WD AT	$25,950	4%
PRO-4X Crew Cab 4WD AT	$33,390	6%
SL Crew Cab 4WD AT	$35,550	7%

Safety Checklist

Crash Test:

Frontal	Very Poor
Side	Very Good

Airbags:

Torso	Standard Front Pelvis/Torso from Seat
Roll Sensing	Yes
Knee Bolster	None

Crash Avoidance:

Collision Avoidance	None
Blind Spot Detection	None
Lane Keeping Assist	None
Backup Camera	Optional*
Pedestrian Crash Avoidance	None

General:

Auto. Crash Notification	None
Day Running Lamps	None

Safety Belt/Restraint:

Dynamic Head Restraints	Standard Front
Adjustable Belt	Standard Front

Note: As of May 2018, all vehicles are required to have a backup camera.
^Warning feature does not meet government standards.
*Backup camera does not meet government standards.

Nissan Frontier

Specifications

Drive	4WD
Engine	4.0-liter V6
Transmission	5-sp. Automatic
Tow Rating (lbs.)	Average-6300
Head/Leg Room (in.)	Average-39.7/42.4
Interior Space (cu. ft.)	Very Cramped-87.7
Cargo Space (cu. ft.)	Very Roomy-33.5
Wheelbase/Length (in.)	125.9/205.5

Ratings—10 Best, 1 Worst

Combo Crash Tests	1
Safety Features	3
Rollover	3
Preventive Maintenance	5
Repair Costs	6
Warranty	1
Fuel Economy	6
Complaints	7
Insurance Costs	5
OVERALL RATING	**2**

Nissan Juke

Nissan Juke

Safety Checklist

Crash Test:
Frontal . . . . Very Poor
Side . . . . Very Poor
Airbags:
Torso . . . Standard Front Pelvis/Torso from Seat
Roll Sensing . . . . Yes
Knee Bolster . . . . None
Crash Avoidance:
Collision Avoidance . . . . None
Blind Spot Detection . . . . None
Lane Keeping Assist . . . . None
Backup Camera . . . . Standard*
Pedestrian Crash Avoidance . . . . None
General:
Auto. Crash Notification . . . Operator Assist.-Fee
Day Running Lamps . . . . Optional
Safety Belt/Restraint:
Dynamic Head Restraints . . . . . . Standard Front
Adjustable Belt . . . . Standard Front

Note: As of May 2018, all vehicles are required to have a backup camera.
^Warning feature does not meet government standards.
*Backup camera does not meet government standards.

At-a-Glance

Status/Year Series Started Unchanged/2011
Twins . . . . –
Body Styles . . . . SUV
Seating 5
Anti-Theft Device . . . . . . Std. Pass. Immobil. & Alarm
Parking Index Rating . . . . Very Easy
Where Made . . . . Oppama, Japan
Fuel Factor:
MPG Rating (city/hwy) Poor-26/31
Driving Range (mi.) . . . . Very Short-331
Fuel Type . . . . Premium
Annual Fuel Cost . . . . Average-$1434
Gas Guzzler Tax . . . . No
Greenhouse Gas Emissions (tons/yr.) . . Average-6.5
Barrels of Oil Used per year Average-11.8

How the Competition Rates

Competitors	Rating	Pg.
Ford Escape	5	137
Mitsubishi Outlander Sport	4	218
Subaru Forester	4	234

Price Range

Price Range	Retail	Markup
S FWD	$20,250	3%
SV FWD	$22,300	4%
SL AWD	$26,940	4%
NISMO RS AWD	$30,020	4%

Nissan Juke

Specifications

Drive . . . . AWD
Engine 1.6-liter I4
Transmission . . . . CVT
Tow Rating (lbs.) . . . . –
Head/Leg Room (in.) Cramped-39.6/42.1
Interior Space (cu. ft.) . . . . Very Cramped-87
Cargo Space (cu. ft.) . . . . Very Cramped-10.5
Wheelbase/Length (in.) 99.6/162.4

The all-new 2018 Nissan Juke will not be available until later in the year. Because the 2017 is still available, we've included it here with its 2017 ratings.

Ratings—10 Best, 1 Worst

Combo Crash Tests	—
Safety Features	3
Rollover	—
Preventive Maintenance	8
Repair Costs	10
Warranty	1
Fuel Economy	—
Complaints	—
Insurance Costs	10

OVERALL RATING —

Nissan Leaf

Nissan Leaf

At-a-Glance

Status/Year Series Started	All New/2018
Twins	—
Body Styles	Hatchback
Seating	5
Anti-Theft Device	Std. Pass. Immobil. & Alarm
Parking Index Rating	Very Easy
Where Made	Smyrna, TN

Fuel Factor:

MPG Rating (city/hwy)	Very Good-126/101
Driving Range (mi.)	Very Short–150
Fuel Type	Electricity
Annual Fuel Cost	Very Good–$750
Gas Guzzler Tax	No
Greenhouse Gas Emissions (tons/yr.)	Very Low-0.0
Barrels of Oil Used per year	Very Low-0.0

How the Competition Rates

Competitors	Rating	Pg.
BMW i3	—	95
Chevrolet Bolt	—	110
Mercedes-Benz B	—	205

Price Range

Price Range	Retail	Markup
S	$30,680	6%
SV	$34,200	6%
SL	$36,790	6%

Safety Checklist

Crash Test:

Frontal	–
Side	–

Airbags:

Torso	Standard Front Pelvis/Torso from Seat
Roll Sensing	No
Knee Bolster	None

Crash Avoidance:

Collision Avoidance	Optional CIB & DBS
Blind Spot Detection	Optional
Lane Keeping Assist	Optional
Backup Camera	Standard*
Pedestrian Crash Avoidance	Optional

General:

Auto. Crash Notification	Operator Assist.-Fee
Day Running Lamps	None

Safety Belt/Restraint:

Dynamic Head Restraints	None
Adjustable Belt	Standard Front

Note: As of May 2018, all vehicles are required to have a backup camera.
^Warning feature does not meet government standards.
*Backup camera does not meet government standards.

Nissan Leaf

Specifications

Drive	FWD
Engine	Electric
Transmission	1-sp. Automatic
Tow Rating (lbs.)	—
Head/Leg Room (in.)	Roomy-41.2/42.1
Interior Space (cu. ft.)	Cramped-92.4
Cargo Space (cu. ft.)	Roomy-24
Wheelbase/Length (in.)	106.3/176.4

Ratings—10 Best, 1 Worst

Combo Crash Tests	7
Safety Features	3
Rollover	9
Preventive Maintenance	6
Repair Costs	6
Warranty	1
Fuel Economy	5
Complaints	8
Insurance Costs	1
OVERALL RATING	**4**

Nissan Maxima

At-a-Glance

Status/Year Series Started........ Unchanged/2016
Twins .... –
Body Styles .... Sedan
Seating................................. 5
Anti-Theft Device ...... Std. Pass. Immobil. & Alarm
Parking Index Rating .... Hard
Where Made........................ Smyrna, TN
Fuel Factor:
  MPG Rating (city/hwy) Average-22/30
  Driving Range (mi.) Long-450
  Fuel Type........................ Premium
  Annual Fuel Cost.................. High-$1782
  Gas Guzzler Tax .... No
  Greenhouse Gas Emissions (tons/yr.).. Average-6.0
  Barrels of Oil Used per year High-13.2

How the Competition Rates

Competitors	Rating	Pg.
Hyundai Sonata	9	164
Mazda 6	5	203
Toyota Camry	8	244

Price Range	Retail	Markup
S	$32,910	7%
SV	$34,890	7%
SR	$38,030	7%
Platinum	$40,340	7%

Nissan Maxima

Safety Checklist

Crash Test:
  Frontal........................... Good
  Side............................ Average
Airbags:
  Torso . . . Standard Front Pelvis/Torso from Seat
  Roll Sensing......................Yes
  Knee Bolster .... None
Crash Avoidance:
  Collision Avoidance ...... Optional CIB & DBS
  Blind Spot Detection .... Optional
  Lane Keeping Assist .... None
  Backup Camera....................Standard*
  Pedestrian Crash Avoidance .... None
General:
  Auto. Crash Notification . . . Operator Assist.-Fee
  Day Running Lamps .... Standard
Safety Belt/Restraint:
  Dynamic Head Restraints .... None
  Adjustable Belt.............Standard Front

Note: As of May 2018, all vehicles are required to have a backup camera.
^Warning feature does not meet government standards.
*Backup camera does not meet government standards.

Nissan Maxima

Specifications

Drive.................................FWD
Engine 3.5-liter V6
Transmission .... CVT
Tow Rating (lbs.) .... –
Head/Leg Room (in.) .... Very Roomy-39.4/45
Interior Space (cu. ft.)................ Average-98.6
Cargo Space (cu. ft.) Cramped-14.3
Wheelbase/Length (in.) 109.3/192.8

Nissan Murano

Nissan Murano

Ratings—10 Best, 1 Worst

Combo Crash Tests	—
Safety Features	4
Rollover	4
Preventive Maintenance	8
Repair Costs	3
Warranty	1
Fuel Economy	4
Complaints	8
Insurance Costs	10
OVERALL RATING	**—**

Nissan Murano

At-a-Glance

Status/Year Series Started	Unchanged/2015
Twins	–
Body Styles	SUV
Seating	5
Anti-Theft Device	Std. Pass. Immobil. & Alarm
Parking Index Rating	Hard
Where Made	Canton, MS

Fuel Factor:

MPG Rating (city/hwy)	Poor-21/28
Driving Range (mi.)	Long-450
Fuel Type	Regular
Annual Fuel Cost	Average-$1553
Gas Guzzler Tax	No
Greenhouse Gas Emissions (tons/yr.)	High-7.5
Barrels of Oil Used per year	High-13.7

How the Competition Rates

Competitors	Rating	Pg.
Cadillac XT5	3	108
Ford Edge	9	136
Jeep Grand Cherokee	4	174

Price Range

Price Range	Retail	Markup
S FWD	$29,740	6%
SV FWD	$32,800	7%
SL AWD	$38,730	7%
Platinum AWD	$40,780	7%

Safety Checklist

Crash Test:
- Frontal ....
- Side ....

Airbags:
- Torso . . . Standard Front Pelvis/Torso from Seat
- Roll Sensing ....Yes
- Knee Bolster .... Standard Driver

Crash Avoidance:
- Collision Avoidance ...... Optional CIB & DBS
- Blind Spot Detection .... Optional
- Lane Keeping Assist .... None
- Backup Camera...................Standard*
- Pedestrian Crash Avoidance .... None

General:
- Auto. Crash Notification . . . Operator Assist.-Fee
- Day Running Lamps .... Standard

Safety Belt/Restraint:
- Dynamic Head Restraints .... None
- Adjustable Belt...............Standard Front

Note: As of May 2018, all vehicles are required to have a backup camera.
^Warning feature does not meet government standards.
*Backup camera does not meet government standards.

Nissan Murano

Specifications

Drive	AWD
Engine	3.5-liter V6
Transmission	CVT
Tow Rating (lbs.)	Very Low-1500
Head/Leg Room (in.)	Cramped-39.9/40.5
Interior Space (cu. ft.)	Roomy-108.1
Cargo Space (cu. ft.)	Very Roomy-39.6
Wheelbase/Length (in.)	111.2/192.4

Ratings—10 Best, 1 Worst

Combo Crash Tests	—
Safety Features	3
Rollover	3
Preventive Maintenance	1
Repair Costs	4
Warranty	1
Fuel Economy	3
Complaints	3
Insurance Costs	10

OVERALL RATING —

Nissan Pathfinder

Nissan Pathfinder

At-a-Glance

Status/Year Series Started. Unchanged/2013
Twins . . . . Infiniti QX60
Body Styles . . . . SUV
Seating 7
Anti-Theft Device . . . . . . Std. Pass. Immobil. & Alarm
Parking Index Rating . . . . Hard
Where Made. Smyrna, TN
Fuel Factor:
  MPG Rating (city/hwy) Poor-19/26
  Driving Range (mi.) Average-422
  Fuel Type. . . . . .Regular
  Annual Fuel Cost . . . . .High-$1700
  Gas Guzzler Tax . . . . .No
  Greenhouse Gas Emissions (tons/yr.). High-8.2
  Barrels of Oil Used per year High-15.0

How the Competition Rates

Competitors	Rating	Pg.
Dodge Durango	2	130
Ford Explorer	3	139
GMC Acadia	2	149

Price Range

Price Range	Retail	Markup
S FWD	$29,990	8%
SV FWD	$32,680	8%
SL 4WD	$37,390	8%
Platinum 4WD	$43,560	8%

Safety Checklist

Crash Test:
  Frontal. . . . .
  Side. . . . .
Airbags:
  Torso . . . Standard Front Pelvis/Torso from Seat
  Roll Sensing. . . . . .Yes
  Knee Bolster . . . . None
Crash Avoidance:
  Collision Avoidance . . . . . . Optional CIB & DBS
  Blind Spot Detection . . . . Optional
  Lane Keeping Assist . . . . None
  Backup Camera. . . . . Optional*
  Pedestrian Crash Avoidance . . . . None
General:
  Auto. Crash Notification . . . Operator Assist.-Fee
  Day Running Lamps . . . . Standard
Safety Belt/Restraint:
  Dynamic Head Restraints . . . . None
  Adjustable Belt. . . . . Standard Front & Rear

Note: As of May 2018, all vehicles are required to have a backup camera.
^Warning feature does not meet government standards.
*Backup camera does not meet government standards.

Nissan Pathfinder

Specifications

Drive. 4WD
Engine 3.5-liter V6
Transmission . . . . CVT
Tow Rating (lbs.) Low-5000
Head/Leg Room (in.) Roomy-41.1/42.3
Interior Space (cu. ft.). . . . . Very Roomy-157.8
Cargo Space (cu. ft.) Cramped-16
Wheelbase/Length (in.) 114.2/197.2

Nissan Rogue   Medium SUV

Ratings—10 Best, 1 Worst

Combo Crash Tests	1
Safety Features	5
Rollover	4
Preventive Maintenance	3
Repair Costs	4
Warranty	1
Fuel Economy	7
Complaints	10
Insurance Costs	10
OVERALL RATING	**3**

Nissan Rogue

Nissan Rogue

At-a-Glance

Status/Year Series Started. Unchanged/2014
Twins . . . . –
Body Styles . . . . SUV
Seating. 5/7
Anti-Theft Device . . . . . . Std. Pass. Immobil. & Alarm
Parking Index Rating . . . . Average
Where Made. Smyrna, TN

Fuel Factor:
MPG Rating (city/hwy) Good-25/32
Driving Range (mi.) Average-402
Fuel Type. . . . . .Regular
Annual Fuel Cost . . . . Low-$1325
Gas Guzzler Tax . . . . .No
Greenhouse Gas Emissions (tons/yr.) . . Average-6.4
Barrels of Oil Used per year Average-11.8

How the Competition Rates

Competitors	Rating	Pg.
Kia Sorento	6	181
Mazda CX-5	4	200
Subaru Outback	8	237

Price Range

Price Range	Retail	Markup
S FWD	$23,820	6%
SV FWD	$25,240	6%
SV AWD	$26,590	6%
SL AWD	$31,310	6%

Safety Checklist

Crash Test:
Frontal. . . . . .Very Poor
Side. . . . . .Very Poor

Airbags:
Torso . . . Standard Front Pelvis/Torso from Seat
Roll Sensing. . . . . .Yes
Knee Bolster . . . . None

Crash Avoidance:
Collision Avoidance . . . . . . Optional CIB & DBS
Blind Spot Detection . . . . Optional
Lane Keeping Assist . . . .Warning Only Optional
Backup Camera . . . . .Standard*
Pedestrian Crash Avoidance . . . . Optional

General:
Auto. Crash Notification . . . Operator Assist.-Fee
Day Running Lamps . . . . Standard

Safety Belt/Restraint:
Dynamic Head Restraints . . . . None
Adjustable Belt. . . . . .Standard Front

Note: As of May 2018, all vehicles are required to have a backup camera.
^Warning feature does not meet government standards.
*Backup camera does not meet government standards.

Nissan Rogue

Specifications

Drive. . . . . .AWD
Engine 2.5-liter I4
Transmission . . . . CVT
Tow Rating (lbs.) . . . . .Very Low-1000
Head/Leg Room (in.) . . . . Very Roomy-41.6/43
Interior Space (cu. ft.). Roomy-105.8
Cargo Space (cu. ft.) . . . . Very Cramped-9.4
Wheelbase/Length (in.) 106.5/182.3

Nissan Sentra Compact

Ratings—10 Best, 1 Worst

Combo Crash Tests	2
Safety Features	2
Rollover	6
Preventive Maintenance	8
Repair Costs	9
Warranty	1
Fuel Economy	9
Complaints	9
Insurance Costs	5
OVERALL RATING	**5**

Nissan Sentra

At-a-Glance

Status/Year Series Started....... Unchanged/2013
Twins ....–
Body Styles .... Sedan
Seating 5
Anti-Theft Device ...... Std. Pass. Immobil. & Alarm
Parking Index Rating .... Easy
Where Made Aguascalientes, Mexico / Kyushu, Japan
Fuel Factor:
  MPG Rating (city/hwy) ...... Very Good-30/39
  Driving Range (mi.) Long-442
  Fuel Type ....Regular
  Annual Fuel Cost .... Very Low-$1098
  Gas Guzzler Tax ....No
  Greenhouse Gas Emissions (tons/yr.)..... Low-5.3
  Barrels of Oil Used per year Low-9.7

How the Competition Rates

Competitors	Rating	Pg.
Ford Focus	5	143
Honda Civic	10	153
Toyota Corolla	8	245

Price Range	Retail	Markup
S MT	$16,990	3%
SV	$18,840	5%
SR	$19,990	5%
SL	$21,500	5%

Nissan Sentra

Safety Checklist

Crash Test:
  Frontal.........................Very Poor
  Side............................... Average
Airbags:
  Torso . . . Standard Front Pelvis/Torso from Seat
  Roll Sensing........................Yes
  Knee Bolster .... None
Crash Avoidance:
  Collision Avoidance ...... Optional CIB & DBS
  Blind Spot Detection .... Optional
  Lane Keeping Assist .... None
  Backup Camera................. Optional*
  Pedestrian Crash Avoidance........... None
General:
  Auto. Crash Notification... Operator Assist.-Fee
  Day Running Lamps .... None
Safety Belt/Restraint:
  Dynamic Head Restraints .... None
  Adjustable Belt.................Standard Front

Note: As of May 2018, all vehicles are required to have a backup camera.
^Warning feature does not meet government standards.
*Backup camera does not meet government standards.

Nissan Sentra

Specifications

Drive.......................................FWD
Engine 2.0-liter I4
Transmission .... CVT
Tow Rating (lbs.) ....–
Head/Leg Room (in.) Average-39.4/42.5
Interior Space (cu. ft.)................ Cramped-95.9
Cargo Space (cu. ft.) Cramped-15.1
Wheelbase/Length (in.) 106.3/182.1

Nissan Titan — Standard Pickup

Ratings—10 Best, 1 Worst

Combo Crash Tests	7
Safety Features	2
Rollover	2
Preventive Maintenance	2
Repair Costs	5
Warranty	1
Fuel Economy	1
Complaints	2
Insurance Costs	8
OVERALL RATING	**1**

Nissan Titan

Nissan Titan

At-a-Glance

Status/Year Series Started	Unchanged/2016
Twins	–
Body Styles	Pickup
Seating	6
Anti-Theft Device	Std. Pass. Immobil. & Alarm
Parking Index Rating	Very Hard
Where Made	Canton, MS

Fuel Factor:

MPG Rating (city/hwy)	Very Poor-15/21
Driving Range (mi.)	Long-448
Fuel Type	Regular
Annual Fuel Cost	Very High-$2135
Gas Guzzler Tax	No
Greenhouse Gas Emissions (tons/yr.)	High-8.4
Barrels of Oil Used per year	Very High-18.3

How the Competition Rates

Competitors	Rating	Pg.
Chevrolet Silverado	7	118
Ford F-150	9	140
Toyota Tundra	–	256

Price Range

	Retail	Markup
S Crew Cab 2WD	$35,230	4%
SV Crew Cab 4WD	$41,400	6%
SL Crew Cab 4WD	$49,910	6%
Platinum Crew Cab 4WD	$55,850	6%

Safety Checklist

Crash Test:

Frontal	Average
Side	Very Good

Airbags:

Torso	Standard Front Pelvis/Torso from Seat
Roll Sensing	Yes
Knee Bolster	None

Crash Avoidance:

Collision Avoidance	None
Blind Spot Detection	Optional
Lane Keeping Assist	None
Backup Camera	Optional*
Pedestrian Crash Avoidance	None

General:

Auto. Crash Notification	Operator Assist.-Fee
Day Running Lamps	Optional

Safety Belt/Restraint:

Dynamic Head Restraints	None
Adjustable Belt	Standard Front

Note: As of May 2018, all vehicles are required to have a backup camera.
^Warning feature does not meet government standards.
*Backup camera does not meet government standards.

Nissan Titan

Specifications

Drive	4WD
Engine	5.0-liter V8
Transmission	6-sp. Automatic
Tow Rating (lbs.)	Very High-12038
Head/Leg Room (in.)	Roomy-41/41.8
Interior Space (cu. ft.)	–
Cargo Space (cu. ft.)	Very Roomy-58.1
Wheelbase/Length (in.)	151.6/242.7

Nissan Versa

Ratings—10 Best, 1 Worst

Combo Crash Tests	1
Safety Features	1
Rollover	4
Preventive Maintenance	9
Repair Costs	9
Warranty	1
Fuel Economy	9
Complaints	5
Insurance Costs	1
OVERALL RATING	**1**

Nissan Versa

Nissan Versa

At-a-Glance

Status/Year Series Started Unchanged/2006
Twins . . . . –
Body Styles . . . . Sedan, Hatchback
Seating 4
Anti-Theft Device . . . . Std. Pass. Immobil.
Parking Index Rating . . . . .Very Easy
Where Made Aguascalientes, Mexico / Kyushu, Japan
Fuel Factor:
MPG Rating (city/hwy) . . . . Very Good-31/40
Driving Range (mi.) . . . . Very Short-373
Fuel Type . . . . .Regular
Annual Fuel Cost . . . . Very Low-$1065
Gas Guzzler Tax . . . . .No
Greenhouse Gas Emissions (tons/yr.) Low-5.1
Barrels of Oil Used per year Low-9.4

How the Competition Rates

Competitors	Rating	Pg.
Chevrolet Sonic	9	119
Ford Fiesta	2	141
Toyota Yaris	5	257

Price Range

	Retail	Markup
S MT	$11,900	2%
S Plus	$14,130	3%
SV	$15,720	3%

Safety Checklist

Crash Test:
 Frontal . . . . .Very Poor
 Side . . . . .Very Poor
Airbags:
 Torso . . . Standard Front Pelvis/Torso from Seat
 Roll Sensing . . . . .Yes
 Knee Bolster . . . . None
Crash Avoidance:
 Collision Avoidance . . . . None
 Blind Spot Detection . . . . None
 Lane Keeping Assist . . . . None
 Backup Camera . . . . Optional*
 Pedestrian Crash Avoidance . . . . None
General:
 Auto. Crash Notification . . . . None
 Day Running Lamps . . . . None
Safety Belt/Restraint:
 Dynamic Head Restraints . . . . None
 Adjustable Belt . . . . .Standard Front

Note: As of May 2018, all vehicles are required to have a backup camera.
^Warning feature does not meet government standards.
*Backup camera does not meet government standards.

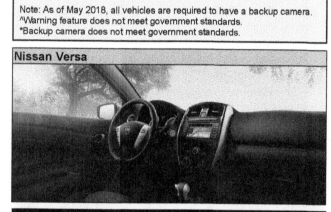
Nissan Versa

Specifications

Drive . . . . .FWD
Engine 1.6-liter I4
Transmission . . . . CVT
Tow Rating (lbs.) . . . . –
Head/Leg Room (in.) Average-39.8/41.8
Interior Space (cu. ft.) . . . . Very Cramped-90.2
Cargo Space (cu. ft.) Cramped-14.9
Wheelbase/Length (in.) 102.4/175.4

Porsche Macan

Ratings—10 Best, 1 Worst

Combo Crash Tests	—
Safety Features	6
Rollover	—
Preventive Maintenance	3
Repair Costs	1
Warranty	7
Fuel Economy	2
Complaints	10
Insurance Costs	5
OVERALL RATING	—

Porsche Macan

Porsche Macan

At-a-Glance

Status/Year Series Started Unchanged/2015
Twins . . . . —
Body Styles . . . . SUV
Seating 5
Anti-Theft Device . Std. Pass. Immobil. & Active Alarm
Parking Index Rating . . . . Hard
Where Made . . . . Leipzig, Germany

Fuel Factor:
MPG Rating (city/hwy) . . . . Very Poor-17/23
Driving Range (mi.) Short-381
Fuel Type . . . . Premium
Annual Fuel Cost . . . . Very High-$2313
Gas Guzzler Tax . . . . No
Greenhouse Gas Emissions (tons/yr.) . . Average-6.6
Barrels of Oil Used per year High-15.0

How the Competition Rates

Competitors	Rating	Pg.
BMW X5	5	98
Cadillac XT5	3	108
Lexus RX	4	193

Price Range

Price Range	Retail	Markup
Base	$47,800	11%
S	$55,400	11%
GTS	$68,900	11%
Turbo	$77,200	11%

Safety Checklist

Crash Test:
Frontal . . . .
Side . . . .

Airbags:
Torso . . Standard Front & Rear Torso from Seat
Roll Sensing . . . . Yes
Knee Bolster . . . . Standard Front

Crash Avoidance:
Collision Avoidance . . . . . . Optional CIB & DBS^
Blind Spot Detection . . . . Optional
Lane Keeping Assist . . . . Optional^
Backup Camera . . . . Optional*
Pedestrian Crash Avoidance . . . . None

General:
Auto. Crash Notification . . . . None
Day Running Lamps . . . . Standard

Safety Belt/Restraint:
Dynamic Head Restraints . . . . None
Adjustable Belt . . . . Standard Front & Rear

Note: As of May 2018, all vehicles are required to have a backup camera.
^Warning feature does not meet government standards.
*Backup camera does not meet government standards.

Porsche Macan

Specifications

Drive . . . . AWD
Engine 3.0-liter V6
Transmission . . . . 7-sp. Automatic
Tow Rating (lbs.) Low-4400
Head/Leg Room (in.) . . . . —
Interior Space (cu. ft.) . . . . —
Cargo Space (cu. ft.) Average-17.7
Wheelbase/Length (in.) 110.5/184.3

Ratings—10 Best, 1 Worst

Combo Crash Tests	2
Safety Features	1
Rollover	2
Preventive Maintenance	8
Repair Costs	10
Warranty	2
Fuel Economy	1
Complaints	5
Insurance Costs	10
OVERALL RATING	**2**

Ram 1500

Ram 1500

Safety Checklist

Crash Test:
Frontal . . . . Very Poor
Side . . . . Poor
Airbags:
Torso . . . Standard Front Pelvis/Torso from Seat
Roll Sensing . . . . Yes
Knee Bolster . . . . None
Crash Avoidance:
Collision Avoidance . . . . None
Blind Spot Detection . . . . None
Lane Keeping Assist . . . . None
Backup Camera . . . . Optional
Pedestrian Crash Avoidance . . . . None
General:
Auto. Crash Notification . . . . None
Day Running Lamps . . . . Standard
Safety Belt/Restraint:
Dynamic Head Restraints . . . . None
Adjustable Belt . . . . Standard Front

Note: As of May 2018, all vehicles are required to have a backup camera.
^Warning feature does not meet government standards.
*Backup camera does not meet government standards.

At-a-Glance

Status/Year Series Started Unchanged/2009
Twins . . . . –
Body Styles . . . . Pickup
Seating 5/6
Anti-Theft Device . Std. Pass. Immobil. & Opt. Pass. Alarm
Parking Index Rating . . . . Very Hard
Where Made . . . . Warren, MI / Saltillo, Mexico
Fuel Factor:
MPG Rating (city/hwy) . . . . Very Poor-13/19
Driving Range (mi.) Short-394
Fuel Type . . . . Regular
Annual Fuel Cost . . . . Very High-$2425
Gas Guzzler Tax . . . . No
Greenhouse Gas Emissions (tons/yr.) Very High-12.0
Barrels of Oil Used per year . . . . Very High-22.0

How the Competition Rates

Competitors	Rating	Pg.
Chevrolet Silverado	7	118
Ford F-150	9	140
Toyota Tundra	–	256

Price Range

	Retail	Markup
Tradesman Reg. Cab 2WD	$27,095	4%
SLT Quad Cab 2WD	$34,945	6%
Sport Crew Cab 4WD	$46,395	9%
Laramie Longhorn Crew Cab 4WD	$53,995	10%

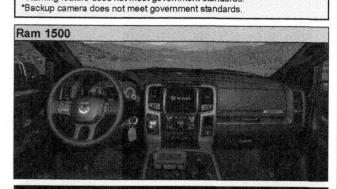

Ram 1500

Specifications

Drive 4WD
Engine 5.7-liter V8
Transmission . . . . 6-sp. Automatic
Tow Rating (lbs.) . . . . Very High-8800
Head/Leg Room (in.) Average-41/41
Interior Space (cu. ft.) Roomy-116.6
Cargo Space (cu. ft.) . . . . Very Roomy-57.5
Wheelbase/Length (in.) 140.5/229

Subaru Crosstrek

Ratings—10 Best, 1 Worst

Combo Crash Tests	5
Safety Features	8
Rollover	4
Preventive Maintenance	4
Repair Costs	8
Warranty	3
Fuel Economy	7
Complaints	—
Insurance Costs	5
OVERALL RATING	**5**

Subaru Crosstrek

At-a-Glance

Status/Year Series Started. . . . . All New/2018
Twins . . . . —
Body Styles . . . . SUV
Seating. 5
Anti-Theft Device . Std. Pass. Immobil. & Active Alarm
Parking Index Rating . . . . Easy
Where Made. . . . . Gunma, Japan
Fuel Factor:
  MPG Rating (city/hwy) Good-27/33
  Driving Range (mi.) . . . . Very Long-488
  Fuel Type. . . . . .Regular
  Annual Fuel Cost. . . . . Low-$1250
  Gas Guzzler Tax .No
  Greenhouse Gas Emissions (tons/yr.). Low-5.0
  Barrels of Oil Used per year Average-11.4

How the Competition Rates

Competitors	Rating	Pg.
Chevrolet Traverse	4	123
Jeep Renegade	1	175
Toyota RAV4	9	252

Price Range	Retail	Markup
Base MT	$21,795	5%
Premium MT	$22,595	5%
Premium AT	$23,595	6%
Limited	$26,295	6%

Subaru Crosstrek

Safety Checklist

Crash Test:
  Frontal. . . . . Average
  Side. . . . . Average
Airbags:
  Torso . . .Standard Front Pelvis/Torso from Seat
  Roll Sensing. . . . . .Yes
  Knee Bolster . . . . Standard Driver
Crash Avoidance:
  Collision Avoidance . . . . . . Optional CIB & DBS
  Blind Spot Detection . . . . Optional
  Lane Keeping Assist . . . . Optional
  Backup Camera . . . . Standard
  Pedestrian Crash Avoidance . . . . Optional
General:
  Auto. Crash Notification. . . Operator Assist.-Fee
  Day Running Lamps . . . . Standard
Safety Belt/Restraint:
  Dynamic Head Restraints . . . . None
  Adjustable Belt. . . . . .Standard Front

Note: As of May 2018, all vehicles are required to have a backup camera.
^Warning feature does not meet government standards.
*Backup camera does not meet government standards.

Subaru Crosstrek

Specifications

Drive. . . . . .AWD
Engine 2.0-liter I4
Transmission . . . . CVT
Tow Rating (lbs.) . . . . —
Head/Leg Room (in.) Average-39/43.1
Interior Space (cu. ft.). Average-100.9
Cargo Space (cu. ft.) Average-20.8
Wheelbase/Length (in.) 104.9/175.8

Ratings—10 Best, 1 Worst

Combo Crash Tests	6
Safety Features	8
Rollover	3
Preventive Maintenance	3
Repair Costs	7
Warranty	3
Fuel Economy	6
Complaints	7
Insurance Costs	1
OVERALL RATING	**4**

Subaru Forester

Subaru Forester

At-a-Glance

Status/Year Series Started Unchanged/2014
Twins . . . . –
Body Styles . . . . SUV
Seating 5
Anti-Theft Device . Std. Pass. Immobil. & Active Alarm
Parking Index Rating . . . . Easy
Where Made . . . . Lafayette, IN
Fuel Factor:
 MPG Rating (city/hwy) Average-24/32
 Driving Range (mi.) Long-430
 Fuel Type . . . . Regular
 Annual Fuel Cost . . . . Low-$1359
 Gas Guzzler Tax . . . . No
 Greenhouse Gas Emissions (tons/yr.) . . Average-6.6
 Barrels of Oil Used per year Average-12.2

How the Competition Rates

Competitors	Rating	Pg.
Chevrolet Trax	10	124
Mazda CX-3	10	199
Mitsubishi Outlander Sport	4	218

Price Range	Retail	Markup
2.5i MT	$22,795	6%
2.5i Premium AT	$26,195	6%
2.5i Touring	$33,090	7%
2.0 XT Touring	$36,090	7%

Safety Checklist

Crash Test:
 Frontal . . . . Poor
 Side . . . . Good
Airbags:
 Torso . . . Standard Front Pelvis/Torso from Seat
 Roll Sensing . . . . Yes
 Knee Bolster . . . . Standard Driver
Crash Avoidance:
 Collision Avoidance . . . . . . Optional CIB & DBS
 Blind Spot Detection . . . . Optional
 Lane Keeping Assist . . . . Optional
 Backup Camera . . . . Standard
 Pedestrian Crash Avoidance . . . . Optional
General:
 Auto. Crash Notification . . . Operator Assist.-Fee
 Day Running Lamps . . . . Standard
Safety Belt/Restraint:
 Dynamic Head Restraints . . . . None
 Adjustable Belt . . . . Standard Front

Note: As of May 2018, all vehicles are required to have a backup camera.
^Warning feature does not meet government standards.
*Backup camera does not meet government standards.

Subaru Forester

Specifications

Drive . . . . AWD
Engine 2.5-liter I4
Transmission . . . . CVT
Tow Rating (lbs.) . . . . Very Low-1500
Head/Leg Room (in.) . . . . Very Roomy-41.4/43
Interior Space (cu. ft.) Roomy-113.1
Cargo Space (cu. ft.) . . . . Very Roomy-34.4
Wheelbase/Length (in.) 103.9/180.9

Subaru Impreza — Compact

Ratings—10 Best, 1 Worst	
Combo Crash Tests	6
Safety Features	8
Rollover	9
Preventive Maintenance	4
Repair Costs	8
Warranty	3
Fuel Economy	4
Complaints	6
Insurance Costs	1
OVERALL RATING	**5**

Subaru Impreza

Subaru Impreza

At-a-Glance

Status/Year Series Started. Unchanged/2017
Twins . . . . –
Body Styles . . . . Sedan, Hatchback
Seating. 5
Anti-Theft Device . Std. Pass. Immobil. & Active Alarm
Parking Index Rating . . . . Easy
Where Made. . . . . Gunma, Japan

Fuel Factor:
MPG Rating (city/hwy) Poor-20/27
Driving Range (mi.) Average-419
Fuel Type. . . . . Regular
Annual Fuel Cost . . . . .Average-$1623
Gas Guzzler Tax . . . . No
Greenhouse Gas Emissions (tons/yr.). . Average-6.5
Barrels of Oil Used per year High-15.0

How the Competition Rates

Competitors	Rating	Pg.
Chevrolet Cruze	8	114
Mazda Mazda3	6	202
Toyota Corolla	8	245

Price Range	Retail	Markup
Base Sedan MT	$18,495	5%
Premium Wagon	$21,795	5%
Sport Sedan AT	$22,895	5%
Limited Wagon	$24,695	6%

Safety Checklist

Crash Test:
Frontal. . . . . Good
Side. . . . . Poor
Airbags:
Torso . . . Standard Front Pelvis/Torso from Seat
Roll Sensing. . . . . .Yes
Knee Bolster . . . . Standard Driver
Crash Avoidance:
Collision Avoidance . . . . . . Optional CIB & DBS
Blind Spot Detection . . . . Optional
Lane Keeping Assist . . . . Optional
Backup Camera. . . . . Standard
Pedestrian Crash Avoidance . . . . Optional
General:
Auto. Crash Notification . . . Operator Assist.-Fee
Day Running Lamps . . . . Standard
Safety Belt/Restraint:
Dynamic Head Restraints . . . . None
Adjustable Belt. . . . . .Standard Front

Note: As of May 2018, all vehicles are required to have a backup camera.
^Warning feature does not meet government standards.
*Backup camera does not meet government standards.

Subaru Impreza

Specifications

Drive. . . . . .AWD
Engine 2.0-liter I4
Transmission . . . . CVT
Tow Rating (lbs.) . . . . –
Head/Leg Room (in.) Roomy-39.8/43.1
Interior Space (cu. ft.). Average-100
Cargo Space (cu. ft.) . . . . Very Cramped-12.3
Wheelbase/Length (in.) 105.1/182.1

Ratings—10 Best, 1 Worst

Combo Crash Tests	10
Safety Features	7
Rollover	3
Preventive Maintenance	2
Repair Costs	9
Warranty	3
Fuel Economy	7
Complaints	4
Insurance Costs	5
OVERALL RATING	**8**

Subaru Outback

Subaru Outback

At-a-Glance

Status/Year Series Started Unchanged/2015
Twins . . . . –
Body Styles . . . . Wagon
Seating 5
Anti-Theft Device . Std. Pass. Immobil. & Active Alarm
Parking Index Rating . . . . Easy
Where Made . . . . Lafayette, IN
Fuel Factor:
  MPG Rating (city/hwy) Good-25/33
  Driving Range (mi.) . . . . Very Long-519
  Fuel Type . . . . Regular
  Annual Fuel Cost . . . . Low-$1310
  Gas Guzzler Tax . . . . No
  Greenhouse Gas Emissions (tons/yr.) . . Average-6.4
  Barrels of Oil Used per year Average-11.8

How the Competition Rates

Competitors	Rating	Pg.
Kia Sorento	6	181
Toyota Highlander	9	247
Volkswagen Atlas	6	259

Price Range

	Retail	Markup
Base	$25,895	6%
Premium	$27,995	6%
Limited	$32,695	7%
3.6R Limited	$35,395	7%

Safety Checklist

Crash Test:
  Frontal . . . . Very Good
  Side . . . . Very Good
Airbags:
  Torso . . . Standard Front Pelvis/Torso from Seat
  Roll Sensing . . . . Yes
  Knee Bolster . . . . None
Crash Avoidance:
  Collision Avoidance . . . . . . Optional CIB & DBS
  Blind Spot Detection . . . . Optional
  Lane Keeping Assist . . . . Optional
  Backup Camera . . . . Standard
  Pedestrian Crash Avoidance . . . . Optional
General:
  Auto. Crash Notification . . . Operator Assist.-Fee
  Day Running Lamps . . . . Standard
Safety Belt/Restraint:
  Dynamic Head Restraints . . . . None
  Adjustable Belt . . . . Standard Front

Note: As of May 2018, all vehicles are required to have a backup camera.
^Warning feature does not meet government standards.
*Backup camera does not meet government standards.

Subaru Outback

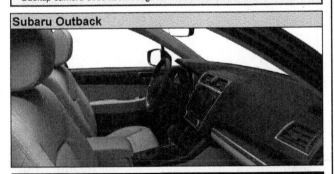

Specifications

Drive . . . . AWD
Engine 2.5-liter I4
Transmission . . . . 6-sp. Automatic
Tow Rating (lbs.) . . . . Very Low-2700
Head/Leg Room (in.) Roomy-40.8/42.9
Interior Space (cu. ft.) Roomy-108.1
Cargo Space (cu. ft.) . . . . Very Roomy-35.5
Wheelbase/Length (in.) 108.1/189.6

Ratings—10 Best, 1 Worst

Combo Crash Tests	—
Safety Features	7
Rollover	7
Preventive Maintenance	8
Repair Costs	10
Warranty	10
Fuel Economy	10
Complaints	—
Insurance Costs	5

OVERALL RATING   —

Tesla Model 3

Tesla Model 3

At-a-Glance

Status/Year Series Started	All New/2018
Twins	—
Body Styles	Sedan
Seating	5
Anti-Theft Device	Std. Passive Alarm Only
Parking Index Rating	Average
Where Made	Fremont, CA

Fuel Factor:

MPG Rating (city/hwy)	Very Good-131/120
Driving Range (mi.)	Very Short-310
Fuel Type	Electricity
Annual Fuel Cost	Very Low-$500
Gas Guzzler Tax	No
Greenhouse Gas Emissions (tons/yr.)	Very Low-0.0
Barrels of Oil Used per year	Very Low-0.0

How the Competition Rates

Competitors	Rating	Pg.
BMW i3	—	95
Chevrolet Bolt	—	110
Mercedes-Benz B	—	205

Price Range

	Retail	Markup
Base	$35,000	6%
Premium	$40,000	6%
Prem. w/Enhanced Autopilot	$45,000	6%

Safety Checklist

Crash Test:
- Frontal ....
- Side ....

Airbags:
- Torso . . . Standard Front Pelvis/Torso from Seat
- Roll Sensing .... Yes
- Knee Bolster .... Standard Front

Crash Avoidance:
- Collision Avoidance ...... Optional CIB & DBS^
- Blind Spot Detection .... Optional
- Lane Keeping Assist .... Optional
- Backup Camera .... Standard
- Pedestrian Crash Avoidance .... None

General:
- Auto. Crash Notification .... None
- Day Running Lamps .... Standard

Safety Belt/Restraint:
- Dynamic Head Restraints .... None
- Adjustable Belt .... None

Note: As of May 2018, all vehicles are required to have a backup camera.
^Warning feature does not meet government standards.
*Backup camera does not meet government standards.

Tesla Model 3

Specifications

Drive	RWD
Engine	Electric
Transmission	CVT
Tow Rating (lbs.)	—
Head/Leg Room (in.)	—
Interior Space (cu. ft.)	—
Cargo Space (cu. ft.)	Cramped-15
Wheelbase/Length (in.)	113.2/184.8

Ratings—10 Best, 1 Worst	
Combo Crash Tests	9
Safety Features	9
Rollover	10
Preventive Maintenance	8
Repair Costs	10
Warranty	10
Fuel Economy	10
Complaints	1
Insurance Costs	1
OVERALL RATING	**10**

Tesla Model S

Tesla Model S

At-a-Glance

Status/Year Series Started	Unchanged/2015
Twins	–
Body Styles	Sedan
Seating	5
Anti-Theft Device	Std. Passive Alarm Only
Parking Index Rating	Hard
Where Made	Fremont, CA

Fuel Factor:

MPG Rating (city/hwy)	Very Good-88/90
Driving Range (mi.)	–
Fuel Type	Electricity
Annual Fuel Cost	Very Low-$650
Gas Guzzler Tax	No
Greenhouse Gas Emissions (tons/yr.)	Very Low-0.0
Barrels of Oil Used per year	Very Low-0.0

How the Competition Rates

Competitors	Rating	Pg.
Buick LaCrosse	5	104
Cadillac XTS	8	109
Mercedes-Benz E	3	208

Price Range	Retail	Markup
75 kWh	$69,500	6%
75D kWh	$74,500	6%
90D kWh	$87,500	6%
P100D kWh	$135,000	6%

Safety Checklist

Crash Test:
Frontal	Good
Side	Very Good

Airbags:
Torso	Standard Front Pelvis/Torso from Seat
Roll Sensing	Yes
Knee Bolster	Standard Front

Crash Avoidance:
Collision Avoidance	Standard CIB & DBS
Blind Spot Detection	Standard
Lane Keeping Assist	Optional
Backup Camera	Standard
Pedestrian Crash Avoidance	None

General:
Auto. Crash Notification	None
Day Running Lamps	Standard

Safety Belt/Restraint:
Dynamic Head Restraints	None
Adjustable Belt	None

Note: As of May 2018, all vehicles are required to have a backup camera.
^Warning feature does not meet government standards.
*Backup camera does not meet government standards.

Tesla Model S

Specifications

Drive	RWD
Engine	Electric
Transmission	CVT
Tow Rating (lbs.)	–
Head/Leg Room (in.)	Average-38.8/42.7
Interior Space (cu. ft.)	Cramped-94
Cargo Space (cu. ft.)	Very Roomy-31.6
Wheelbase/Length (in.)	116.5/196

Ratings—10 Best, 1 Worst

Combo Crash Tests	10
Safety Features	9
Rollover	9
Preventive Maintenance	8
Repair Costs	10
Warranty	10
Fuel Economy	10
Complaints	2
Insurance Costs	8
OVERALL RATING	**10**

Tesla Model X

Tesla Model X

At-a-Glance

Status/Year Series Started. Unchanged/2017
Twins . . . . –
Body Styles . . . . SUV
Seating 7
Anti-Theft Device . . . . Std. Passive Alarm Only
Parking Index Rating . . . . Very Hard
Where Made. .Fremont, CA
Fuel Factor:
  MPG Rating (city/hwy) . . . . Very Good-89/90
  Driving Range (mi.) . . . . –
  Fuel Type. . . . . Electricity
  Annual Fuel Cost . . . . Very Low-$700
  Gas Guzzler Tax . . . . .No
  Greenhouse Gas Emissions (tons/yr.). Very Low-0.0
  Barrels of Oil Used per year . . . . Very Low-0.0

How the Competition Rates

Competitors	Rating	Pg.
Audi Q7	3	89
BMW X5	5	98
Buick Enclave	4	101

Price Range

Price Range	Retail	Markup
75D kWh	$79,500	6%
90D kWh	$93,500	6%
100D kWh	$96,000	6%
P100D kWh	$140,000	6%

Safety Checklist

Crash Test:
  Frontal. . . . . Very Good
  Side. . . . . Very Good
Airbags:
  Torso . . . Standard Front Pelvis/Torso from Seat
  Roll Sensing. . . . . .Yes
  Knee Bolster . . . . .Standard Front
Crash Avoidance:
  Collision Avoidance . . . . . . Standard CIB & DBS
  Blind Spot Detection . . . . Standard
  Lane Keeping Assist . . . . Optional
  Backup Camera. . . . . Standard
  Pedestrian Crash Avoidance . . . . None
General:
  Auto. Crash Notification . . . . None
  Day Running Lamps . . . . Standard
Safety Belt/Restraint:
  Dynamic Head Restraints . . . . None
  Adjustable Belt. . . . . None

Note: As of May 2018, all vehicles are required to have a backup camera.
^Warning feature does not meet government standards.
*Backup camera does not meet government standards.

Tesla Model X

Specifications

Drive . . . . .AWD
Engine . . . . Electric
Transmission . . . . CVT
Tow Rating (lbs.) . . . . –
Head/Leg Room (in.) Roomy-41.7/41.2
Interior Space (cu. ft.). Roomy-120
Cargo Space (cu. ft.) Roomy-26
Wheelbase/Length (in.) 116.7/198.3

Ratings—10 Best, 1 Worst

Combo Crash Tests	—
Safety Features	2
Rollover	9
Preventive Maintenance	4
Repair Costs	3
Warranty	2
Fuel Economy	7
Complaints	9
Insurance Costs	1
OVERALL RATING	**—**

Toyota 86

Toyota 86

At-a-Glance

Status/Year Series Started........ Unchanged/2017
Twins . . . . —
Body Styles . . . . .Coupe
Seating. 4
Anti-Theft Device .Std. Pass. Immobil. & Active Alarm
Parking Index Rating . . . . .Very Easy
Where Made. Gunma, Japan
Fuel Factor:
  MPG Rating (city/hwy) Good-25/34
  Driving Range (mi.) . . . . .Very Short-375
  Fuel Type. . . . . .Premium
  Annual Fuel Cost . . . . .Average-$1570
  Gas Guzzler Tax . . . . .No
  Greenhouse Gas Emissions (tons/yr.). . Average-6.4
  Barrels of Oil Used per year Average-11.8

How the Competition Rates

Competitors	Rating	Pg.
Buick Cascada	–	100
Mazda MX-5	–	204

Price Range

	Retail	Markup
Base MT	$26,255	5%
Base AT	$26,975	5%
Special Edition MT	$29,155	5%
Special Edition AT	$29,875	5%

Safety Checklist

Crash Test:
  Frontal. . . . .
  Side. . . . .
Airbags:
  Torso . . .Standard Front Pelvis/Torso from Seat
  Roll Sensing. . . . . .Yes
  Knee Bolster . . . . .Standard Front
Crash Avoidance:
  Collision Avoidance . . . . None
  Blind Spot Detection . . . . None
  Lane Keeping Assist . . . . None
  Backup Camera. . . . . None
  Pedestrian Crash Avoidance . . . . None
General:
  Auto. Crash Notification. . . Operator Assist.-Fee
  Day Running Lamps . . . . Standard
Safety Belt/Restraint:
  Dynamic Head Restraints . . . . None
  Adjustable Belt. . . . . None

Note: As of May 2018, all vehicles are required to have a backup camera.
^Warning feature does not meet government standards.
*Backup camera does not meet government standards.

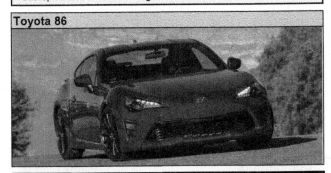
Toyota 86

Specifications

Drive. . . . . .RWD
Engine 2.0-liter I4
Transmission . . . . 6-sp. Automatic
Tow Rating (lbs.) . . . . —
Head/Leg Room (in.) . . . . Very Cramped-37.1/41.9
Interior Space (cu. ft.). . . . . Very Cramped-76.5
Cargo Space (cu. ft.) . . . . Very Cramped-6.9
Wheelbase/Length (in.) 101.2/166.7

Toyota 4Runner

Toyota 4Runner

Ratings—10 Best, 1 Worst

Combo Crash Tests	1
Safety Features	4
Rollover	1
Preventive Maintenance	9
Repair Costs	4
Warranty	2
Fuel Economy	2
Complaints	9
Insurance Costs	10
OVERALL RATING	**2**

Toyota 4Runner

At-a-Glance

Status/Year Series Started....... Unchanged/2006
Twins ..... Lexus GX, Lexus RX, Toyota Highlander
Body Styles .... SUV
Seating.................................. 5/7
Anti-Theft Device ...... Std. Pass. Immobil. & Alarm
Parking Index Rating .... Average
Where Made................... Tahara, Japan
Fuel Factor:
MPG Rating (city/hwy) .... Very Poor-17/21
Driving Range (mi.) Long-428
Fuel Type........................Regular
Annual Fuel Cost .... Very High-$1976
Gas Guzzler Tax ....No
Greenhouse Gas Emissions (tons/yr.)Very High-10.0
Barrels of Oil Used per year .... Very High-18.3

How the Competition Rates

Competitors	Rating	Pg.
Buick Enclave	4	101
Chevrolet Tahoe	4	122
Volvo XC90	8	268

Price Range	Retail	Markup
SR5 2WD	$34,410	9%
SR5 Premium 4WD	$38,115	9%
TRD Pro	$42,675	9%
Limited 4WD	$44,760	9%

Safety Checklist

Crash Test:
Frontal.........................Very Poor
Side............................Poor
Airbags:
Torso . . . Standard Front Pelvis/Torso from Seat
Roll Sensing.......................Yes
Knee Bolster ....Standard Front
Crash Avoidance:
Collision Avoidance .... None
Blind Spot Detection .... None
Lane Keeping Assist .... None
Backup Camera....................Standard*
Pedestrian Crash Avoidance .... None
General:
Auto. Crash Notification . . . Operator Assist.-Fee
Day Running Lamps .... Standard
Safety Belt/Restraint:
Dynamic Head Restraints ......Standard Front
Adjustable Belt................Standard Front

Note: As of May 2018, all vehicles are required to have a backup camera.
^Warning feature does not meet government standards.
*Backup camera does not meet government standards.

Toyota 4Runner

Specifications

Drive...............................4WD
Engine 4.0-liter V6
Transmission .... 5-sp. Automatic
Tow Rating (lbs.) Low-4700
Head/Leg Room (in.) Average-39.3/41.7
Interior Space (cu. ft.)........... Very Roomy-128
Cargo Space (cu. ft.) ....Very Cramped-9
Wheelbase/Length (in.) 109.8/190.2

Ratings—10 Best, 1 Worst

Combo Crash Tests	8
Safety Features	10
Rollover	7
Preventive Maintenance	6
Repair Costs	4
Warranty	2
Fuel Economy	5
Complaints	8
Insurance Costs	5
OVERALL RATING	**8**

Toyota Avalon

Toyota Avalon

At-a-Glance

Status/Year Series Started........ Unchanged/2013
Twins .... Lexus ES
Body Styles .... Sedan
Seating 5
Anti-Theft Device ...... Std. Pass. Immobil. & Alarm
Parking Index Rating .... Average
Where Made.................. Georgetown, KY

Fuel Factor:
MPG Rating (city/hwy) Average-21/31
Driving Range (mi.) Average-418
Fuel Type........................ Regular
Annual Fuel Cost .... Average-$1496
Gas Guzzler Tax .... No
Greenhouse Gas Emissions (tons/yr.)..... High-7.5
Barrels of Oil Used per year High-13.7

How the Competition Rates

Competitors	Rating	Pg.
Cadillac XT5	3	108
Chevrolet Impala	4	116
Ford Taurus	3	147

Price Range	Retail	Markup
XLE	$33,500	11%
XLE Premium	$36,700	11%
Touring	$37,900	11%
Hybrid Limited	$42,800	11%

Safety Checklist

Crash Test:
Frontal........................... Average
Side............................ Very Good

Airbags:
Torso . Std Front & Rear Pelvis/Torso from Seat
Roll Sensing............................Yes
Knee Bolster ....Standard Front

Crash Avoidance:
Collision Avoidance ...... Standard CIB & DBS
Blind Spot Detection .... Optional
Lane Keeping Assist .... Optional
Backup Camera................... Standard
Pedestrian Crash Avoidance .... Optional

General:
Auto. Crash Notification... Operator Assist.-Fee
Day Running Lamps .... Standard

Safety Belt/Restraint:
Dynamic Head Restraints .... None
Adjustable Belt................Standard Front

Note: As of May 2018, all vehicles are required to have a backup camera.
^Warning feature does not meet government standards.
*Backup camera does not meet government standards.

Toyota Avalon

Specifications

Drive.....................................FWD
Engine 3.5-liter V6
Transmission .... 6-sp. Automatic
Tow Rating (lbs.) .... Very Low-1000
Head/Leg Room (in.) Cramped-37.6/42.1
Interior Space (cu. ft.)............. Average-103.63
Cargo Space (cu. ft.) Cramped-16
Wheelbase/Length (in.) 111/195.3

Toyota Camry

Ratings—10 Best, 1 Worst	
Combo Crash Tests	9
Safety Features	10
Rollover	8
Preventive Maintenance	6
Repair Costs	3
Warranty	2
Fuel Economy	8
Complaints	—
Insurance Costs	5
OVERALL RATING	**8**

Toyota Camry

Toyota Camry

Safety Checklist

Crash Test:
Frontal . . . . Very Good
Side . . . . Good
Airbags:
Torso . Std Front & Rear Pelvis/Torso from Seat
Roll Sensing . . . . Yes
Knee Bolster . . . . Standard Front
Crash Avoidance:
Collision Avoidance . . . . . . Standard CIB & DBS
Blind Spot Detection . . . . Optional
Lane Keeping Assist . . . . Optional
Backup Camera . . . . Standard
Pedestrian Crash Avoidance . . . . Standard
General:
Auto. Crash Notification . . . Operator Assist.-Fee
Day Running Lamps . . . . Standard
Safety Belt/Restraint:
Dynamic Head Restraints . . . . None
Adjustable Belt . . . . Standard Front

Note: As of May 2018, all vehicles are required to have a backup camera.
^Warning feature does not meet government standards.
*Backup camera does not meet government standards.

Toyota Camry

At-a-Glance

Status/Year Series Started . . . . All New/2018
Twins . . . . —
Body Styles . . . . Sedan
Seating 5
Anti-Theft Device . . . . . . Std. Pass. Immobil. & Alarm
Parking Index Rating . . . . Average
Where Made . . . . Georgetown, KY
Fuel Factor:
MPG Rating (city/hwy) Good-28/39
Driving Range (mi.) . . . . Very Long-513
Fuel Type . . . . Regular
Annual Fuel Cost . . . . Very Low-$1146
Gas Guzzler Tax . . . . No
Greenhouse Gas Emissions (tons/yr.) . Very Low-4.6
Barrels of Oil Used per year Low-10.3

How the Competition Rates

Competitors	Rating	Pg.
Ford Fusion	4	144
Nissan Altima	4	219
Subaru Legacy	7	236

Price Range

Price Range	Retail	Markup
LE	$24,000	9%
XSE	$29,000	10%
XLE Hybrid	$32,250	9%
XSE V6	$34,950	10%

Specifications

Drive . . . . FWD
Engine 2.5-liter I4
Transmission . . . . 8-sp. Automatic
Tow Rating (lbs.) . . . . —
Head/Leg Room (in.) Cramped-38.3/42.1
Interior Space (cu. ft.) Average-100.4
Cargo Space (cu. ft.) Cramped-15.1
Wheelbase/Length (in.) 111.2/192.1

Ratings—10 Best, 1 Worst	
Combo Crash Tests	4
Safety Features	9
Rollover	6
Preventive Maintenance	9
Repair Costs	7
Warranty	2
Fuel Economy	8
Complaints	10
Insurance Costs	3
OVERALL RATING	**8**

Toyota Corolla

Toyota Corolla

At-a-Glance	
Status/Year Series Started	Unchanged/2014
Twins	–
Body Styles	Sedan
Seating	5
Anti-Theft Device	Std. Passive Immobil. Only
Parking Index Rating	Easy
Where Made	Princeton, IN
Fuel Factor:	
MPG Rating (city/hwy)	Good-27/36
Driving Range (mi.)	Average-402
Fuel Type	Regular
Annual Fuel Cost	Low-$1208
Gas Guzzler Tax	No
Greenhouse Gas Emissions (tons/yr.)	Low-5.8
Barrels of Oil Used per year	Average-10.6

How the Competition Rates

Competitors	Rating	Pg.
Ford Focus	5	143
Honda Civic	10	153
Nissan Sentra	5	228

Price Range	Retail	Markup
L	$18,500	6%
LE	$18,935	8%
SE AT	$20,445	8%
XSE	$22,680	8%

Safety Checklist

Crash Test:
- Frontal .... Poor
- Side .... Average

Airbags:
- Torso . . . Standard Front Pelvis/Torso from Seat
- Roll Sensing .... Yes
- Knee Bolster .... Standard Driver

Crash Avoidance:
- Collision Avoidance ...... Standard CIB & DBS
- Blind Spot Detection .... None
- Lane Keeping Assist .... Standard
- Backup Camera .... Standard
- Pedestrian Crash Avoidance .... Optional

General:
- Auto. Crash Notification .... None
- Day Running Lamps .... Standard

Safety Belt/Restraint:
- Dynamic Head Restraints .... None
- Adjustable Belt .... Standard Front

Note: As of May 2018, all vehicles are required to have a backup camera.
^Warning feature does not meet government standards.
*Backup camera does not meet government standards.

Toyota Corolla

Specifications

Drive	FWD
Engine	1.8-liter I4
Transmission	4-sp. Automatic
Tow Rating (lbs.)	Very Low-0
Head/Leg Room (in.)	Cramped-38.3/42.3
Interior Space (cu. ft.)	Average-97.5
Cargo Space (cu. ft.)	Very Cramped-13
Wheelbase/Length (in.)	106.3/182.6

Ratings—10 Best, 1 Worst

Combo Crash Tests	—
Safety Features	6
Rollover	6
Preventive Maintenance	10
Repair Costs	9
Warranty	2
Fuel Economy	8
Complaints	10
Insurance Costs	8
OVERALL RATING	**—**

Toyota Corolla iM

Toyota Corolla iM

At-a-Glance

Status/Year Series Started Unchanged/2015
Twins . . . . —
Body Styles . . . . Hatchback
Seating 5
Anti-Theft Device . . . . Std. Passive Immobil. Only
Parking Index Rating . . . . .Very Easy
Where Made . . . . .Tsutsumi, Japan
Fuel Factor:
  MPG Rating (city/hwy) Good-28/36
  Driving Range (mi.) Long-436
  Fuel Type . . . . .Regular
  Annual Fuel Cost . . . . Low-$1181
  Gas Guzzler Tax . . . . .No
  Greenhouse Gas Emissions (tons/yr.) Low-4.7
  Barrels of Oil Used per year Average-10.6

How the Competition Rates

Competitors	Rating	Pg.
Honda Civic	10	153
Mazda Mazda3	6	202
Volkswagen Jetta	7	262

Price Range

	Retail	Markup
Hatchback MT	$18,750	8%
Hatchback AT	$19,490	8%

Safety Checklist

Crash Test:
  Frontal . . . .
  Side . . . .
Airbags:
  Torso . . . Standard Front Pelvis/Torso from Seat
  Roll Sensing . . . . .Yes
  Knee Bolster . . . . Standard Driver
Crash Avoidance:
  Collision Avoidance . . . . . . Standard CIB & DBS
  Blind Spot Detection . . . . None
  Lane Keeping Assist . . . . None
  Backup Camera . . . . Standard
  Pedestrian Crash Avoidance . . . . None
General:
  Auto. Crash Notification . . . . None
  Day Running Lamps . . . . Standard
Safety Belt/Restraint:
  Dynamic Head Restraints . . . . None
  Adjustable Belt . . . . .Standard Front

Note: As of May 2018, all vehicles are required to have a backup camera.
^Warning feature does not meet government standards.
*Backup camera does not meet government standards.

Specifications

Drive . . . . .FWD
Engine 1.8-liter I4
Transmission . . . . CVT
Tow Rating (lbs.) . . . . —
Head/Leg Room (in.) Average-39.7/41.7
Interior Space (cu. ft.) Cramped-90.4
Cargo Space (cu. ft.) Average-20.8
Wheelbase/Length (in.) 102.4/170.5

Ratings—10 Best, 1 Worst

Combo Crash Tests	8
Safety Features	10
Rollover	3
Preventive Maintenance	7
Repair Costs	6
Warranty	2
Fuel Economy	2
Complaints	10
Insurance Costs	8
OVERALL RATING	**9**

Toyota Highlander

Toyota Highlander

At-a-Glance

Status/Year Series Started Unchanged/2014
Twins . . . . . . Lexus GX, Lexus RX, Toyota 4Runner
Body Styles . . . . SUV
Seating 7/8
Anti-Theft Device . . . . . . Std. Pass. Immobil. & Alarm
Parking Index Rating . . . . Hard
Where Made . . . . Princeton, IN
Fuel Factor:
MPG Rating (city/hwy) . . . . Very Poor-18/24
Driving Range (mi.) Short-389
Fuel Type . . . . Regular
Annual Fuel Cost . . . . High-$1812
Gas Guzzler Tax . . . . No
Greenhouse Gas Emissions (tons/yr.) Very High-9.0
Barrels of Oil Used per year High-16.5

How the Competition Rates

Competitors	Rating	Pg.
Dodge Durango	2	130
Ford Explorer	3	139
Volkswagen Atlas	6	259

Price Range	Retail	Markup
LE I4 FWD	$30,630	10%
LE Plus AWD	$36,520	10%
Limited AWD	$43,140	10%
Hybrid LTD Platinum	$47,880	10%

Toyota Highlander

Safety Checklist

Crash Test:
Frontal . . . . Average
Side . . . . Very Good
Airbags:
Torso . . . Standard Front Pelvis/Torso from Seat
Roll Sensing . . . . Yes
Knee Bolster . . . . Standard Driver
Crash Avoidance:
Collision Avoidance . . . . . . Standard CIB & DBS
Blind Spot Detection . . . . Optional
Lane Keeping Assist . . . . Standard
Backup Camera . . . . Standard
Pedestrian Crash Avoidance . . . . Optional
General:
Auto. Crash Notification . . . Operator Assist.-Fee
Day Running Lamps . . . . Standard
Safety Belt/Restraint:
Dynamic Head Restraints . . . . None
Adjustable Belt . . . . Standard Front

Note: As of May 2018, all vehicles are required to have a backup camera.
^Warning feature does not meet government standards.
*Backup camera does not meet government standards.

Specifications

Drive . . . . AWD
Engine 3.5-liter V6
Transmission . . . . 6-sp. Automatic
Tow Rating (lbs.) . . . . Very Low-2000
Head/Leg Room (in.) . . . . Very Roomy-40.7/44.2
Interior Space (cu. ft.) . . . . Very Roomy-144.9
Cargo Space (cu. ft.) Cramped-13.8
Wheelbase/Length (in.) 109.8/191.1

Toyota Prius | Compact

Ratings—10 Best, 1 Worst

Combo Crash Tests	5
Safety Features	9
Rollover	7
Preventive Maintenance	9
Repair Costs	5
Warranty	2
Fuel Economy	10
Complaints	4
Insurance Costs	5
OVERALL RATING	**7**

Toyota Prius

Toyota Prius

At-a-Glance

Status/Year Series Started........ Unchanged/2016
Twins .... –
Body Styles .... Hatchback
Seating... 5
Anti-Theft Device .... Std. Passive Immobil. Only
Parking Index Rating .... Very Easy
Where Made.................... Tsutsumi, Japan
Fuel Factor:
  MPG Rating (city/hwy) .... Very Good-54/50
  Driving Range (mi.) .... Very Long-589
  Fuel Type............................. Regular
  Annual Fuel Cost .... Very Low-$705
  Gas Guzzler Tax .... No
  Greenhouse Gas Emissions (tons/yr.) . Very Low-2.8
  Barrels of Oil Used per year .... Very Low-6.3

How the Competition Rates

Competitors	Rating	Pg.
Chevrolet Volt	7	125
Ford C-MAX	5	134
Volkswagen Golf	5	261

Price Range

	Retail	Markup
One	$23,475	6%
Three	$26,735	7%
Four	$29,135	7%
Four Touring	$30,015	7%

Toyota Prius

Safety Checklist

Crash Test:
  Frontal........................... Average
  Side.............................. Average
Airbags:
  Torso . . . Standard Front Pelvis/Torso from Seat
  Roll Sensing.........................Yes
  Knee Bolster .... Standard Driver
Crash Avoidance:
  Collision Avoidance ...... Standard CIB & DBS
  Blind Spot Detection .... Optional
  Lane Keeping Assist .... Optional
  Backup Camera .... Standard
  Pedestrian Crash Avoidance .... Optional
General:
  Auto. Crash Notification. . . Operator Assist.-Fee
  Day Running Lamps .... Optional
Safety Belt/Restraint:
  Dynamic Head Restraints .... None
  Adjustable Belt................Standard Front

Note: As of May 2018, all vehicles are required to have a backup camera.
^Warning feature does not meet government standards.
*Backup camera does not meet government standards.

Toyota Prius

Specifications

Drive.............................FWD
Engine 1.8-liter I4
Transmission .... CVT
Tow Rating (lbs.) .... –
Head/Leg Room (in.) .... Very Cramped-34.4/42.3
Interior Space (cu. ft.)................ Cramped-93.1
Cargo Space (cu. ft.) Roomy-24.6
Wheelbase/Length (in.) 106.3/178.7

Ratings—10 Best, 1 Worst

Combo Crash Tests	2
Safety Features	3
Rollover	6
Preventive Maintenance	9
Repair Costs	5
Warranty	2
Fuel Economy	10
Complaints	9
Insurance Costs	5
OVERALL RATING	**5**

Toyota Prius C

Toyota Prius C

At-a-Glance

Status/Year Series Started	Unchanged/2013
Twins	–
Body Styles	Hatchback
Seating	5
Anti-Theft Device	Std. Passive Immobil. Only
Parking Index Rating	Very Easy
Where Made	Iwata, Japan

Fuel Factor:

MPG Rating (city/hwy)	Very Good-53/46
Driving Range (mi.)	Very Long-471
Fuel Type	Regular
Annual Fuel Cost	Very Low-$741
Gas Guzzler Tax	No
Greenhouse Gas Emissions (tons/yr.)	Very Low-3.6
Barrels of Oil Used per year	Very Low-6.6

How the Competition Rates

Competitors	Rating	Pg.
Chevrolet Sonic	9	119
Fiat 500	2	132
Mitsubishi Mirage	3	216

Price Range

	Retail	Markup
One	$20,630	5%
Two	$21,430	6%
Three	$22,855	7%
Four	$24,965	7%

Safety Checklist

Crash Test:
Frontal	Poor
Side	Very Poor

Airbags:
Torso	Standard Front Pelvis/Torso from Seat
Roll Sensing	No
Knee Bolster	Standard Driver

Crash Avoidance:
Collision Avoidance	Standard CIB & DBS
Blind Spot Detection	None
Lane Keeping Assist	Warning Only Optional
Backup Camera	Optional
Pedestrian Crash Avoidance	None

General:
Auto. Crash Notification	Operator Assist.-Fee
Day Running Lamps	Standard

Safety Belt/Restraint:
Dynamic Head Restraints	None
Adjustable Belt	None

Note: As of May 2018, all vehicles are required to have a backup camera.
^Warning feature does not meet government standards.
*Backup camera does not meet government standards.

Toyota Prius C

Specifications

Drive	FWD
Engine	1.5-liter I4
Transmission	CVT
Tow Rating (lbs.)	–
Head/Leg Room (in.)	Cramped-38.6/41.7
Interior Space (cu. ft.)	Very Cramped-87.4
Cargo Space (cu. ft.)	Average-17.1
Wheelbase/Length (in.)	100.4/157.3

Toyota Prius Prime

Compact

Ratings—10 Best, 1 Worst	
Combo Crash Tests	—
Safety Features	10
Rollover	6
Preventive Maintenance	9
Repair Costs	7
Warranty	2
Fuel Economy	10
Complaints	5
Insurance Costs	5

OVERALL RATING —

Toyota Prius Prime

Toyota Prius Prime

At-a-Glance

Status/Year Series Started	Unchanged/2017
Twins	—
Body Styles	Sedan
Seating	4
Anti-Theft Device	Std. Passive Immobil. Only
Parking Index Rating	Very Easy
Where Made	Tsutsumi, Japan

Fuel Factor:

MPG Rating (city/hwy)	Very Good-55/53
Driving Range (mi.)	Very Long-611
Fuel Type	Regular
Annual Fuel Cost	Very Low-$680
Gas Guzzler Tax	No
Greenhouse Gas Emissions (tons/yr.)	Very Low-1.3
Barrels of Oil Used per year	Very Low-3.0

How the Competition Rates

Competitors	Rating	Pg.
Chevrolet Volt	7	125
Ford C-MAX	5	134
Volkswagen Jetta	7	262

Price Range	Retail	Markup
Plus	$27,100	4%
Premium	$28,800	4%
Advanced	$33,100	4%

Safety Checklist

Crash Test:
- Frontal . . . .
- Side . . . .

Airbags:
- Torso . . . Standard Front Pelvis/Torso from Seat
- Roll Sensing . . . . Yes
- Knee Bolster . . . . Standard Front

Crash Avoidance:
- Collision Avoidance . . . . . . Standard CIB & DBS
- Blind Spot Detection . . . . Optional
- Lane Keeping Assist . . . . Optional
- Backup Camera . . . . Standard
- Pedestrian Crash Avoidance . . . . Standard

General:
- Auto. Crash Notification . . . . None
- Day Running Lamps . . . . Standard

Safety Belt/Restraint:
- Dynamic Head Restraints . . . . None
- Adjustable Belt . . . . Standard Front

Note: As of May 2018, all vehicles are required to have a backup camera.
^Warning feature does not meet government standards.
*Backup camera does not meet government standards.

Toyota Prius Prime

Specifications

Drive	FWD
Engine	1.8-liter I4
Transmission	CVT
Tow Rating (lbs.)	—
Head/Leg Room (in.)	Roomy-39.4/43.2
Interior Space (cu. ft.)	Cramped-91.5
Cargo Space (cu. ft.)	Average-19.8
Wheelbase/Length (in.)	106.3/182.9

Toyota Prius V

Ratings—10 Best, 1 Worst

Rating	
Combo Crash Tests	6
Safety Features	7
Rollover	5
Preventive Maintenance	9
Repair Costs	7
Warranty	2
Fuel Economy	10
Complaints	9
Insurance Costs	5
OVERALL RATING	**9**

Toyota Prius V

At-a-Glance

Status/Year Series Started. Unchanged/2013
Twins . . . . –
Body Styles . . . . Wagon
Seating 5
Anti-Theft Device . . . . Std. Passive Immobil. Only
Parking Index Rating . . . . Easy
Where Made. . . . . .Tsutsumi, Japan
Fuel Factor:
MPG Rating (city/hwy) . . . . Very Good-44/40
Driving Range (mi.) . . . . Very Long-501
Fuel Type. . . . . .Regular
Annual Fuel Cost . . . . Very Low-$873
Gas Guzzler Tax . . . . .No
Greenhouse Gas Emissions (tons/yr.). Very Low-4.3
Barrels of Oil Used per year Low-7.8

How the Competition Rates

Competitors	Rating	Pg.
Ford Fusion Energi	8	145
Kia Optima	9	178
Subaru Legacy	7	236

Price Range	Retail	Markup
Two	$26,675	7%
Three	$28,060	7%
Four	$29,695	7%
Five	$30,935	7%

Safety Checklist

Crash Test:
Frontal. . . . . Poor
Side. . . . . Very Good
Airbags:
Torso . . . Standard Front Pelvis/Torso from Seat
Roll Sensing. . . . . .Yes
Knee Bolster . . . . Standard Driver
Crash Avoidance:
Collision Avoidance . . . . . . Standard CIB & DBS
Blind Spot Detection . . . . None
Lane Keeping Assist . . . .Warning Only Optional
Backup Camera. . . . . Standard
Pedestrian Crash Avoidance . . . . None
General:
Auto. Crash Notification. . . . . None
Day Running Lamps . . . . Standard
Safety Belt/Restraint:
Dynamic Head Restraints . . . . None
Adjustable Belt. . . . . .Standard Front

Note: As of May 2018, all vehicles are required to have a backup camera.
^Warning feature does not meet government standards.
*Backup camera does not meet government standards.

Toyota Prius V

Specifications

Drive. . . . . .FWD
Engine 1.8-liter I4
Transmission . . . . CVT
Tow Rating (lbs.) . . . . –
Head/Leg Room (in.) Cramped-39.6/41.3
Interior Space (cu. ft.). Average-97.2
Cargo Space (cu. ft.) . . . . Very Roomy-34.3
Wheelbase/Length (in.) 109.4/182.3

Toyota RAV4

Small SUV

Ratings—10 Best, 1 Worst	
Combo Crash Tests	7
Safety Features	9
Rollover	3
Preventive Maintenance	4
Repair Costs	7
Warranty	2
Fuel Economy	5
Complaints	10
Insurance Costs	10
OVERALL RATING	**9**

Toyota RAV4

At-a-Glance

Status/Year Series Started........ Unchanged/2013
Twins .... –
Body Styles .... SUV
Seating 5
Anti-Theft Device .... Std. Passive Immobil. Only
Parking Index Rating .... Easy
Where Made.... Woodstock, Ontario / Tahara, Japan
Fuel Factor:
MPG Rating (city/hwy) Average-22/29
Driving Range (mi.) Short-392
Fuel Type................................Regular
Annual Fuel Cost..............Average-$1489
Gas Guzzler Tax ....No
Greenhouse Gas Emissions (tons/yr.).. Average-7.2
Barrels of Oil Used per year High-13.2

How the Competition Rates

Competitors	Rating	Pg.
Ford Escape	5	137
Honda HR-V	5	156
Hyundai Tucson	8	165

Price Range	Retail	Markup
LE FWD	$24,410	7%
XLE FWD	$25,500	7%
SE AWD	$30,190	7%
Limited AWD	$32,305	7%

Toyota RAV4

Safety Checklist

Crash Test:
Frontal........................... Average
Side............................ Very Good
Airbags:
Torso . . . Standard Front Pelvis/Torso from Seat
Roll Sensing...............................Yes
Knee Bolster .... Standard Driver
Crash Avoidance:
Collision Avoidance ...... Standard CIB & DBS
Blind Spot Detection .... Optional
Lane Keeping Assist .... Optional
Backup Camera.................... Standard
Pedestrian Crash Avoidance .... Optional
General:
Auto. Crash Notification .... None
Day Running Lamps .... Standard
Safety Belt/Restraint:
Dynamic Head Restraints .... None
Adjustable Belt................Standard Front

Note: As of May 2018, all vehicles are required to have a backup camera.
^Warning feature does not meet government standards.
*Backup camera does not meet government standards.

Toyota RAV4

Specifications

Drive.....................................AWD
Engine 2.5-liter I4
Transmission .... 6-sp. Automatic
Tow Rating (lbs.) .... Very Low-1500
Head/Leg Room (in.) Average-39.8/42.6
Interior Space (cu. ft.).......... Average-101.9
Cargo Space (cu. ft.) ..... Very Roomy-38.4
Wheelbase/Length (in.) 104.7/179.9

252

Ratings—10 Best, 1 Worst

Combo Crash Tests	—
Safety Features	8
Rollover	2
Preventive Maintenance	6
Repair Costs	4
Warranty	2
Fuel Economy	1
Complaints	9
Insurance Costs	10
OVERALL RATING	—

Toyota Sequoia

At-a-Glance

Status/Year Series Started	Unchanged/2008
Twins	—
Body Styles	SUV
Seating	8
Anti-Theft Device	Std. Pass. Immobil. & Alarm
Parking Index Rating	Very Hard
Where Made	Princeton, IN

Fuel Factor:

MPG Rating (city/hwy)	Very Poor-13/17
Driving Range (mi.)	Short-384
Fuel Type	Regular
Annual Fuel Cost	Very High-$2528
Gas Guzzler Tax	No
Greenhouse Gas Emissions (tons/yr.)	Very High-12.8
Barrels of Oil Used per year	Very High-23.5

How the Competition Rates

Competitors	Rating	Pg.
Buick Enclave	4	101
Chevrolet Suburban	2	121
Volvo XC90	8	268

Price Range

	Retail	Markup
SR5 2WD	$48,300	10%
Sport 2WD	$51,015	10%
Limited 4WD	$60,020	10%
Platinum 4WD	$67,235	10%

Toyota Sequoia

Safety Checklist

Crash Test:
Frontal . . . .
Side . . . .

Airbags:
Torso . . . Standard Front Pelvis/Torso from Seat
Roll Sensing . . . . Yes
Knee Bolster . . . . Standard Front

Crash Avoidance:
Collision Avoidance . . . . . . Standard CIB & DBS
Blind Spot Detection . . . . Optional
Lane Keeping Assist . . . . None
Backup Camera . . . . Standard
Pedestrian Crash Avoidance . . . . None

General:
Auto. Crash Notification . . . . None
Day Running Lamps . . . . Optional

Safety Belt/Restraint:
Dynamic Head Restraints . . . . None
Adjustable Belt . . . . Standard Front & Rear

Note: As of May 2018, all vehicles are required to have a backup camera.
^Warning feature does not meet government standards.
*Backup camera does not meet government standards.

Toyota Sequoia

Specifications

Drive	4WD
Engine	5.7-liter V8
Transmission	6-sp. Automatic
Tow Rating (lbs.)	Average-7100
Head/Leg Room (in.)	Very Cramped-34.8/42.5
Interior Space (cu. ft.)	—
Cargo Space (cu. ft.)	Average-18.9
Wheelbase/Length (in.)	122/205.1

Toyota Sienna   Minivan

Ratings—10 Best, 1 Worst

Combo Crash Tests	6
Safety Features	9
Rollover	5
Preventive Maintenance	2
Repair Costs	4
Warranty	2
Fuel Economy	3
Complaints	3
Insurance Costs	5
OVERALL RATING	**2**

Toyota Sienna

Toyota Sienna

At-a-Glance

Status/Year Series Started Appearance Change/2004
Twins .... –
Body Styles .... Minivan
Seating 7/8
Anti-Theft Device ...... Std. Pass. Immobil. & Alarm
Parking Index Rating .... Hard
Where Made.................... Princeton, IN
Fuel Factor:
  MPG Rating (city/hwy) Poor-18/25
  Driving Range (mi.) Average-412
  Fuel Type....................... Regular
  Annual Fuel Cost .... High-$1784
  Gas Guzzler Tax .... No
  Greenhouse Gas Emissions (tons/yr.).... High-8.6
  Barrels of Oil Used per year High-15.7

How the Competition Rates

Competitors	Rating	Pg.
Chrysler Pacifica	8	127
Honda Odyssey	9	157
Kia Sedona	–	180

Price Range	Retail	Markup
L FWD	$29,750	8%
SE FWD	$36,110	8%
XLE Premium FWD	$39,505	9%
LTD Premium AWD	$47,310	9%

Safety Checklist

Crash Test:
  Frontal........................... Average
  Side.............................. Average
Airbags:
  Torso . . . Standard Front Pelvis/Torso from Seat
  Roll Sensing........................ Yes
  Knee Bolster .... Standard Driver
Crash Avoidance:
  Collision Avoidance ...... Standard CIB & DBS
  Blind Spot Detection .... Optional
  Lane Keeping Assist .... None
  Backup Camera.................. Standard
  Pedestrian Crash Avoidance .... None
General:
  Auto. Crash Notification... Operator Assist.-Fee
  Day Running Lamps .... Optional
Safety Belt/Restraint:
  Dynamic Head Restraints ...... Standard Front
  Adjustable Belt........ Standard Front & Rear

Note: As of May 2018, all vehicles are required to have a backup camera.
^Warning feature does not meet government standards.
*Backup camera does not meet government standards.

Toyota Sienna

Specifications

Drive....................................... FWD
Engine 3.5-liter V6
Transmission .... 6-sp. Automatic
Tow Rating (lbs.) Low-3500
Head/Leg Room (in.) Average-41/40.5
Interior Space (cu. ft.).... Very Roomy-164.4
Cargo Space (cu. ft.) ..... Very Roomy-39.1
Wheelbase/Length (in.) 119.3/200.2

Toyota Tacoma Compact Pickup

Ratings—10 Best, 1 Worst

Rating	
Combo Crash Tests	1
Safety Features	8
Rollover	2
Preventive Maintenance	9
Repair Costs	4
Warranty	2
Fuel Economy	3
Complaints	4
Insurance Costs	8
OVERALL RATING	**2**

Toyota Tacoma

At-a-Glance

Status/Year Series Started....... Unchanged/2016
Twins .... –
Body Styles .... Pickup
Seating................................ 4
Anti-Theft Device ...... Std. Pass. Immobil. & Alarm
Parking Index Rating .... Very Hard
Where Made..... San Antonio, TX / Tijuana, Mexico
Fuel Factor:
MPG Rating (city/hwy) Poor-19/23
Driving Range (mi.) Long-435
Fuel Type............................Regular
Annual Fuel Cost ....High-$1783
Gas Guzzler Tax ....No
Greenhouse Gas Emissions (tons/yr.)..... High-7.3
Barrels of Oil Used per year High-16.5

How the Competition Rates

Competitors	Rating	Pg.
Chevrolet Colorado	2	112
Nissan Frontier	1	221

Price Range

Price Range	Retail	Markup
SR Access Cab 2WD	$24,575	7%
SR5 Access Cab 2WD	$26,660	7%
SR5 Dbl Cab 4WD V6	$33,220	8%
Limited Sport Dbl. Cab 4WD V6	$39,250	8%

Toyota Tacoma

Safety Checklist

Crash Test:
Frontal.........................Very Poor
Side...........................Very Poor
Airbags:
Torso ... Standard Front Pelvis/Torso from Seat
Roll Sensing.....................Yes
Knee Bolster ....Standard Front
Crash Avoidance:
Collision Avoidance ...... Standard CIB & DBS
Blind Spot Detection .... Optional
Lane Keeping Assist .... None
Backup Camera................... Standard
Pedestrian Crash Avoidance .... None
General:
Auto. Crash Notification............... None
Day Running Lamps .... Standard
Safety Belt/Restraint:
Dynamic Head Restraints .... None
Adjustable Belt..............Standard Front

Note: As of May 2018, all vehicles are required to have a backup camera.
^Warning feature does not meet government standards.
*Backup camera does not meet government standards.

Toyota Tacoma

Specifications

Drive...4WD
Engine 2.7-liter I4
Transmission .... 6-sp. Automatic
Tow Rating (lbs.) Low-3500
Head/Leg Room (in.) Roomy-39.7/42.9
Interior Space (cu. ft.)........... Very Cramped-57.5
Cargo Space (cu. ft.) .... Very Roomy-33.5
Wheelbase/Length (in.) 127.4/212.3

Toyota Tundra — Standard Pickup

Ratings—10 Best, 1 Worst

Combo Crash Tests	—
Safety Features	10
Rollover	2
Preventive Maintenance	6
Repair Costs	5
Warranty	2
Fuel Economy	1
Complaints	9
Insurance Costs	10
OVERALL RATING	**—**

Toyota Tundra

Toyota Tundra

Toyota Tundra

At-a-Glance

Status/Year Series Started. Unchanged/2007
Twins . . . . —
Body Styles . . . . Pickup
Seating. 5/6
Anti-Theft Device . . . . . . Std. Pass. Immobil. & Alarm
Parking Index Rating . . . . Very Hard
Where Made. . . . . San Antonio, TX
Fuel Factor:
  MPG Rating (city/hwy) . . . . Very Poor-13/18
  Driving Range (mi.) Short-392
  Fuel Type. . . . . .Regular
  Annual Fuel Cost . . . . Very High-$2474
  Gas Guzzler Tax . . . . .No
  Greenhouse Gas Emissions (tons/yr.) Very High-8.9
  Barrels of Oil Used per year . . . . . . Very High-20.6

How the Competition Rates

Competitors	Rating	Pg.
Chevrolet Silverado	7	118
Ford F-150	9	140
Nissan Titan	1	229

Price Range

Price Range	Retail	Markup
SR Reg. Cab 2WD 5.7 V8	$32,390	8%
SR5 Dbl. Cab 4WD 5.7 V8	$37,150	8%
Limited Crew Max 4WD 5.7 V8	$45,300	8%
1794 Edition Crew Max 5.7 V8	$50,130	8%

Safety Checklist

Crash Test:
  Frontal. . . . . .Very Poor
  Side. . . . .
Airbags:
  Torso . . . Standard Front Pelvis/Torso from Seat
  Roll Sensing. . . . . .Yes
  Knee Bolster . . . . .Standard Front
Crash Avoidance:
  Collision Avoidance . . . . . . Standard CIB & DBS
  Blind Spot Detection . . . . Optional
  Lane Keeping Assist . . . . None
  Backup Camera. . . . . Standard
  Pedestrian Crash Avoidance . . . . None
General:
  Auto. Crash Notification. . . . . None
  Day Running Lamps . . . . Standard
Safety Belt/Restraint:
  Dynamic Head Restraints . . . . . .Standard Front
  Adjustable Belt. . . . . Standard Front & Rear

Note: As of May 2018, all vehicles are required to have a backup camera.
^Warning feature does not meet government standards.
*Backup camera does not meet government standards.

Toyota Tundra

Specifications

Drive. 4WD
Engine 5.7-liter V8
Transmission . . . . 6-sp. Automatic
Tow Rating (lbs.) . . . . Very High-10000
Head/Leg Room (in.) Average-39.7/42.5
Interior Space (cu. ft.). . . . . —
Cargo Space (cu. ft.) . . . . Very Roomy-67.1
Wheelbase/Length (in.) 145.7/228.9

Ratings—10 Best, 1 Worst

Combo Crash Tests	2
Safety Features	2
Rollover	5
Preventive Maintenance	10
Repair Costs	10
Warranty	2
Fuel Economy	9
Complaints	9
Insurance Costs	3
OVERALL RATING	**5**

Toyota Yaris

Toyota Yaris

At-a-Glance

Status/Year Series Started	Unchanged/2012
Twins	–
Body Styles	Hatchback
Seating	5
Anti-Theft Device	Std. Passive Immobil. Only
Parking Index Rating	Very Easy
Where Made	Iwata, Japan

Fuel Factor:

MPG Rating (city/hwy)	Very Good-30/36
Driving Range (mi.)	Very Short-360
Fuel Type	Regular
Annual Fuel Cost	Very Low-$1133
Gas Guzzler Tax	No
Greenhouse Gas Emissions (tons/yr.)	Low-5.6
Barrels of Oil Used per year	Low-10.3

How the Competition Rates

Competitors	Rating	Pg.
Chevrolet Sonic	9	119
Fiat 500	2	132
Mitsubishi Mirage	3	216

Price Range

Price Range	Retail	Markup
L 2 Door MT	$15,635	4%
L 4 Door AT	$16,760	4%
LE 4 Door	$17,660	4%
SE 4 Door	$19,060	4%

Toyota Yaris

Safety Checklist

Crash Test:
Frontal	Poor
Side	Very Poor

Airbags:
Torso	Standard Front Pelvis/Torso from Seat
Roll Sensing	No
Knee Bolster	Standard Driver

Crash Avoidance:
Collision Avoidance	Standard CIB & DBS
Blind Spot Detection	None
Lane Keeping Assist	Warning Only Optional^
Backup Camera	None
Pedestrian Crash Avoidance	None

General:
Auto. Crash Notification	Operator Assist.-Fee
Day Running Lamps	Optional

Safety Belt/Restraint:
Dynamic Head Restraints	None
Adjustable Belt	None

Note: As of May 2018, all vehicles are required to have a backup camera.
^Warning feature does not meet government standards.
*Backup camera does not meet government standards.

Toyota Yaris

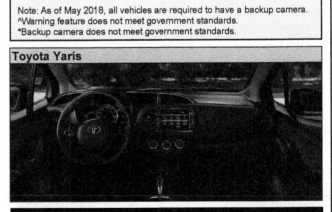

Specifications

Drive	FWD
Engine	1.5-liter I4
Transmission	4-sp. Automatic
Tow Rating (lbs.)	–
Head/Leg Room (in.)	Cramped-39.3/40.6
Interior Space (cu. ft.)	Very Cramped-85.1
Cargo Space (cu. ft.)	Cramped-15.6
Wheelbase/Length (in.)	98.8/155.5

Ratings—10 Best, 1 Worst

Combo Crash Tests	5
Safety Features	2
Rollover	5
Preventive Maintenance	9
Repair Costs	10
Warranty	2
Fuel Economy	9
Complaints	3
Insurance Costs	5
OVERALL RATING	**6**

Toyota Yaris iA

Toyota Yaris iA

At-a-Glance

Status/Year Series Started Unchanged/2017
Twins . . . . –
Body Styles . . . . Sedan
Seating 5
Anti-Theft Device . . . . Std. Passive Immobil. Only
Parking Index Rating . . . . Very Easy
Where Made . . . . Salamanca, Mexico
Fuel Factor:
  MPG Rating (city/hwy) . . . . Very Good-32/40
  Driving Range (mi.) Average-408
  Fuel Type . . . . Regular
  Annual Fuel Cost . . . . Very Low-$1045
  Gas Guzzler Tax . . . . No
  Greenhouse Gas Emissions (tons/yr.) . Very Low-4.1
  Barrels of Oil Used per year Low-9.4

How the Competition Rates

Competitors	Rating	Pg.
Chevrolet Cruze	8	114
Ford Focus	5	143
Volkswagen Beetle	3	260

Price Range

Price Range	Retail	Markup
Sedan MT	$15,950	4%
Sedan AT	$17,050	4%

Safety Checklist

Crash Test:
  Frontal . . . . Poor
  Side . . . . Average
Airbags:
  Torso . . . Standard Front Pelvis/Torso from Seat
  Roll Sensing . . . . Yes
  Knee Bolster . . . . None
Crash Avoidance:
  Collision Avoidance . . . . None
  Blind Spot Detection . . . . None
  Lane Keeping Assist . . . . None
  Backup Camera . . . . Standard
  Pedestrian Crash Avoidance . . . . None
General:
  Auto. Crash Notification . . . Operator Assist.-Fee
  Day Running Lamps . . . . Standard
Safety Belt/Restraint:
  Dynamic Head Restraints . . . . None
  Adjustable Belt . . . . Standard Front

Note: As of May 2018, all vehicles are required to have a backup camera.
^Warning feature does not meet government standards.
*Backup camera does not meet government standards.

Toyota Yaris iA

Specifications

Drive . . . . FWD
Engine 1.5-liter I4
Transmission . . . . 6-sp. Automatic
Tow Rating (lbs.) . . . . –
Head/Leg Room (in.) Cramped-38.2/41.9
Interior Space (cu. ft.) . . . . Very Cramped-85.9
Cargo Space (cu. ft.) . . . . Very Cramped-13.5
Wheelbase/Length (in.) 101.2/171.7

Volkswagen Atlas

Medium SUV

Ratings—10 Best, 1 Worst	
Combo Crash Tests	9
Safety Features	7
Rollover	4
Preventive Maintenance	3
Repair Costs	1
Warranty	10
Fuel Economy	3
Complaints	—
Insurance Costs	5
OVERALL RATING	**6**

Volkswagen Atlas

Volkswagen Atlas

At-a-Glance

Status/Year Series Started. . . . . All New/2018
Twins . . . . —
Body Styles . . . . SUV
Seating. 7
Anti-Theft Device . . . . . . Std. Pass. Immobil. & Alarm
Parking Index Rating . . . . Hard
Where Made. . . . . .Chattanooga, Tennessee
Fuel Factor:
  MPG Rating (city/hwy). Poor-18/25
  Driving Range (mi.) Short-383
  Fuel Type. . . . . .Regular
  Annual Fuel Cost . . . . .High-$1784
  Gas Guzzler Tax . . . . .No
  Greenhouse Gas Emissions (tons/yr.). . Average-7.2
  Barrels of Oil Used per year High-16.5

How the Competition Rates

Competitors	Rating	Pg.
Acura MDX	7	80
GMC Acadia	2	149
Toyota Highlander	9	247

Price Range	Retail	Markup
S FWD	$30,500	4%
SE FWD V6	$34,990	4%
SEL 4Motion V6	$42,690	4%
SEL Premium 4Motion V6	$48,490	4%

Safety Checklist

Crash Test:
  Frontal. . . . . Good
  Side. . . . . Very Good
Airbags:
  Torso . . . . Standard Front Torso from Seat
  Roll Sensing. . . . . .Yes
  Knee Bolster . . . . None
Crash Avoidance:
  Collision Avoidance . . . . . . Optional CIB & DBS
  Blind Spot Detection . . . . Optional
  Lane Keeping Assist . . . . Optional
  Backup Camera. . . . . Standard
  Pedestrian Crash Avoidance . . . . Optional
General:
  Auto. Crash Notification. . . Operator Assist.-Fee
  Day Running Lamps . . . . Standard
Safety Belt/Restraint:
  Dynamic Head Restraints . . . . None
  Adjustable Belt. . . . . .Standard Front

Note: As of May 2018, all vehicles are required to have a backup camera.
^Warning feature does not meet government standards.
*Backup camera does not meet government standards.

Volkswagen Atlas

Specifications

Drive. . . . . .FWD
Engine 3.6-liter V6
Transmission . . . . 8-sp. Automatic
Tow Rating (lbs.) Low-5000
Head/Leg Room (in.) Roomy-41.3/41.5
Interior Space (cu. ft.). . . . . .Very Roomy-153.7
Cargo Space (cu. ft.) Average-20.6
Wheelbase/Length (in.) 117.3/198.3

259

Volkswagen Beetle

Ratings—10 Best, 1 Worst

Combo Crash Tests	3
Safety Features	1
Rollover	7
Preventive Maintenance	5
Repair Costs	3
Warranty	10
Fuel Economy	7
Complaints	8
Insurance Costs	1
OVERALL RATING	**3**

Volkswagen Beetle

Volkswagen Beetle

At-a-Glance

Status/Year Series Started	Unchanged/2012
Twins	–
Body Styles	Hatchback, Convertible
Seating	4
Anti-Theft Device	Std. Pass. Immobil. & Alarm
Parking Index Rating	Very Easy
Where Made	Puebla City, Mexico

Fuel Factor:

MPG Rating (city/hwy)	Good-25/33
Driving Range (mi.)	Average-407
Fuel Type	Regular
Annual Fuel Cost	Low-$1310
Gas Guzzler Tax	No
Greenhouse Gas Emissions (tons/yr.)	Average-6.5
Barrels of Oil Used per year	Average-11.8

How the Competition Rates

Competitors	Rating	Pg.
Kia Soul	7	182
Subaru Impreza	5	235
Toyota Yaris iA	6	258

Price Range

	Retail	Markup
S Coupe AT	$19,995	4%
SE Coupe AT	$22,450	4%
SEL Convertible AT	$30,275	4%
SEL R-Line Coupe AT	$32,550	4%

Safety Checklist

Crash Test:
Frontal	Poor
Side	Poor

Airbags:
Torso	Standard Front Torso from Seat
Roll Sensing	No
Knee Bolster	None

Crash Avoidance:
Collision Avoidance	None
Blind Spot Detection	Optional
Lane Keeping Assist	None
Backup Camera	Optional
Pedestrian Crash Avoidance	None

General:
Auto. Crash Notification	Operator Assist.-Fee
Day Running Lamps	Standard

Safety Belt/Restraint:
Dynamic Head Restraints	None
Adjustable Belt	None

Note: As of May 2018, all vehicles are required to have a backup camera.
^Warning feature does not meet government standards.
*Backup camera does not meet government standards.

Volkswagen Beetle

Specifications

Drive	FWD
Engine	1.8-liter I4
Transmission	6-sp. Automatic
Tow Rating (lbs.)	–
Head/Leg Room (in.)	Cramped-39.4/41.3
Interior Space (cu. ft.)	Very Cramped-85.1
Cargo Space (cu. ft.)	Cramped-15.4
Wheelbase/Length (in.)	100/168.4

Ratings—10 Best, 1 Worst

Combo Crash Tests	5
Safety Features	6
Rollover	5
Preventive Maintenance	3
Repair Costs	7
Warranty	10
Fuel Economy	7
Complaints	3
Insurance Costs	1
OVERALL RATING	**5**

Volkswagen Golf

Volkswagen Golf

At-a-Glance

Status/Year Series Started........ Unchanged/2015
Twins ....Audi A3
Body Styles .... Hatchback
Seating....................................5
Anti-Theft Device ...... Std. Pass. Immobil. & Alarm
Parking Index Rating ....Very Easy
Where Made.. Puebla, Mexico / Wolfsburg, Germany
Fuel Factor:
  MPG Rating (city/hwy) Good-25/36
  Driving Range (mi.) Short-383
  Fuel Type........................Regular
  Annual Fuel Cost ....Low-$1268
  Gas Guzzler Tax ....No
  Greenhouse Gas Emissions (tons/yr.).. Average-6.2
  Barrels of Oil Used per year Average-11.4

How the Competition Rates

Competitors	Rating	Pg.
Kia Soul	7	182
Mazda Mazda3	6	202
Nissan Sentra	5	228

Price Range	Retail	Markup
S Hatchback AT	$19,895	4%
S Sportswagon AT	$22,680	4%
SE Sportswagon AT	$27,030	4%
SEL Sportwagon AT	$29,970	4%

Safety Checklist

Crash Test:
  Frontal........................... Average
  Side............................. Average
Airbags:
  Torso ...Standard Front Pelvis/Torso from Seat
  Roll Sensing.........................Yes
  Knee Bolster .... None
Crash Avoidance:
  Collision Avoidance ...... Optional CIB & DBS
  Blind Spot Detection .... Optional
  Lane Keeping Assist .... Optional
  Backup Camera................... Standard
  Pedestrian Crash Avoidance .... None
General:
  Auto. Crash Notification... Operator Assist.-Fee
  Day Running Lamps .... Standard
Safety Belt/Restraint:
  Dynamic Head Restraints .... None
  Adjustable Belt...............Standard Front

Note: As of May 2018, all vehicles are required to have a backup camera.
^Warning feature does not meet government standards.
*Backup camera does not meet government standards.

Volkswagen Golf

Specifications

Drive.....................................FWD
Engine 1.8-liter I4
Transmission .... 6-sp. Automatic
Tow Rating (lbs.) .... –
Head/Leg Room (in.) Cramped-38.4/41.2
Interior Space (cu. ft.).............. Cramped-93.5
Cargo Space (cu. ft.) Roomy-22.8
Wheelbase/Length (in.) 103.8/167.5

Ratings—10 Best, 1 Worst

Combo Crash Tests	7
Safety Features	3
Rollover	7
Preventive Maintenance	5
Repair Costs	4
Warranty	10
Fuel Economy	8
Complaints	6
Insurance Costs	3
OVERALL RATING	**7**

Volkswagen Jetta

At-a-Glance

Status/Year Series Started. Unchanged/2011
Twins . . . . –
Body Styles . . . . .Sedan
Seating. 5
Anti-Theft Device . . . . . . Std. Pass. Immobil. & Alarm
Parking Index Rating . . . . Easy
Where Made. . . . . .Puebla, Mexico
Fuel Factor:
  MPG Rating (city/hwy) Good-28/39
  Driving Range (mi.) . . . . Very Long-465
  Fuel Type. . . . . .Regular
  Annual Fuel Cost . . . . Very Low-$1146
  Gas Guzzler Tax . . . . .No
  Greenhouse Gas Emissions (tons/yr.). Very Low-4.6
  Barrels of Oil Used per year Low-10.3

How the Competition Rates

Competitors	Rating	Pg.
Ford Focus	5	143
Nissan Sentra	5	228
Toyota Corolla	8	245

Price Range

Price Range	Retail	Markup
S MT	$17,895	4%
SE AT	$21,995	4%
SEL AT	$24,995	4%
GLI AT	$28,995	4%

Volkswagen Jetta

Safety Checklist

Crash Test:
  Frontal. . . . . Average
  Side. . . . . Very Good
Airbags:
  Torso . . . Standard Front Pelvis/Torso from Seat
  Roll Sensing. . . . . .Yes
  Knee Bolster . . . . None
Crash Avoidance:
  Collision Avoidance . . . . . . Optional CIB & DBS
  Blind Spot Detection . . . . Optional
  Lane Keeping Assist . . . . None
  Backup Camera. . . . . .Standard*
  Pedestrian Crash Avoidance . . . . None
General:
  Auto. Crash Notification. . . Operator Assist.-Fee
  Day Running Lamps . . . . Standard
Safety Belt/Restraint:
  Dynamic Head Restraints . . . . None
  Adjustable Belt. . . . . .Standard Front

Note: As of May 2018, all vehicles are required to have a backup camera.
^Warning feature does not meet government standards.
*Backup camera does not meet government standards.

Volkswagen Jetta

Specifications

Drive. . . . . .FWD
Engine 1.4-liter I4
Transmission . . . . 6-sp. Automatic
Tow Rating (lbs.) . . . . –
Head/Leg Room (in.) . . . . Very Cramped-38.2/41.2
Interior Space (cu. ft.). Cramped-94.1
Cargo Space (cu. ft.) Cramped-15.7
Wheelbase/Length (in.) 104.4/183.3

Volkswagen Passat Intermediate

Ratings—10 Best, 1 Worst

Combo Crash Tests	5
Safety Features	3
Rollover	7
Preventive Maintenance	5
Repair Costs	5
Warranty	10
Fuel Economy	7
Complaints	3
Insurance Costs	1
OVERALL RATING	**4**

Volkswagen Passat

Volkswagen Passat

At-a-Glance

Status/Year Series Started........ Unchanged/2012
Twins .... –
Body Styles ....Sedan
Seating..5
Anti-Theft Device ...... Std. Pass. Immobil. & Alarm
Parking Index Rating .... Average
Where Made.................. Chattanooga, TN

Fuel Factor:
MPG Rating (city/hwy) Good-25/36
Driving Range (mi.) .... Very Long-536
Fuel Type........................Regular
Annual Fuel Cost.................. Low-$1268
Gas Guzzler Tax ....No
Greenhouse Gas Emissions (tons/yr.)..... Low-5.0
Barrels of Oil Used per year Average-11.4

How the Competition Rates

Competitors	Rating	Pg.
Acura TLX	9	82
Ford Fusion	4	144
Volvo S60	9	265

Price Range

	Retail	Markup
S 1.8T	$22,440	4%
R-Line 1.8T	$23,975	4%
SE 1.8T	$25,495	4%
SEL Premium V6	$33,995	4%

Safety Checklist

Crash Test:
Frontal........................Very Poor
Side...........................Very Good

Airbags:
Torso . . . Standard Front Pelvis/Torso from Seat
Roll Sensing............................Yes
Knee Bolster .... None

Crash Avoidance:
Collision Avoidance ...... Optional CIB & DBS
Blind Spot Detection .... Optional
Lane Keeping Assist .... None
Backup Camera.................Standard*
Pedestrian Crash Avoidance........... None

General:
Auto. Crash Notification... Operator Assist.-Fee
Day Running Lamps .... Standard

Safety Belt/Restraint:
Dynamic Head Restraints .... None
Adjustable Belt...............Standard Front

Note: As of May 2018, all vehicles are required to have a backup camera.
^Warning feature does not meet government standards.
*Backup camera does not meet government standards.

Volkswagen Passat

Specifications

Drive.......................................FWD
Engine 1.8-liter I4
Transmission ....6-SP. Automatic
Tow Rating (lbs.) ....–
Head/Leg Room (in.) Cramped-38.3/42.4
Interior Space (cu. ft.)..............Average-102
Cargo Space (cu. ft.) Cramped-15.9
Wheelbase/Length (in.) 110.4/191.9

Volkswagen Tiguan Small SUV

Ratings—10 Best, 1 Worst

Combo Crash Tests	—
Safety Features	3
Rollover	3
Preventive Maintenance	3
Repair Costs	4
Warranty	10
Fuel Economy	4
Complaints	—
Insurance Costs	10
OVERALL RATING	**—**

Volkswagen Tiguan

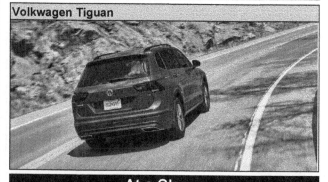
Volkswagen Tiguan

At-a-Glance

Status/Year Series Started. . . . . All New/2018
Twins . . . . —
Body Styles . . . . SUV
Seating. 7
Anti-Theft Device . . . . . . Std. Pass. Immobil. & Alarm
Parking Index Rating . . . . Average
Where Made. . . . . .Puebla, Mexico
Fuel Factor:
  MPG Rating (city/hwy) Poor-22/27
  Driving Range (mi.) . . . . Very Short-367
  Fuel Type . . . . .Regular
  Annual Fuel Cost . . . . .Average-$1531
  Gas Guzzler Tax . . . . .No
  Greenhouse Gas Emissions (tons/yr.). . Average-6.1
  Barrels of Oil Used per year High-13.7

How the Competition Rates

Competitors	Rating	Pg.
Ford Escape	5	137
Lexus NX	5	191
Toyota RAV4	9	252

Price Range

Price Range	Retail	Markup
S FWD	$25,195	4%
SE FWD	$28,930	4%
SEL 4Motion	$33,850	4%
SEL Premium 4Motion	$37,550	4%

Safety Checklist

Crash Test:
  Frontal. . . . .
  Side. . . . .
Airbags:
  Torso . . . Standard Front Pelvis/Torso from Seat
  Roll Sensing. . . . . .Yes
  Knee Bolster . . . . None
Crash Avoidance:
  Collision Avoidance . . . . . . Optional CIB & DBS
  Blind Spot Detection . . . . None
  Lane Keeping Assist . . . . Optional^
  Backup Camera. . . . . .Standard*
  Pedestrian Crash Avoidance . . . . None
General:
  Auto. Crash Notification. . . Operator Assist.-Fee
  Day Running Lamps . . . . Standard
Safety Belt/Restraint:
  Dynamic Head Restraints . . . . None
  Adjustable Belt. . . . . .Standard Front

Note: As of May 2018, all vehicles are required to have a backup camera.
^Warning feature does not meet government standards.
*Backup camera does not meet government standards.

Volkswagen Tiguan

Specifications

Drive. . . . . .FWD
Engine 2.0-liter I4
Transmission . . . . 8-sp. Automatic
Tow Rating (lbs.) . . . . Very Low-1500
Head/Leg Room (in.) Cramped-39.6/40.2
Interior Space (cu. ft.). Roomy-123.9
Cargo Space (cu. ft.) . . . . .Very Cramped-12
Wheelbase/Length (in.) 109.8/185.1

Ratings—10 Best, 1 Worst

Combo Crash Tests	7
Safety Features	7
Rollover	8
Preventive Maintenance	5
Repair Costs	6
Warranty	8
Fuel Economy	7
Complaints	9
Insurance Costs	5
OVERALL RATING	**9**

Volvo S60

Volvo S60

At-a-Glance

Status/Year Series Started........Unchanged/2011
Twins .... –
Body Styles ....Sedan
Seating.....................................5
Anti-Theft Device . Std. Pass. Immobil. & Active Alarm
Parking Index Rating .... Average
Where Made.................. Torslanda, Sweden

Fuel Factor:
MPG Rating (city/hwy)..............Good-25/36
Driving Range (mi.) .... Very Long-516
Fuel Type.............................Regular
Annual Fuel Cost..................Low-$1268
Gas Guzzler Tax ....No
Greenhouse Gas Emissions (tons/yr.).. Average-6.2
Barrels of Oil Used per year Average-11.4

How the Competition Rates

Competitors	Rating	Pg.
Acura TLX	9	82
Audi A6	7	86
Subaru Legacy	7	236

Price Range	Retail	Markup
T5 Dynamic FWD	$33,950	6%
T5 Inscription FWD	$36,800	6%
T5 Inscription Platinum AWD	$42,800	6%
T6 R-Design Platinum AWD	$47,400	6%

Safety Checklist

Crash Test:
Frontal........................ Very Good
Side...........................Very Poor

Airbags:
Torso . . .Standard Front Pelvis/Torso from Seat
Roll Sensing...........................Yes
Knee Bolster .... None

Crash Avoidance:
Collision Avoidance ......Standard CIB & DBS
Blind Spot Detection .... Optional
Lane Keeping Assist .... Optional
Backup Camera....................Optional*
Pedestrian Crash Avoidance......... Optional

General:
Auto. Crash Notification. . . Operator Assist.-Fee
Day Running Lamps .... Standard

Safety Belt/Restraint:
Dynamic Head Restraints .... None
Adjustable Belt.............Standard Front

Note: As of May 2018, all vehicles are required to have a backup camera.
^Warning feature does not meet government standards.
*Backup camera does not meet government standards.

Volvo S60

Specifications

Drive.......................................FWD
Engine 2.0-liter I4
Transmission .... 8-sp. Automatic
Tow Rating (lbs.) .... –
Head/Leg Room (in.) Average-39.3/41.9
Interior Space (cu. ft.)................Cramped-92
Cargo Space (cu. ft.) ....Very Cramped-12
Wheelbase/Length (in.) 109.3/182.5

Ratings—10 Best, 1 Worst

Combo Crash Tests	—
Safety Features	7
Rollover	6
Preventive Maintenance	2
Repair Costs	6
Warranty	8
Fuel Economy	7
Complaints	2
Insurance Costs	10
OVERALL RATING	—

Volvo V60

Volvo V60

At-a-Glance

Status/Year Series Started........ Unchanged/2015
Twins .... —
Body Styles .... Wagon
Seating.................................... 5
Anti-Theft Device . Std. Pass. Immobil. & Active Alarm
Parking Index Rating .... Average
Where Made............... Torslanda, Sweden
Fuel Factor:
　MPG Rating (city/hwy)............. Good-25/36
　Driving Range (mi.) .... Very Long-516
　Fuel Type........................Regular
　Annual Fuel Cost.................. Low-$1268
　Gas Guzzler Tax ....No
　Greenhouse Gas Emissions (tons/yr.).. Average-6.2
　Barrels of Oil Used per year Average-11.4

How the Competition Rates

Competitors	Rating	Pg.
Lincoln MKZ	4	197
Toyota Camry	8	244
Volkswagen Jetta	7	262

Price Range	Retail	Markup
T5 Dynamic FWD	$38,250	6%
T5 Cross Country AWD	$41,850	6%
T6 R-Design Platinum AWD	$49,100	6%
Polestar	$61,600	6%

Safety Checklist

Crash Test:
　Frontal. . . . .
　Side. . . . .
Airbags:
　Torso . . . Standard Front Pelvis/Torso from Seat
　Roll Sensing. . . . . .Yes
　Knee Bolster . . . . None
Crash Avoidance:
　Collision Avoidance . . . . . . Standard CIB & DBS
　Blind Spot Detection . . . . Optional
　Lane Keeping Assist . . . . Optional
　Backup Camera. . . . . Optional*
　Pedestrian Crash Avoidance . . . . Optional
General:
　Auto. Crash Notification. . . Operator Assist.-Fee
　Day Running Lamps . . . . Standard
Safety Belt/Restraint:
　Dynamic Head Restraints . . . . None
　Adjustable Belt. . . . . .Standard Front

Note: As of May 2018, all vehicles are required to have a backup camera.
^Warning feature does not meet government standards.
*Backup camera does not meet government standards.

Volvo V60

Specifications

Drive. . . . . .FWD
Engine 2.0-liter I4
Transmission . . . . 8-sp. Automatic
Tow Rating (lbs.) Low-3500
Head/Leg Room (in.) Cramped-38.7/41.9
Interior Space (cu. ft.). Cramped-92
Cargo Space (cu. ft.) Roomy-28
Wheelbase/Length (in.) 109.3/182.5

Volvo XC60 Medium SUV

Ratings—10 Best, 1 Worst

Combo Crash Tests	—
Safety Features	10
Rollover	4
Preventive Maintenance	5
Repair Costs	6
Warranty	8
Fuel Economy	5
Complaints	—
Insurance Costs	10
OVERALL RATING	—

Volvo XC60

Volvo XC60

At-a-Glance

Status/Year Series Started. . . . . All New/2017
Twins . . . . —
Body Styles . . . . SUV
Seating 5
Anti-Theft Device . Std. Pass. Immobil. & Active Alarm
Parking Index Rating . . . . Average
Where Made. . . . . Ghent, Belgium

Fuel Factor:
MPG Rating (city/hwy) Average-22/28
Driving Range (mi.) . . . . Very Long-458
Fuel Type. . . . . Premium
Annual Fuel Cost . . . . .High-$1830
Gas Guzzler Tax . . . . .No
Greenhouse Gas Emissions (tons/yr.). . Average-6.1
Barrels of Oil Used per year High-13.7

How the Competition Rates

Competitors	Rating	Pg.
Audi Q7	3	89
BMW X5	5	98
Lexus RX	4	193

Price Range

Price Range	Retail	Markup
T5 Dynamic FWD	$40,950	6%
T5 Inscription AWD	$42,950	6%
T6 Dynamic AWD	$46,950	8%
T6 R-Design AWD	$51,000	6%

Safety Checklist

Crash Test:
   Frontal. . . . .
   Side. . . . .
Airbags:
   Torso . . . Standard Front Pelvis/Torso from Seat
   Roll Sensing. . . . . .Yes
   Knee Bolster . . . . Standard Driver
Crash Avoidance:
   Collision Avoidance . . . . . Standard CIB & DBS^
   Blind Spot Detection . . . . Standard
   Lane Keeping Assist . . . . Standard
   Backup Camera. . . . . Optional*
   Pedestrian Crash Avoidance . . . . Standard
General:
   Auto. Crash Notification. . . Operator Assist.-Fee
   Day Running Lamps . . . . Standard
Safety Belt/Restraint:
   Dynamic Head Restraints . . . . None
   Adjustable Belt. . . . . .Standard Front

Note: As of May 2018, all vehicles are required to have a backup camera.
^Warning feature does not meet government standards.
*Backup camera does not meet government standards.

Volvo XC60

Specifications

Drive. . . . . .AWD
Engine 2.0-liter I4
Transmission . . . . 8-sp. Automatic
Tow Rating (lbs.) Low-3500
Head/Leg Room (in.) . . . . Very Cramped-38/41.5
Interior Space (cu. ft.). . . . . Very Roomy-132.6
Cargo Space (cu. ft.) Roomy-29.7
Wheelbase/Length (in.) 112.8/184.6

Volvo XC90 Large SUV

Ratings—10 Best, 1 Worst

Combo Crash Tests	9
Safety Features	10
Rollover	3
Preventive Maintenance	3
Repair Costs	2
Warranty	8
Fuel Economy	5
Complaints	2
Insurance Costs	10
OVERALL RATING	**8**

Volvo XC90

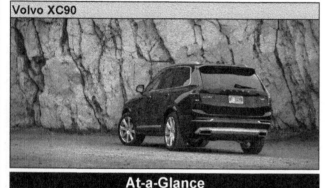

Volvo XC90

At-a-Glance

Status/Year Series Started. Unchanged/2015
Twins . . . . –
Body Styles . . . . Wagon
Seating. 7
Anti-Theft Device . Std. Pass. Immobil. & Active Alarm
Parking Index Rating . . . . Hard
Where Made. . . . . Torslanda, Sweden
Fuel Factor:
  MPG Rating (city/hwy) Average-22/28
  Driving Range (mi.) . . . . Very Long-458
  Fuel Type. . . . . Premium
  Annual Fuel Cost . . . . High-$1830
  Gas Guzzler Tax . . . . .No
  Greenhouse Gas Emissions (tons/yr.). . Average-6.0
  Barrels of Oil Used per year High-13.7

How the Competition Rates

Competitors	Rating	Pg.
Buick Enclave	4	101
Chevrolet Tahoe	4	122
Infiniti QX80	–	171

Price Range

Price Range	Retail	Markup
T5 Momentum FWD	$45,750	6%
T5 R-Design FWD	$51,150	6%
T6 Inscription AWD	$57,050	6%
T8 Excellence AWD	$104,900	6%

Safety Checklist

Crash Test:
  Frontal. . . . . Very Good
  Side. . . . . Good
Airbags:
  Torso . . . Standard Front Pelvis/Torso from Seat
  Roll Sensing. . . . . .Yes
  Knee Bolster . . . . Standard Driver
Crash Avoidance:
  Collision Avoidance . . . . . . Standard CIB & DBS
  Blind Spot Detection . . . . Standard
  Lane Keeping Assist . . . . .Standard^
  Backup Camera . . . . .Standard*
  Pedestrian Crash Avoidance . . . . Standard
General:
  Auto. Crash Notification . . . Operator Assist.-Fee
  Day Running Lamps . . . . Standard
Safety Belt/Restraint:
  Dynamic Head Restraints . . . . None
  Adjustable Belt . . . . . . .Standard Front and Rear

Note: As of May 2018, all vehicles are required to have a backup camera.
^Warning feature does not meet government standards.
*Backup camera does not meet government standards.

Volvo XC90

Specifications

Drive . . . . .AWD
Engine 2.0-liter I4
Transmission . . . . 8-sp. Automatic
Tow Rating (lbs.) Low-5000
Head/Leg Room (in.) Cramped-38.9/40.9
Interior Space (cu. ft.). Roomy-119.6
Cargo Space (cu. ft.) Cramped-15.8
Wheelbase/Length (in.) 117.5/194.8

ELECTRIC VEHICLES

So you're considering an electric vehicle? You're not alone! A recent survey by the Consumer Federation of America found that about one-third of potential car buyers would consider an EV. So it's no surprise that 16 major auto manufacturers have 31 new electric vehicles on the market with choices ranging from subcompacts to the luxury laden Tesla. While they're still more expensive than the corresponding gas powered vehicles, EV prices are on the way down and their benefits may warrant the added expense.

Energy from electricity is something we are all familiar with and, in fact, take for granted. We live in a plug-in world where most electrically powered products are extraordinarily convenient and highly functional. Imagine every night doing the same thing with your car as you do with your cell phone—simply plugging it in for the power it needs the next day. And then getting into a nearly silent, clean running car that glides effortlessly out of your driveway and likely has faster pickup than your gas powered car.

While there are a number of environmental reasons for buying an electric vehicle, the simplicity of operation, quiet ride, high tech feel and responsive performance are also major benefits. When you consider the complexity of a gasoline powered engine (most of us can't even identify the items under the hood!) and associated maintenance costs, the simplicity of electric power is refreshing, understandable, and very reliable. Owners of EVs report very low maintenance costs as there's very little to maintain.

SHOULD I EVEN CONSIDER AN ELECTRIC?

The big question most consumers have about EVs is: will I run out of power at the worst time possible—or anytime! Who hasn't needed a flashlight or tried to make a cell phone call only to find the battery is dead. In addition, many of us find it hard to imagine that the same type of engine that runs our blender, sewing machine or drill could possibly power a car! Finally, will I easily be able to plug this thing in at home? These concerns often dissuade people from looking further into the purchase of an electric vehicle.

The fact is, according to a recent analysis of consumer readiness for electric vehicles, 42% of car buyers meet the typical driving patterns, charging needs, and model preferences of the electric vehicles already on the market. Of households, 56% have access to charging, 95% transport 4 or fewer passengers, 79% don't require hauling, and 69% drive less than 60 miles on weekdays, well within the range of most battery-electric vehicles. Bottom-line, there's an excellent chance that an EV will meet your driving needs.

WHAT ARE MY CHOICES?

EVs come in various sizes, styles and price ranges. In addition, there are various types of EVs. The industry is trying to settle on acronyms to describe the different types, but here's a simple overview:

All Electric:

BEVs (Battery Powered Electric Vehicles) simply have a battery and an electric motor which powers the car. They are the simplest and "purest" form of electric vehicle. Because they depend solely on battery power, the battery systems have to be large which increases the cost of these vehicles. In addition to charging up at home, there are a growing number of publically available charging stations (over 17,000 to date) in shopping centers, employee parking lots, and along the highway. The range of these vehicles is from 68-238 miles per charge.

Electric with Built-In Charging Systems:

EREVs (Extended Range Electric Vehicles) have a gas powered auxiliary power source, that can recharge the battery if you run low on power before getting home or to a charging station. They tend to have smaller batteries and depend on the auxiliary gas powered recharger in place of a larger battery. The battery range on these vehicles is from 53-81 miles. There are only two vehicles in this category and they are a bit different from each other. The BMW i3 has an auxiliary gas engine that simply recharges the battery; it does not power the vehicle. The Chevy Volt has a gas engine that can both recharge the battery and run the vehicle. At various times both the electric motor and gas motor will power the Volt. With the auxiliary recharging engines, the range is 150 miles for the BMW i3 and 420 miles for the Chevy Volt. When the Volt reaches about 37 mph, the gas engine kicks in regardless of the state of the battery.

Dual Electric and Gasoline Vehicles:

PHEVs (Plug in Hybrid Electric Vehicles) have both an electric and gasoline motor which power the wheels at separate times. They are different from the now common hybrid vehicles, because you can plug them in to recharge. If your daily mileage is low, then these can be used like exclusively electric vehicles. Because the gasoline engine will kick in when the battery depletes, the range of these vehicle is similar to gasoline powered vehicles. The electric range is 11-27 miles per charge and the gasoline engine range is 330-600 miles.

WHAT ABOUT CHARGING?

There are three basic types of charging systems, two of which will work in your home.

Level 1: This is the simplest and least expensive system to set up in your home. All you need is a dedicated circuit (nothing else being used on the circuit) and a common household outlet. Level 1 charging is the slowest method because it uses standard 120 volt household current. Your electric vehicle will come with a Level 1 charging cord that you plug into a regular household outlet. The cord comes with a control box

which monitors charging. Typically, it will take about an hour to get 4.5 miles of range. Complete charging times range from 3 to 57 hours.

Level 2: This requires a dedicated 240 volt circuit, the same one you would need for an electric dryer or other large appliance. First, your home has to have 240 electrical service (all newer homes will) and second, if there is not a readily available line, it will have to be run to where it is needed from the circuit breaker box. Not only will this require an electrician, but if walls or ceilings are disturbed, carpentry, drywall and painting may also be necessary. In addition, once the circuit is available, you will need a special device to plug into the circuit which monitors the electrical charge to the car. Depending on features, these devices can range from $500-$2500. Before these costs scare you off, it is worth investigating the actual cost (you may be lucky enough to have a circuit box in your garage or very close) and determine if your utility company will offer any financial assistance (many do as they want to sell you more electricity). In addition, you need to consider the fact that this installation will save you hundreds of dollars in gasoline costs as well as being much more convenient than going to a gas station to refuel. Typically an hour's charging will provide 24 miles of driving. Complete charging times range from 1.5 to 12 hours.

Level 3 or DC Fast Charge: This feature enables the car to be connected to a public charging station, many of which have very fast charging systems. This is great if you have an EV and your office provides charging

stations or you're on the road and find one on the highway or in a shopping center. You can get up to 40 miles of range with just 10 minutes of charging. Overall charging times can be as low as 20 minutes.

One of the issues the industry is struggling with is a universal plug. There are three types of fast charge plugs, one of which is proprietary to the Tesla. Tesla does offer adaptors that can be used in the various types of outlets. If you are planning to charge your vehicle at work, be sure to check out the DC fast charge plug before you buy. Final Note: Because EVs are so quiet, pedestrians may not hear them coming so the government is considering requiring some type of added noise making capacity. When driving an EV use care when around pedestrians.

FOLLOWING IS *THE CAR BOOK'S* SNAPSHOT GUIDE TO THE 2018 EVs:

This is a very basic guide to many of the key features on today's EVs. It's important to take a good, long test drive in order to make a selection that best meets your needs and to get the details behind the features that are really important to you.

You'll find the following items in the EV snapshot:

Range: The first number is how far you can go on a single charge on just battery power. The second number shows the range with auxiliary power. In some cases that auxiliary power just recharges the battery, in other cases it powers the wheels just like a gas engine. In addition to the estimated range, we have provided two comparative ratings. The first rating is the total electric range which includes the range added with an auxiliary recharging engine. The second includes the range with the auxiliary engine that directly powers the wheels. This range is compared to the range of standard gasoline engines. The ratings for electric and electric + auxiliary vehicles range compares just these vehicles. Beware, driving with a "lead foot" and using heat and air conditioning will reduce your range.

Charging Time: This is the total time for a complete charge using Level 1 and Level 2 systems. We did not include the DC fast charging time because there is significant variation in the power of public stations.

MPGe: This is the equivalent of the traditional gasoline miles per gallon converted to electricity (thus the small 'e' at the end). While it is not actually miles per gallon, it gives you a way to compare the efficiency of EVs with gas powered vehicles. We've presented the 'combined' mileage rating which combines highway and city driving. The rating following the estimate compares the mileage with all other electric vehicles running on just battery power.

Introduction: This is the year the vehicle was first introduced. The longer the production time, the more likely the manufacturer is to have worked out any bugs. On the other hand, more recent introductions will contain more sophisticated technology and safety features.

Price: This is the manufacturer's suggested retail price which gives you a general idea of EV pricing. It's important to

check for federal and local rebate programs and to comparison shop. Car pricing is notoriously variable and that's no different for EVs. To get the best price consider using the services of the non-profit CarBargains program (page 68).

Size Class/Seating: This provides a general idea of the size of the car. Most consumers compare vehicles within the same size class.

On Board Charger: The greater the KW (kilowatt) rating, the faster the charger. In addition we indicate which vehicles have DC Fast Charging (Level 3) built-in which enables you to take advantage of speedy (and sometimes free) public charging facilities.

Auxiliary Power/MPG: This indicates whether or not (and what kind) of auxiliary power the vehicle may have. There are two types—engines that recharge the battery and engines that drive the wheels. For electric vehicles with auxiliary engines that power the car, we've included the EPA combined MPG estimate. The rating following the estimate compares the mileage with all other gasoline powered vehicles in *The Car Book*. See the descriptions on pages 271-272.

Crash Test Rating: Not all EVs have been crash tested. This tells you which one's were crash tested and how they performed using *The Car Book's* rating system based on government's tests. (See page 19.)

Safety Features: Safety has become critically important to today's car buyer, so we've identified 3 key safety features and indicated if the EV has those features. AEB stands for *Automatic Emergency Braking* – this system automatically applies the

brakes if a collision is imminent. We do not indicate, here, if the vehicle has other forms of automatic braking technologies such as brake assist or forward crash warning. *Rear Cameras* have become one of the best ways to avoid the tragic consequences of hitting a small child as well as serve as a wonderful parking assistant. *Lane Assist* moves you back into your lane if you're drifting. We do not indicate if the car simply provides a warning.

Warranty: Warranties vary so here's how the car's overall warranty stacks up in comparison with all other warranties.

Battery Warranty: Electric vehicle batteries are relatively new products and critical to the car's operation. As such, you want to be sure that your *battery* comes with a good, long warranty.

Interior Space/Cargo Space: This is another indication of the car's size. The ratings are relative compared to all of the vehicles in the *The Car Book*.

Parking Index: This rating takes into consideration the vehicle's key dimensions and determines an estimate for 'ease of parking' compared to other models. This is a general guide and no substitute for a good long test drive.

Sales: This indicates November 2017 year to date total sales for the 2017 version of the vehicle indicating the general popularity of the EV.

For more complete information on many of these vehicles, please see the corresponding vehicle on the car ratings pages.

Audi A3 Plug-in Hybrid

Introduction:	2016
Range:	17 mi.– Vry. Short/Aux. Power–430 mi.–Long
Charging Time:	Level 1 (8 hrs.)–Fast/Level 2 (2.5 hrs.)–Fast
MPGe:	Electric-86–Low

On Board Charger:	3.3 kW
Auxiliary Power/MPG:	Yes (PHEV)/MPG-39–Very High
Crash Test Rating:	—
Safety Features	AEB–Yes*; Rear Camera–Yes; Lane Asst–Yes*
Warranty:	4 years/50,000 mi.
Battery Warranty:	8 years/100,000 mi.
Size Class/ Seating:	Compact/5
Interior/Cargo Space:	89 cf–Vry. Cramped/13.6 cf–Cramped
Parking Index:	Easy
Sales:	2,607
Price:	$37,900 (MSRP)
Notes:	*Indicates optional feature

BMW 330e

Introduction:	2016
Range:	14 mi.–Vry. Short/Aux. Power - 350 - Vry. Short
Charging Time:	Level 1 (10 hrs.) - Avg/Level 2 (2.2 hrs.) - Vry. Fast
MPGe:	71 - Very Low

On Board Charger:	3.5 kW
Auxiliary Power/MPG:	Yes (PHEV)/MPG-30-High
Crash Test Rating:	-
Safety Features	AEB-Yes*; Rear Camera-Yes*; Lane Asst-No
Warranty:	4 years/50,000 mi.
Battery Warranty:	8 years/100,000 mi.
Size Class/ Seating:	Compact/5
Interior/Cargo Space:	96 cf-Cramped/13 cf-Cramped
Parking Index:	Average
Sales:	3,778
Price	$44,100
Notes:	*Indicates optional feature

BMW 530e

Introduction:	2017
Range:	16 mi.–Vry. Short/Aux. Power - 370 - Vry. Short
Charging Time:	Level 1(7 hrs.) - Fast/Level 2 (3 hrs.) - Fast
MPGe:	72 - Low

On Board Charger:	3.5 kW
Auxiliary Power/MPG:	Yes (PHEV)/MPG-29-High
Crash Test Rating:	-
Safety Features	AEB-Yes; Rear Camera-Yes; Lane Asst-Yes
Warranty:	4 years/50,000 mi.
Battery Warranty:	8 years/100,000 mi.
Size Class/ Seating:	Mid-Size/5
Interior/Cargo Space:	99 cf-Average/10 cf-Very Cramped
Parking Index:	Average
Sales:	3,066
Price	$51,200
Notes:	*Indicates optional feature

BMW 740e

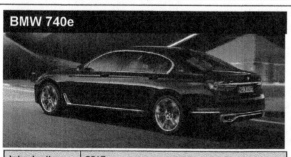

Introduction:	2017
Range:	14 mi.–Vry. Short/Aux. Power - 340 - Vry. Short
Charging Time:	Level 1(12 hrs.) - Avg/Level 2 (3 hrs.) -Fast
MPGe:	64 - Very Low

On Board Charger:	3.7kW
Auxiliary Power/MPG:	Yes (PHEV)/MPG-27-High
Crash Test Rating:	-
Safety Features	AEB-Yes*; Rear Camera-Yes; Lane Asst-Yes*
Warranty:	4 years/50,000 mi.
Battery Warranty:	8 years/100,000 mi.
Size Class/ Seating:	Large/5
Interior/Cargo Space:	114 cf-Roomy/14.8 cf-Cramped
Parking Index:	Very Hard
Sales:	640
Price	$89,100
Notes:	*Indicates optional feature

BMW i3

Introduction:	2014
Range:	81 mi.–Long/Aux. Power–180 mi.–Vry. Short
Charging Time:	Level 1 (10 hrs.)–Average/Level 2 (3 hrs.)–Fast
MPGe:	Electric-124–Very High

On Board Charger:	7.4 kW; DC fast charge optional
Auxiliary Power/MPG:	Optional (EREV)/MPG-39–Very High
Crash Test Rating:	—
Safety Features	AEB–Yes*; Rear Camera–Yes*; Lane Asst–No
Warranty:	4 years/50,000 mi.
Battery Warranty:	8 years/100,000 mi.
Size Class/ Seating:	Subcompact/4
Interior/Cargo Space:	83.1 cf–Vry. Cramped/2.8 cf–Vry. Cramped
Parking Index:	Very Easy
Sales:	5,604
Price	$42,400 (MSRP)/$46,250 w/battery ext.
Notes:	*Indicates optional feature

BMW i8

Introduction:	2014
Range:	15 mi.–Vry. Short/Aux. Power–330 mi.–Vry. Short
Charging Time:	Level 1 (3.5 hrs.)–Vry. Fast/Level 2 (1.5 hrs.)–Vry. Fast
MPGe:	Electric-76–Low

On Board Charger:	5 kW; DC fast charge standard
Auxiliary Power/MPG:	Yes (PHEV) /MPG-28–High
Crash Test Rating:	—
Safety Features	AEB–Yes*; Rear Camera-Yes; Lane Asst-No
Warranty:	4 years/50,000 mi.
Battery Warranty:	8 years/100,000 mi.
Size Class/ Seating:	Compact/4
Interior/Cargo Space:	80.9 cf.–Vry. Cramped/4.7 cf–Vry. Cramped
Parking Index:	Hard
Sales:	408
Price	$136,500 (MSRP)
Notes:	*Indicates optional feature

BMW x5 xDrive Plug-in Hybrid

Introduction:	2016
Range:	14 mi.–Vry. Short/Aux. Power–540 mi.–Vry. Long
Charging Time:	Level 1 (3.7 hrs.)–Vry. Fast/Level 2 (2.7 hrs.)–Fast
MPGe:	Electric-56–Very Low

On Board Charger:	3.5 kW
Auxiliary Power/MPG:	Yes (PHEV)/MPG-24–Average
Crash Test Rating:	—
Safety Features	AEB–Yes*; Rear Camera–Yes*; Lane Asst–No
Warranty:	4 years/50,000 mi.
Battery Warranty:	8 years/100,000 mi.
Size Class/ Seating:	Medium SUV/5
Interior/Cargo Space:	cf– /34.2 cf–Very Roomy
Parking Index:	Very Hard
Sales:	4,517
Price	$63,045 (MSRP)
Notes:	*Indicates optional feature

Cadillac CT6 Plug-in

Introduction:	2017
Range:	31 mi- Avg./Aux. Power - 440 - Long
Charging Time:	Level 1 (12.5 hrs.) - Avg./Level 2 (4.5 hrs.) - Avg.
MPGe:	62 - Very Low

On Board Charger:	3.6kW
Auxiliary Power/MPG:	Yes (PHEV)/MPG-26-Average
Crash Test Rating:	-
Safety Features	AEB-No; Rear Camera-Yes; Lane Asst-Yes*
Warranty:	4 years/50,000 mi.
Battery Warranty:	8 years/100,000 mi.
Size Class/ Seating:	Mid-Size/5
Interior/Cargo Space:	106 cf-Roomy/10.6 cf-Vry. Cramped
Parking Index:	Hard
Sales:	179
Price	$75,095
Notes:	*Indicates optional feature

Chevrolet Bolt

Introduction:	2017
Range:	238 mi.–Vry. Long
Charging Time:	Lvl. 1 (51 hrs.) - Vry. Slow/Lvl. 2 (9 hrs.) - Vry. Slow
MPGe:	119 - Very High

On Board Charger:	7.2 kW; DC fast charge optional
Auxiliary Power/MPG:	No
Crash Test Rating:	–
Safety Features	AEB-No; Rear Camera-Yes; Lane Asst-No
Warranty:	3 years/36,000 mi.
Battery Warranty:	8 years/100,000 mi.
Size Class/ Seating:	Subompact/5
Interior/Cargo Space:	95 cf.–Cramped/16.9 cf–Average
Parking Index:	Very Easy
Sales:	20,070
Price	$36,620
Notes:	

Chevrolet Volt

Introduction:	2011, All new model in 2016
Range:	53 mi.–Average/Aux. Power–420 mi.–Avg.
Charging Time:	Level 1 (13 hrs.)–Avg./Level 2 (4.5 hrs.)–Avg.
MPGe:	Electric-106–High

On Board Charger:	3.6 kW
Auxiliary Power/MPG:	Yes (EREV)/MPG-42–Very High
Crash Test Rating:	5 Stars
Safety Features	AEB–Yes*; Rear Camera–Yes; Lane Asst–Yes*
Warranty:	3 years/36,000 mi.
Battery Warranty:	8 years/100,000 mi.
Size Class/ Seating:	Compact/5
Interior/Cargo Space:	90 cf–Vry. Cramped/10.6 cf–Vry. Cramped
Parking Index:	Easy
Sales:	18,412
Price	$33,995 (MSRP)
Notes:	*Indicates optional feature

Chrysler Pacifica

Introduction:	2017
Range:	33 mi.–Short/Aux. Power - 570 - Vry. Long
Charging Time:	Level 1(12 hrs.) - Average/Level 2 (2 hrs.) - Vry. Fast
MPGe:	84 - Low

On Board Charger:	6.6kW
Auxiliary Power/MPG:	Yes (PHEV)/MPG-32-High
Crash Test Rating:	5 stars
Safety Features	AEB-Yes*; Rear Camera-Yes; Lane Asst-Yes*
Warranty:	3 years/36,000 mi.
Battery Warranty:	10 years/100,000 mi.
Size Class/ Seating:	Minivan/7
Interior/Cargo Space:	165 cf-Vry. Roomy/32.3 cf-Vry. Roomy
Parking Index:	Very Hard
Sales:	3,817
Price	$41,995
Notes:	*Indicates optional feature

Fiat 500e

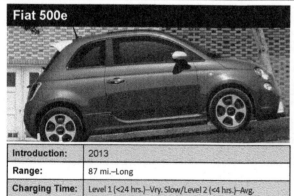

Introduction:	2013
Range:	87 mi.–Long
Charging Time:	Level 1 (<24 hrs.)–Vry. Slow/Level 2 (<4 hrs.)–Avg.
MPGe:	116–Very High

On Board Charger:	6.6 kW
Auxiliary Power/MPG:	None
Crash Test Rating:	–
Safety Features	AEB–No; Rear Camera–Yes*; Lane Asst–No
Warranty:	4 years/50,000 mi.
Battery Warranty:	8 years/100,000 mi.
Size Class/ Seating:	Subcompact/2
Interior/Cargo Space:	71.6 cf–Vry. Cramped/7 cf–Vry. Cramped
Parking Index:	Very Easy
Sales:	5,210
Price	$31,800 (MSRP)
Notes:	*Indicates optional feature

Ford C-Max Energi

Introduction:	2013
Range:	20 mi.–Short/Aux. Power–550 mi.–Vry. Long
Charging Time:	Level 1 (7 hrs.)–Fast/Level 2 (2.5 hrs.)–Fast
MPGe:	Electric-88–Low

On Board Charger:	3.3 kW
Auxiliary Power/MPG:	Yes (PHEV)/MPG-38–Very High
Crash Test Rating:	4 stars
Safety Features	AEB–No; Rear Camera–Yes; Lane Asst–No
Warranty:	3 years/36,000 mi.
Battery Warranty:	8 years/100,000 mi.
Size Class/ Seating:	Midsize/5
Interior/Cargo Space:	99.7 cf–Avg./19.2 cf–Avg.
Parking Index:	Average
Sales:	7,704
Price	$31,770 (MSRP)
Notes:	

Ford Focus Electric

Introduction:	2012
Range:	76 mi.–Long
Charging Time:	Level 1 (20 hrs.)–Slow/Level 2 (3.6 hrs.)–Average
MPGe:	105–High

On Board Charger:	6.6 kW
Auxiliary Power/MPG:	None
Crash Test Rating:	—
Safety Features	AEB–No; Rear Camera–Yes; Lane Asst–No
Warranty:	4 years/36,000 mi.
Battery Warranty:	8 years/100,000 mi.
Size Class/ Seating:	Compact/5
Interior/Cargo Space:	90 cf–Vry. Cramped/14.2 cf–Cramped
Parking Index:	Easy
Sales:	1,704
Price	$29,170 (MSRP)
Notes:	Limited availability

Ford Fusion Energi

Introduction:	2013
Range:	20 mi.–Short/Aux. Power–550 mi.–Vry. Long
Charging Time:	Level 1 (7 hrs.)–Fast/Level 2 (2.5 hrs.)–Fast
MPGe:	Electric-88–Low

On Board Charger:	3.3 kW
Auxiliary Power/MPG:	Yes (PHEV)/MPG-38–Very High
Crash Test Rating:	5 stars
Safety Features	AEB–Yes*; Rear Camera–Yes; Lane Asst–No
Warranty:	3 years/36,000 mi.
Battery Warranty:	8 years/100,000 mi.
Size Class/ Seating:	Midsize/5
Interior/Cargo Space:	102.8 cf–Roomy/8.2 cf–Vry. Cramped
Parking Index:	Average
Sales:	8,757
Price	$33,900 (MSRP)
Notes:	*Indicates optional feature

Hyundai IONIQ Electric

Introduction:	2017
Range:	124 mi- Very Long
Charging Time:	Level 1 (9 hrs.) - Fast/Level 2 (4 hrs.) - Average
MPGe:	136 - Very High

On Board Charger:	6.6kW
Auxiliary Power/MPG:	No
Crash Test Rating:	—
Safety Features	AEB-Yes*; Rear Camera-Yes; Lane Asst-No
Warranty:	5 years/60,000 mi.
Battery Warranty:	10 years/100,000 mi.
Size Class/ Seating:	Compact/5
Interior/Cargo Space:	96.2 cf-Cramped/23.8 cf-Roomy
Parking Index:	Very Easy
Sales:	353
Price	$29,500
Notes:	*Lifetime battery warranty for original owner

Hyundai Sonata Plug-in Hybrid

Introduction:	2016
Range:	27 mi.–Short/Aux. Power–600 mi.–Vry. Long
Charging Time:	Level 1 (8.7 hrs.)–Fast/Level 2 (2.7 hrs.)–Fast
MPGe:	Electric–99–Average

On Board Charger:	3.3 kW
Auxiliary Power/MPG:	Yes (PHEV)/MPG–40–Very High
Crash Test Rating:	—
Safety Features	AEB–No; Rear Camera–Yes; Lane Asst–No
Warranty:	5 years/60,000 mi.
Battery Warranty:	10 years/100,000 mi.
Size Class/ Seating:	Midsize/5
Interior/Cargo Space:	106.1 cf–Roomy/9.9 cf–Vry. Cramped
Parking Index:	Easy
Sales:	2,340
Price	$34,600 (MSRP)
Notes:	*Lifetime battery warranty for original owner

Kia Soul EV

Introduction:	2015
Range:	93 mi.–Long
Charging Time:	Level 1 (24 hrs.)–Vry. Slow/Level 2 (4.5 hrs.)–Avg.
MPGe:	105–High

On Board Charger:	6.6 kW; DC fast charge optional
Auxiliary Power/MPG:	None
Crash Test Rating:	—
Safety Features	AEB–No; Rear Camera–Yes; Lane Asst–Yes
Warranty:	5 years/60,000 mi.
Battery Warranty:	7 years/150,000 mi.
Size Class/ Seating:	Compact/5
Interior/Cargo Space:	97.1 cf–Avg./18.8 cf–Avg.
Parking Index:	Very Easy
Sales:	1,953
Price	$33,950 (MSRP)
Notes:	Only available in CA, GA, HI, MD, NJ, NY, OR, TX, and WA.

Mercedes-Benz B-Class

Introduction:	2014
Range:	87 mi.–Long
Charging Time:	Level 1 (22 hrs.)–Slow/Level 2 (3.5 hrs.)–Average
MPGe:	84–Low

On Board Charger:	10 kW
Auxiliary Power/MPG:	None
Crash Test Rating:	—
Safety Features	AEB–Yes; Rear Camera–Yes; Lane Asst–No
Warranty:	4 years/50,000 mi.
Battery Warranty:	8 years/100,000 mi.
Size Class/ Seating:	Midsize/5
Interior/Cargo Space:	—/21.6 cf–Avg.
Parking Index:	Very Easy
Sales:	633
Price	$41,450 (MSRP)
Notes:	

Mercedes-Benz C350e

Introduction:	2016
Range:	11 mi- Vry. Short/Aux. Power - 410 - Average
Charging Time:	Level 1 (4 hrs.) - Vry. Fast/Lvl 2 (1.75 hrs.) - Vry. Fast
MPGe:	51 - Very Low

On Board Charger:	3.6kW
Auxiliary Power/MPG:	Yes (PHEV)/MPG-30-High
Crash Test Rating:	—
Safety Features	AEB-Yes; Rear Camera-Yes; Lane Asst-Yes*
Warranty:	4 years/50,000 mi.
Battery Warranty:	8 years/100,000 mi.
Size Class/ Seating:	Compact/5
Interior/Cargo Space:	91 cf-Vry. Cramped/11.8 cf-Vry. Cramped
Parking Index:	Very Easy
Sales:	803
Price	$45,490
Notes:	*Indicates optional feature

Mercedes-Benz S550e Plug-in Hybrid

Introduction:	2016
Range:	14 mi.–Vry. Short/Aux. Power–450 mi.– Long
Charging Time:	Level 1 (4.5 hrs.)–Vry. Fast/Level 2 (2 hrs.)–Vry. Fast
MPGe:	Electric-58–Very Low

On Board Charger:	3.3 kW
Auxiliary Power/MPG:	Yes (PHEV)/MPG-26–Average
Crash Test Rating:	—
Safety Features	AEB–Yes; Rear Camera–Yes; Lane Asst–Yes*
Warranty:	4 years/50,000 mi.
Battery Warranty:	8 years/100,000 mi.
Size Class/ Seating:	Large/5
Interior/Cargo Space:	112 cf–Roomy/13.9 cf–Cramped
Parking Index:	Very Hard
Sales:	640
Price:	$95,650 (MSRP)
Notes:	*Indicates optional feature

Nissan Leaf

Introduction:	2011
Range:	107 mi.–Vry. Long
Charging Time:	Level 2 (NA)/Level 1 (NA)
MPGe:	114–Very High

On Board Charger:	6.6 kW; DC fast charge optional
Auxiliary Power/MPG:	None
Crash Test Rating:	4 stars
Safety Features	AEB–No; Rear Camera–Yes; Lane Asst–No
Warranty:	3 years/36,000 mi.
Battery Warranty:	8 years/100,000 mi.
Size Class/ Seating:	Compact/5
Interior/Cargo Space:	92.4 cf–Cramped/24 cf–Avg.
Parking Index:	Very Easy
Sales:	11,128
Price:	$32,100/$35,120 (MSRP)
Notes:	

Porsche Cayenne S E-Hybrid

Introduction:	2015
Range:	14 mi.–Vry. Short/Aux. Power–480 mi.–Vry. Long
Charging Time:	Level 1 (11 hrs.)–Average/Level 2 (3.6 hrs.)–Average
MPGe:	Electric-47–Very Low

On Board Charger:	3.6 kW
Auxiliary Power/MPG:	Yes (PHEV)/MPG 22–Low
Crash Test Rating:	—
Safety Features	AEB–Yes*; Rear Camera–Yes*; Lane Asst–Yes*
Warranty:	4 years/50,000 mi.
Battery Warranty:	7 years/70,000 mi.
Size Class/ Seating:	Midsize SUV/5
Interior/Cargo Space:	—/20.5 cf–Avg.
Parking Index:	Hard
Sales:	1,551
Price:	$77,200 (MSRP)
Notes:	*Indicates optional feature

Porsche Panamera S E-Hybrid

Introduction:	2013
Range:	16 mi.–Vry. Short/Aux. Pwr.–540 mi. –Vry. Long
Charging Time:	Level 1 (>11 hrs.)–Average/Level 2 (2.3 hrs.)–Vry. Fast
MPGe:	Electric-51–Very Low

On Board Charger:	3.6 kW
Auxiliary Power/MPG:	Yes (PHEV)/MPG-25–Avgerage
Crash Test Rating:	—
Safety Features	AEB–Yes*; Rear Camera–Yes*; Lane Asst–Yes*
Warranty:	4 years/50,000 mi.
Battery Warranty:	7 years/70,000 mi.
Size Class/ Seating:	Large/5
Interior/Cargo Space:	—/11.8 cf–Vry. Cramped
Parking Index:	Very Hard
Sales:	18
Price:	$96,100 (MSRP)
Notes:	*Indicates optional feature

Smart forTwo Electric Drive

Introduction:	2011
Range:	68 mi.–Average
Charging Time:	Level 1 (13 hrs.)–Avg./Level 2 (6 hrs.)–Slow
MPGe:	107–High

On Board Charger:	3.3 kW
Auxiliary Power/MPG:	None
Crash Test Rating:	—
Safety Features	AEB–No; Rear Camera–Yes*; Lane Asst–No
Warranty:	4 years/50,000 mi.
Battery Warranty:	4 years/50,000 mi.
Size Class/ Seating:	Subcompact/2
Interior/Cargo Space:	45.4 cf–Vry. Cramped/7.8 cf–Vry. Cramped
Parking Index:	Very Easy
Sales:	415
Price	$25,000 (MSRP)
Notes:	Offers Battery Rental program, *indicates opt. feature

Tesla Model 3

Introduction:	2017
Range:	210 mi.–Vry. Long
Charging Time:	Level 1 (57 hrs.)–Vry. Slow/Level 2 (12 hrs.)–Vry. Slow
MPGe:	126–Very High

On Board Charger:	7.7 kW
Auxiliary Power/MPG:	None
Crash Test Rating:	—
Safety Features	AEB–Yes; Rear Camera–Yes; Lane Asst–Yes
Warranty:	4 years/50,000 mi.
Battery Warranty:	8 years/unlimited mi.
Size Class/ Seating:	Intermediate/5
Interior/Cargo Space:	–/15.0 cf–Cramped
Parking Index:	Average
Sales:	712
Price	$35,000 (MSRP)
Notes:	

Tesla Model S

Introduction:	2012
Range:	208 mi.–Vry. Long
Charging Time:	Level 1 (52 hrs.)–Vry. Slow/Level 2 (10 hrs.)–Vry. Slow
MPGe:	101–Average

On Board Charger:	11 kW; DC fast charge optional
Auxiliary Power/MPG:	None
Crash Test Rating:	5 stars
Safety Features	AEB–Yes; Rear Camera–Yes; Lane Asst–Yes
Warranty:	4 years/50,000 mi.
Battery Warranty:	8 years/unlimited mi.
Size Class/ Seating:	Large/5
Interior/Cargo Space:	94 cf–Cramped/31.6 cf–Vry. Roomy
Parking Index:	Hard
Sales:	22,085
Price	$71,070 (MSRP)
Notes:	

Tesla Model X

Introduction:	2016
Range:	238 mi.–Vry. Long
Charging Time:	Level 1 (57 hrs)–Vry. Slow/Level 2 (12 hrs)–Vry. Slow
MPGe:	Electric-93–Average

On Board Charger:	10 kW; DC fast charge optional
Auxiliary Power/MPG:	None
Crash Test Rating:	5 stars
Safety Features	AEB–Yes; Rear Camera–Yes; Lane Asst–Yes
Warranty:	4 years/50,000 mi.
Battery Warranty:	8 years/unlimited
Size Class/ Seating:	Mid-Size/7
Interior/Cargo Space:	120 cf–Roomy/26 cf–Roomy
Parking Index:	Very Hard
Sales:	18,015
Price	$80,000 (MSRP)
Notes:	

Toyota Prius Prime

Introduction:	2017
Range:	25 mi.–Short/Aux. Power - 640 - Vry. Long
Charging Time:	Level 1 (5.5 hrs.) - Fast/Level 2 (2 hrs.) - Vry. Fast
MPGe:	133 - Very High

On Board Charger:	3.3kW
Auxiliary Power/MPG:	Yes (PHEV)/MPG-54-Very High
Crash Test Rating:	-
Safety Features	AEB-Yes*; Rear Camera-Yes; Lane Asst-Yes
Warranty:	3 years/36,000 mi.
Battery Warranty:	8 years/100,000 mi.
Size Class/ Seating:	Mid-Size/5
Interior/Cargo Space:	91.5 cf-Cramped/19.8 cf-Average
Parking Index:	Very Easy
Sales:	18,516
Price	$27,100
Notes:	*Indicates optional feature

Volvo XC90 Plug-in Hybrid

Introduction:	2016
Range:	14 mi.–Vry. Short /Aux. Pwr.–350 mi.–Vry. Short
Charging Time:	Level 1 (7 hrs.)–Fast/Level 2 (2.5 hrs.)–Fast
MPGe:	Electric-53–Very Low

On Board Charger:	3.5 kW
Auxiliary Power/MPG:	Yes (PHEV)/MPG-25– Average
Crash Test Rating:	5 stars
Safety Features	AEB–Yes; Rear Camera–Yes; Lane Asst–Yes
Warranty:	4 years/50,000 mi.
Battery Warranty:	4 years/50,000 mi.
Size Class/ Seating:	Midsize SUV/7
Interior/Cargo Space:	103.8 cf–Roomy/15.4 cf–Cramped
Parking Index:	Hard
Sales:	1,828
Price	$68,100 (MSRP)
Notes:	

VW e-Golf

Introduction:	2015
Range:	83 mi.–Long
Charging Time:	Level 1 (20 hrs.)–Slow/Level 2 (4 hrs.)–Avg.
MPGe:	116–Very High

On Board Charger:	7.2 kW; DC fast charge standard
Auxiliary Power/MPG:	None
Crash Test Rating:	—
Safety Features	AEB–Yes*; Rear Camera–Yes; Lane Asst–No
Warranty:	4 years/50,000 mi.
Battery Warranty:	8 years/100,000 mi.
Size Class/ Seating:	Compact/5
Interior/Cargo Space:	93.5 cf–Cramped/22.8 cf–Avg.
Parking Index:	Easy
Sales:	3,191
Price	$28,995 (MSRP)
Notes:	*Indicates optional feature